Transforming International Criminal Justice

Transforming International Criminal Justice

Retributive and restorative justice in the trial process

Mark Findlay and Ralph Henham

WILLAN
PUBLISHING

Published by

Willan Publishing
Culmcott House
Mill Street, Uffculme
Cullompton, Devon
EX15 3AT, UK
Tel: +44(0)1884 840337
Fax: +44(0)1884 840251
e-mail: info@willanpublishing.co.uk

Published simultaneously in the USA and Canada by

Willan Publishing
c/o ISBS, 920 NE 58th Ave, Suite 300
Portland, Oregon 97213-3644, USA
Tel: +001(0)503 287 3093
Fax: +001(0)503 280 8832
e-mail: info@isbs.com
website: www.isbs.com

First published 2005

ISBN 1-84392-078-6

British Library Cataloguing-in-Publication Data
A catalogue record for this book is available from the British Library

Project management by Deer Park Productions, Tavistock
Typeset by GCS, Leighton Buzzard, Beds
Printed and bound by T.J. International, Padstow, Cornwall

Contents

List of figures and tables

Figures

Tables

Table of cases

Table of legislation

Introduction

This book sets out an agenda to transform international criminal trials and thereby the delivery of international criminal justice (ICJ)[1] to victim communities. The progress of the book itself charts a transformation of thinking about the comparative analysis of trial process. The product has a potential to advance the boundaries of ICJ through wider access and inclusivity in an environment of rights protection.

It commences with an investigation of social theory supporting a model of the trial as a process of decision-making. In order to interrogate and apply this model to international criminal trials, the comparative analysis of examples from the trial traditions most influential over international trial process is attempted. Detailed analysis of trial transcripts from Italy and England is the empirical focus for such analysis, and the challenges inherent in this methodology are explored.

The comparative analysis applied suggests the importance of understanding both the fact and value of trial decision-making. The trial as process presents opportunities to examine the synthesis and difference behind procedural influences over ICJ. The decision model identifies and applies the uniform importance of discretion in decision-making, the centrality of lay and professional relationships in trial decision processes, and the significance of truth in forming the substance of the principal decisions in the process.

---

1 We use ICJ as the acronym for international criminal justice throughout the text even though it is more commonly applied to the International Court of Justice.

At this point an important pathway of influence in the process is analysed – the relationship between the judge and the victim in the sentencing process. This case study identifies the relevance of normative frameworks as a context for understanding how the decision process is materialized in practice. But more than about rules and procedures, such an understanding rests on discovering how discretion moves important decision relationships and how these in turn are constructed and operated through a feature of influence. Addressing the particular problems facing the judge/victim relationship when translated into contexts of international criminal trials demands a radical rethinking of trial process and the engagement with other important ICJ paradigms. Transformation in this setting will rely on enhancing the moral legitimacy of ICJ through wider access, greater inclusion and a more protected victim voice in the process and outcomes of ICJ.

The radical dimension of the book is in its argument for the harmonization of restorative and retributive justice within ICJ. The manifesto for how trial transformation is to be achieved gives the authors confidence that the new international criminal trial will invigorate ICJ as a force for global governance.

Foundations

The genesis of this book is the pressing need to provide theoretical and empirical insights into the relatively recent phenomenon of ICJ and its manifestation in the principles and practices of international criminal trials. In addition to the creation of international structures to investigate and try crimes of global significance, there is emerging an international jurisprudence on criminal law (and procedural hybrids to support and develop this) which requires integrated analysis. Such developments are formal and informal in nature and context, reflecting predominantly retributive and restorative aspirations for penality and reconciliation respectively.

The present pace and form of change in ICJ appears largely as the product of global political imperatives (Christie 1977: 1–15; Scharf 1999). The nature of these imperatives has necessitated the operation of formal trials and their resultant penal sanctions within the two broad and divergent Western criminal justice traditions (Anglo-American common law and Western European civil law) exemplified in the adversarial and inquisitorial trial forms. Outside this, the jurisdictions of the developing world in particular are adapting restorative and 'truth-focused' justice paradigms to manage crimes of international significance.

The internationalization of criminal trial institutions especially has, therefore, prompted debates about synthesizing formal styles of criminal procedure (Findlay 2001a). However, this is by no means a straightforward matter involving a conventional bifurcated consideration of separate criminal justice procedural traditions. It requires comparative research within the realms of politics, policy and politicization at the local and global level. It demands an interrogation of alternative justice approaches in contest for ICJ constituencies and outcomes. With formal justice process, action and human relationships (Henham and Findlay 2001c) for decision-making require analysis as drivers of justice, rather than remaining content with a dry and narrow discussion of competing constitutional legalities. For the less formal ICJ paradigms, the expectations of states in transition and their victim communities are important contexts for analysis. The book confronts and attempts to harmonize these alternative justice directions.

In broad terms, our analysis is motivated by the twin desires. First to provide a basis for understanding what the internationalization of criminal justice signifies as a fusion of ideology and structure, and second a concern that the institutions of ICJ should forge morally legitimate connections between the allocation of individual responsibility for international crimes and the principles for distributive justice which post-conflict societies and transitional cultures demand. We consider that some accommodation between the relativity of global and local justice is necessary for the fulfilment of these aspirations. As we argue and demonstrate progressively throughout what follows, comparative contextual analysis (CCA)[2] provides a methodology for predicting how legitimate expectations for justice can be translated into practice. It also shows us that for a truly ICJ, mechanisms of truth and accountability must grow from the consciousness of victim communities.

The victim focus for ICJ can stimulate a new era in *collaborative justice*.[3] Collaboration between the principal parties to a justice

---

2 CCA is a unique methodology for comparative research where the detailed interrogation of context precedes any analysis of similarity and difference. It is a thematic process directed and designed to explore relationships of agency rather than institutional or structural frameworks.

3 This concept is developed and operationalized in the context of trial transformation in Chapter 8.

resolution, and the justice paradigms they legitimate, will ensure *communities of justice*[4] internationally.

Progress of thinking

This book initially focuses on criminal trial practices and processes in a variety of local and regional domestic contexts. The object is to produce evaluations of decisions and relationships we regard as essential to understanding the operation of trial process at the international level. The context of the criminal trial is selected as a focus on procedural comparison for its symbolic significance and essential connection with the negotiation and imposition of penal sanctions, a primary political purpose behind the internationalization of justice (Findlay 2001a: 27). The trial setting for the analysis of ICJ is initially chosen because it provides a stage common to all jurisdictions where the purposes and power relations of penality are given public expression through the rituals of punishment. Whilst recognizing the significance of pre-trial decision-making, our research *locus* is where the ideological and policy dimensions of penality are played out and hence where issues of synthesis and difference in alternative justice traditions and paradigms[5] can best be explored beyond normative models.

We restrict the discussion of synthesis and difference to alternative trial traditions as they influence the manifestation of formal ICJ. From this we contrast formal and informal ICJ paradigms to seek inspiration over a newly legitimated influence for global governance.

What follows is based on some fundamental assumptions. The first is that an understanding of internationalization presupposes that the trial processes of ICJ institutions[6] reflect domestic procedural contexts where it is possible to make generalizations about issues of similarity and difference in trial traditions. This is because such a foundation, and resultant traditions, reflect a merging or hybridization of inquisitorial and adversarial trial forms.

---

4   Again, Chapter 8 describes and justifies the notion of communities of justice as the appropriate constituencies (and promoters) of ICJ.
5   These go beyond the conventional interest of trial justice in retribution. In different traditions of trial procedure there may be differential emphasis on deterrence, community protection, reform and restitution as motivators for justice and punishment. Alternative to trial justice there is emerging in ICJ an active interest in restoration and reconciliation.
6   Findlay (2002a, 2002b) Henham (2002b, 2003a, 2003b).

Implicit in this is the second assumption – namely, that the study of internationalization and comparativism go hand in hand. In other words, an appreciation of the relationship between international and national trial processes necessitates a theoretical and methodological commitment to comparative analysis at many levels. International trial processes need to be understood in terms which are able to make sense of their origins. This implies that an understanding of the content and parameters of international trial procedure depends upon an ability to comprehend the origins and significance of structure and process. It also serves to draw a conceptual distinction between the creation and development of new, exclusive forms of international trial process and those reflecting accommodation or compromise across otherwise separate justice paradigms.

Our commitment to internationalization and comparativism is also driven by a need to gauge the extent to which international trial practice conforms with particular human rights considerations,[7] or indeed, to question whether reflecting trial practice against such concerns is an adequate measure of ICJ. Opening up access to a more inclusive and accountable trial process is intended to entrench human rights commitments in ICJ through wider trial contexts. To complete the ICJ picture we range into alternative justice resolutions and ask whether the 'rights protections' institutionally on offer through international trial process might also enhance and promote restorative outcomes and victim expectations. More generally, we also engage with broader criminological themes concerning the relationship between postmodernity and the penality of ICJ, such as the reconfiguration of the relationship between citizen and state in the context of the new international world order. Justice as a crucial component of global governance is a concluding challenge.

Originally, the book is concerned with two inter-related dimensions of international justice research. First, it seeks to explain the development and application of comparative contextual analysis (CCA),[8] an innovative approach developed by the authors for the international and comparative analysis of criminal trials. In describing CCA the book is arguing for a fresh understanding of transitional trial process and a

---

7   When discussing the notion of rights here (see Findlay 2001c; Henham 2004), much of the focus is on individualized protections. Particularly in our reflections on restorative justice we would not limit rights to first-generation but, rather, include third-generation and communal rights, as well as paradigms within which rights compete and are modified in a contested process.

8   First presented in Findlay (1999a).

radical change in the approach to comparative method in sociolegal studies. We explore the building blocks for effective comparative analysis and go on to apply these to understanding trials within and across certain jurisdictional settings. These have resonance for incorporating restorative dimensions within a transformed international trial process. The arguments are introduced through a presentation about crucial features of the trial and ways in which these can be analysed within a model of the trial as decision-making. The reasons for this model are made clear, as is the novel notion of the trial comprising pathways of influence towards common and predictable outcomes in a variety of analytical and practical contexts. Internationalization is discussed along with other important levels for analysis. Our thesis is that ICJ can only be understood through the comparative contextualization of regional and local trial processes/institutions responsible for their own versions of justice. We make clear that any effective comparative trial case studies must grow from a consideration of theorizing, modelling and methodologies for comparative criminal justice. A natural consequence is to explore international justice processes which supplement or augment trial potential. This then has to be followed by a deep understanding of trial justice in individual/operational contexts, to precede any comparative exercise. Knowledge in context will suggest the limits to universalization (Findlay 1999a, 1999c, 2001a). The trial, examined as a component of ICJ in specific cultural contexts, will allow for a critique of its process, and the emergence of a blueprint for its transformation, being as it is currently the institutional face of ICJ.

In essence, Parts I and II are a comparative study of criminal justice focusing on the trial process and its transformation. They examine theoretical models and political applications of criminal justice through detailed empirical analysis, in order to explore the underlying relationship of theory and empirical study, applying the outcome in theory-testing and policy evaluation at several jurisdictional levels.

The methodology of CCA enables a multi-dimensional exploration of contexts (local, regional and global) that recognizes the importance of difference within an agenda of synthesis (Findlay 2001a: 26–53) in process and paradigms. The methodology incorporates a detailed examination of trial practice in nominated settings, a comparative exploration of process across these settings, and an extrapolation of universal understandings about decision-making going forward to engage the common components of ICJ. In so doing comparison is possible on the domestic, regional and international level. It will be thematic and sensitive to the original and developmental contexts of similarity and difference. The process of decision-making in the determination of justice outcomes is the overarching context within which comparison is maintained. Agency facilitating process is preferred to a consideration of normative frameworks and structures as representing the 'people action' that is the trial.

To inform a comparative analysis of justice as a process that makes, substantiates and stimulates crucial and common relationships becomes a central consideration. This analysis is facilitated through accommodating the unique application of discretion within crucial decision pathways. What makes this book important is that it takes the task of comparison seriously, and interrogates the trial as a dynamic decision-making process at several levels of interaction. Essential to this understanding is a foundational and intimate inquiry into how trial decisions come about within different jurisdictional settings (local, regional, international), and what binds trial decision-making together. The natural outcome of considering *pathways of influence* operating here in decision-making, rather than more static decision structures in the trial, makes possible a transformational analysis, one where trial justice may also participate in restorative options to victim communities.

International trial focus

The trial is the focus of analytical interest because of its significance as a symbol of developing ICJ in its institutional sense. The assumption is that the structure and process of the public trial will necessarily legitimate ICJ, whenever it is employed.

The leap from domestic jurisdictional and process comparison to speculation concerning ICJ is achieved by a conventional search for universal themes and institutional foundations, complemented by a more radical exposition of the mechanics of decision-making and the influences which mould discretion. Our work examining comparative criminal justice traditions, formal and informal, and ICJ trends confirms the significance of the trial as a potent symbol of justice in action at the international level (Findlay 2001a; Henham 2003a).

In any procedural tradition much happens beyond the trial to bring about criminal justice resolutions. However, at the level of representation at least, the trial is now what tends to declare, demonstrate and determine ICJ in a formal sense. Furthermore, the trial is the most public display of interactive decision-making in the justice process, and is what the public, the politician and the policy-maker equate with justice in action.

The trial, therefore, is a crucial theatre for ICJ. Within the trial (and the different trial traditions we examine), the principal relationships which produce decisions and outcomes may be viewed as *pathways to justice* where a range of influences can be identified, interactions measured and outcomes predicted. We argue that this is a crucial common theme from the local to the international trial. These relationships can be exclusive or inclusive (of lay participation, its influence and legitimate expectations), and the manner in which they facilitate or impede the essential interaction of the trial becomes critical in evaluating justice outcomes (Henham and Findlay 2001c).

The context in which these relationships operate (in regional and international justice institutions in particular) is supposedly governed by a fair trial 'rights' paradigm. We identify access and inclusion as the primary indicators of fairness to all, particularly lay participants in the trial action. The degree to which this is achieved indicates much about the nature and limits of ICJ, and its potential as a reliable producer of fair outcomes. For example, sentencing (as a consequence of trial decision-making) provides a focus for how these various trial 'pathways' converge to confirm or deny justice against a 'rights' based procedural model. At present, that model can prefer the interests of one side while at the same time having difficulty recognizing and balancing the equally legitimate rights of others. Sentencing can be seen as the crucial outcome wherein a variety of earlier decision pathways (even those pre-trial) need to be considered. It will also suggest how 'new' classes of global interest and influence (i.e. victim communities) need not be driven away from formal justice routes simply because retributive outcomes are not sufficient for their wider collective expectations.

The context of the book is internationalization. The discussion of trial process is directed towards an informed interpretation of international criminal trials. As a crucial context for the achievement of comparative analysis, internationalization is presented against other layers of location which might be domestic and regional. From each layer is drawn common themes such as societal values, moral action, community, citizenship, reintegration and inclusion which enable an understanding of how concepts of justice translate from one location to another. Internationalization is a truly transitional context.

Internationalization is also deeply paradoxical. In its current manifestations it is heavily reliant on homogeneous notions of community. However, the 'international community' is anything but pluralist. Rather, the new world order is coterminous with competing and conjectural notions of community at more local and regional levels where citizenship is problematic and the inclusion and exclusion it provides tend to challenge simple determinations of criminal responsibility. This has telling implications for restorative justice paradigms and argues for their protection within a rights-based and dominant (universal) institutional framework. Restorative justice advocates are wary of any institutional co-option for fear that it might compromise the cultural relativity and relevance of indigenous restorative processes. Their locality, it is argued, is their legitimacy. We agree but suggest that in such relative and ungoverned localities grow the seeds of 'rights-denial' along with selective victim inclusion.

At the same time, at the international level, institutions of trial and penality are anxious to confirm model liberal democratic notions of justice by identifying the individual responsibilities of those whose actions put them outside the global polis. The presence of such a profound paradox does not prevent a consideration of restorative justice processes within and beyond the international trial. In fact it suggests the need to integrate retributive and restorative processes if ICJ is to achieve its most inclusive potentials for global governance.

Analytical underpinning

During the course of our analysis we elaborate our commitment to the concept of the trial as a processual activity. Our understanding of process as a social phenomenon recognizes that it:

- is a recursive activity;
- has 'objectivity' as structure;
- occurs through social interaction;
- is enabled by rules and resources; and
- is patterned through communication structures/systems.

We take the view that the dimensions involved in the creation and patterning of processual activity exist over time and space, across cultures and from global to local contexts. We also maintain that the relationship between human agency and process is crucial, because it is through the discretionary decision-making process that the relative realities of fact and value merge. Consequently, where the fact/value distinction is drawn we do so, as Tamanaha (1997) suggests, 'standing on the ground' in context, and not proposing a perspective-free versus a perspective-bound contrast. The distinction between values and facts as functionally separate aspects of experience is therefore depicted in commonsense terms, within the action of the trial.

Finally, we suggest that understanding outcomes depends on deconstructing crucial sites for decision-making within the trial in terms of the relationships between trial participants. We therefore conceptualize decision-making in the context of process in terms of a series of frames of action each of which recursively contributes to mould the trial process and its outcomes – what we describe as pathways of decision-making. Such a conceptualization moves beyond the notion of decision sites and their relative significance as process variables and focuses on context; more specifically, the cultural contexts in which significant trial relationships are created and merge to determine the exercise of discretionary power at significant decision sites in the trial process.

The book's next analytical dimension is both instrumental and aspirational in that it purports to suggest how CCA can help us to move towards the development of viable and meaningful conceptions of ICJ and their development.[9] In other words, whilst we seek to describe how the theoretical and methodological imperatives of CCA can underpin the rational development of international criminal procedure and penal sanctions, we also suggest the direction which this should take in advocating a conceptualization of the international criminal trial that repositions its purpose in terms of restorative justice (RJ).[10] The reasons

---

9   As Braithwaite suggests: 'impartiality is not neutral on the law. It stands for justice and protecting the victims of human rights abuses, for being clear that abuses of human rights are wrong and must stop' (2002a chap 6).

10 See, further, Braithwaite and Pettit (1990); Zehr (1990); Zedner (1994); Dignan and Cavadino (1996); Dignan (1999a); Findlay (2000c); Braithwaite (1989a, 2002a); Johnstone (2002); Hirsch *et al.* (2003). Dignan (1999a) suggests that the philosophy upon which RJ is based can best be summarized in terms of three principles:

1   Responsibility – to engage with offenders to try to bring home the consequences of their actions and an appreciation of the impact they have had on the victim(s) of their offences.

2   Restoration – to encourage and facilitate the provision of appropriate forms of reparation by offenders towards either their direct victims (provided which are agreeable) or the wider community.

3   Reintegration – to seek reconciliation between victim and offender where this can be achieved and, even in cases where this is not possible, to strive to reintegrate both victims and offenders within the community as a whole following the commission of an offence.

for this are essentially contextualized in the aspirations of global victim communities. In this respect, the analysis of these may emerge out of appreciating a significant pathway of influence within the international trial process as it stands (victim/judge) and how it needs to grow in a rights-based context.

However, our analysis reaches far beyond conventional contemporary expectations for RJ. It involves an approach which aims to succeed in restating the rationality of the international trial as a process which is primarily engaged in the pursuit of 'truth', and that this should not only be seen in terms which are relevant to victims or victim communities. We therefore envisage a major task for CCA is to produce insights into the meaning of morally relative concepts such as 'truth', 'justice' or 'fairness'. These then are suggested as essential connections between ICJ and global governance. For example, a significant issue which links the international and domestic dimension is the nature of the trial process as a transformative mechanism – the extent to which the trial process (especially sentencing) can link together notions of morality, law and behaviour around the 'truth' of the verdict. The resolution of this issue has significant practical implications for determining the extent to which international forms of penality can engage with notions of 'truth' and 'justice' in global communities, problematic as we suggest these are. It also raises some significant theoretical questions about how law is (or can be) implicated in this process. The analysis, if it is to be genuinely reflective of the widest ICJ concerns as they are currently developing, cannot stop there.

How can competing rationalizations for process be prioritized? Surely, the positioning of RJ (as with other justifications for sanction relationships and the establishment of truth beyond the notion of individual liability) depends on context. In the third part we play with contexts, which are victim centred, in order to test and balance trial purposes which work towards punishment, and/or could incorporate reconciliation. The search for truth should be a common component of both, procedurally and in terms of outcomes.

However, in essence the problem remains that of how to rationalize ICJ in terms which envisage the trial as the means for giving effect to the priorities for justice suggested by the context of a particular social conflict. At present the justification for penality around which it is easiest to mobilize (in the sense of a symbolic global response) is retribution. As the underlying rationale for punishment this tends to preclude any constructive engagement with RJ themes (Zedner 1994). Yet, if we look at the trial as an institution whose social function is the pursuit of 'truth' (from contested fact/value) this provides a rationale which can claim universal appeal, and which resonates with RJ.

We therefore have to look carefully at what the international trial is for and what the process signifies. In common with the justice paradigms from which their rules and procedures are drawn, international criminal institutions provide a forum where the guilt or innocence of the accused is established according to designated norms of international procedure. Clearly, in practice this does not necessarily provide a context for 'truth',[11] let alone reconciliation (Drumbl 2001). It is axiomatic that guilt does not necessarily equate with 'truth' in terms of what actually took place, nor (therefore) does it equate with any basic notion of 'justice' – either in terms that the process has convicted the correct person of the correct crime, or that the consequential penalty is appropriate.[12]

Accordingly, if the norms that regulate proof and establish guilt do not necessarily deliver 'truth' in the context of any conventional trial paradigm, it has to be decided how the rationale of the international trial[13] can be transformed so that it sits comfortably with the idea that the process exists for the purpose of facilitating outcomes of 'truth' which have meaning for all parties to social conflict and their political audience. Here, if truth-finding within the trial process better points to restoration through the acceptance of responsibility, rather than the adversarial proof of individual liability, then trial professionals should have the discretion to move towards such an outcome. An apparently fundamental obstacle to this derives from the current dialectical nature of the trial process as a sanctioning mechanism. Hence, the communicative and relational context of the trial experience is (unlike mediation) not aimed at establishing the grounds for shared understandings or, as Habermas (1981) suggests, mutual or joint attempts at interpretation aimed at consensus. As Mannozzi (2002a) describes, conventional modelling of the perpetrator/victim relationship sees it as dualistic and paradoxical; whilst being connected by crime the two parties are at the same time divided by it. We suggest that relationships between people in the process hold the key. The pathways of influence which formulate and emerge out of these relationships constantly search for moral 'truths' and, at the same time, mechanisms for

---

11 For a detailed interrogation of truth as it is distilled in jury verdicts, see Maher (1988).

12 A process may, of course, be judged as 'just' or 'fair' according to the criteria set by particular normative paradigms.

13 Adjusting or modifying the model is inadequate. See Dignan and Cavadino (1996).

restoration within an atmosphere of allocated responsibility. Analysing these pathways of influence rather than concentrating on their outcomes makes an argument for transforming trial process to meet the needs of ICJ more apparent. The important point is that, as with perpetrators and victims, reunification within the terms of the penal process is as a pair of 'opposites' and opponents. Our task in redefining the rationality for trial process in the resolution of social conflict is therefore to facilitate the possibilities for sharing and proposing new (peaceful) interpretations or, to put it another way, providing the context for the construction of shared (or common) interpretations of 'truth' out of the contested fact framework.[14]

In this book we carefully examine the rationales for trial process at the local and global level, concentrating particularly on what it means (represents), and for whom. In so doing we adopt the following conceptualization of trial process (processual paradigm) in terms of the interaction between law and moral behaviour:

- Process may be seen to represent particular values – moral justifications.

- These values are embodied as process in the form of ethical (normative) principles.

- Process may be seen in terms of its 'reality' – where fact and value merge (this constitutes the explanatory endeavour).

- Process may be seen in terms of outcome – what does this 'reality' actually represent in terms of these values/ethics (this has to be an explanation of what outcome *is* against what it *represents*)? But,

- Principally, relationships of decision-making and the pathways of influence which contextualize these.

If we look at the relationship between process and purpose diagrammatically, then as Figure I.1 shows, process can be conceived as a transformation (negotiation) that mirrors both justification and legitimacy.

---

14 Note that Christodoulidis (2000) questions the capacity of legal rules to bring about reconciliatory functions. He argues that law is over-deterministic and incapable of proceeding beyond the categorical abstractions imposed by the reductive nature of legal rules. He suggests that essentially complex reflexive ethical decisions cannot be reached solely within a legal context, nor can it address the phenomenological connections between conflict and social identity necessary to produce reconciliation.

Figure I.1 Conceptualizing the relationship between legitimacy and justification

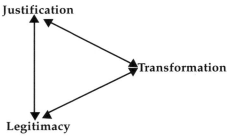

Moral values or justifications represent ideological positions that may either be designated as *hegemonic*, such as power, authority, social control, imperialism, repression, or *relational* – justice (as identified through integrated sentencing, truth, reconciliation, humanitarianism). This discussion of truth cannot be divorced from the purposes of truth-seeking: reconciliation, but within the context of the determination of guilt.

Ethical principles are represented in procedural norms (due process principles) and human rights paradigms. These principles are ensured through more open and accountable discretion in the decision process. Rights are represented through access to and inclusion within an accountable justice process. In our discussion of the new international trial the justification is to better recognize victim communities. The transformation is of a normative framework and its process which is more accessible and inclusive. Legitimacy is enhanced through the accountable exercise of these rights for disenfranchised victims, and this in turn sees trial decision-making more in tune with victim expectations. We argue that process integration must take place at each of these three levels:

1 *Justification* – ideological level – reconciliation of the hegemonic and the relational.

2 *Transformation* – reconciliation of normative principles.

3 *Legitimacy* – reconciliation of communities.[15]

Trial process integration is achieved through the accountable exercise of professional discretion (such as judicial) within crucial pathways of

---

15 We recognize significantly differing interpretations of 'community' and their implications. See, for example, Cotterrell (1997), Weisberg (2003b).

influence (such as judge/victim). In order to accommodate new intentions for trial justice the authority and role of professionals within decision relationships will need to change and will stand as essential evidence of wider trial transformation (see Chapter 8).

Our trial paradigm provides a rational structure for a menu of collaborative justice resolutions.[16] It must be conceptualized as both vertical and lateral in its effects; vertical because, as pointed out, the moral justification for action (through process) must engage with (be legitimate) in the eyes of significant others (such as judges and victims) – lateral, because each level of our paradigm requires some accommodation (reconciliation) with our motivation for change. Hence, ideology, process and legitimacy are infused with the same moral purpose[17] and imperatives for shared interpretations through communication. The accommodation of relational justifications requires a moral commitment that takes the form of direct participation by significant others in the normative process. For instance, within trial justice the empowerment of the victim must have more potential than simply to legitimate retributive sentencing agendas. Victims' interests will constrain judges to recognize the importance of RJ outcomes for the benefit of generic victims who, after all, are the justification of international criminal jurisdiction.

Conventional process models are not conceived as transformative in the sense we are suggesting is necessary for the integration of restorative themes.[18] The current retributive paradigm for international

---

16 Collaborative justice is well revealed in transitional cultures where custom-based justice resolutions predominate. In such settings, formal, state-sponsored criminal justice is required to recognize custom in order to share in its legitimacy and outreach. The difficulty presented in such collaborations is the potential for the formal justice institutions to distort and disorient the custom resolutions. This is a consequence of contextual dislocation without the institutions which are importing the custom-based resolutions being transforming in order to accommodate unfamiliar regulatory conditions and resolutory motivations.

17 We advance the connection between morality and community. For ICJ foundational moralities exist within the 'global community' and are symbolic more than actual because of this. They require enunciation as a crucial component of the development of global communities and their justice.

18 Packer (1968), for example, provides a typology, a heuristic device concerned to identify norms operating within the criminal justice system that express principles appealing to the value positions adopted by crime control and due process. Ashworth (1998), by contrast, suggests a normative rights paradigm mainly concerned with the identification of principles of substantive and procedural fairness. For further elaboration, see Chapter 3. For an evaluation of how a victim's perspective may be modelled for the criminal justice process, see Dignan and Cavadino (1996) and, for restorative themes and law, Walgrave (2002).

sentencing (for example) firmly espouses the virtues of balance and proportionality in the punishment of wrongdoing, and deterrence. The gravity of the crime is seen as the primary consideration: 'sentences to be imposed must reflect the inherent gravity of the criminal conduct of the accused.'[19] This paradigm continues to maintain for the pluralistic cultures of most Western liberal democracies. The immediate consequence for these democracies is that the state's punishment apparatus increasingly exists merely as a symbolic focus for social control,[20] the moral basis upon which it legitimately exercises the power of punishment (the state's consideration for the powers citizens have autonomously ceded to it as part of the social contract) having diminished.[21] The ideological framework for international penality must equally recognize that the responsibility to protect citizens of the 'global community' against certain consequential aspects of criminality also requires a firm commitment to prevent the exclusion of significant minorities from participating in the processes of ICJ.[22] This exclusion extends to participation in the creation of structures and processes which are instrumental in the protection of human rights through agency action in the process as well as through normative endorsement.

In pluralistic cultures the ideologies for the processes which seek to resolve disputes between individuals and the interests of an identifiable community, are fragmented and contingent. Arguably, a broader basis for process legitimacy is possible if we recognize that the rights infringed by crime are not just those of victims *but are held in common socially* (Braithwaite and Pettit 1990). Zedner (1994) suggests that the wider social purposes of particular forms of conflict resolution include the following imperatives:

- The reassertion of normative order.
- The re-establishment of the rights and obligations of citizens.
- The interpretation and development of law and policy.
- The elaboration and maintenance of (legal) ideology.

---

19 This view was again reinforced recently by the ICTY in the Plavsi judgment: *Prosecutor* v. *Biljana Plavsi* (Case no. IT-00-39 & 40/1-S).
20 As such it is vulnerable to populist pressure against rational policy development.
21 And diminished all the more so when the place of the state is in part replaced by amorphous notions like the 'global community' and 'international organizations'.
22 The redefinition and colonization of conflict situations are crucial determinants of the relationship between citizen and state. See Christie (1977).

In their present manifestation international criminal trial structures fail to deliver resolutions that comply with such criteria. Grounded in retributive justifications borne out of ideologies which seek to control and dominate rather than tolerate pluralism, their legitimacy is symbolic not actual; they represent oppression rather than a force for truth, reconciliation and unity.

It is easy to see how these components accord with the foundations of good governance. If they are strongly incorporated within and promoted by ICJ then the impact of justice on global governance will be enhanced. What are the contexts of global justice within which the transformed trial can operate to help achieve this?

The development of a penality and process which advance community interests through reintegration depends upon the existence of the kind of communitarianism that is founded on relationships of interdependency, trust and group loyalty (Braithwaite 1989a: 85). The global community on the other hand is about dominion. The absence of any infrastructure for social renewal which accompanies the immediate aftermath of violent confrontation and humanitarian catastrophe necessarily means that the impetus for ideological, normative and structural change must initially be externally driven.

A unifying force that governs the conceptualization of rights and social structure is the notion of individualism. Its implication that individual *collective* concern for others *as a moral imperative* is a significant legitimation for national and international structures of penality and justice resolution. The value system of individualism sustains a shared moral culture which transcends national boundaries and predetermines ideologies of criminal justice. The difficulty remains in envisaging the moral basis upon which law's authority is claimed to rest in terms of shared beliefs or sentiments. This is where the communitarian underpinnings of RJ allow for a repositioning of the 'rights' paradigm which guarantees regional and ICJ. How is it possible to *identify* transnational values of individualism in forms of international regulatory power, such as structures designed for the implementation of international penal norms, purporting to be grounded in principles of fairness and justice? The answer lies in the translation of individualized rights concerns into the restorative arena where rights are endorsed but only in a communitarian endeavour. The context of ICJ serving the interests of the global community makes this progression more logical than it may be in other levels of justice delivery which we study. CCA will reveal this and it is indicative of the way in which this analysis flows from the local to the global.

In addition, we must understand the categories of meaning the parties themselves give to their dispute (Caplan 2001) and how these can be negotiated for the restorative purpose. Different sets of norms may be invoked by the same people in different circumstances. The continual negotiation of rules and behaviour may produce situations where contested norms are counterpoised against unequal power; in which case, those at ease with all possibilities have an advantage over those who are not. This is the conventional context of the adversarial trial which is the international model for justice resolution. It demands modification through restorative pathways of influence if the generic rights of global communities are to receive sufficient recognition beyond individualized guilt. A study of the constraints which inform the social organization of undisputed areas of social life reveals many of the underlying forces that influence social control. These take on new meaning through restorative transformation guaranteed within the retributive boundaries of the trial.

The notion of individualism and its collective expression can be further refined in this context for, as Braithwaite (2002a: 264) argues, RJ, which values fairness and justice rather than neutrality (or partiality?), can be used to develop the value framework for deliberating the relative merits of normative action. This is so important for ICJ which currently is bifurcated between the restorative and retributive paradigms, and as a result access to normative rights protections within the formal justice institutions such as the trial is unacceptably selective (see Chapter 7). Public accountability of RJ militates against the domestication of injustice. RJ can be used to engage a plurality of stakeholders and so structurally facilitate the remedying of imbalances of power because of the subjective variant of a global community referent. However, neither of these benefits should be seen as compensation for vast victim communities being asked to choose restorative or retributive processes, institutional rights protection or community accountability.

An important issue in looking at ICJ is to determine what new frameworks of justice operate through the internationalization process. We conclude our text reflecting on the crucial component of collaboration in the transition to a truly inclusive, accessible and accountable criminal justice. Collaboration is imagined in terms of form and constituent relationships. In form, the quality of the relationship between the culture of state justice and the culture of private (civil) justice is crucial, as is the transition of sponsorship from domestic to international 'states'. Regarding the collaboration of civil and state justice, there must be a reciprocal relationship between them – at once enriching and checking – the law filtering down to its indigenous roots and back up again from indigenous deliberation styles.[23] When weaknesses in indigenous disputing are identified they can be remedied through enforceable rights. This is where recourse to a transformed trial justice at the international level becomes crucial.

ICJ, released from a retributive paradigm alone, and further legitimated through a wider victim constituency, will gain the legitimacy and potential more directly to influence global governance, particularly in post-conflict societies. Notions of RJ as peacemaking following global and social conflict call for identification of key stakeholders and negotiation about the reasons for disintegration. This is similar to our interest in the analysis of pathways of influence within the trial setting.

Perhaps in the global context a rethinking of the notion of restorative as collaborative justice is necessary. As Findlay (2000a: 398) suggests:

- The community context is complex.
- Responsibilty to collaborate is unclear.
- To whom that responsibility is owed is unclear.
- Which victims are to be restored is unclear.

There is a need to identify the proponents of custom-based (indigenous) resolution and those with an investment in the rejuvenation of the international process. There is no reason why these should be separated by trial justice. Home-grown restorative mechanisms can influence trial decision-making so that within international concerns for humanity as the victim, trial justice may incorporate a wide array of restorative 'pathways of influence', tailored to the local situation from which they emerged.

In the case of transitional cultures, Findlay (2000a: 407) argues for the development of an interactive model for justice delivery. Education and training are needed to achieve the transition to collaborative justice involving victims, immediate community, perpetrators, police, community agencies and sentencers. It may be argued that the globalized notion of penality is in itself a transitional culture that represents communities within and beyond state boundaries. The one factor that holds them together is a common humanitarian focus. This is obvious where the victim is humanity and the offender may be a political movement

---

23   Weisberg (2003b) cautions against the view that RJ is necessarily a reform of justice, or recapture, of an indigenous moral systems. In this sense, contemporary legal forms 'may thwart the recapture of the authentic'.

designed to segment the global community. The trial can address such divisiveness by establishing boundaries of legality within which RJ is both qualified and possible. The focus of the trial will naturally shift with this change in constituency. The purpose of the trial may shift as access and inclusion for a wider constituency is made possible. Conflict resolution will receive recognition along with punishment. Criminalization in its more domestic understanding has already been reframed through consideration of crimes against humanity, and the determination of truth in favour of actionable individual liability.[24] Outcomes for the international trial will develop in order to recognize such change. All these developments, we argue, are essentially reliant on collaboration between parties to the trial, and those 'communities of justice' as yet not drawn into the protective decision-making environment of trial justice.

Crucial to our analysis of such relationship-reliant collaboration are pathways to decision-making within the trial process. Analytically, these are the legitimate focus for CCA. The analyses in what follows, of pathways of influence, argue for the significance of human agency over structure. The trial is envisaged as a continuum of decision sites relevant to outcome wherein fact/value is negotiated to produce the objectivity of process through outcome. However, the significance of this negotiation remains relative at the subjective level (individual and collective). In order to engage with relevant pathways of influence trial participants and *significant others* must be made to feel that they can claim 'ownership' – that the process is legitimate – that they somehow can have an input in the resolution of those negotiations. They must, in other words, have access to and be significantly included both in the process and the outcome of transformed trial justice. This will be because it is now built upon a shared premise – that the purpose of the process is genuinely pluralistic – to negotiate, transform and re-construct social structure and social life in communities ravaged by war and atrocity.

This is not just a question of education and training trial participants to accept inevitable change. Collaborative justice is a much broader concept as conceived at the global level. Within the trial, our research reveals that it is the relationships between the principal players which enable justice to emerge (or not) as the case may be. This is the same (or more so) for restorative decision-making. Incorporation of this within a trial paradigm will enable the diversity of reintegrative justice with the

---

24   Not to say the latter, along with retribution, are not worthy residual concerns for expanded frames of ICJ.

benefit of a reliance on wider institutional authority and processes of legitimation. Different justice dimensions then collaborate within an accountable, yet dynamic and tolerant institutional framework of the international trial.

Collaborative decision-making creates communities of justice which translate just outcomes through the negotiation of influence. In the international context it is essential to have a safe platform for such negotiation and the trial provides that predetermined framework for relationships to influence just outcomes and restorative pathways to peace that build global communities in safety and integrity. What we are talking about is using the international trial process as a vehicle for the promotion of peace. The book explains how this can be achieved through collaborative justice reliant as it is on the development of *communities of justice* internationally.

Structure of the text

The text is developed in three parts. The first addresses the issue of comparative research into trial process, whilst the second part is devoted to case studies on comparative trial practice and their thematic development towards crucial pathways of influence (judge/victim). The third part speculates on trial transformation and the merger of retributive and restorative ICJ.

Chapter 1 explores the challenges of sociolegal analysis in a comparative domain. Issues such as context, comparison, interaction and interpretation are discussed. The operationalization of the conceptual framework for the analysis is proposed, and the essential connections between theory and methods for CCA argued for. This chapter presents the hard thinking about theorizing and the importance to be placed on comparative analysis grounded in resilient and dynamic theory-building.

More particularly, Giddens' structuration theory is elaborated to provide a set of organizing and interpretative constructs which are capable of identifying elements and processes crucial to the application of rules and resources, by participants during the course of the criminal trial. The theory is developed to recognize structural, organizational and interactive levels of analysis within context. The purpose, therefore, is to use structuration theory as a sensitizing device providing a suitable framework against which to model the major dimensions of decision-making in the criminal trial. Examples of the way in which the theoretical foundation is to be employed and augmented are set out.

Chapter 2 attacks conventional approaches to criminal justice modelling as (variously) atheoretical, overly ideological, heuristic, distractingly normative or as failing to give context its due. A contextual model is then proposed for the analysis of trial process, and trial decisions in particular. Essentially, it is argued that the comparative contextual model facilitates the integration of theoretical and methodological propositions derived from positivist, ethnographic and grounded theory approaches. We explain how the incorporation of particular evaluators for inclusion in the model should follow on from an examination of particular trial contexts. The connections between theory, the contextual model and process are elaborated.

This chapter also looks forward to the manner in which trial decision-making models can facilitate the analysis and application of different ICJ paradigms. As later discussed in Chapter 7, comparative analysis of trial decision-making (modelled and applied) holds out the prospect to determine if restorative and retributive justice aspirations can both exist within international trial process. This may lead to an augmenting of the model and a transformation of trial process. The key, in our thinking, to modelling both trial and justice decision-making at large is the workings of pathways of influence. Relationships between judges (adjudicators) and victims are an example to test these trial-to-trial, local-to-global and between-justice paradigms.

Chapter 3 exemplifies the essence of comparison for the project and the need to approach it anew. The place of context is ventured as is the unique approach we adopt to context-based comparison, and the link between context and objectivity. The trial process is seen both as a context and object for analysis. Within the process, structure and function, procedural traditions, rules and practice, personalities and discretion, and sites for decision-making are each reviewed as useful foci for analysis. In particular when addressing the implementation of an integrated methodology for examining trial decision-making in different contexts, data such as trial narrative are interrogated and the question asked how meaning might be added to their limitations. The importance of an integrated methodology, also relying on observation and commentary, is argued for. Such a methodology will reveal what is behind trial process as decisions, and on the comparative level enable speculation about trial justice, local to global.

Our comparative commitment is trial to trial, on the level of decision-making relationships. The common pathways of influence that evolve should then provide a platform for looking at trial justice local to global, and then to speculate from the trial to RJ paradigms.

Consistent with our commitment to the decision-making model for the trial, the methodology should offer insights into the 'pathways of influence' flowing through crucial decision relationships in the trial. These pathways are where subjective and objective understandings of trial process have a common framework in comparison.

We concede the challenge in presenting a convincing comparative analysis at various levels, but we have been working on just that core challenge for years now. Regarding the significance of the trial as a methodological focus it is important to remember its inversion in the internationalized setting. While in local and even regional criminal justice traditions the trial may be overshadowed by the operational significance of pre- and post-trial process, the trial is the essential embodiment of ICJ. Even so, we caveat our interest, accepting what has gone before and what will follow. Our emphasis is on the trial as a process of decision-making and this depends on the widest interpretation of the trial as such. Our focus on sentencing allows for a marriage of speculation between institutions and process in terms of essential output measures for justice in any popular level.

A rejection of modelling criminal justice process (particularly for the purposes of comparison) forgets that a book such as this builds on our work of deep theorizing, and a tested pilot methodology for comparing Italian and English trials (Henham and Findlay 2001c). Further, methodology which works out of deep theorizing and creative comparative modelling, should enable credible speculation on the transformation of ICJ, presented in Chapter 7.

Part II introduces the aspirations for the comparative case studies. These as presented cannot be the definitive individual analyses of trial processes from the chosen jurisdictions. Nor are the narrative data held out as being representative or sufficient for a full comparative analysis of trials in context (jurisdiction to jurisdiction, local to global). Rather, this is an opportunity to suggest from limited but no less provocative research terrain, the extent to which satisfying comparison is possible, and develop insights for internationalization. In particular, the theme of lay/professional interaction in the trial process, and its significance in ensuring fair trial, is emphasized. Such relationships are the context for pathways of influence and we will generalize from these in order to draw common themes from local/comparative to international trial contexts. In particular, the example of victim/judge interaction is detailed in order both to explain one pathway of influence and to identify a common relationship for comparative application.

There is an emphasis in Chapters 4–6 on the verdict delivery and sentencing stages. Further, the importance of discretion in the relationship between, say, judges and victims, lay and professional judges, jurors and lawyers is interrogated in detail, which provides unique descriptive and analytical understandings of how trials work. It also provides the substance for our investigation of common pathways of influence in trial settings at several levels of analysis.

Part II develops the suggestion that an enhanced rights focus in the international criminal trial offers three important possibilities for the significant pathway of decision-making influence, judge/victim. Initially, broadening and improving access for a wider range of victim communities to trial rights will enliven the place of victims in trial decision-making and give them greater presence in determining formal justice outcomes. Incorporated within the transformation of trial decision-making, part of which a rejuvenation of judicial discretion will provide (as posited in Chapter 6), the judge/victim relationship will act as a stimulus for a wider consideration of trial rights, away from protections and towards opportunities for access.[25] It might also develop a critical pathway of influence making sense of, and showing the way for, the incorporation of RJ within the international trial.

In Chapter 4 a complete murder trial transcript, and a number of vignettes of examination in other Italian trials, suggest the dynamics between lay and professional participants. It also reveals clues for a more specific investigation of the relationship between judges and victims. The Italian jurisdiction is chosen because, as a consequence of recent procedural reform at least, it is a trial style experiencing fundamental change. This revision of normative frameworks and the hybrid justice form which ensues may not be all it seems in practice, and here our earlier considerations of procedural synthesis are implicitly critiqued. This level of interpretation is important in addressing the limitations of narrative analysis. Inter-related themes, such as the influence of a rights paradigm, novel presentations of evidence, the role of the judge as mediator, the importance of pre-trial interrogation, and the tone and significance of narrative forms, are set out in this chapter. From these the contextual model is applied and tested, setting the agenda for the analysis of common law narratives in Chapter 5. The ground is prepared for examining the significance of decision-making

---

25   Recognizing the instrumentality of judicial discretion as a means for transforming trial decision-making we argue is insufficient without processual norms of accountability that mirror the substantive content of rights and provide for their realization as a meaningful social reality. As we suggest in Chapter 6, the judge/victim relationship stimulus enables and develops the norms of access and accountability, but only where a commitment towards a transformed trial process has already been made.

relationships (lay/professional) and extracting the influences which formulate these relationships and their decision-making outcomes. The importance of discretion is suggested, then developed as an essential tool for trial transformation when applied in more detail to the victim/ judge relationship (Chapter 6).

A particular feature of Chapter 4 is the identification of themes which may support the later contention that the trial can be transformed to support wider international justice paradigms. For instance, the importance of evidence production and fact-finding, essential to the common goal of truth in retributive and restorative processes, is revealed through a close examination of the relationships in the process which provide 'facts' for trial decision-making. The connection between facts and 'truth' (moral or otherwise) seems important for both retributive and RJ processes. The argument that the trial is uniquely and universally well-suited to produce facts is reflected upon. If confirmed through comparative analysis, then this may be one of other themes to support the mutuality of retribution and restoration as outcomes for international trials. This is contested and developed in detail in Part III.

In Chapter 5, through the interrogation of common law trial transcripts similar in form and content to those reviewed in the previous chapter, we take the comparative investigation of trial decisions one context further. Comparative contextual analysis reveals a detailed understanding of another trial style, and sets out themes for comparing harmony and dissonance in trial decision-making as it may evolve at regional and international levels, influenced as they seem to be by both local procedural traditions (civil and common law).

The common law referent is selected as the other major procedural influence on the internationalization of criminal justice. Reflecting on the issues which emerge from the Italian experience (and the application of our analytical model), Chapter 5 employs structural and integrated process levels of analysis in order to speculate on crucial components and variants to trial process, and within each trial context. These themes have emerged in Chapter 4 and are now compared with the decision-making narrative declared through English judgments. The model of trial decision-making is also tested to see if there are some common levels of significance in the apparent pathways of influence described or suggested in the narrative.

Such comparative analysis then allows for the identification and manipulation of those contextual elements common to trial decision-making, in order to produce universal themes ripe for testing in regional and international justice contexts. Preparatory to this we also reflect on fair trial influences in both procedural paradigms in this and the preceding chapter, particularly from the point of access to justice. The access consideration is important in the examination of the victim/judge pathway of influence and its present constrictions within ICJ. The 'rights' paradigm for trial decision-making is important in regional and international trial processes. It also presents a common language when, in our concluding part, we propose a transformed trial model to support transforming ICJ.

Chapters 4 and 5 reveal the first stage of CCA – that being the deep individual analysis of social contexts prior to engaging in comparison. These two domestic traditions of trial process are explored employing a uniform analysis into narrative revealing common decision-making themes.[26] Comparison is possible once the domestic contextual investigation is performed, not simply around issues of similarity and difference, within and between the two contexts. Relying on our theory of trial justice and our model of trial decision-making, the intimate, individual contextual analysis offers up the significance of the judge/victim relationship interrogated in Chapter 6. This then enables a discussion of pathways of influence in the process that has particular relevance to international trials and their potential for exploring trial-centred ICJ.

Chapter 6 has two distinct purposes. The first is to interrogate the relationship between victims and judicial officers in the construction of the sentence. This important relationship of influence in the setting of penality is at the heart of RJ. It is a somewhat flawed relationship in the international trial context because of the current incapacity of the trial to meet retributive and restorative aspirations of many significant global victim communities. The English and Italian trial models are interrogated further in order to establish the manner in which often-competing interests are integrated to satisfy sometimes-competing sentencing principles. This leads on to the second purpose, which is to reflect these relationships against the 'fair-trial' aspirations of regional and international justice institutions and the difficulties they will face in realizing them through the sentencing style.

The victim/judge pathway of influence exhibits contemporary thinking and political policy about appropriate purposes for justice. This is alluded to but not clearly or harmoniously enunciated in the divided paradigms of ICJ (see Part III). The trial therefore becomes an interesting comparative context in which the real and the symbolic

---

26 So saying, the narrative produced out of the two different trial traditions is distinctly different in form, content and meaning.

significance of victim communities (uniquely constructed in ICJ) emerge in the evaluation of justice coverage and quality.

The rights of lay participants were a critical theme emerging from the contextual analysis of trial traditions, especially as they connected with trial professionals in decision-making. Transposed into the inter-national setting (and with particular relevance to the judge/victim relationship) themes of access, inclusion and accountability represent developing trial rights. Judicial discretion, and its accountable application, is suggested as a reconciling normative 'rights' framework with the challenge to expand trial access and inclusion to a range of new outcomes and processes.

It is the relationship between the victim and trial professionals (the judge in particular) which sets up an important pathway of influence in trial decision-making. Parts II and III are linked by the analysis of expectations held out for that relationship, their achievement in com-parative contexts, and the manner in which this relates to the processes and purposes of ICJ. A 'rights' paradigm for justice is a reason for arguing the inclusion of RJ processes and outcomes within the trial process to meet the widest expectations of victim communities. To achieve this will depend in no small part on a renegotiation of lay/professional participation, represented by the judge/victim relation-ship in particular. Questions are raised concerning whether this needs a redesigned normative framework for the international trial, and where the exercise of discretion sits with all this.

As the second purpose we also want to look at the manner in which the international sentencing principal and international trial insti-tutions recognize the significance of the judge/victim relationship and how this is compatible with what is revealed through our comparative analysis of trials. If, as we suspect, the victim's (community's) desire is for restoration and retribution, what features of their pathway of influence support these within the trial and what may need to be transformed in order to achieve them? How common are the features of this relationship in working towards restorative and retributive outcomes? Answers to these issues should provide some empirical basis for the speculation on inclusive justice in the following chapter.

The revolutionary thinking in the book is in Part III and, as such, its summary deserves more detail and integrated argument than we have so far introduced for the other two parts. Part III works from the indication that access, inclusion and accountability will drive a new form of international trial process more sensitive to the interests of victim communities. Greater access for victims to transformed trial justice will generate a closer examination of victim interests in the trial beyond its current retributive priority. It will also invite a critical review of victim inclusion in the processes of trial decision-making. Access to trial justice is one issue for a refocusing of trial pathways of influence. Yet without making the victim's voice more prominent and better recognized within trial decisions, the balance of influence might be little changed. The under-emphasis of inclusion has meant that recent attempts to further introduce victims within the trial seem little more than symbolic. Victim communities have turned instead to alternative justice paradigms in order that their involvement may be, for them, more meaningful. The challenge for the final part of this book is to transform trial decision-making to meet the needs of victim communities for greater access and inclusion. With this motivation in mind it is argued that trial process and outcomes should embrace and incorporate where possible the essential features of alternative justice paradigms to seemingly better satisfy inclusivity in particular.[27] RJ, for instance, should become a more significant concern within the victim/ judge decision site if the trial, and its reflection of the rights of trial contestants, incorporates and supports those justice principles which to date have conventionally be seen as an alternative to trial process.[28]

In an international justice context in particular, disempowered victim communities tend to reject the trial in favour of less formal alternative resolution processes, or have been redirected away from the trial and its accountable processes (e.g. Gacaca sessions in Rwanda). As a result, those communities, and the alternative justice paradigms they utilize, tend to be accorded a lower political legitimacy by international organizations when compared with more formal ICJ, wherein the trial is considered paramount.[29] From this perspective the relative merits of RJ processes and outcomes, and their compatibility with the trial, tend to be removed from the debate regarding harmonization (Delmas-Marty and Spencer 2002). The paradox here is that victim communities in turn invest legitimacy in the alternative process and not the trial.

In Chapter 7 we argue that while choice and diversity in justice paradigms are important for contextual sensitivity, there is no need for an essentially dichotomous analysis here (see Zedner 1994; Schiff 1996;

---

27 No doubt this will also require some modification in the essentials of alternative paradigms in order to ensure a collaborative and comfortable 'best fit'.

28 As the chapter progresses we recognize and address the arguments that any such incorporation is either inappropriate or ill-conceived. ICJ, we say, provides a unique context wherein this marriage is in the best interests of victim communities and of the trial as a forum for their advancement.

29 Note the clear equation of ICJ with public trial institutions such as the ICC.

Daly 1998). If a transformed trial process (see Chapter 8 for details) opens up access to processes and outcomes protected by a strong rights framework, then this is the challenge for the trial and ICJ on which it relies. In this instance the rights are those of victims and victim communities as well as accused persons. The protection of lay participation is the motivation behind a consideration of rights here.

To ensure the impact of these rights guarantees, and in achieving this help in transforming the trial, Chapter 8 details that there will need to be much more than a shift in substantive and procedural norms. Professional participants in the trial in particular, and the communities they service, will need to embrace inclusivity and wider contexts of community responsibility for trial justice.

The third significant motivation for the opening up of a transformed and potentially restorative trial process is the enhancement of accountability. This is vital for the development of a more accessible and inclusive ICJ which better protects the rights of lay participants. Again as flagged in Chapters 6 and 7 and discussed more fully in Chapter 8, the expanding of accountability is through the enhancement of judicial discretion in the direction of lay participants in the trial, their support communities and their legitimate interests. This requires accountability to be structured around the significant decision relationships in the trial such as the judge and victim. A consequence will be diversion away from rigid normative ascription to the predominant rights of one party, or professionalism removed from community responsibility.

It would be naïve to think that greater accountability is an essential consequence of trial transformation. It has to be both a force for transformation and a measure of its achievement but in both it needs management through a new normative framework. This is not to say the ICJ currently does not allow for judicial discretion to promote victim interests and accountability. Proposed here is that trial transformation should rely on more accountable processes, a genuine, pervasive and inclusive rights-consciousness, and in turn produce these features as trial outcomes.

As a measure of the rights impact of the transformed trial, accountability will be the corollary of increased access both in terms of the justification for and practice of new trial justice. Chapter 6 identifies accountability as the determining factor for procedural norms governing trial transformation, as well as the rationale for inclusive[30] ICJ

---

30 By inclusivity here we mean the greater effective involvement of lay participants, their significant communities and their legitimate interests within the widest range of trial decision-making.

policy. This is the 'best practice' foundation for criminal trial relation-ships, as they should currently operate in their widest sense. Chapter 7 builds on this to analyse the arguments for trial transformation which would complement and reshape normative governance through accountable, discretionary applications. Chapter 8 details how this works.

For inclusion to be effective, it requires norms of accountability These norms in the procedures and substance of trial justice as it stands may be simply rhetorical and devoid of any intention to broaden access and participation.[31] The exercise of discretion to facilitate trial decision-making and to reconcile the fact/value dichotomy in trial tasking can, however, be used to transform processual norms into more inclusive outcomes.[32] This then locates discretion as a means of interpreting, modifying and applying transformed process rationales such as inclusivity. Norms of accountability (as evidence and consequences of a rights paradigm in ICJ) will in the transformed trial govern, and be governed by, the discretionary pathways of influence at the heart of trial decision-making. Chapter 6 shows how the judge/victim pathway requires this. The decision relationships, and their product, will work then towards a more integrated penality, as well as enjoying diversion to restorative outcomes preceding sentence and punishment. In so doing trial decisions must reflect and confirm those substantive and procedural norms endorsing inclusivity.

Accountability is a resonant theme complementing the individual responsibility focus of both retributive and restorative justice (addressed in Chapter 6). It is essential to the aspirations of the International Criminal Court (ICC). It is a measure of the rights impact and the coverage of ICJ, and will confirm its legitimacy and relevance for interested communities. The trial can be its medium since our model determines it as a process, with definitive trajectories and path-ways of influence which they determine. The RJ process, if brought within the trial, will tend to soften the fact/value divide of the trial as it stands, by providing more meaningful access to victims and their communities in situations where retributive justice alone may limit appropriate relief from a victim and community perspective.

Chapter 7 develops various levels of argument for the positioning of other justice paradigms within the trial. The operational relevance of the trial in the delivery of ICJ is put against its symbolic significance

31   For instance, victim impact.
32   These would include an expanded array of outcomes anticipated by victims and their communities through alternative/RJ processes operating currently in ICJ.

and the question is posed: how can the trial be transformed so its symbolic and practical relevance might be drawn closer together? In addition, the need to locate the development of restorative ICJ within a rights-based process that does not require the essential compromise of one pathway of influence, is advanced.

Chapter 8 has the purpose of materializing the process and outcomes of the transformed trial. This will be achieved by engaging with the dimensions (structures) of international trial justice we have mentioned earlier (ideological,[33] jurisdictional, institutional and interactive). In order to manage the scope of this endeavour, the discussion in Chapter 8 limits the contentious elements of transformation policy down to a focus on a few indicative themes. We utilize the concept of legitimacy as a binding theme. How can the trial enhance its legitimacy as an essential deliverer of ICJ through the integration of other justice forms and what are the critical consequences of these?

Chapter 8 commences with a selective interrogation of the essence of the trial. What are the crucial components of trial practice and institutions particularly within the context of ICJ? What essentially cannot be reconfigured at the risk that we are left with something that cannot claim to be a trial? In this it is still necessary to see the trial in a dynamic light, not bound by single normative and institutional representations.[34]

It is natural from a discussion of essence that we can look at what is available for change. This is put against the discussion in Chapter 7 of why and where change should occur. Here we rehearse the difficulties associated with any transformation. Several preconditions for change (such as the repositioning of the professional in trial decision-making), posed in Chapter 7, are given some critical, practical edge here. The nature of change is introduced closely around the argument that such transformation needs to promote greater access to trial justice and thereby the advancement of accessible rights through fair trial (such as inclusion and accountability).

---

33 The issue of ideology may not be explicitly addressed as part of our application of structuration theory; rather it is implicit from the fact that we seek to advance a case for change based on what we regard as a sound moral argument – namely, that the process as it stands fails to offer legitimacy to those chiefly affected (victims/communities). It is also through this dimension that the ideologies of communities of justice are reconciled at the local and global level.

34 The importance of a search for truth rather than simply an adversarial struggle over facts and evidence is proposed as a progressive indicator of trial development. Also this position prepares the way for a smoother incorporation of restorative dimensions.

The transformed trial is cited throughout this part as working to support *communities of justice*. Early in the chapter notions like this and the associated process of collaborative justice are invested with clear definition, as is their importance identified for the transformed trial (and hence ICJ) process.

The transformed trial will confront some fundamental problems for criminal justice in general and these are identified as significant challenges and potential impediments to change. For instance, this part indicates the need to re-emphasize a process designed to determine individual liability, in connecting with the collective moral view.

Looking at ideology, jurisdiction, institution and interaction as contexts wherein trial transformation might be achieved (or resisted) in turn throws up a couple of interconnected critical themes, themes which may in fact argue against the discreet utility of any such particular context. Jurisdiction, for instance, is not simply about whether the new trial straddles the civil and the criminal in its possible processes and outcomes. It also requires a discussion of the trial without the constraints of its particular normative framework. Our analytical method of comparative contextual analysis (CCA) requires just such a multi-level comparison to apply in order that dynamics of change are fully appreciated. The transformed trial will, of necessity, involve an expansion of decision-making boundaries. The throughput of process in terms of information, involvement and decision outcomes is considered as a part of transformation dynamics beyond any representation of jurisdiction. This will obviously require a challenge to conventional trial jurisdiction (power and authority). Here the importance of transparency and accountability as a brake on un-inhibited change receives prominence in the discussion of Chapter 8 (as it did in Chapters 6 and 7).

Some of the themes related to truth-seeking as an important purpose for the transformed trial work down from the meta to the more micro analysis. The analysis of this purpose, in particular as an indicator of trial transformation, links themes in other contexts for change. An example is refining just how truth-seeking supports the introduction of restorative process but at the same time may seem to confound retributive concerns about guilt. A way to incorporate these concerns might be through the chapter's careful discussion of the role of evidence in establishing truth and apportioning guilt/responsibility, leading on to sentence.

The lay/professional relationship, the importance of authority structures in decision-making processes, and the manner in which the professional will need to be repositioned within these processes, pose some paradoxes brought about by transformation which we raise but perhaps cannot here be entirely resolved. An example is with legal representation and the manner in which it is said to protect the rights of lay participants, but might also be accused of distancing the lay voice from crucial decision processes.

In all this the analysis Part III is governed by current and possible expectation for trial outcomes. While recognizing the place of the present retributive drivers behind these outcomes, it is necessary to suggest disconnections between truth-finding and verdict, verdict and trial determination, if a harmonious integration of justice paradigms is not to produce a subjugation of particular legitimate expectations from ICJ (such as retributive below restorative). To assist this redesigning the allocation of responsibility within the trial is important. A revised normative framework (suggested in Chapter 6) must precede and accompany this, as outlined in Chapters 7 and 8. The connection between responsibility and liability will not always follow and a discussion of the tension between non-impunity and amnesty directs the analysis of this theme of legitimate trial outcomes as much towards truth and responsibility as it does towards guilt and liability. This draws on the discussion of how restorative and retributive justice will be incorporated within the transformed trial, foreshadowed and argued for in Chapter 7.

Throughout Chapter 8 we confront and develop a selection of themes in transformation. Surrounding these is the importance of a normative structure more than tolerating change. Discretion with judicial supervision is a function of how this structure will be operationalized within the new trial, and the problems associated with this are noted. Discretion to adapt trial types and purposes is also important when we examine the link between retributive and restorative trial justice. Three possibilities for the relationship might be advanced to include:

1 where retribution can be better achieved with the assistance of restorative processes (diversion) – see the establishment of truth and the use of amnesties;

2 where there is a mix of both, and where progressive components of both give a better overall satisfaction of client interest; and

3 where one takes precedence over the other.

In each and all of these settings transformation can occur by the discretionary activation of procedural norms which bring representatives of outside agencies and communities of victims into a redirected trial process aimed at enhanced outcomes. This is just the type of issue on which to develop transformational justice policy, which this book advocates and explores throughout.

Chapter 8 concludes with a consideration of what the trial will look like at certain selected sights of decision-making. This may mean an expansion of the trial particularly into what we see at present as pre-trial concerns. This is not of necessity a complete picture but more indicative of policy directions and whose responsibility it might be to create and promote change. A consideration of who will be responsible for the selection of alternative paradigms in the process and when and how and why, are given as detail of this.

The book concludes that overarching satisfaction with justice requirements is a guide to the activation of different paradigms and their priority. We are not singularly advocating local agendas in post-conflict societies as the only measure of justice satisfaction, utility and, as a result, success. This book is about real global concerns for justice and just governance. Part III returns full circle to the issue of legitimacy of the trial within ICJ more generally, and its place as a force for global governance and peacemaking.

Part 1

Chapter 1

Theorizing the contextual analysis of trial process

Introduction

The main purpose of this chapter is to provide a comprehensive account of the theoretical position adopted by the authors in the comparative contextual analysis (CCA)[1] of trial process. The development of CCA is driven by the need to provide a theoretically informed methodology capable of addressing two interconnected purposes:

1 To examine the manner in which civil law and common law process styles are influencing the operation and development of international criminal trials

2 To understand how the essentials of criminal trial process and practices in chosen jurisdictions (national and international) are constructed, negotiated and relate to one another.

More particularly, the achievement of these aspirations necessarily requires reflection on the most appropriate theoretical framework to inform the comparative endeavour and creative methodologies for dealing with jurisdictional idiosyncrasies and transitional processes which challenge comparison at a variety of levels.[2]

---

1 See Findlay (1999a) for initial formulation of this concept.
2 For a full discussion of our methodological aspirations, see Findlay (2001a, 2002a), Henham and Findlay (2002), Henham (2003a).

This chapter concentrates on describing the theoretical under-pinning to the project and of CCA more broadly. The theoretical base is designed to support both inductive and deductive methodologies whilst maintaining critical awareness of the comparative challenge. The flexibility of our theoretical position is ultimately driven by the desire to achieve particular policy outcomes through appropriate methodological devices. These include the capacity to prefer particular trial practices for the achievement of international criminal justice (ICJ). We, therefore, anticipate that through the adoption of such method-ologies will emerge (and be confirmed) certain theoretical insights into:

- the place of the trial within criminal justice;
- the essential mechanisms of decision-making within the trial;
- key procedural components within the trial which accord with (or challenge) ideologies of criminal justice;
- common issues and relationships across levels of trial analysis; and
- motivations behind the form of international criminal trial process and hence ICJ.

It is axiomatic that research such as this cannot advance unless (or until) it is informed by theory, and the proof of empirical research implies the need to approach the observation of trial phenomena with some theoretical predisposition. For example, in the context of analytical induction, the essential place of discretion in the operation of trial traditions, and its ability to generate a procedural environment within which internationalization may be achieved conventionally, provides a method for theorizing the language of decision-making. In this sense the trial is theorized as a series of decisions, the relationships which produce these decisions and their contexts. Yet, whether theory motivates a language for research (such as discretion), or whether the research data build a language to inform theory, the analysis of trial practice will enable a more theoretically balanced analysis of policy goals as an applied purpose for the theoretical exercise. In the present case it is to reveal what comprises ICJ in the sense of a trial, and what alternative processes of resolution might offer.

We now propose to illustrate how (and on what basis) we have developed elements of social theory in the criminal justice context to accommodate and underpin the CCA of criminal trials.

Levels of analysis

Comparative analysis of the criminal trial process raises significant theoretical difficulties. These involve recognition that, in developing any theoretical foundations we are governed by the following:

1 Significance of context[3] – the need to understand the interaction between legal and social processes in the trial setting.[4] These may be ideologically driven.

2 The requirement to disentangle competing interests and relationships that comprise the trial environment and produce its essential decisions – in this the theoretical context must be capable of identifying and accommodating the rival agendas of respective trial participants in order that the ideological significance of the trial *as* a social *process* can be contextualized.

3 The continual presence of symbolic as well as process concerns – here the theoretical accommodation must also extend beyond symbolism to conceptualize power and locate symbolic elements in the trial process as significant in the recursive practices of decision-making in the courtroom.

4 The difficulty of drawing out from the description of processes and the narrative of players interpretations of social action and actual behaviour – in this sense, the theoretical framework, whilst not being prescriptive of narrative and descriptive interpretations, must both facilitate their understanding as representing recursively organized processes and provide a conceptualization of these processes which will sustain a reliable and valid methodology.

---

3 See Findlay (1999a) for a detailed elaboration of the nature and significance of this concept.

4 The trial setting provides a stage common to all jurisdictions where the purposes and power relations of penality are given public expression through the rituals of punishment. Whilst recognizing the significance of pre-trial decision-making, the project's trial focus is deliberately chosen as the *locus* where the ideological and policy dimensions of penality are played out and hence where issues of synthesis and difference can be best explored. The contextual analysis of legal and social processes (as interactive phenomena) at comparable sites for decision-making within the trial setting is, therefore, crucial to this endeavour. Although it is acknowledged that legal processes *are* social processes, these phenomena are treated as both theoretically and methodologically distinct for reasons elaborated later.

5 The challenge provided by narrative analysis – conceptualizing the trial process as capable of accommodating notions of difference and synthesis within competing procedural traditions.

6 The various levels (and contexts) of comparison – internal and external, not dichotomous.

7 The challenge of specificity versus universality (for the purposes of comparison).

8 Finally, the importance of sites for decision-making and shared practices (relationships) with emphasis on the dynamics of process (human interaction) rather than structure or function.

The theoretical problems and underlying assumptions informing comparative trial research require a cohesive theoretical framework within which both the research methodology and the empirical findings can be located, and the links between them identified. That CCA requires an appreciation of the social reality of historical, social, political and economic variables as impacting on the trial process means it becomes necessary to deconstruct ways in which criminal justice processes are conceptualized and operate in respective jurisdictions. This involves a recognition that, along with any shift in trial context, the normative significance of process may represent different philosophical interpretations of what constitutes epistemologically accepted empirical 'truths'.

The moral validity of principles about punishment is contextually contingent, as are the symbols and structures which manifest these (Norrie 1996b; Henham 1999a). As a consequence, a theoretical framework for this research should be capable of elucidating both objective and subjective conceptions of process (Henham 2000a). Norrie (1996b) suggests this theorizing should emphasize the dialectic form of justice within different cultures by recognizing that external, or purely historical and structural, accounts of process fail to account for human subjectivity and ambivalence about justice (as a search for common threads both at the level of ideology and process). As our discussion will develop, this holds especially true for emerging representations of ICJ.

Recognizing the moral and cultural relativity of concepts such as 'justice' and 'fairness' requires a contextual appreciation of the subjectivity of trial participants' experiences in terms of these measures. Such terms may, nevertheless, be justifiable according to particular 'objective' criteria. The deconstruction of participant experience in a trial so contextualized offers a phenomenological account of process and its ideological significance. It also enables us to identify the major dimensions of what might constitute comparable justice referents across jurisdictional boundaries and provides linkage to process. The process representation on which this book will rely is trial decision-making in various comparative contexts and through unique personal relationships.

There must, therefore, be recognition that social theory is generally capable of conceptualizing the sociohistorical context and consequences, but not the human subjectivity, of moral action. This is highly significant in terms of its methodological implications for any analysis of the criminal trial process. Ideally such analysis should be capable of providing mechanisms of 'description and explanation' of social phenomena which comprise trial decisions and that reflect internal/external (objective/subjective) experiences of social reality for trial participants, and hence the basis for comparison we have selected.

The methodological capability of research instruments must, therefore, reflect that fact–value distinction[5] in the following, where appropriate:

1 Descriptive analysis of information available to the court.
2 How such information is assimilated as an 'objective' process.
3 How this both structures and impacts on decision-making processes.[6]
4 Identification of points where judicial perceptions of case material are shared.
5 Wider contextual exploration of discretionary decision-making in a manner conducive to the comparative endeavour.

At the comparative level of different jurisdictions the research theory and methodology must also reflect the dimensions of cultural diversity, spatial and temporal relativity. It must also be both simultaneously relevant at the one-dimensional (local) and multi-dimensional (global) level of analysis. Notwithstanding, theory and methodology must also be equally sensitive to the distorting effect of simple, false or rigid conceptual dichotomies, while maintaining a reflexive and critical analytical stance.

---

5 Between which the moral challenge of subjective trial justice and objective principles of penalty are shared.
6 The relative importance attached to decision-making in some jurisdictions is acknowledged.

Contextual analysis, as a precursor to the comparative endeavour, tends to highlight the unique features of each trial and by so doing cautions against viewing the objects of comparison as simple or opposing. For instance, the theoretical approach to the comparative project must acknowledge the cultural significance of the legal and social variables chosen for analysis within particular jurisdictions in terms of the reasons for their selection and their effects. Coincidently, it should also recognize the global forces that provide an international focus for the recognition of certain legal rules that transcend the boundaries of the unitary state.[7]

Comparison

As suggested earlier, in order to appreciate the trial beyond its localized manifestations, a contextual analysis needs to be comparative at many levels. The identified interest in globalization (Findlay 1999a)[8] and the internationalization of criminal procedure suggest several dualities that dominate the CCA to follow. Initially, the comparison will be within context (e.g. the trial as an essential institutional feature of traditions of criminal justice within nominated legal cultures). Concurrently, the comparison of context with context (e.g. locality and globe) will evolve. The latter holds out much for critically appreciating the representations of trial justice, and the interests which promote them. To achieve its fullest potential within the theme of globalization (internationalization), comparative research should, therefore, concentrate:

- within a nominated cultural[9] context;
- across two or more contexts within the same culture;

---

7 It must also be capable of conceptualizing what happens to them during this transformation. For further discussion in the context of the narrative impact of the European Convention on Human Rights on English sentencing praxis, see Henham (2000c) and, more generally, Campbell, E. (1999).

8 With globalization defined as the collapsing of time and space for processes of communication, some of the central features which distinguish trial traditions (such as jurisdiction and judicial language) are for us conveniently under challenge as essential distinguishers of trial process.

9 Culture is employed here in preference to notions such as society and community because, while culture is a relative concept, it relies on common forms and functions which allow for comparisons of civilization and social development. In the comparative exercise, referent cultures are a useful locator when examining social relationships and behaviours in transition.

- across time and space within a culture in transition;
- culture to culture; and (not or)
- simultaneously at the local and global levels (Findlay 1999a: vii).

The trial assumes a variety of social functions dependent on context. These may coexist while contradicting or challenging any single understanding of trial justice. With the criminal trial being culturally relative, it has the potential within any particular culture to represent criminal justice. The popular knowledge of justice (both local and global) anticipates and endorses this. However, the trial's existence and representation at a global level may argue for the unity and generalization of justice.

Recently, Findlay (1999a) argued the virtues of CCA when examining the relationship between crime and globalization. This means an interactive project where context is employed over *community* or *culture*, to enable comparative analysis without sacrificing specificity. Context is seen as an actual place. CCA provides the potential to reconcile 'an acute sensitivity to the peculiarities of the local', with 'the universalizing imperative'. The novelty in this approach to comparative analysis is not the rediscovery of context. Rather it is in the multilevelled applications which context invites. Nelken identifies the need to ensure, when analysing any feature of criminal justice, that it 'resonates' with the rest of the culture in context before a comparison is advanced.

Cultural ideals and values of criminal justice do not necessarily reflect their wider diffusion in the culture. In many societies there is a wide gulf between legal and general culture, as where the criminal law purports to maintain principles of impersonal equality before the law in societies where clientilistic and other particular practices are widespread (Nelken 1997b: 563; also Findlay 1997a).

The recognition of difference is crucial to the success of CCA and not just for the purpose of sounding simplistically preferential. There potential is therefore through comparison, to understand the complexity of culture and not only seek explanations for features of culture, such as crime and justice. Comparative investigation turns into the hermeneutic exercise of trying to use evidence about crime and its control to resolve puzzles about culture (Nelken 1994: 225).

An enlivening, if underdeveloped, capacity of comparative analysis is to move away from 'cause and effect' as a narrow frame of analytical reference. When examining institutions and strategies of crime control, a causal focus tends both to distort the place and purpose of criminal justice, and the motivations for the analytical project. CCA recognizes the possibility of simultaneously viewing crime and control from several dimensions. This emphasis on interaction and transition avoids simplistic assumptions about criminal justice, and the unfounded construction of policy. It should also prevent the abstraction of effective social control mechanisms from their essential contextual supports, to the extent where an appreciation of the impact of context over control is lost.

Research into trial traditions as a focus for comparative legal/cultural analysis has regularly suffered from what David Nelken refers to as 'comparison by juxtaposition' (1997b). This may be explained through answers to Nelken's question about what the comparison is supposed to be achieving. Rather than the style of analysis, it might be 'the disguised hegemonic project and the avowed search for global legal concepts' (Zedner 1995: 519), which is laid open to criticism. The inclusion of comparative analysis amongst the characteristics of intellectual and administrative imperialism is only to be expected when contextual actuality is overlooked or underplayed. Where the comparative project breaks down into an exercise in justification rather than analysis is when context is marginalized.

Recognizing these challenges to the comparative project we remain convinced of the value of the trial as the procedural focus for the research. Across each major procedural style serious crime is tried. Serious crime is also far more likely to be defended and therefore tried. Serious crimes and their trial have produced many of the procedural safeguards around which criminal justice traditions have grown. In practice there may prove to be less that divides the adversarial from the inquisitorial trial. For instance, the more complex the case the more that the significance of documentary evidence will prevail. And there is little doubt that the ideology of criminal justice in both traditions takes the trial as its manifestation. This is confirmed by the paramount place of the trial in the institutionalization of ICJ.

Challenges for theory

Following on from the preceding discussion it may be postulated that within the comparative context there are three levels of analysis that hold good from culture to culture, across time and space and simultaneously at the local and global levels:[10]

---

10   This analytical distinction is not intended to obscure the fact that such levels reflect various aspects of complex interdependent social processes.

1 *Legal* – concerning the nature and function of norms established by legislation. Substantive legal rights that might be accorded to participants in the trial process and legal procedure would also fall into this category. More widely, instrumental relationships between legal form, policy and power may be analysed within this context. This is the common or preferred level for comparative legal/procedural analysis.

2 *Organizational* – concerning the channels and agencies involved in the communication of information relevant to the trial process.[11] It is concerned with strategic rationales (both official and bureaucratic) for the operation and function of legal norms and the organizational 'reality' of discretionary justice as constrained (or promoted) by power and social control variables. Sociology of law is comfortable here.

3 *Interactive* – concerning the social reality of decision-making within the courtroom.[12] This deals essentially with interactive analysis of the relationship between social action and decision-making in the trial process. The ethnographies of the court and the trial take this approach. Little if any work explores each and all.

As presented these different levels of analysis appear to pose major theoretical problems since several theoretical approaches have possible relevance to the different levels of analysis. At the conceptual level it therefore becomes necessary to recognize and reconcile the implications for synthesis of distinct analytical categories revealed through contextual analysis for participating jurisdictions. For example, theoretical approaches that might be relevant to legal aspects of the research such as conflict or Marxist perspectives are also relevant to its interactive aspects, whilst other theoretical formulations such as due process paradigms might be more appropriate for unravelling the complexities of organizational aspects of the research. Furthermore, several possibly relevant theories deal with different levels of abstraction and cannot readily be conceptually related to one another. A clear example of this problem is the link between due process paradigms and Marxist theory, the former focusing on legalistic criteria such as the operation of the presumption of innocence[13] and the latter

---

11 This includes the role of the police and the judiciary in pre-trial process.
12 Decision-making beyond the courtroom which impacts on the trial process is addressed.
13 This example bears most resemblance to adversarial systems.

focusing on higher-order concepts such as alienation, suppression and class domination. Secondly, as suggested, some theoretical approaches are unable to demonstrate a link with wider social theory and, being conceived in such isolation, cannot then be integrated with other approaches which take account of such deficiency to construct a coherent whole.

In summary, a social theory which would serve as a coherent framework for the comparative contextual analysis of trial process needs to deal satisfactorily with the following points:

1 The sociolegal nature of the research.

2 The different levels of abstraction required by the different levels of analysis.

3 The need to adopt a non-deterministic and reflexive approach to understanding human behaviour that recognizes the intentionality of mind and action and at the same time not prohibit the potential for universalization.

4 The capacity to deal with both objective and subjective conceptions of social reality.

5 The ability to conceptualize social processes within and between cultures, at the local and global level and across time and space.

6 The ability to conceptualize links between ideology, power and policy as social processes.

7 The ability to support several methodologies which have applicability to a number of theoretical approaches.

8 The reflexive capacity to respond to theoretical ideas generated by the research process, as a tool for theory development (Glaser and Strauss 1967; Strauss 1987).

Comparativism enables not only a consideration of object in various contexts and from different levels and perspectives of analysis, but also it tolerates paradox and dialectic, both essential in any understanding of criminal justice institutions and processes. Particularly for a consideration of the trial in transition (towards its international forms) more global levels of analysis rely on paradox.

Globalization is paradox. It may be harmonious and diverse; one culture and all cultures. Primarily, it is a process reliant on crucial social relationships to defeat and deny time and space. The setting of the trial and its various sites for decision-making demonstrate these relationships. The trend to internationalize and fuse criminal trial procedures is a natural consequence of modernization as well as sharing the social, political and economic priorities which characterize the modern. As with modernization the theatre of international trials can marginalize and reintegrate, unify and divide.

The unity of globalization is as yet more convincing at a symbolic level. Criminal justice, and the trial as its exemplar, represents unequivocal symbols around which global ethics are confirmed. Crime control claims an irrefutable mandate for global order, and a symbolic terrain across which order rules. The trial has become public proof of this.

Any theoretical framework for explaining the internationalization of criminal trials will depend on a recognition of dialectics:

- The structural and the operational.
- The symbolic and the actual.
- The ideology and the function.
- Rule and process.

Developing structuration theory in a comparative context

A social theory that satisfies the criteria summarized above which we utilize as a framework for the CCA of trial process is the theory of structuration formulated by Giddens (1979, 1982, 1984). This provides a particular macro-theoretical account of the reflexive relationship between human agency and social structure. Giddens' theory presents a non-dogmatic, flexible formulation providing a set of sensitizing concepts that has great potential for empirical application (Layder 1994). The theory attempts to redress the balance between structuralism, functionalism and phenomenologically derived positions by suggesting that social structures, institutions and systems 'exist only insofar as they are continually produced and reproduced via the duality of structure' (Giddens 1977). Giddens' notion of human action entails the two concepts of 'knowledgeability' and 'capability'. Knowledgeability distinguishes between discursive and practical consciousness or rather as between what social actors are able to say about their activities and what they are not able to formulate discursively but which is knowledge utilized in the course of social interaction or particular courses of conduct. This dichotomy is lacking in functionalist approaches. Capability is simply the process whereby individuals choose between alternative courses of conduct (decision-making is described as a subcategory of capability).

A crucial factor in Giddens' analysis of action is the concept that the unintended consequences of human action are involved in social reproduction and that they themselves become conditions of action subject to their rationalization by social actors. This process is regarded as integral to the reproduction of social systems and to the virtual existence of structure (Giddens 1982).

Giddens' notion of institutions refers to structured social practices which exist over time and space and which receive the support and acknowledgement of society by consensus, whereas structure refers to 'rules and resources instantiated in social systems but having only a virtual existence'.[14] Giddens' view, therefore, distinguishes between system and structure regarding each as existing only through the process of structuration.[15] Structure is regarded as property of a particular social system, not of the activities of social actors, and structural properties seen as non-temporal and non-spatial existing only as particular moments in the constitution of social systems. Social institutions, therefore, are the medium through which structural properties (rules and resources) are applied in the 'continuity of daily life'. The recursive feature of the organization of social practices is the fact that structural properties both enable and constrain the production of social practices. Therefore, in Giddens' view, both rules and resources constitute the medium through which institutional practices are created and reproduced in social institutions.

14 Giddens (1982: 9, emphasis added) describes the theory of structuration in the following terms: 'The structured properties of society, the study of which is basic to explaining the long-term development of institutions "exist" only in their instantiation in the structuration of social systems, and in the memory traces (reinforced or altered in the continuity of daily social life) that constitute the knowledgeability of social actors. But institutionalised practices "happen" and are "made to happen" through the application of resources in the continuity of daily life. Resources are structured properties of social systems but "exist" only in the capability of actors, in their capacity to "act otherwise". This brings me to an essential feature of the theory of structuration, the thesis that the organisation of social practices is fundamentally *recursive*. Structure is both the medium and the outcome of the practices it – recursively organises.'

15 This may be seen as a criticism of structuration theory in that Giddens precludes the possibility that structures may have some objective existence that does not depend on the human actions that reproduce them. As Layder (1994: 157) points out, 'This makes it very difficult to understand social systems as patterns of domination which endure and have effect beyond the situation of their actual implementation in practice'.

In relation to theoretical abstraction, it remains crucial for our understanding of the processes of social reproduction involved in trial decision-making to use theory as a mechanism for conceptual and contextual integration. By adopting theory as reflexivity, capable of providing the conceptual apparatus for linking varying levels of theoretical abstraction which enable us to account for law as part of social structure and signify political and economic imperatives, abstraction is not to be regarded as delimiting, as distancing the object of inquiry from any meaningful account that may be given of it, but rather the reverse.

It is the need to explain process involving different levels of analysis that demands a theoretical account of process capable of accommodating conceptual diversity. Thus, at the empirical level, the limiting factor which circumscribes our theoretical mission concerns the nature of trial decision-making within the project's two complementary and interactive spheres:

1 The internationalization of criminal trial process.
2 The analysis of competing process styles at work within national (jurisdictional), regional and international criminal trials.

Structuration theory is being employed here as a conceptual vehicle to facilitate the deconstruction of the processes of social reproduction which comprise the criminal trial and justice determination thereby. As with any theory (at whatever level of abstraction) it is partial and needs to be refined in terms of its applicability to the trial process through the development of a heuristic model designed to address specific elements of process in the comparative dimension.

At the macro level, structuration theory provides conceptual flexibility and, paradoxically, some coherence to lower-order theoretical formulations. Macro-theory is consequently both a starting point and a unifying factor in the conceptualization of process. It is not used to postulate a particular definitive theory of knowledge (i.e. an epistemology of the trial process) but, rather, in the sense of suggesting *some* variables which *may* allow us to understand the nature and social context of trial decision-making, being the essence of process.

Structuration theory provides an epistemological framework for conceiving of a dynamic process of social reproduction at a higher-order level. It is a facilitator, or vehicle for theory development, as well as a theoretical statement. These qualities are given equal emphasis throughout the ensuing discussion.

Structuration has the potential to:

- do away with unnecessary dualities and break down artificial barriers between contexts;

- emphasize action and interaction over structure and motivation;

- contextualize agency within social action, revealing an inter-dependence of social features; and

- harmonize macro and micro human interaction (i.e. sentencing against the human connection between judges and victims). This does not produce simple conflation but rather recognizes both difference and synergy for the purposes of comparison. For harmonization, there is no need to extract (or abstract) from content to produce analysis. The interaction, which is an essential feature of trial decision-making, can then become the subject for research.

Structuration theory acts as a sensitizing perspective from which to view relationships between structure and agency which depend for their relative existence on context (involving jurisdiction, institution and locality). Context so envisaged is dynamic across time and space.

By envisaging 'action in context' in this way structuration enables fact and value to be observed as part of the same dynamic. There is no need to maintain a sharp distinction between observations in context and normative judgements. In this way it is easy to 'add value' and meaning to observations in context. The application of context within structuration therefore becomes crucial to the reconciliation of the subjective and the objective. Values and facts are naturalistically conceived as distinct features of the research and the trial experience.

Within this conceptual framework we later elaborate the need for a contextual model as a heuristic device. This postulates specific ways in which we may need to proceed in order to comprehend the nature of process within different contexts by suggesting contrasting (yet com-plementary) ways of conceptualizing trial decision-making. These paradigms may be based on existing theoretical positions which deal with different levels of abstraction implicit in process interaction, but the model is neither theoretically, not methodologically, prescriptive. The testing of theoretical propositions and data generated from grounded theory methodologies collectively informs the refinement and development of the macro-theoretical position – the processual interrogation of trial decision-making. Different methodologies required to fulfil the demands imposed by modelling reflect different ways of conceiving of the relationship between theory and the production of 'new' knowledge about the trial process. These methodologies are driven by the need to understand comparative context for the purpose of understanding international, political/cultural outcomes. A contextual model is, therefore, in reality a *locus* for testing various (possibly competing) versions of what constitutes the process of trial decision-making.

We must accept, therefore, that any theoretical position is both limiting and normative, and that the significance of this lies in the relationship between theory and methodology (Findlay and Henham 2001). Hence, whilst admitting that theoretical statements reflect normativity, we expect that the normativity of context (as revealed through the adoption of appropriate methodologies) will assist us to advance our theoretical appreciation (modelling) of process (Henham and Findlay 2001c). Again, this recognition points to the fact that *any* theory we can bring to bear on this issue may be fragmented or provide inadequate explanations at varying levels of abstraction. Because structuration theory permits us to develop a model for deconstructing contextuality which tolerates (accommodates) inductive and deductive methodologies, it allows us to make statements about the normativity of context at several levels. It allows us to go deep into trial decision-making, across various trial decision-making structures, and out to consider the trial within ICJ.

Operationalizing the conceptual framework

Before further engaging in any assessment of whether structuration theory is capable of fulfilling the criteria listed above, it is necessary to develop and explain in more detail those specific aspects of comparative trial research which fall to be conceptualized within its theoretical framework. If we accept that the trial process can be reduced to a number of interconnected decision-making sites we can further postulate which variables may be involved in the decision-making process, their relative significance and the factors which determine their importance.[16] In specific terms this analysis would necessitate information on:

---

16 It is anticipated that within the larger project will emerge a range of more specific research exercises covering significant sites of decision-making in the trial such as the presentation of evidence, the role of the prosecutor, the role of the judge, verdict delivery and sentencing.

1 decision-making sites in the trial process;
2 describing how the purposes of the trial are meant to be negotiated and resolved;
3 the prescribed roles of participants;
4 sites of anticipated social interaction;
5 how evidence should be processed and the form it takes;
6 who is supposed to have access and to what features of the process;
7 the place of trial players within the process, and how they relate;
8 their symbolic significance;
9 the way players and decisions influence one another; and
10 the levels of meaning in the decision-making narrative. This fore-shadows our recognition of difficulties in reconciling levels of meaning and distilling meaningful inferences.

Consequently, the initial theoretical mission in deconstructing the criminal trial is to provide a vehicle that can conceptually link the relevant players in the trial process to specific actions required (or performed) by them within decision-making sites as well as their interaction. Structuration theory facilitates the conceptualization of these processes at a level which permits us to focus on the patterns of social relationships in the criminal trial over time and space and examines the nexus between social structure, institutions and systems of the criminal process and the reasons, motivations, and reflexive behaviour of trial participants. Therefore, in terms of the different levels of analysis suggested earlier, the present research can be conceptualized within the theoretical framework provided by the theory of structuration in the following terms (interactive as they would be in their application):

- *Legal* – the nature, function and discretionary choices presented by legal rules and principles. Substantive legal rights accorded to trial participants, legal procedure and relationships between legal form, policy and social control variables may be regarded as aspects of structural properties (rules and resources). Rules also include conventions, presumptions and discretion. Allocative resources include material resources enabling an organization and/or its human participants to function effectively, whilst authoritative resources might include the status and hierarchical position of trial participants. Resources are linked to power by focusing on a person's transformative capacity (i.e. their ability to effect change).

- *Organizational* – strategic rationales for the operation and function of the trial process may be envisaged as part of a system existing as regular reproducible social practices – namely, as modes of social interaction where structural properties are implemented. This analytical level, therefore, encompasses information regarding communication structures that impact on the roles of significant players in the trial process and influence the outcome of courtroom interaction. Analytical links between symbolism, ideology and power may also be explored at this level.

- *Interactive* – the social reality of decision-making within the courtroom may be seen as forming part of the process of the application of structural properties by social actors through the mechanism of social institutions. This level is, therefore, concerned with *actual* decision-making processes in the courtroom and would reflect the fact that discretionary choices (the capability of social actors to act otherwise) determine the conditions of structuration, i.e. the continuity or transformation of structures (rules and resources), and, therefore, the reproduction of systems. It is also important to note that discretionary power and the *locus* (jurisdictional setting) which determine the conditions of its exercise are patterned through the activities of trial participants who recursively create the meaning and social reality of discretion as both action and structure.

The main points above can be summarized diagrammatically in terms of structuration theory, as shown in Figure 1.1.

If we now return to assess the extent to which structuration theory is capable of fulfilling the theoretical criteria for the comparative contextual analysis of the criminal trial listed earlier, the following conclusions may be drawn:

1 Regarding the sociolegal nature of the research – the theory of structuration locates legal rules and principles as an element of structure and, therefore, as part of the essential mechanism for the reproduction of social systems. Therefore, the law is not examined in isolation and *then* related to other features of the social system such as power, authority and social control.

2 Concerning the need for the theory to relate to different levels and context of abstraction – since structuration theory was developed at a high level of abstraction utilizing higher-order concepts, lower-order theoretical formulations can therefore, be subsumed, evaluated or rejected within this framework.

19

3 Regarding the need for a non-deterministic theory – the theory of structuration does not adopt the position that human action is determined by social causes.

4 On the need to deal with both objective and subjective conceptions of social reality – structuration theory does offer some explanation of the origins of subjectivity through emphasizing the recursive nature of the organization of social practices through the application of structured properties by social actors (Giddens 1982). In fact, human agency is regarded as an a priori condition accounting for the existence and maintenance of structural properties. At the micro level, structuration theory facilitates the understanding and appreciation of the interaction between human agency and moral context because of the recursiveness in structure that both creates and maintains the condition of its existence.

5 On the need to conceptualize across and between cultures, at the local and global level and across time and space – structuration theory permits an examination of the structured pattern of social relationships within any particular society over time and space including established or institutionalized practices such as the trial process.

6 On the wider relationships between law and power, authority and social control – Giddens attempts to link the concept of power to that of action in describing power as the capability of individual social actors to secure their own ends even against the will of others. Thus, Giddens asserts that 'power in social systems can thus be treated as involving reproduced relations of *autonomy* and *dependence* in social interaction' (Giddens 1982). The relationship between ideology and policy can be envisaged in terms of those factors which influence relations of autonomy and dependence in the trial process; for example, the link between managerialism and access to justice.

7 Regarding the ability to sustain methodological diversity – this is implicit in point (2) above and related to the ability of structuration theory to provide a credible framework for identifying the links between conceptual ideas and quantitative or qualitative data by facilitating their presentation as an intelligible form of empirical 'truth', the epistemological significance of which (although as in all cases contestable) can be presented in coherent/rational terms.

8 This argument is also relevant regarding the reflexive capacity of structuration theory and to the wider notion that, despite

imperfections, it provides a powerful and flexible set of sensitizing concepts. Its significance lies in its relevance to the overall orientation of social research, that as Giddens (1984) suggests, should:

- recognize that social research has a necessary cultural, ethnographic or 'anthropological' aspect to it;
- be sensitive to the complex skills which actors have in co-ordinating the contexts of their day-to-day behaviour; and
- be sensitive to the time-space institution of social life.

Figure 1.1 Conceptualizing the structuration of trial process

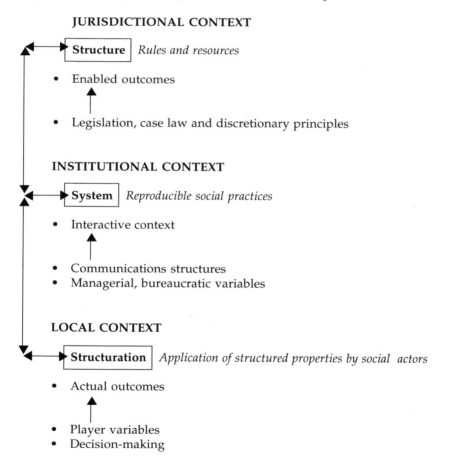

JURISDICTIONAL CONTEXT

| **Structure** | *Rules and resources* |

- Enabled outcomes

- Legislation, case law and discretionary principles

INSTITUTIONAL CONTEXT

| **System** | *Reproducible social practices* |

- Interactive context

- Communications structures
- Managerial, bureaucratic variables

LOCAL CONTEXT

| **Structuration** | *Application of structured properties by social actors* |

- Actual outcomes

- Player variables
- Decision-making

Particularly important in the present context is Giddens' assertion that 'sociological descriptions have the task of mediating the frames of meaning within which actors orient their conduct. But such descriptions are interpretative categories which also demand an effect of translation in and out of the frames of meaning involved in sociological theories' (1984).

In summary, therefore, structuration theory's strategic significance in comparative contextual analysis of the trial process is its ability to provide a set of organizing or interpretative constructs to identify elements and processes concerned in the recursive nature of the application of rules and resources by trial participants. Whilst acknowledging that a high level of abstraction is necessary to provide a coherent framework for the legal, organizational and interactive aspects of the research, it is important to recognize the potential difficulty of relating abstract conceptual formulations directly to specific research findings, or to integrate more specific concepts and processes identified as central concerns of other theoretical approaches. This necessitates the consideration and development of a heuristic model; a theoretically grounded device that allows us to link what is discovered to existing knowledge (Henham and Findlay 2001c).

The issue of what may constitute appropriate linkage between theory and empirical reality or, indeed, whether any is necessary, clearly raises fundamental epistemological questions which entail distinct theoretical and methodological choices. The point we make, therefore, is that since the epistemological position directly determines what any methodology will produce, it is crucial for research which seeks to understand levels of meaning and context that this linkage remains flexible enough to accommodate competing or complementary ontological commitments. These concerns are reflected in our development of modelling for the research described in the following chapter (Henham and Findlay 2001c).

Consistent with Giddens' advice regarding the selective application of structuration theory as a sensitizing device (1984: 326), this interpretation does not try to account for the 'meaning' of action; rather it postulates its use as a processural paradigm or sensitizing construct[17] designed to elucidate the dimensions of decision-making. In this connection processes of decision-making may be conceptualized in

---

17 The 'sensitizing' concept is one which is designed to convey the notion of a perspective that is very open to reflecting changes in the situational contexts of discretionary decision-making and their implications for the manufacture of trial process.

their contextualization as a series of frames of action. As such, the context of trial process may be envisaged in terms of a series of decision sites, being pathways of decision-making wherein each outcome depends upon understanding how and why relationships between trial participants are resolved at crucial sites for decision-making within the trial. More revealing perhaps are the relationships of influence which determine the pathways and their decision outcomes. Each such frame of action contributes to mould the trial process since each pathway is dependent upon influences that shape, drive and emanate from these relationships. Socio-historic accounts of the manufacture and move-ment of process are dependent on the constituents of previous frames of action in as much as instantiation recursively contributes to our understanding of contextualized social action and interaction through process.

Thus, context[18] is three-dimensional and *dynamic* across time and space, whilst the relationship between structure and agency depends for its relative existence upon the context from which it comes, which is never separate or autonomous. As such the relativity of each frame of action is established through our ability to consider interaction within the context of the frame against past and present action outcomes.[19] Hence, our analysis envisages the various dimensions of decision-making, their contextualization and comparison in terms of a series of frames which comprise a moving picture: contextualized social action. Taking the example of rights concerns within trials, therefore, the reality of rights can be seen as dependent on their engagement with or translation into (or out of) social action. They can be envisaged as principles that require reflection against (and cannot be autonomous from) structure and action within context, and context in transition.

Particularly important in the present context is Giddens' (1984) assertion that sociological descriptions are implicated in the task of mediating the frames of meaning within which actors orient their

---

18 'Context' is employed here as a central concept within the analysis in preference to overworked notions such as 'community', 'society' or 'culture'. The interactive and actual connotations of 'context', along with the often artificial and extreme notions of community, society and culture within representations of criminal justice, promote contextual analysis. Consequently, as an object of contextual analysis, the trial is not limited to rules, institutions, people, situations or reactions. The trial is more effectively understood as relationships which develop within the dynamics of its selected context.

19 According to Giddens, context involves (1) the time/space boundaries (usually having symbolic or physical markers) around interaction strips; and (2) the co-presence of actors.

conduct. Structuration theory facilitates the adoption of methodologies which allow us to signify the objective/subjective meaning of social action by conflating the theoretical and empirical imperatives dictated by epistemological controversies. For instance, if one is seeking to understand the individual and institutional capacity of juries to comprehend, it may be essential to locate the question within the contemporaneity of issues in the trial. In so doing the contextuality of *process* in terms of its objectivity (both conceptual and concrete) and the subjective account of that objectivity (in terms of its phenomenological content) are revealed (Henham and Findlay 2001c). The crucial point is that the relative realities of fact and value are merged in process (Tamanaha 1997). Consequently, where the fact/value distinction is drawn in this research we do so as Tamanaha suggests 'standing on the ground', in context and not proposing a perspective-free versus a perspective-bound contrast. It is argued that one cannot view the world beyond context (perspective), and that a fact/value distinction only has relevance within the researchers' actions in a real world, where values and facts are naturalistically conceived as functionally distinct aspects of experience. The distinction, therefore, is drawn in commonsense terms, within the action of the trial.

To summarize, structuration theory distinguishes analytical levels for the purpose of comparison and seeks to go beyond a consideration of influences over agency in order to explain decision-making.[20] Discretion as a unique facilitator for the decision-making process recurs throughout our analysis and is an important universal theme for our methodology.

Structuration is also interested in what influences the moment of interaction as well as that moment. For discretion this means the negotiation of decisions, and the structures of status, which pre-determine the direction and application of discretion.

It suggests that dualism and dichotomy (such as between agency and structure) have no relative reality in context, and that abstraction is necessary in order to deconstruct the mechanisms of structuration for comparative analysis.[21] Nevertheless, applying levels of analysis or components of context for analysis does not endorse their autonomy within social action. Within certain contexts and across contexts in transition there is no reason why the macro and the micro, or indeed structure, human action and 'practical consciousness', should not be

---

20 This is the process wherein pathways of influence can be identified and analysed.
21 This will demonstrate inclusion and exclusion as a consequence of decisions as discretion is exercised under identifiable influences.

extracted and abstracted for the purpose of analysis. It may be the outcome of their interaction within particular contexts which becomes the legitimate focus for comparative analysis. Contextual boundaries such as instantiation may therefore be employed as important components for comparison if harmony or dissonance is the interest.

As described, the criminal trial process is conceptualized within the theoretical framework provided by the theory of structuration at three inter-related levels of social reality: legal, organizational and interactive. These levels constitute the components of a process model that envisages human agency as the *dynamic* variable which reproduces of the social reality within trial process through structuration. This is a social reality that is shaped by the dimensions of fact/value dependent upon context (e.g. the determination of evidence). At the macro level, structuration theory provides a higher plane of theoretical formulation for understanding how process is created through human agency and the way in which the different fields of analysis are implicated in this dynamic. At the micro level, these fields are examined in comparative context in relation to particular aspects of the trial process. This is achieved by focusing on specific decision sites which have relevance for the issue under investigation, looking at them as if they were literally a micro-representation of structuration and examining those crucial aspects of human agency which operate within that particular context to produce sentence outcomes.

If we take victim participation in the criminal trial process for the purposes of illustration, what we are looking for are those factors that are relevant to understanding the way in which the three levels we have identified are actually implicated through the human decision-making that is structuration in creating the conditions that determine inclusivity or exclusivity for victims within the trial. This decision-making is discretionary and influenced by contextual factors within and beyond the trial itself that will determine the direction and outcome of the process. Comparative contextual analysis seeks to determine the meaning of what is happening in context – what are these different pathways of influence that feed into the decisions relating to victim inclusivity? How are they constituted and what is their significance for outcome? How are the three levels of analysis implicated in our understanding of this process? In broader terms, we examine how and why value is added to fact and what this means for outcome in a micro-representation of structuration in action. Figure 1.2 purports to show how the three analytical levels of this model relate to one another by providing an overview of the trial decision-making process as structuration.

Figure 1.2 Modelling the relationship between structuration and trial decisions

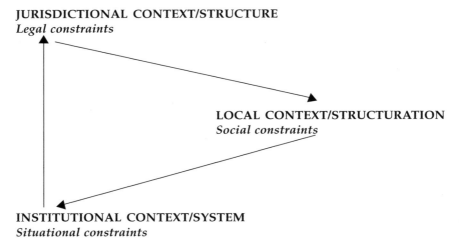

JURISDICTIONAL CONTEXT/STRUCTURE
Legal constraints

LOCAL CONTEXT/STRUCTURATION
Social constraints

INSTITUTIONAL CONTEXT/SYSTEM
Situational constraints

Note: Each decision site model is a micro-representation of structuration adapted to show the predominant influences on discretionary decision-making within the framework for action suggested by structuration theory

It is important to note that discretionary power and the *locus* (jurisdictional setting) which determines the conditions of its exercise is patterned through the activities of trial participants who recursively create the meaning and social reality of discretion as both action and structure. It is the need to explain process involving different levels of analysis that demands a theoretical account of process capable of accommodating conceptual diversity. Thus, at the empirical level, the limiting factor which circumscribes our theoretical mission concerns the nature of trial decision-making. The interaction of these levels of analysis produced in our pilot methodology (described in Chapter 4) the particular understanding of pathways of influence. Jurisdictional constructs lead on to organizational process opportunities creating contexts for interaction through decision-making. The requirement to decide legal questions is followed by a means for decisions within comparative institutional frameworks, which are contextualized by specific factors of decision-making and discretionary mechanisms. In this respect the analysis (as with the decision-making being analysed) proceeds down identifiable decision pathways, formulated through pressures from players and institutional patterns, formulating a process with features and functions of influence.

Linking theory and method

As we describe in Chapter 4, our methodology involves the identification, description and analysis[22] of communication structures and interactive processes in trial narrative through contextual analysis. The methodology facilitates the deconstruction of narrative by developing an approach which combines inductive and deductive strategies. These allow us to signify the objective/subjective meaning of social action by conflating the theoretical and empirical imperatives dictated by epistemological controversies, such as the fact-finding process. In so doing, the contextuality of process in terms of its objectivity (both conceptual and concrete) and the subjective account of that objectivity (in terms of its phenomenological content) are revealed. The comparability of contextual analyses and the methodological capability of revealing sites of synthesis or difference depend on being able to appreciate the reality of process as manufactured at different levels of abstraction, as objective or subjective phenomena for each participant jurisdiction. Equally important, when researching the trial, is the capacity to move from the abstract to the actual employing decision sites, and pathways of influence in the trial as the common mechanism for context and comparison.

Structuration theory provides a wider contextual dimension to this approach. By emphasizing the recursive nature of the process of structuration it suggests flexibility capable of conceptualizing what is actually happening in the courtroom in processural terms, but also permits symbolic and ideological referents to be contextualized through analysis of the trial as process across cultures and in time and space. In this way the study that follows can examine what goes on in any trial, what it means to the participants, how common themes connect with trial principle, and the manner in which various justice paradigms get translated into any and many trials.

As such symbolism and power are located in our understanding of the trial as a reproducible social practice through the mechanism of the narrative which reflects the continuous context of decision-making in the courtroom. This can be augmented through observational and experiential methods determined as they are by hierarchies of status, and the relationships between lay and professional players. Con-

---

22 Where necessary, narrative is supplemented by various ethnographic approaches, including direct non-participant observation, interviewing and contextual commentary.

ceptually, it is therefore important to recognize what Giddens refers to as the 'dialectic of control', which emphasizes the significance of social context and the power balance existing at the individual and group level. The reproduction of power relations relies heavily on symbolic structures in the trial context. Consequently, the ontology of structure and institutional power are intimately connected to the phenomenology of individual reason and motivation.

In terms of structuration theory narrative may be regarded as a record of reproduced relations (systems) whilst its official status and authority are conceived in terms of structure. Even so, these structures of status have little meaning without the application of power and authority through pathways of influence, at specific trial sites. Ideological, power and social control variables are reflected in narrative in so far as they impact on the social interaction which constitutes the process of structuration, i.e. the extent of their effect on the reproduced relations of autonomy and dependence in social interaction. Part of the means affecting the capability of individual social actors to secure their own ends is the linkage between ideology and policy, mediated through the symbolism of the criminal trial process. However, we would not go so far as Giddens and conflate action and structure to the extent that the latter fails to have any objective reality except in so far as it reflects the reasons, motivations and reflexive behaviour of individuals. Instead we would favour, as a sensitizing perspective, the distinction between the context and situational circumstances of interaction drawn by Bourdieu,[23] which acknowledges the possibility of objectivism in social relations. With this acknowledgement, structure takes on a role, along with agency, relationships and decisions as action in order to explain the process of the trial. The difficulty here, as noted earlier in our discussion of comparative analysis, is remaining true to the cultural relativity of certain contextual forms of trial while searching for and utilizing universal characteristics of the trial across which comparison may be mounted. The model of the trial as sites for decision-making, relationships between decision-making parties and essential pathways of influence producing decisions, allows for subjective analysis within universalized process forms, as well as reproducible senses of structure and agency.

Twining recognizes generalization in narrative analysis as both 'necessary and dangerous' (1999: 69). On generalizations in relation to the reasoning of legal decision-making he observes:

---

23   For critical analysis, see Layder (1994).

They are necessary as the glue in inferential reasoning, and they can also be used in the formation of hypotheses, to fill in gaps in stories, and, as a last resort, as anchors for parts of a story for which no particular evidence is available ... they are dangerous because, especially when unexpressed they are often in-determinate in terms of frequency, level of abstraction, empirical reliability, defeasibility, identity (which generalisation?), and power (whose generalisation?) (1999: 72).

Much the same could be said for the construction and application of analytical universals within and across contexts and levels of analysis. The use of models helps soften some of the difficult interfaces between universals, and subjective methodologies. Additionally, the distinction between action and value in narrative can be readily conceptualized in terms of our contextual modelling, which is capable of locating the mechanism of the narrative in the context of decision-making in a criminal trial (with its specific audiences, players, processes, insti-tutions, power relations and symbolic structures, etc.) and lends itself to reconstruction at the various comparative levels discussed earlier. Such analytical levels are relevant from culture to culture, vertically or horizontally (from local to international jurisdictions) and hold good for the analysis of decision-making in a socio-historic context.

We now turn to consider further the relationship between action and narrative in the criminal trial process and its conceptualization by structuration theory. A diagrammatical representation of this relation-ship is presented in Figure 1.3. Structuration theory conceptualizes the nature and direction of the flow in Figure 1.3 as between action and narrative in terms of a recursive and reflexive process. The trial is apposite as a process which is both recursive and reflexive in practice.

Figure 1.3   Conceptualizing the relationship between action and narrative in structuration theory

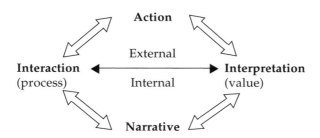

Therefore, the transition from action to narrative proceeds through interaction (process) as objectivity, and interpretation (value) as subjectivity.

The relationship between action and narrative is recursive in that it depends on the application of structured properties by social actors (structuration) in an interactive context, i.e. through the trial as a reproducible social practice (system). Narrative is, consequently, a representation of that reality. However, both interpretation and interaction reflect the objective and subjective dialectic between action and narrative. In other words, both interaction (as process) and interpretation (as value) have an external and internal dynamic which is present in the trial narrative.[24] For instance, trial transcripts often represent the question-and-answer format of evidence production. This narrative is governed by normative conventions such as the rules of evidence and procedure. It is also made both universal and predictable by the structures of status which govern the conversation. Hence, the narrative itself records dimensions of the formal process required (structure) but does not permit us to understand how each player in the trial process subjectively interprets any aspect of the process. A narrative simply records the way in which formal requirements are interpreted (acted upon) as external processes. Each narrative will declare different versions of meaning through the text but, as with the record of evidence, so much is left unsaid and left to the interpretation of the advocate, the judge, and sometimes the jury.

Developing theory and methodology

Informed by the preceding theoretical analysis a selection of major contested trials from common law and civil law jurisdictions are later examined and compared in detail. It is not intended that these trials should be representative of procedural styles beyond the desire that they involve offences and circumstances common to the trial practice of the style concerned. In addition, efforts are made to ensure that (as far as possible) there is some commonality between the trials in terms of the matters in content and form. Trials are, therefore, selected on the

---

24　It would be wrong to suggest that the trial, then, is simply another arena in which to recall the fact/value debate in social science. As a close reading of the role of evidence in the trial reveals, we are more likely to be examining a conflation of fact/value; in the form of value-added facts. Distilling this process of adding value to fact (subjectifying the objective) is a challenge for interactive methodologies.

basis of measures of comparability,[25] and accepted indicators of difference.[26] However, such indicators only act as a focus for comparability since a wider spectrum of relevant issues existing within participating jurisdictions is revealed through the contextual analysis of the variables included in the trial decision-making process at particular trial decision sites.[27]

The comparative contextual analysis of procedural sites within trials necessarily depends on establishing the principal points of decision-

---

25 Measures of comparability:

- Trial length.
- Charges.
- Number and nature of accused.
- Pre-trial documentation.
- Expert evidence.
- Contested issues of procedure.
- Judicial intervention.
- Frameworks for decision-making.
- Outcome.

The categories developed here do not denote the final categories for analysis. It is also important to note that similar action may be redefined in some jurisdictions. Both measures of comparability and difference are expected to evolve during the research process.

26 Accepted indicators of difference:

- Nature of indictment.
- Role of the prosecutor.
- Significance of documentary evidence.
- Role of defence advocate.
- Accused's rights, and the requirement on the accused to participate.
- Role of the victim.
- Nature of adjudicator.
- Mechanisms for verdict.
- Appeals.

It is important to remember that as much as synthesis is a theme of the procedural analysis in internationalization, so is the identification of difference. In order to enable comparison, common procedural sites need to be located within actual trials. This is where the comparative analysis of procedural difference crucially depends on uniformity within and across stages of the trial (tradition to tradition). These sites focus on principal points of decision-making in the trial and the players involved. Another common theme to lubricate the exploration of difference is the exercise of discretion. Discretion may also highlight some interesting degrees of difference in the operation of comparable sites for decision-making. Difference, and its characteristics, therefore, are also appropriate contextual issues for generalization where appropriate.

27 A number of principal decision sites are common to most jurisdictions, whether adversarial or inquisitorial, i.e. prosecutorial decisions, pre-trial hearings, course of

making and identifying the players involved for particular jurisdictions, along with the pathways of influence which produce the decisions documented in the trial narrative. As mentioned earlier, the trial is deliberately chosen as the common domain for analysis since, whatever emphasis is given to pre-trial procedures, it provides a setting where public expression is given to the ideological and policy dimensions of penality. It, therefore, provides the most appropriate forum for exploring issues of synthesis and difference as between competing jurisdictions.[28]

Apart from contextualizing the basis for comparison, expert commentary also determines the extent to which relevant issues may be addressed by whatever trial narrative is available (or accessible) for a particular jurisdiction. The questions that need to be asked of the narrative in this context are as follows:

- What information on the trial process does it provide (for example, who makes decisions, where, when, and for what purpose)?

- What are the respective roles of the trial participants?

- How do they interact?

- How do trial participants conceptualize and process information as formal (evidence), or informal (understandings) discourse, what form does it take and what is kept from them?

- Who has access to what features of the process?

- What pathways of influence are created and how do they operate in order that any particular trial decision is achieved?

---

trial, verdict delivery, appeal. These sites are meant to hold good wherever the place of trial. The relevance of place for each site is revealed through contextual analysis. Note that police activities are included within the term 'prosecutorial decisions', and the interaction of trial participants within the term 'course of trial'.

28 The foregoing analysis depends on there being some measure of agreement as to the status of any narrative record produced, and the possibility that (as with the dossier in France – Vogler 1996) pre-trial (or other) documentation may subsequently assume the status of trial record. Where narrative (of whatever status) is deficient trial observation, personal interview and expert commentary should provide the basis for comparison. Notwithstanding the well-known methodological limitations of such techniques in social research (Sarantakos 1993), the status of the narratives produced requires to be established. In particular, it is necessary to establish some measures for comparability in terms of the reliability and validity of the research methods employed (Punch 1998).

The links existing between the methodology to be applied to trial narrative and key elements in structuration theory relate primarily to those elements of structure requiring action (e.g. legislation, case law and discretionary principles, as well as the status of the participants identified and empowered by these) which determine trial players, actions and narrative. These links are conceptualized in Figure 1.4. In this conceptualization structuration itself is conceived as a reciprocal process that allows narrative to reveal actual descriptions of players, actions and issues in context as interactive processes.

Figure 1.4   Conceptualizing narrative analysis as structuration

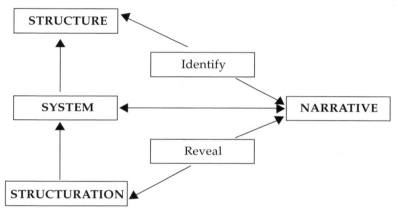

Thus, the methodology is complementary in that it deconstructs the transcript through a process of inductive and deductive influence that, in effect, reflects how the trial exists as a recursive process and how decisions are achieved within it. The development of theory through inductive and deductive methodologies is mediated through the heuristic capabilities of the contextual model (elaborated in Chapter 2) (as illustrated in Figure 1.5). As we will discuss in more detail in the next chapter, this is achieved through the model's capacity to direct and accommodate data production relevant to both theory verification and theory generation (Henham and Findlay 2001c). Further, modelling allows for another technology in comparative contextual analysis in that the model provides a platform for universalizing decision-making in the trial. It enables the sensitive comparison of different structures and agencies which come together through the trial process, but do so under common decision relationships and aspirations.

Figure 1.5 Modelling the reciprocal relationship between theory and methodology

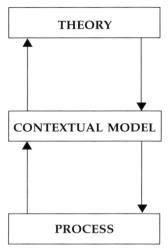

INDUCTIVE   DEDUCTIVE

As described, levels and layers of meaning are revealed through contextual analysis in the comparative dimension. The model is designed to facilitate the comparative essence of our work. Thus, the connections between issues may be identified and explored by employing a deductive methodology, or the interactive process may be described using ethnographic methodologies (even limited to expert commentary on the narrative, if observation and participation are not possible). At the level of inference and meaning this aspect of the methodology will produce accounts of how rules, procedures, processes and status structures are conceptualized and understood by trial participants and enable us to interpret narrative representations of interaction at different trial sites. By exploring the 'objectivity' or common experience of process whilst also deconstructing its 'subjectivity' for each interpretant, the methodology seeks to describe the construction of decision-making as social reality for all participants, including the judge (Rogers and Erez 1999).[29] Through the application

---

29 In summary, therefore, through combining elements of qualitative and quantitative methodologies in the contextual model, a number of the advantages suggested by Bryman (1992) are achieved. For example:

of a common decision-making model we hope that comparison will be advanced in an atmosphere which appreciates the subjective processes of different decision sites.

In terms of combining the two approaches in the contextual model as applied to narrative analysis, we see them as equally important (as complementary aspects of a recursive process) and interactive, in the sense of informing each other, and, therefore, heuristically valuable in explanatory and predictive terms;[30] hence the link to policy. This is because in order to make sense of any cross-cultural comparisons of processual activity, especially the way in which pathways of influence impact on the operation of procedural rules, we need to be able to provide culturally convincing accounts of what process means in a particular context as an objectively verifiable fact, and (crucially) how each participant in the criminal trial process perceives their reality of what is going on (both for themselves and as regards the actions of others). Consequently, the matching of objective and subjective perceptions of social reality and how they merge together in process decisions can be understood and evaluated (together with the perceived significance of those decisions once made) as determinants of trial outcomes.

Returning to our example of victim participation, we might then be in a position to understand why and how the attitudes and penal philosophies of judges influence their approach to evaluating victim evidence at various points in the trial, whilst for the victim (as outsider) their immediate concerns regarding what they expect from the process and its wider significance in terms of the community (for example, its impact for social control) can be appreciated. These collective under-standings are vital to an informed debate about what ICJ actually 'is' and its likely future direction.

---

1   Structure and process – quantitative research is especially efficient at getting to the 'structural' features of social life, whilst qualitative studies are usually stronger in terms of 'processual' aspects.

2   Qualitative research may facilitate the interpretation of relationships between variables – although quantitative research readily allows the researcher to establish relationships among variables, it is often weak in exploring the reasons for them.

3   Relationship between macro and micro levels – quantitative research can often tap large-scale, structural features of social life, qualitative research more readily addresses small-scale, behavioural aspects.

30   These terms are not used here in any positivist sense.

Conclusion

In this chapter we have argued that structuration theory facilitates the adoption of methodologies that allow us to signify the objective/subjective (external/internal) meaning of social action in the trial by conflating the theoretical and empirical imperatives dictated by contemporary epistemological controversies. In doing so, the contextuality of process in terms of its objectivity (both conceptual and concrete) and the subjective account of that objectivity (in terms of its phenomenological content) are revealed.

Understanding process in comparative contexts is about being able to deconstruct, understand and evaluate the different levels of meaning attributed to trial events by participants in different jurisdictions. Our development of structuration theory conceptualizes the nexus between structure and agency as fluid, dynamic and recursive. We operationalize structuration in the trial context through modelling, which exposes the interface between action and structure in processual decision-making. In concrete terms this means that the relative realities of trial participants' experiences are revealed and the extent of their cultural equivalence understood. We therefore maintain that, for CCA, structuration theory provides a valuable vehicle for conceptualizing how *process* is created and sustained which holds good across time and space, and both within and across cultures.

However, we also emphasize that the incorporation of structuration theory in the mission of CCA distinguishes levels for the purpose of comparison and seeks to go beyond a consideration of influences over agency in order to explain decision-making in terms of what people do through predetermined relationships of interest. In our application of structuration theory within CCA we use Giddens' advice (1984: 326) and do so selectively, and as a sensitizing device. We identify some essential preconditions to interaction (legal, organizational and interactive) which precede the comparative analysis of social action. In so doing we recognize that these levels of understanding are ways of considering interconnected aspects of the same social practice. From a theoretical point of view this may be seen as a context for the application of structuration, as part of comparative analysis.

Dualism and dichotomy (such as between agency and structure) have no relative reality in context and, as issues of comparative influence, suggest, that abstraction may be necessary to understanding the mechanisms of structuration. Not so when agency and structure merge within the decision-making of the trial and the pathways of influence which predetermine these. This does not mean that by applying levels of analysis or components of context for analysis the process endorses (as Vaughan 2001 suggests) their autonomy within social action. On the contrary, CCA uses dualism to emphasize integration, difference to expose synthesis, and dissonance to reveal harmony (see Findlay 1999a: Epilogue).[31] Dualism is little more than poles or contextual boundaries for delimiting the action of agency. Within certain contexts and across contexts in transition there is no reason why those factors which influence the moment of interaction should not be extracted and abstracted for the purpose of analysis. It may be the outcome of interaction, whether at the macro or micro level, within particular contexts which becomes the legitimate focus for comparative analysis. Hence, CCA may stand beyond, or strive for more than, structuration in the manner it addresses change, since its mission is to explore theories of transition and change (Henham and Findlay 2001c).

---

31 Through the creative use of paradox we claim to overcome Tamanaha's (1997: chap. 1) critique of sociolegal studies that it employs contextuality in apprehension of grand theory, and that it employs dichotomies oversimply in order to avoid the examination of practical law in action.

Chapter 2

Criminal justice modelling and trial process

Introduction

In the previous chapter we provided a detailed account of the theoretical foundations developed to underpin our critical examination of the internationalization of criminal trial process and provided an evaluation of those influential process styles at work within national and international criminal trials (Henham and Findlay 2001c). This chapter builds and expands upon our discussion of the development of modelling for the research described in this book. We regard this as crucial to the comparative endeavour from two perspectives:

1   To provide a heuristic device; a theoretically grounded construct that allows us to link what is discovered to existing knowledge and facilitates the process of analytical induction, whereby the naturalistic observation of social phenomena provides (and confirms) theoretical insights into the trial process.

2   To provide systematic evaluation regarding the operation of existing criminal justice models and their ideological context in order to allow us to test certain assumptions about preferred criminal justice processes based on such models. The ultimate purpose of this exercise is to draw attention to the limitations and potentials of criminal justice modelling in order to construct a workable policy matrix. This will provide an evaluative tool which will enable the comparative evaluation of justice delivery identified within and beyond the present project.

We begin by embarking on a focused critique of specific paradigms,[1] before developing the arguments which sustain the adoption of a contextual model. The chapter concludes with an assessment of the challenges that face operationalizing the contextual model in the comparative dimension.

Levels of modelling

The traditional approach of comparativists can best be described as template analysis, or what Nelken (1997b) refers to as 'comparison by juxtaposition'.[2] In this, an atheoretical model is constructed of postulates which exemplify the empirical practice pertaining in one particular jurisdiction, usually a Western industrialized democracy such as the USA or the UK; in essence, a model based on adversarial practice. The crucial point is that the resulting model is treated as valid; it is used as a measure against which to evaluate others and, as some have suggested (Zedner 1995), merely disguises, or exemplifies, a more sinister trend towards ideological imperialism to be achieved through intellectual and administrative infiltration of key cultural processes.

The so-called template approach to modelling is fundamentally flawed since it is patently invalid to attempt to measure the principles of an adversarial system against those of an inquisitorial model (or vice versa) without a consideration of context, both within and across cultures (Leigh 1977; Findlay 1999a; Henham and Findlay 2001a). As Vogler (2000) points out, the template approach simply produces accounts of process in different jurisdictions which have been distorted by the dominant perspective since, although the tasks to be achieved by criminal procedure are basically the same, 'the ways in which such tasks are accomplished are so various and so functionally different as to defy universal categorisation'. Much of this modelling reflects the preoccupation of comparative law scholarship with anthropological/ historical reviews of particular systems and policy arguments advancing the benefits of one style over another. Similarly, political modelling has proved of limited utility in analysing criminal justice systems (Vogler 2000), whilst recent developments in behavioural law and economics have yet to deliver convincing models of criminal justice process (Rostain, 2000).

---

1 For characterization and evaluation of traditional approaches to criminal justice modelling, see Henham and Findlay (2002).
2 This is well evidenced in the cultural imperialism of much restorative justice policy-making (see Findlay 2000c).

In identifying these apparently different levels of modelling we recognize that they also represent and portray particular conceptions of the nature and function of modelling social processes. They reflect one-dimensional perspectives of modelling which in our view need to be understood as aspects of a more holistic appreciation of the purpose of modelling for comparative contextual analysis.[3] Figure 2.1 illustrates the inter-relationship of these various perspectives (or levels) of modelling. This suggests not only the inter-relationship of component levels within the model, but also that this conception is a necessary precursor to the deconstruction of context through the adoption of appropriate methodologies. Therefore, the ideological commitments which underpin theoretical models must be acknowledged in the heuristic endeavour, as should their reflection in the context(s) where normative principles (rights) operate, and against which they fall to be evaluated. Similarly, the ideological context may itself inform the progress and direction of the heuristic task through the process of theory generation. Further, the affiliation of context (beyond broad notions of society and space) demands recognition of the objects of inquiry as motivations for eventual comparison. For the trial, the process requires contextualization, which will necessitate or perhaps stimulate the development of modelling.

Figure 2.1 The relationship between contextualization and modelling

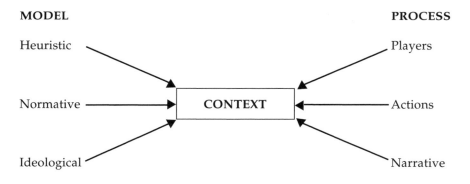

MODEL

Heuristic

Normative

Ideological

PROCESS

Players

CONTEXT

Actions

Narrative

---

3   As argued in Chapter 1, in order to appreciate the object of inquiry beyond its localized manifestations contextual analysis needs to be comparative at many levels. Contextual analysis must precede any such comparison since context is dynamic and essentially interactive.

As for the process outcomes (or foci) for contextual analysis (which may precede the settling of any model), these are driven by a concern for discretionary decision-making.[4] Players (lay/professional), their actions (through obligation and discretion) and the trial narrative (form, source, status) relate and interact within context. Their conceptualization (i.e. symbolic, structural, functional) will tend preferentially to complement particular perspectives of modelling. For instance, actions within the trial may reveal ascription to rights protection. The authority of professional players may be crucially dependent on ideologies of independence. The narrative (limited as it may be) is a voice for the trial process which enables some discovery of relationships and interaction.

The connection between model and process through context exercises our inquiry into methodology. Modelling is anticipated to provide a platform for generalization, informed by the relativities of context and process.

In recognizing the need for conceptual synthesis in modelling for the comparative project we remain sensitive to our legitimate expectations for modelling and the reasons underlying its choice. In this exercise, we are not just about comparing the crucial features of process within any chosen model. Nor do we limit external comparison to observations across similar jurisdictional levels. Put simply, the problem for comparative contextual analysis is that any model sophisticated enough to conceptualize the social reality (i.e. the external/internal, higher/lower aspects of trial process) at comparative levels[5] needs to be developed *before* the contextual analysis takes place which would permit the incorporation of constructs that may allow the making of *valid* (i.e. meaningful) comparisons.[6] This paradox presents acute

---

4 It might be argued that discretionary decision-making is a suspect or perhaps overly relative inspiration for comparative analysis of trial processes. We would counter, however, that all trials are about decisions, their players and their outcomes. Even where crucial decision-making precedes the trial and crucially informs its outcome, it is still essential that the trial legitimates such decision-making. Considerations of decisions and their sites in the trial promote recognition of power and authority as the context for decision-making. In addition, decision-making represents the interactive relationships within the trial which initially require analysis within and across process contexts.

5 See Findlay (1999a) – comparative levels within context, concurrently context to context, across time and space within a context in transition, and simultaneously at local and global levels.

6 Without this, the essential relativity of contextual analysis may disintegrate the power of generalization offered by modelling.

difficulties in modelling at the comparative level since it is precisely this need to identify and delineate context and facilitate its understanding through the model which remains paramount. Context is a social phenomenon involving people, places and institutions. The interactive, immediate and actual connotations of context promote contextual analysis. If we conceptualize context as including (but not confined to) physical space, institutional process, patterns of relationships, boundaries of permission which may designate such relationships and individual variation examined in relationship to a particular representation of the trial (as a series of sites for decision-making), it becomes necessary to visualize a model which is conceptually capable of facilitating the analytical deconstruction of the legal, organizational and interactive dimensions of the trial across jurisdictions (Henham and Findlay 2001c).

Postulating a model which permits the evaluation of these complex dimensions within and across contexts allows phenomenological accounts of context to emerge for each participating jurisdiction. These must be contextually understood as essential precursors to the comparative phase. In other words, the emerging model permits the elements of contrasting styles to be compared and evaluated because it facilitates the gathering of the information (data) necessary to evaluate them, as well as allowing for and anticipating contextual relativities. It is for this reason that we argue for a contextual model which is theoretically neutral (but reflexive) as regards those prerequisites to be included, since it incorporates methodologies appropriate to both theory verification and theory generation which transcend the limitations imposed by template analysis and militate against the inherent dangers of ideological imperialism. Thus, both theory and method are available at different levels of abstraction and are capable of revealing the social reality of trial process at the local and global levels (Findlay 1999a).

Having advanced the case for conceptual synthesis in our overall approach to developing a contextual model for the project, we now turn our attention to a more detailed evaluation of existing criminal justice paradigms and decision-making models before elaborating our alternative contextual approach to modelling the criminal trial process.

Developing the contextual model (1)

Criminal justice paradigms

The bareness of criminal justice modelling has long been recognized and the components of Packer's normative models of the criminal process have been subjected to considerable critical scrutiny in recent years (Ashworth 1994, 1998; Sanders and Young 2000). It is not our purpose here to revisit these debates; suffice to say that we are deprived of models that look much beyond Garland's work on penality (1990) at the process of criminal justice and allow for the introduction of the insights of social theory.[7] Further, the atheoretical relativism of much criminal justice modelling presents additional difficulties.[8] For example, justice modelling (or other models incorporating notions of fairness based on political, managerial or economic paradigms)[9] provides inadequate analytical devices for comparative analysis. Although heuristically valuable, such paradigms are nevertheless contextually relative (in a moral and normative sense). They are also functionalist in nature, since the specific variables (principles) present in each model collectively contribute towards constructing a particular measure of 'justice' or 'fairness' in the criminal process. Similarly, rights modelling in the criminal justice context must be capable of accommodating notions of power and social control if it is not to be conceived as morally relative and democratically suspect (Campbell 1999).

As we describe, the contextual model is conceived solely for the purpose of describing the recursive process of decision-making in a criminal trial. As such the model allows for consideration of particular aspects of different (possibly conflicting) justice paradigms represented in inquisitorial and adversarial systems[10] to be identified and contextualized within the explanatory framework provided by structuration theory (Henham and Findlay 2001). Taking the notion of

---

7 Notable exceptions are Steven Box's work on power and mystification (1983), Blumberg on systems analysis (1967), Chambliss on critical theory (1969) and Schur on deinstitutionalization (1971).

8 For us relativism in analysis is cordoned off in context. In this way the relativity of any issue for analysis can be explored, awaiting its subsumption into the generality (universalizing) of modelling to follow.

9 See, for example, Hudson (1987) and Hutton (1995). A way around the problem might be achieved if one were able to delineate objectively the 'major dimensions' of fairness. See further Matza (1964).

10 The problematic nature of this distinction in trial practice is explored in Findlay (2001a).

justice as an example, it is contextualization which gives cultural form to justice and identifies the particular limitations on its role in modelling (Findlay 1999a). Particular forms of criminal justice modelling can be seen as paradigms of how relations of autonomy and dependence in the social interaction of the courtroom are reproduced in certain ways. However, the contextual model is multi-dimensional and non-prescriptive[11] as regards context, comparison or purpose.

In recognizing these limitations this book seeks to counter the conventional wisdom typified by much past criminal justice modelling, particularly the tendency to treat areas (decision-making sites) as self-contained entities as opposed to structures within a wider social system (Low 1978).[12] It is essentially concerned with providing sociological insights into discretionary decision-making within and relevant to, the trial process, whilst acknowledging that the relative paucity of adequate theoretically grounded constructs available for the evaluation of criminal justice processes reflects deeper controversies concerning the boundaries which (should) exist between the sociology of law and sociology (Nelken 1998: 407; Cotterrell 1999: 182) and their methodological implications (Banakar 2000).

The debate between Cotterrell and Nelken regarding the extent to which sociological insights should be used in the interpretation of legal ideas has significant epistemological and methodological repercussions in the present context (Henham 2001a: 253). Particularly relevant is Nelken's (1998) affirmation that there are not one but several 'legal realities' and that legal reasoning and the process of legal reasoning has numerous contexts.[13] Hence, although there is broad agreement between Cotterrell and Nelken regarding the need for legal sociology to address the sociolegal contexts of legal decision-making, Nelken distances himself from Cotterrell's suggestion that legal contexts should only be interpreted sociologically.

The Cotterrell/Nelken debate raises two key issues for this research endeavour. The first relates to Cotterrell's (1999a: 182) insistence on the need to understand the moral power of the law and, secondly, the methodological implications of the related demystification of the

---

11 Here 'non-prescriptive' is used in the sense of accommodating methodologies derived from disparate theoretical positions.

12 The project's theoretical requirements necessitate an appreciation of the conceptual rigidity of structural and functional accounts as a basis for criminal justice modelling and an ability to conceptualize the interactive (re)construction of discretionary decision-making processes as recursively organized human action.

13 Here, however, he tends to determine context within a form of specific legal or social analysis (i.e. critical legal context, law in context).

internal/external distinction in conceptualizing legal thought and decision-making processes. For example, the inter-relationship between the normative and analytical aspects of legal decision-making is particularly significant in the sentencing process of England and Wales. Sentencing decisions require judges to adhere to judicial techniques and analytical justifications (such as those required by the principles of statutory interpretation), whilst also reflecting legalistic concepts (such as culpability) in the choice of an appropriate sanction against a background of guideline judgements and principles which are not binding in the legal sense. Thus, the debate concerning the normative character of law has an added dimension in that the discretionary character of sentence decision-making requires judges to justify and signify legal rules as morally appropriate since sentencers effectively operationalize policy-justified principles of punishment by transforming law into appropriate sanctions through the criminal (punishment) process. Therefore, law's moral power in sentencing is achieved through its capacity to shape social reality through the recursively organized practices of the criminal process.

In order to appreciate the transformation of normative principles as morally significant (as an aspect of social reality) it consequently becomes necessary to understand law's capacity to achieve this, which can only be addressed by examining the epistemological and methodological questions raised by conceptualizing 'social reality'. Hence, the relationship between legal reasoning and punishment in sentencing must be systematically and empirically explained as a form of 'social reality'. The implications of this for sentence modelling are profound in that a satisfactory paradigm should be capable of conceptualizing both the nature of legal reasoning in the analytical sense and its sociological significance as process for trial participants and the wider community.[14] The normative character of the 'social reality' of law and legal processes also raises the secondary difficulty of conceptualizing the 'meaning' of social action and its linkage to policy formation (Nelken 1998: 419).[15]

---

14 Although acknowledging the significance of context for comparative sentencing research, Davies (2002) does not develop a model for the comparative contextual understanding of the relationship between law and social process in judicial discretionary decision-making.

15 Another example might be with the institution and practice of the jury. Imbued with so many expectations for justice, and a function which is largely ideological, the jury is often attacked for not complying with or advancing social policy. See Duff and Findlay (1997).

Therefore, in the sentencing context, we are essentially concerned with law's capacity to shape the social reality of sentencing as a normative phenomenon. In short, the transformation of the moral to the normative through sentencing *law and* the sentencing *process* both constitutes and reproduces the social reality of sentencing. In the wider context of this project, the implications for modelling concern the need to appreciate and conceptualize how the moral meaning in law is transformed into normative guides to conduct through discretionary decision-making in the comparative dimension.

In summary, existing criminal justice paradigms display several weaknesses which have influenced our consideration of modelling for the project:

1 An inability to accommodate the different levels of abstraction required by different levels of analysis.

2 An inability to support methodologies which may have applicability to a number of theoretical approaches.

3 A failure to represent trial decision-making as an interactive social process.

4 An inability to provide the reflexive capacity to facilitate theory generation.

5 A failure to reflect the relationship between the processes of legal reasoning and discretionary decision-making.

6 A failure to provide adequate mechanisms for representing the meaning of social action across time and space and both within and across cultures at all levels of comparison (Findlay 1999c).

We now propose to examine various contemporary models of discretionary decision-making in order to establish the extent to which they are capable of responding to these limitations before elaborating the basis for our contextual model for the comparative contextual analysis (CCA) of trial process.

Decision-making models

This section provides an account of contributions to criminal justice modelling by legal theory, the sociology of law and mainstream sociological interpretations. The analysis is designed to assess the relative significance of such models to furthering our understanding of discretionary decision-making in the trial process. We, therefore, draw attention to their fundamental methodological implications where appropriate.

An approach centred on *legal formalism* would regard any discretionary decision within the trial process as essentially concerned with the judicial interpretation and application of statutory provisions and would largely ignore the interactions between legal and social processes. Legal formalism would, therefore, determine what view might be taken of the role of discretion in decision-making, particularly in relation to the process of giving reasons for decisions and determining their validity. It would also unrealistically delineate the parameters of procedural justice, without recognition of their everyday interpretation through discretion.

The conceptual defects of legal formalism can be illustrated if we look at the ambivalent nature of sentencing principles. In common law jurisdictions, such as England and Wales, sentencing principles are not objectively accorded the status of substantive rules of law, either in terms of their internal validity, nor as precedent (external validity). Secondly, sentencing principles are morally prescriptive in that they provide guidance to judges on how they ought to react when faced with certain factual configurations and reach reasoned (i.e. rational) judgements in consequence. Sentencing principles, therefore, postulate a normatively desirable course of action (expected sentencing behaviour) which is a reflection, not of the strict juridical application of a legal rule (legal formalism) but the use of sentencing discretion to express what is in reality a matter of sentencing policy, i.e. the acceptable boundaries for the exercise of judicial discretion within the statutory framework of maximum sentences in particular types of cases. A third conceptual problem relates to the fact that it is not possible to subject the role of sentencing principles in the sentence decision-making process to the same analytical scrutiny as might apply to the process of deductive legal reasoning typified by legal formalism. In essence, therefore, the sentencing decision reflects interconnected judgements regarding a defendant's legal and moral accountability.

Legal formalism, although pivotal to the substantive development of law, does not, therefore, extend beyond doctrinal analysis, or the mechanical model,[16] i.e. an approach concerned with the regularity and

---

16 For example, the work of Thomas (1979, 1982) in developing sentencing jurisprudence. Lovegrove (1989) provides an illustration of this kind of approach through the development of sentencing decision models describing judges' sentence determination in relation to single and multiple counts. Lovegrove's *mathematical model* comes closest to providing an analytical device capable of

predictability of conduct – the external aspect of rules (Hart 1961). However, Hart is unable to account empirically for what distinguishes positive acceptance from compulsion and, indeed, he postulates that moral acceptability and obligations are not fundamental prerequisites to the creation of a legal rule. Such a model is clearly substantially deficient in failing to recognize the possible linkage between the internal validity of law and its moral validity (Fuller 1969). This failure is accentuated in the sentencing context since, as they contain normative imperatives, sentencing principles can be regarded as a combination of legal and moral norms that reflect a conception of 'justice' (i.e. a morality of sanctioned punishment) supportive of judicial and/or executive ideology. In this sense, therefore, sentencing jurisprudence is suggestive of how sentencing law ought to be applied in a social context through the medium of a sentencing decision. This position is consistent with that of American realists (such as Llewellyn 1960b) who were prepared to acknowledge that formal rules did not necessarily decide cases; rather judicial decisions provided (in essence) a guide towards a communitarian philosophy of punishment. It is also consistent with the notion of law as an integrative mechanism (Cotterrell 1992: 71) and a Durkheimian analysis (Durkheim 1982), which might suggest that the function of punishment, as expressed in sentencing law and practice, is to reflect and reaffirm society's moral opprobrium (Garland 1990: 52–4). The significance of such an approach for modelling is its *capacity* to conceptualize the normative significance of trial rules and process as representing a form of moral legitimacy derived through the recursive exercise of judicial and/or state power. This is a conceptualization notably lacking in contemporary paradigms of discretionary decision-making process.

Furthermore, if we were to adopt an analytical model of the trial and its place in criminal justice which centred around legal formalism, we not only have the potential of distraction from actuality, but also this

conceptualizing the interpretation and application of current sentencing policy and practice. This is achieved by operationalizing the major components which typify tariff sentencing, and providing a decision strategy model which is further refined into an algebraic model capable of testing the propositions and general predictions generated by the decision model. The main weakness in Lovegrove's approach is the crucial absence of any conceptualization of ideology, power and social control as judicial and institutional variables instrumental in policy determination. Therefore, in deconstructing the mechanisms of sentencing discourse, Lovegrove's paradigm neglects its social context and thus presents an incomplete account of the transformation of normative principles in sentencing behaviour as symbolic punishment.

approach will compound the distorting impact of symbolism and ideology. For instance, if the statutes of trial procedure and rules of court practice from either general procedural style are compared, this may highlight linguistic and processural similarities and differences. But this may not shed much light beyond the political and procedural aspirations of either tradition. It may be a long way off revealing synthesis in practice, whether this be evidenced much beyond courtroom compromise (Findlay 2001a). Further, trial players in the competing traditions may have such different roles and powers as to make comparison without initial contextualization at the level of offence or sites of decision-making of limited relevance.

Modelling in the sociological context necessarily reflects theoretical developments and is characterized by its emphasis on 'explaining' discretionary decision-making as a form of human behaviour. Until recently, the theorizing of legal ideas or the process of discretionary reasoning involved in decision-making (such as sentencing) has received scant attention from scholars in the field.[17] An additional complicating factor stems from the political imperatives that have provided the impetus for sociological inquiry. These have not always been motivated by a desire to understand discretionary decision-making as an intrinsic or holistic aspect of judicial behaviour, but rather (as in the case of sentencing) by the retributive concerns of regulating the disparities revealed by official statistics. Hence, sentencing research has largely proceeded on the basis of attempting to explain why general 'inequality' rather than 'equality' exists in sentencing decisions.

Notwithstanding, even a more reflexive naturalistic view of legal rules and procedural justice does not enable us to understand the significance of the interaction between legal and social processes in decision-making, since these are regarded as essentially ideological issues. However, analyses of the nature of the sentence decision-making process by criminologists reinforce the view that the *actual* process of decision-making (as opposed to its significance) does involve the analysis of information relating to legal rules in the light of legal *and* social constraints. For example, Hogarth's (1971) model of sentencing behaviour is grounded in a phenomenological approach to the study of sentencing. Hogarth summarizes the main elements of the phenomenologically derived model in the following passage:

---

17 A notable exception is McBarnet (1981b).

the model which finally emerged was one that viewed sentencing as a dynamic process in which the facts of the cases, the constraints arising out of the law and the social system, and other features of the external world are interpreted, assimilated and made sense of in ways consistent with the attitudes of the magistrates concerned (1971: 382).

Significantly, Hogarth identified the three most important variables in explaining sentencing behaviour to be the penal philosophies and attitudes of magistrates, the characteristics of the communities where courts are situated and the nature and extent of information available to magistrates before sentence. Hogarth appears to provide an early validation of the contextual approach in his emphasis on the key inter-relationship of variables; namely, that magistrates' attitudes and beliefs tended to reflect those of the local penal culture and their selection of what they considered to be 'essential information' for sentencing. Regrettably, Hogarth's deconstruction of sentencing behaviour was constrained by the adoption of purely positivist research methodologies. Hogarth's *human process model* is, nevertheless, significant in that it seeks to suggest factors that are responsible for structuring discretionary (sentencing) decisions, although it does not 'explain' decisions in individual cases.

As suggested earlier, criminal justice modelling has largely reflected the positivist concern with identifying and measuring 'explanatory' variables in the search to understand inconsistencies in discretionary decision-making in the trial process. In so doing it has failed to explain the basis upon which the social agents involved rationalize their own behaviour (Rock 1973), or reflect the postmodern emphasis connecting power with knowledge which suggests the need to expose the ideological significance of all forms of communication process (Foucault 1980). The accompanying methodological switch to various forms of qualitative research suggests instead research designs which are capable of deconstructing discretionary trial decisions in terms of the meanings, purposes, motivations and intentions of trial participants, their ideological predilections and those of the state (Hodgson 2001).

Understanding context additionally requires an appreciation that courtroom interaction necessarily proceeds according to norms which are characteristic of authority-permeated relationships (Emerson 1969). For example, Goffman (1961) notes how hearings may be conducted on the basis of 'transformation rules' which enable officials to act in ways that in normal interaction would clearly violate appropriate rules of behaviour, whilst postmodern legal scholarship has tended to suppress notions of human subjectivity since it negates concepts of self-determinism, rational choice and autonomous rights (Salter 1996). Norrie (1996b) suggests how constructs such as 'subjectivity' must be understood in their contradictory aspects which necessitates a dialectical understanding of how socio-historically defined propositions are promoted and obstructed by law. As McBarnet (1981b: 160) points out, however, the paradox lies in the fact that it is judicial discretionary decision-making which sustains the rhetoric of judicial authority, yet retains the capacity to deny it in individual cases:

> structural factors also provide some of the means for bridging the ideological gap. The doctrine of the separation of powers provides a multi-headed state and with it the potential to extol the rhetoric in one sector and deny it in another ... The rhetoric lives on in [the] statute but is routinely negated in the courts by judicial reasoning.
>
> Beneath judicial reasoning itself structural factors are also at work. Just as the techniques of advocacy are themselves only adaptations to a particular form of proof, so the techniques of judicial reasoning are themselves significant only in a particular form of law.
>
> ... The conflicting rhetoric of due process and practical demands for crime control are [thus] both simultaneously maintained and the gap between rhetoric and practice is managed out of existence (1981b: 160, 161).

Qualitative methodologies have increasingly been successful in deconstructing discretionary decision-making in terms of the meanings, purposes, motivations and intentions of trial participants, their ideological predilections and those of the state. The naturalistic method and the need to gain a 'holistic' or contextual overview of the decision-making process is more consistent with Tata's (1997) approach and the so-called *narrative model*. This suggests that (in sentencing, for example) a 'schematic-holistic' or 'whole case' approach is necessary whereby decisions are constituted and reconstituted according to 'context', 'audience'. Therefore, decisions are seen as unstructured, relative, pragmatic and situational. 'Reasons' are suspect (*post hoc*) including Appeal Court narrative.[18] This approach emphasizes the

---

18 'Largely constructed and typified by the criminal process even before they reach the judge' (Tata 1997).

innate subjectivism and contextual relativity of legal and social constraints. In recognising that there may be a tendency to exaggerate the *process* of decision-making at the expense of appreciating the unique construction of each decision, the *narrative model* implicitly acknowledges the pivotal significance of demographic and psychological variables in decision-making. Therefore, the ethnography of discretionary decision-making behaviour consists of developing methodologies of access to the subjective experiences of social actors. Crucially, this involves the contextualization of decision-making experience by 'description' and its interpretation.[19] However, the transition from 'description' to contextualization is a difficult one, so far inadequately addressed by decision-making models. This is all the more so when it is an interactive and dynamic relationship which is the object of inquiry. It entails a commitment to cultural interpretation – the need to uncover the shared cultural meanings of trial participants in addition to revealing the subjectivism of social action. As earlier declared, this is possible through a sensitive contextual analysis which precedes and then informs both modelling and comparative analysis.

In this respect, useful insights are provided by Rogers and Erez (1999: 269) in their study of the cultural interpretation of 'objectivity' in sentencing among legal professionals in South Australia. Rogers and Erez found the need to contextualize this 'construct' arose from the differing perceptions which legal practitioners had regarding certain actions as either objective or subjective when asked about their experiences and opinions of the operation of victim impact statements. Using various qualitative techniques they attempted to 'decode' the symbolic references that the various legal practitioners ascribed to the linguistic, social and relational constructs of the term 'objectivity' in their particular practices (1999: 269). The result was an attempt to 'explain' how the definition of objectivity is produced through the analysis of the subjective experiences of legal professionals as a constantly changing process. The significance of this approach is that it represents a rare attempt to fix the meaning or contextualize an interactive process by deconstructing the subjectivity of trial participants' subjective experiences. Hence, the methodology is culturally contextual in that it suggests ways in which the objectivity of process is constructed subjectively.

---

19 This may involve an exploration of what is not said as well as what is said, and of impressions. In order to get the most out of narrative in the trial context it may be necessary to add value through a variety of participant observation methodologies. See Casanovas (1999).

Casanovas (1999) goes further than this in suggesting that legal decisions are produced through and by changing structures of collective behaviour which do not rely solely on the consciousness of individuals, but on the enacting power of networks that modulate their interactive and co-ordinated behaviour. Decisions are, therefore, the result of a kind of 'collective reasoning' and can be perceived as emerging properties of a 'collective situation' where solutions are proposed in the knowledge (consciously or otherwise) that they will be accepted and legitimated by relevant trial participants (i.e. 'pragmatic contexts' – the cognitive result of patterning professional relationships). Casanovas argues that the reconstruction of the 'reality' of the courtroom can only be modelled at the micro-situational level to ensure the asymmetry of human interaction and cognition.

In what follows we argue that the contextual model provides a broader construct which permits the integration of the theoretical and methodological postulates of positivist, ethnographic and grounded theory approaches. It focuses on the context of decision-making in a criminal trial (with its specific audiences, players, processes, institutions, power relations and symbolic structures, etc.) and lends itself to reconstruction at various analytical levels which are relevant from culture to culture, vertically or horizontally (from local to international jurisdictions) and hold good for the analysis of decision-making in a socio-historic context. In all these respects the relativity of context is celebrated in order to prepare the detailed understandings essential for CCA.

The contextual model

We suggest that there are two fundamental challenges for criminal justice modelling which remain unresolved at both the institutional and comparative level:

1 The need to appreciate and conceptualize how the moral meaning in law is transformed into normative guides to conduct.

2 To 'explain' satisfactorily the *process* (behaviour) which is the social reality of discretionary decision-making in the criminal trial.

In short, the challenge is to develop a model which addresses the normative significance of law as an aspect of the social reality of the decision-making process in the comparative dimension. We would argue that an examination of *law and process* must explain how law is transformed into normative guides to conduct.[20] To understand law's capacity to achieve this end requires an appreciation of the relationship between legal reasoning and discretionary decision-making, both analytically (as legal formalism) and sociologically (as process). Therefore, to understand the capacity for law to shape or reinforce our modes of understanding the social reality of trial procedure (Cotterrell 1998b: 182) and thereby appreciate the moral power of law, we need to conceptualize legal thought and decision-making *as a process*. The process is the context for analysis, in its stages and its comparative forms, always against its social and legal reality. This does not require law's reality to be subsumed or distorted by sociological interpretations, but rather an acknowledgement that sociological insights are capable of providing conceptual settings which facilitate the deconstruction of different legal discourses (and systems) and enable us to understand how each discourse constructs 'inside' and 'outside' from the internal points of view of *both* law and sociology (Nelken 1998: 419). Neither can be excluded from the domain of context where an interactive process such as the trial is to be understood in terms of its constituent decision-making.

Recognizing the relativity of context and process and the nexus between legal reasoning and trial practice also recognizes the plurality of legal interpretations and conflates the necessity to conceptualize the object/subject or action/value dialectic in sentence modelling. Contextuality suggests a methodology capable of informing law's characteristics, legal reasoning and our interpretation of the actions of legal participants with sociological dimensions which penetrate the temporality and cultural relativity of conventional accounts. This is provided, of course, that context and contextuality are given wide methodological range, not bound within any model or discourse for law, society or justice.

Consequently, we argue that the limitations of legal formalism may be remedied by utilizing a combination of the *human process* and *narrative* models in analysis to provide a *contextual model* of discretionary decision-making which accommodates comparativism (Henham and Findlay 2001a). In contextualizing decision-making it is, therefore, seen as legitimate to describe and analyse the psychological appropriation and assimilation of relevant information as an objective (external) process and consider the extent to which trial participants appear to share similar, uniform and comparable images of relevant

---

20 Any emphasis or predisposition towards a consideration of the constituents of process is eschewed by Casanovas (1999).

case material and legal rules in the context of perceived audience expectation (as consistent with the *narrative* model).

The methodology implicit in the contextual model involves the identification, description and analysis of communication structures and interactive processes through contextual analysis. The model accommodates methodologies which facilitate the deconstruction of social reality in the trial process by developing an approach which combines inductive and deductive strategies. These permit us to signify the objective/subjective meaning of social action by conflating the theoretical and empirical imperatives dictated by epistemological controversies. In so doing, the contextuality of process in terms of its objectivity (both conceptual and concrete) and the subjective account of that objectivity (in terms of its phenomenological content) are revealed.

Any methodology compatible with the contextual model must, therefore, be capable of responding to the objective/subjective dimensions of interpretation and be sensitive to different levels of reasoning and understanding attributed to action and process by trial participants. Inferential meanings can be revealed at different levels of analysis through the adoption of interpretative methodologies designed to discover the subjective significance of action for each participant in the trial process. This may be achieved by juxtaposing methodologies and contrasting common areas where knowledge is limited or understandings apparently are concealed. Contextual analysis therefore aims to identify where 'shared meanings' (in their broadest sense) of the trial process exist. This is achieved by focusing on the construction of the 'objectivity' and 'subjectivity' of relevant information, communication relationships and processes, and social action at the legal, organizational and interactive levels of analysis. In terms of combining elements of qualitative and quantitative method-ologies in the contextual model, they are seen as equally important (as complementary aspects of a recursive process) and interactive, in the sense of informing each other, and, therefore, heuristically valuable in explanatory and predictive terms.

In the following section we intend to elaborate this descriptive account of the contextual model by suggesting how the concept may be operationalized.

Developing the contextual model (2)

As described, the contextual model proposes that information (data) appropriate to both inductive and deductive methodologies are filtered (directed) through what are designated as appropriate evaluators *of context*. In the contextual model so far elaborated we have selected evaluators which derived from *human process* and *narrative* paradigms of discretionary decision-making behaviour. These will include players, actions and their stories. However, these are not exhaustive of evaluative paradigms which may comprise the contextual model in either a substantive or temporal sense. We suggest that others may be included depending on the subject matter under investigation. In other words, the contextual model we portray is reflexive as regards subject matter and the recursive nature of trial process (and its different relationships, stages and levels). Hence, discrete evaluative paradigms (whether related to theory verification or theory generation) may be regarded as submodels consisting of evaluative postulates that direct appropriate methodologies; for example, the narrative paradigm is suggestive of ethnographic methodologies.

To summarize, the initial formulation of the model derives from a deconstruction of context(s) against an application of insights from existing theory which are thought likely to have the potential to infuse the analysis with meaningful comparative conclusions.[21] Although the selection of theoretical postulates for modelling is necessarily pre-determined, their verification and modification, and the ultimate content of the model, are, therefore, dependent on contextual analysis.

The twin components of the contextual modelling approach can be summarized as follows:

- *Evaluators of context* – these are theoretical propositions selected on the basis that they are likely to provide some conceptual insights that will contribute to our understanding of the particular social phenomenon chosen for analysis. The focus is on *process* or, more particularly, the construction of process in comparative context.

- *Evaluation in context* – this refers to the *practice* of comparative contextual analysis; utilizing those interpretative methodologies which have been dictated by the theoretical positions chosen on the basis of the problem posed.

Hence, *evaluators of context* may be regarded as consisting of 'accepted knowledge' which is tested against 'reality' and becomes modified by

---

21 This is not the same as theoretical determinism since the outcome is dependent on the independent variables generated through the deconstruction of context.

the 'emerging knowledge' produced through the recursive process of *evaluation in context*. The latter gradually allows us to modify (and/or confirm) accepted knowledge through theory verification, whilst the process of theory generation may suggest confirmation, integration and postulate new evaluators. Essentially, the model, initially at least (or at the formulation stage), must follow on from a deconstruction of context(s) (Henham and Findlay 2002).

This dichotomy is crucial to the understanding of the manner in which context is applied for the understanding of particular jurisdictions, and then the interrogation of relativity and generality at any comparative level. Regarding evaluation in context, we refer to the practice of utilizing chosen methodologies dictated by the contextual model's focus on particular evaluative paradigms for understanding specific social interactions within the trial process. The significance of this at the comparative level is crucial since it is this activity which will deliver descriptions and evaluations of process which possess contextual significance at the legal, organizational and interactive levels of analysis.

Whether particular methodologies are directed by deductive or inductive paradigms, information (data) is filtered (again) back through the contextual model.[22] In terms of theory generation this involves the process of inductive inference through evaluation against first-order concepts. In this sense the elaboration of categories and inductive development of concepts through the systematic examination of data produces modelling of recurrent social practices, such as the trial process, particularly sensitive to understanding the nature of problem-solving and decision-making. For theory verification, data are evaluated against the postulates of the evaluative paradigm chosen for analysis. However, the contextual model encourages mixed methodologies to facilitate the interpretation of relationships between variables and provide a bridge between macro and micro levels of analysis. Hence, a naturalistic method may be used to explore the complexities of trial narrative together with interviewing and observational studies of the trial process (Punch 1998: chap. 11).

Our modelling of methodological imperatives suggests a pragmatic (yet principled) approach which permits the penetration of the internal aspects of fact/value within trial decision-making. For instance, by reducing decisions on penalty down through the manner in which the

---

22 This notion of a contextual model is where the phases of contextualization and modelling collide. Within this notion we have the potential for a model crucially informed by preceding contextual analysis.

judge's discretion is influenced by the harm to the victim and the mitigation of the accused's liability then what lies behind the negotiation of justice through sentencing should be more apparent. At the same time, the decision site model will show how these understandings enable us to appreciate the meaning of process in all its complexity.

Let us take as an example victim participation in the trial process. Theory verification through the contextual model may entail operationalizing methodologies to test postulates relating to an ideologically derived theory of process (see Carlen 1976). These methodologies will be designed to reveal to what extent victim participation takes place and assess its significance in terms of political, economic and sociological propositions relevant to that theory. Theoretical statements may, therefore, be refined or made as a result that (in turn) produce normative principles for the future operation of the criminal justice process (or part thereof), or validate assumptions made regarding the integrity of existing processes. Alternatively, contextual modelling may permit us to examine the relevance of several contested theoretical accounts of discretionary decision-making. Since it is capable of accommodating theoretical propositions conceived at different levels of abstraction, this enables us to hypothesize about the macro and micro dimensions of decision-making over time, space and context. Such modelling may, therefore, include theoretical evaluators that address:

- the conceptualization of process;
- the relationship between law and moral action;
- the nature and significance of judicial discretionary decision-making as social interaction;
- the symbolism of process; and
- the relationship between power and sentencing.

The conceptual dimensions of discretionary decision-making which eventually emerge will depend upon our perception and evaluation of context; each such context providing the *locus* for testing various (possibly competing) versions of social reality at several conceptual levels of interpretation and meaning. Contextual analysis therefore counteracts the tendency towards one-dimensionalism, undue generalization and those weaknesses identified in our earlier analysis of criminal justice modelling by facilitating a wide range of methodologies for the investigation of designated interactions occurring within the trial process.

Modelling and comparativism

The problem of paradox and relativity in modelling poses a significant problem for comparativism. One solution to this might be to envisage modelling as recursive and developmental in achieving the necessary degree of contextuality. Yet such a position would not sustain our claim for drawing upon more uniform theoretical and analytical themes through our constant reference to context. We, therefore, suggest the following three-staged approach to modelling:

1 *Formulation* – where the construction of the model may only occur following an examination of context and speculation on comparative applications.

2 *Application* – once a model has been broadly proposed its general themes are used to inform the comparative endeavour (in its many facets as part of comparative contextual analysis).

3 *Revision* – the utility of the model is constantly tested (and where necessary adapted) through reflection on its relevance to the outcomes of comparative contextual analysis and its exposure to other individual contexts.

Consequently, the contextual model may be regarded as recursive but having specific paths of influence. If we regard *evaluators of context* as emerging knowledge – what can such evaluators tell us regarding legal, policy, empirical, theoretical and comparative paradigms within and across jurisdictions at the macro and micro levels? Again, in general terms, such emerging knowledge becomes modified through the recursive process of contextualization in which *evaluation in context* gradually allows us to modify (and/or confirm) accepted knowledge through theory verification, whilst theory generation may suggest confirmation, integration and postulate new evaluators. However, the need for greater specificity suggests the identification of themes for analysis drawn from the initial jurisdictional or procedural context needs to be added with value or at least given verification as generalizable (or suitably constant for comparison) by reflection against a model. The model, initially at least (or at the formulation stage), must follow on from a deconstruction of context (or contexts) and an application of likely theories which will infuse the model with its comparative potential.

Our call for the overthrow of conventional criminal justice modelling is implicit in the prioritizing of contextual analysis since, unlike conventional modelling, we do not prepare the model and then test context against it. We engage context, and with actual knowledge of process we formulate models that will then inform the comparative endeavour whilst at the same time being tested and evaluated through it.

At the comparative level the purpose of modelling is to enable us to draw *meaningful* comparative conclusions which relate to issues of difference and possible harmonization of trial procedures. To return to our example of victim participation in the trial process, a conclusion may be reached which suggests that in most jurisdictions, victim participation is in fact a mystification of what is in reality the state's ideological and political commitment towards increased social control, therefore making no appreciable difference to trial process in either common law or civil law systems. However, in reaching such a conclusion the contextualization of several crucial concepts is necessary:

1 The notion of victim.
2 Participation and interaction.
3 The significance of process and outcome.
4 The ideological and socio-historical context.

In short, we require a 'complete' understanding and appreciation of what is happening in the trial process in a particular jurisdiction and its wider social significance. For comparative analysis there must exist comparable definitions, experiences and understandings of what trial participants understand by the happening of a particular trial event and its significance. This will include commonality and difference. Further, it implies the need for mechanisms which facilitate the identification of 'objective' criteria across jurisdictional boundaries and methodologies that are cognizant of subjectivity. The contextual model significantly provides for such methodologies but, crucially, we cannot rely simply on a comparison of subjectivities. The point here is that the subjective appreciation of process is intimately connected to its 'objective existence' – an existence external to human subjectivity. The contextual model, therefore, acknowledges the 'objectivity' of process as existing through the criteria by which human participants in the trial process recognize external reality, i.e. reality as objects, events or states occurring with or without the intervention of human agency.[23]

---

23 The extent to which social phenomena are instrumental in shaping social life has preoccupied sociologists for decades.

Recognition of the 'objectivity' of process is consequently dependent on connections made between subjectivity and objective reality. The significance of this dichotomy for comparativism is that the contextual model allows us to explore common definitions of process or 'objectivity' whilst also deconstructing the 'subjectivity' for each interpretant (Rogers and Erez 1999). Therefore, the construction of discretionary decision-making is described within and across cultures in context.

We suggest that to achieve comparability in the approach to contextual analysis necessitates a focus on those units of comparison listed in Figure 2.2. Whilst we can speculate where there may be points of difference and synthesis at particular sites for discretionary decision-making (Henham and Findlay 2001c: 29–30), the crucial issue is whether comparability exists subjectively as regards what is described as objective experience. Therefore, the significance of trial phenomena across jurisdictions (particularly discretionary decision-making) depends on the extent to which contextual analysis is successful in revealing subjective consensus regarding the meaning and function of process. It is the degree of consensus which will determine the relevance of comparativism to policy-making across the international dimension. The role of the contextual model is to ensure that possible outcomes are evaluated *in context and across contexts* in ways which

Figure 2.2   Units of comparison

• *What does the trial process signify?*	Penality Penal philosophy Principles of punishment
• *What are the formal objectives of the trial process?*	Policy objectives System objectives
• *How are these objectives achieved?*	Nature of process Decision sites
• *Who takes part? When and what are their roles and their status?*	System objectives Subsystem objectives
• *How does the trial process relate to other aspects of the criminal process?*	Significance of pre- and post-trial phases
• *What opportunities exist for negotiation or diversion from the process?*	Bargaining Alternative mechanisms
• *When and how are the interests of the accused, victims and the public protected?*	Process protection Rights law

remain 'sensitive' to each participating jurisdiction.

Linking principle and policy

Having been directed to the appropriate phenomena and employed appropriate methodologies by the contextual model, how do we evaluate the outcomes in a 'meaningful' way? One answer to this question is to evaluate the evidence against a range of desired policy outcomes at the international and domestic level by utilizing various measures, such as efficiency. However, there must be equal recognition that such measures are legally and culturally loaded as are (for example) notions of 'fair trial' and 'access to justice' goals. Emphasis should, therefore, be placed on searching for procedural alternatives (or hybrids) consistent with process aspirations and ideological principle (Norrie 1993).

As argued in the Introduction, our challenge is to suggest CCA can help us to move towards the development of viable and meaningful conceptions of international criminal justice (ICJ). Our aspirations for the development of international trial penality are driven by the realization that the notions of trial justice and relational justice must be reconciled in order to legitimize the punishment of those who breach international criminal law in the eyes of both the victor and the vanquished. The repositioning of restorative and retributive justice within the framework of the trial represents a challenge for theory and method in the sociolegal analysis of process. It requires an acknowledgement on our part that the modelling for CCA has an ideological goal – the legitimation of trial justice. However, we would argue that this does not in any sense weaken or distort the integrity of our analytical approach; rather, it strengthens it, precisely because the theory and method of contextual analysis exist in order to reveal the foundations for legitimacy and justice within the trial. We, therefore, regard contextual modelling as a transformative technology which is designed to lay bare the relativity of contexts for achieving justice. By identifying and deconstructing the creation and pathways of influence within the trial form we seek to provide information about how the contexts of justice are created and forged in discretionary decisions. Relationships between trial participants (such as judge and victim) provide the context for exploring the boundaries of trial legitimacy and its potential for change. Comparative contextual modelling allows us to move from trial to trial (global to local) and compare relative understandings of this interface between fact and value.

Summary

The foregoing analysis has argued the case for a heuristic model which facilitates contextual analysis of the criminal trial process. The main characteristics of this approach can be summarized as follows:

- The contextual analysis of trials deals with the *process* of *how* law may be transformed into normative guides to conduct. It examines the relationship between the processes of legal reasoning and decision-making and allows for *various* sociological perspectives to be used as interpretative devices.

- Descriptions of the *meaning* of social action are revealed through the model by conflating the objective/subjective dimensions of social reality and accommodating empirical imperatives dictated by epistemological controversies.

- The contextual model suggests that phenomenological description and explanation incorporate accounts of process and its *meaning*. Therefore, it addresses not only the transformation of law and process as social reality, but concerns itself with the phenomenological construction of transformation and process, both individually and collectively as shared experience. Different levels and layers of meaning may be examined, as may process at the legal, organizational and interactive levels of analysis.

- The contextual model is atheoretical, accommodates both inductive and deductive methodologies and is subject to constant reappraisal and modification. Theoretical input determines the level of abstraction required in analysis.

- Social theory may provide a vehicle for conceptualizing how *process* is created and sustained, which holds good across time and space and both within and across cultures (Henham and Findlay 2001c). In approaching the recursivity of process the contextual model focuses on the ways in which each frame of action contributes to our understanding of the whole.

- The contextual model is employed to direct methodologies to the *relevant* aspects of process (decision sites) through the development of inductive and deductive theoretical positions.

- Although the epistemological issue between Cotterrell (1998b) and Nelken (1998) regarding sociology's capacity to interpret law and legal ideas remains unresolved, contextual analysis does at the very least provide a novel way of conceptualizing the *process* of discretionary decision-making. If, as is suggested, we *do* adopt Cotterrell's view that sociological insights provide a legitimate vehicle for describing how law's moral power is transformed into meaningful action, contextual analysis does provide conceptual linkage between how 'knowledge' is constructed and the various dimensions of its empirical reality.

- In accepting Cotterrell's prescription for extending the interpretative aspect of legal theory by suggesting that sociological insights might usefully illuminate how the moral meaning in law should be reflected in sociolegal research, we correspondingly acknowledge the conceptual and empirical link to policy. The contextual model facilitates conceptual linkage between sources of morality and ways whereby legal ideas and practices are made morally meaningful to citizens through policy prescriptions such as the penality of communitarianism. Thus, the transition of law's moral power through policy consists in the description and explanation of law as an objective phenomenon and an interactive process.

In this and the preceding chapter we have explained the theoretical and methodological foundations of CCA and suggested why it provides an analytical framework for understanding the complexities of trial decision-making whether at the global or local level. This is a crucial precursor to our later explanation of how comparative contextual modelling and its application in deconstructing the social reality of decision-making in international trials can provide us with the knowledge necessary to evaluate the prospects for trial transformation through the accommodation of retributive and restorative aspirations within the trial process. We begin our journey towards this objective in the next chapter by providing a detailed exposition of how the methodology of CCA can lay bare influences on the exercise of discretionary power within trial relationships and provide accurate understandings of the jurisdictional contexts in which they operate.

Chapter 3

Methods for analysing trials comparatively

Introduction

This chapter commences with recognition of our essential commitment to comparativism, and the need to approach it anew for the purposes of sociolegal research within the context of internationalism. Context-based comparison, and the link between context and objectivity, is the simple driver for the methodology described in detail as the chapter progresses, and applied empirically in Chapters 4, 5 and 6.

The trial process is both a context and object for analysis. Its process, structure and function, procedural traditions, rules and practice, personalities and discretion, and sites for decision-making are each reviewed as useful foci for comparative analysis. In particular, when addressing the implementation of an integrated methodology for examining trial decision-making in different contexts, data such as trial narrative are interrogated and the question asked how meaning might be added to address its limitations? The importance of an integrated methodology, also incorporating observation and expert commentary, is argued for. Such a methodology will reveal what is behind trial process as decisions, and on the comparative level will enable speculation about trial justice processes, local to global.

Our initial comparative commitment is trial to trial, on the level of decision-making relationships. The common pathways of influence which evolve from these should then provide a platform for looking at trial justice local to global in terms of common parties and interests, and universal relationships. A more detailed understanding of these in their context and comparison prompts the question, 'where to the international criminal trial?' and suggests that the analysis should extrapolate from the trial to restorative justice paradigms (as we do in Chapters 7 and 8). This is an attempt to match the expectations of trial participants, the reality of their relationships and the limitations of trial processes leading to a need for transformation in the international setting. The importance of the rights protections offered by the trial is the stimulus to suggest a widening of its orbit into areas of justice delivery now seen as alternative (see Chapter 7). The remainder of the book will attempt just such an exercise, to provide the empirical basis through specific contextual comparison and interrogation of the relationships which emerge therefrom, for predictions about the transformation of the trial and thereby the promotion of inclusive notions of ICJ.

An analytical exercise on a limited number of trials in England and Italy is introduced in detail in this chapter and then comparative contextual analysis (CCA) of the Italian and English trial decision sites is developed in Chapters 4 and 5. Chapter 6 integrates these contexts along with the understandings of international justice institutions, around the victim/adjudicator relationship. Discretion and account-ability as forces for trial transformation are posed against the challenge for trial transformation within designated normative (rights) frame-works.

This chapter concludes by proposing a methodological agenda for the case-study work to follow and the essential issues in trial decision-making to be addressed. This methodology needs to be capable of managing the analysis of relationships and generalizing the crucial form and nature of trial decision-making.

Consistent with our commitment to the decision-making model for the trial, the methodology proposed here should offer insights into the 'pathways of influence' flowing through crucial decision relationships in the trial. The relationships form between significant lay and pro-fessional players at crucial decision sites in the process. The notion of pathways indicates a process where subjective and objective under-standings of trial decision-making have a common framework in comparison. They reveal how decisions are settled and what interests prevail in their foundation. Pathways are also crucial motivators for trial transformation, exhibiting as they do some interests that the trial presently is unable to achieve (see Chapters 6 and 7).

We concede the challenge in presenting a convincing comparative analysis of the trial at various levels, and ultimately with a policy development agenda for ICJ. However, it is comparison beyond jurisdictional context alone, moving from local to global as well as within and beyond trial models of justice, that enables speculation on transforming the trial to assist in making ICJ more inclusive (see Chapter 7).

The comparative exercise is engaged coincidentally at several interconnecting levels and contexts, compatible with contemporary understandings of internationalism (local, regional and global). International justice paradigms provide a unique context for comparison wherein the established traditions can be critically evaluated and transformations of trial justice proposed. The contradictions and contests within internationalism are well evidenced in the development of ICJ and provide a dynamic platform for evaluating developing trial process and its place within the new justice paradigm. Old concepts such as professional authority, and access to justice and victim impact take on a new significance within the context of ICJ. The trial therefore has to adapt to the changes in some of its fundamental pathways of influence.

On the significance of the trial as a methodological focus, it is important to remember its transitions in form, substance and symbolism from the jurisdictional to the internationalized setting. Whilst in local and even regional criminal justice traditions the trial may be overshadowed by the operational significance of pre- and post-trial process, the trial is the essential embodiment of ICJ. Even so, we caveat our interest accepting what has gone before and what will follow the trial as a central justice event.

The trial, we later argue, can and should be transformed to incorporate the major principles motivating ICJ from the perspective of victim communities. Thereby, the trial can insure inclusion rather than exclusion of those communities that may not have satisfactory access to retributive justice, while at the same time requiring the broader social benefits of restoration.

As already established, our emphasis is on the trial as a process of decision-making, and this depends on the widest interpretation of the trial model as such. Decision-making is seen in this context as:

- the site for the decision;
- the discretion which enables the decision;
- the relationship between decision participants; and
- the pathways of influence which determine the relationship and the decisions which emerge.

The latter becomes a key to understanding the common themes open for analysis, context to context.

Our focus (in Chapter 6) on sentencing as the decision site allows for informed speculation based on comparison between crucial trial institutions and process outcomes, particularly in terms of essential output measures for formal, retributive justice such as verdict and sentence. At a popular culture level, these are what trial justice is all about. The relationship between the judge and the victim in the achievement of such outcomes is a useful and novel frame of reference for comparative analysis as discussed in Chapter 6, if we are to explore the capacity of the trial to satisfy developing expectations for justice from a variety of international 'communities'.

In that chapter and the analysis of the judge/victim/sentencing pathway, discretion is identified as the force for trial decision-making, the language of trial relationships and the device for negotiating pathways of influence. Discretion drives sentencing through clear formal and informal prescriptions which are evident in the narrative under examination. The relationship between the judge and the victim in creating a sentence is chosen particularly as a revealing lay/professional connection where the influence of the victim is gaining recognition in ICJ. The distinguishers of power and authority between the judge and the victim (the professional and the lay participant) determine to some extent the pathway of influence in victim/judge trial relationships, as do their political context. Recent efforts at a political level to promote victim impact (see Chapter 6) reveal the manner in which context inextricably moderates the negotiation of power and influence in dynamic decision-making relationships. Power and authority, along with popular legitimacy, may be variables determining what can be adequately universalized from this pathway of influence, context to context. For instance, whilst victim and judge differ trial to trial, their participation in sentencing has become essential.

A newly developed political context concerning the status of victim participation has impacted on their trial relationship and, as Chapter 6 reveals, the pathway of influence this relationship generates has become a uniform feature of contemporary trial justice. Comparisons of this common pathway, trial to trial, will show much about trial process within various contexts and as a characteristic of new justice paradigms at other levels of community engagement such as the international. This is particularly the case if we have chosen as we have a decision site (sentencing) at the heart of trial justice, as a crucial context for comparison.

Essential to the foundations of the methodology applied in Part II is the theorizing and modelling expanded in the preceding two chapters. A standard criticism of modelling criminal justice process (particularly for the purposes of comparison) ignores that a book such as this builds on our work of deep theorizing and a tested comparative methodology for analysing trials in different jurisdictional contexts (see Findlay and Henham 2001). Therefore, modelling is also grounded in context, and is only applied in order to give the eventual comparison, context to context, a sharper edge.

Further, methodology working out of such theorizing and creative comparative modelling enables credible speculation on the transformation of ICJ, presented in Chapter 7, even where the development of the paradigm is in its earliest stages and empirical understandings are as yet formative.

The essence of comparison

To predict and evaluate the project's methodology we embark on a limited exercise where CCA is applied to the decision-making process in certain common law, and Italian civil law trials.[1] A wider comparative evaluation of trial decision relationships would involve critically reviewing international trial process and analysing competing paradigms of international and national justice contexts. We venture there in a speculative sense in Part III but there is much more to do in a wider comparative endeavour. This could be achieved empirically by developing comparative trial analysis, local to local (in a wider range of procedural traditions). With the understandings achieved concerning the nature of trial decision-making, we continue to explore these in regional contexts and then in the international tribunal processes. Layers of comparative analysis would build on each other to reveal an appreciation of ICJ through its strategic institutional development.[2]

---

1 Due to the nature of the transcripts available to us this will mean examining fragments of two Italian trials against our experience of similar trial practice in English and Australian jurisdictions. Further, we will specifically interrogate the full sentencing transcripts of two English trials, and one murder trial in Italy.
2 This would, to some extent require an acceptance of ICJ as evolving from national jurisdictions on to an international process. However, it would not necessarily exclude those arguments that have international criminal law as a product of international instruments and agency (see Wu 2004).

The trial is a challenging focus for comparative analysis. Despite different types of trial in and across various jurisdictions it remains a centrepiece for criminal justice resolutions in many procedural traditions, particularly now ICJ. It uniformly involves professional and lay participants communicating, interacting and making decisions. It produces narrative as evidence of its decisions.[3]

The trial consists of observable human interactions at various levels of formality. It is contextualized by rules and procedures, within conventions and traditions of practice, and is preceded and followed on by processes and outcomes, the influence of which may be observed in the trial, and its consequences beyond. The analysis of important sites for decision-making within the trial enables specific and general comparisons for a variety of purposes.[4]

The trial assumes several important social functions dependent on context.[5] These may be apparent and often implicit in wider expectations about criminal justice and social control. As such, a comparative dimension when researching the trial even in functional terms is required if the significance of essential components of trial decision-making is to be determined. The direction of such analysis (local to global) is more important when arguing that the trial in its purposes can support other justice paradigms because of common objectives (see Chapters 6 and 7).

It is also crucial when considering the transformation of trial justice within a dynamic environment like internationalism, to recognize the extent to which the trial satisfies the more encompassing expectations for justice, and what is possible to remedy its shortcomings. At this

---

3 Obviously the nature, extent and accessibility of trial transcript (as an essential tool of our method) will vary within trial stages and across different trials, courts and jurisdictions. This is a challenge for comparative analysis.

4 Here we are interested in the manner in which trial decision sites and their relationships exhibit characteristics which identify the trial under review, and represent common themes of process which translate into other process traditions, or not as the case may be. Whilst conducting this comparison across traditions, the same process features are available to reflect on the trial regionally and internationally.

5 For the purposes of this work context means social space at any particular time or place. It is not limited to theoretical or analytical paradigms such as law in context while it may incorporate these. The use of context is not prescriptive, whilst it relies on identified boundaries and relationships. It is essentially a very flexible and relative mechanism to facilitate comparative analysis, whilst exhibiting common, transferable themes. It is not loaded with meanings from its other uses in legal and social science research such as 'law in context'. Simply, context is considered to provide many and varied boundaries for analysis which might be as rigid as the concept of jurisdiction or as fluid as victims' rights.

point we might be cautioned for expecting too much of the trial in ensuring criminal justice, particularly at the international level (see Chapter 7). But within the international context the political reality has been to require a place of prominence for the trial and, from this, other justice initiatives are deemed alternative.

The trial lends itself to comparative analysis initially and essentially dependent on the recognition (and technical application) of social context.[6] This context includes issues such as due process and fairness along with their cultural interpretations and procedural protections.[7] Trials exist within the wider realm of criminal justice and rely on participants and procedures with specific and predetermined cultural roles. The interaction of these should then provide a ground for proposing harmony and dissonance across different trial contexts.

Being culturally relative (i.e. a construct of a traditional collective context),[8] the criminal trial has the potential within any particular social setting to represent criminal justice. However, the trial's existence and representation at a more global level may argue for the unity and universality of trial justice, reliant on common ideologies, procedures and institutions. In so saying we are not suggesting harmony as a consequence from some logical synthesis of procedural traditions (see Findlay 2000; Delmas-Marty 2002).

At the comparative level research methodology of this type should recognize and reflect cultural diversity, spatial and temporal relativity, whilst being simultaneously relevant at the one-dimensional (local) and multi-dimensional (global) levels[9] of analysis. Notwithstanding, it

---

6 The obvious social context is the legal tradition in which the trial operates. However, the analysis would not be confined to this and could explore anything from contexts of professional and lay participation to negotiations of justice.

7 Such a rights paradigm for the operation of the trial, and the principles of justice it offers out, is particularly potent at regional and international levels of comparison. With this in mind, there is a further argument for including as much of international justice within the protections of the trial process as is possible.

8 Here culture applies to legal and wider social cultures. It is not a term of art nor is it retiring into overworked generalizations about the process of social cohesion. Culture is used to represent a particular collective context drawn together within a tradition of doing things.

9 It might be argued that because globalization is a collapsing of time and space that it cannot be represented through context and is not amenable to comparison. We disagree. Globalization offers a new context where time and space may not be crucial but where political, economic and social boundaries as symbols, ideologies and dynamics provide context. Appreciating the comparative endeavour as more than static and open to environments in tradition, globalization (being such an environment) offers another consequent level for comparative analysis.

71

must also be equally sensitive to the distorting effect of simple, false or rigid conceptual dichotomies. For instance, there may be no model or uniform criminal trial, or even two competing trial styles. However, decision relationships in trials do seem constant. The variants are considerable whilst common themes remain.

Comparative research into the social context (space, presence and boundaries) of the trial requires methodologies compatible with contextually specific issues (like styles of decision-making) as well as more universal relationships, processes and institutions if it is to draw the most from an investigation of trial process.[10]

An effective research method will confront the contradiction of specificity and universality. The trial, like many other social phenomena, cannot be understood outside its particular social environment, without appreciating as a universal social 'fact' common to the legal cultures being examined; it possesses essential forms and features with the potential to be generalized. It is the context of the trial and its representation which gives these universal themes and issues (such as particular trial participants and anticipated trial outcomes) their reality.

In this respect, our model of trials as processes of decision-making in which common sites and pathways of influence feature, enables the specific application of trial decisions to be conceptualized within a uniform frame of reference. This is crucial for the comparative phase in CCA.

Comparison is the essential research endeavour which this review of methodology is intended to support. It is not, however, simply the comparison of an apple with an apple, or apples and oranges which is attempted here. The selected methodology has the capacity to dissect the apple and the orange, to understand its components and to examine it within the context of being fruit (or a process of decision-making, or whatever) prior to analysing the apple and the orange in any other comparative context. To know the context of your referent is a challenge in itself when it comes to examining the trial within very different procedural traditions. This becomes the essence then of any comparative endeavour, to know the referents well, rather than generalizing or simplifying as model states to facilitate strained or ill-informed comparison.

---

10   Hopefully the analysis supported by the methodology will be active in identifying these subjective and objective features.

Through the development of comparative methodologies, critically evaluated against the research task, will emerge (and be confirmed) certain insights into:

- the place of the trial within criminal justice;
- the essential mechanisms of decision-making within the trial;
- key procedural components within the trial which accord with (or challenge) ideologies of criminal justice;
- the reasons for (and resilience of) difference within (and between) trial traditions;
- common issues and relationships across levels of trial analysis;
- essential connections between trial form, process and tradition;
- the interaction between trial participants and its meaning;
- the pathways of influence which determine trial decision-making, and the commonality of their components across contexts, and;
- motivations behind the form of international criminal trial process.

The methodological capability of comparative trial research technologies should demonstrate:

1 descriptive analysis of information available to the court;
2 how such information is assimilated as an 'objective' process;
3 how this both structures and impacts on decision-making processes;
4 identification of points where judicial perceptions of case material are shared;
5 wider contextual exploration of discretionary decision-making in a manner conducive to the comparative endeavour; and
6 all this to reveal the place of practice and symbolism in trial justice.

Accepting the utility of comparative research into trial decision-making, and its possibility, what remains is to determine how it can be achieved. Context is crucial for the comparative endeavour. Context is not a complex term of art. It is the specific and grounded situation in which particular trial decisions are achieved. Obviously it has different manifestations and levels which provide a challenge for comparativism beyond simple or crude duality or simplified dichotomies. Connected with this is the need to recognize universal and relative frameworks for analysis. Again, if simple dichotomies are avoided here in favour of viewing trial decision-making as adding value to fact, then the context tool can be both specific to the styles and cultures of trial decision-making and at the same time loaded with potential for universal themes.

The trial sites for decision-making are offered out as the contextual grounding wherein relativist and universal issues interact and inform trial process as well as its analysis.

Context and comparativism

When it becomes clear that laws are not nearly so certain as was assumed, and that organisational and situational requirements often affect the actor's interpretation of laws, the sociologist may tend to forget about the rules and to interpret behaviour almost purely as a response to other situational factors. The proper interpretative path is tricky but always exciting to traverse: to see rules as a context for the behaviour of legal men (Skolnick 1966: 27).

Skolnick's emphasis on understanding the 'law in action' provides recognition both of the problematic nature of law and of law's capacity for problem-solving. It is essentially a plea for context; a need to understand how individuals interpret and transform principles and associated rules within legal institutions. In a wider sense context also requires an appreciation of the forces of power and domination shaping the organizational and institutional imperatives that produce the social behaviour in question. It is, therefore, concerned with revealing interconnections of power and domination as they are developed in the interactive process of the criminal trial. As we have described, context is directed to how social, cultural, political and economic factors relate to institutional processes, relationship patterns and individual variation in the criminal trial (Henham and Findlay 2001a). It gives reality to the forms and features of the criminal trial and has the potential for generalization.

Contextual analysis, as the initial phase of the comparative endeavour, individually interrogates each issue to be explored and thereby cautions against viewing the objects of comparison as model or opposing.

Contextual analysis is essentially interactive. As an object of such analysis the trial is not considered only as rules, institutions, people, situations, or reactions. The trial is more effectively understood as relationships that develop along with the dynamics of its selected context. For instance, if one were to inquire into the role of the judge in delivering sentence it would also now be important to inject the influence of the victim and the part his or her suffering plays in the calculation of appropriate penalties (see Chapter 6). The politics behind the relationship is the type of environmental determinant making context unique and temporal.

Essential for the motivation of these relationships is the representation of the trial as a series of decisions. These decisions are made by trial participants based on the influence of evidence and narrative which may be contested. The status of particular trial participants is in large measure designated by the decisions required of them, or of their role in producing a particular decision at a crucial site in the interconnected decision-making process. The trial is a progress through inter-related sites for decision-making. These are submodels that provide the context in which specific trial decisions (as action) will be analysed (see Chapters 4 and 5). The context for an understanding of the trial as decision-making depends on participants, their status and connection, as well as the narrative they produce and the rules governing their practice. These are all constituents of their influence within a particular decision site. The negotiation of this relationship and influence to produce decisions is dynamic and indicative, a pathway to further decisions and further developments in process. Trial decisions, however, may not necessarily prove dependent on any or all of these.

CCA recognizes the possibility of viewing trial decision-making from several contextual dimensions, enabling different levels of analysis.[11] The contextual models[12] from the trial as decision-making outcomes, through trial sites for decision-making, and down to trial decisions, each envisage several levels or directions of analysis (see Chapters 4 and 5). As later demonstrated we investigate narratives from trials in two jurisdictions in order to reveal details about how evidence is presented; how participants elicit the facts; how decision-making is shaped by relationships which determine process outcomes; how human rights guarantees protect the testimony of certain

---

11 Comparativism also tolerates paradox and dialectic, both essential in any understanding of contemporary criminal justice institutions and processes such as the trial. Particularly for a consideration of the trial in transition (towards its international forms) the more global levels of analysis rely on paradox (see Findlay 1999: Epilogue). The trend to internationalize and fuse criminal trial procedures is a natural consequence of modernization as well as sharing the social, political and economic priorities which characterize the modern. As with modernization the theatre of international trials can marginalize and reintegrate, unify and divide.

12 For a detailed discussion of contextual modelling, see Henham and Findlay (2002).

participants; and the connection that any or all of these might have to rules and conventions. In doing this we intend to deconstruct decision relationships and the influence which determines them. Such insights will simultaneously provide for the analysis of fair trial (and issues such as access and expectations for justice in particular) or down to comparative roles of the players (lay and professional) within the trial. In addition, the greater knowledge of trial decision-making on a comparative jurisdictional level, and regionally in a rights framework, should enable informed projection on ICJ, and the trial's place therein.[13]

As a consequence of its initial particularity, CCA works in fluid analytical terrain and backgrounds on the move, such as developing ICJ. Through comparison locally and globally, the activity of the trial process is available for research[14] and not just static images of the process, bound within any particular tradition, despite the initial importance of these normative considerations in constructing a context for later comparison (see Chapter 6). This emphasis on interaction and transition avoids simplistic assumptions about how the trial works within criminal justice and any limited construction of policy which might tend to result.

Analysis that is reliant on grounding in social context should also prevent the abstraction of institutions and functions of the trial from their essential legal, moral and political supports, and their transition (see Chapter 6). One of the purposes of CCA is to appreciate the development of the referent as well as the transformation of its social context. ICJ, analysed with the benefit of local and regional comparisons (in transition), will be understood as a rapidly developing process, rather than as normative principles, legislative procedures or structures and agency alone.

Context

Our socio-legal thinking is always situated in a context where experience is vital for knowledge, and awareness of consequences is essential in understanding process.

---

13 This assumes that ICJ is to some extent a product of the institutional and procedural convergence of important criminal justice agencies (local and regional) such as the trial.

14 This is not to overlook or diminish the significant access problems which are presented when approaching trials in progress, or seeking trial transcript for the purposes of research. In different jurisdictions different rules and conventions apply governing access and thereby complicating the comparative endeavour. See Findlay (2001a).

Within this analytical paradigm, context is any particular and nominated social space in which the object for analysis resides. As a methodological tool it involves:

- things within a social space (along with the manner in which these are subjectively perceived by players and decision-makers);
- the connections between these things (decision relationships);
- the boundaries around the existence and relationship of these things (sites for decision-making);
- the forces at work within the space that produce transformation (pathways of influence); and
- the relationship with other designated and influential contexts (process).

In this regard context provides the domain for analysis, identifies the things to be analysed and to some extent explains the way they are. In addition, context requires that the things being researched cannot be removed from their social world. In fact it is this social world that gives them meaning and is as much an essential issue for research and comparison as the thing itself.

However, to call for more contextual reference in research may mean little without recognising complementary model states: 'The call to context in the late twentieth century [in socio-legal studies] reflects a critical argument that prevailing legal and political norms have used the form of abstract, general and universal prescriptions, while neglecting the experiences and needs of ... people' (Minow and Spelman 1990: 1632–3). In this respect context is far from neutral. In the comparative exercise the relativity of context is as significant as are efforts to generalize and model. It is the reconciliation of these competing aspirations for comparative research which remains a challenge for the application of context.

The key concern in the application of context in comparative research is which contexts are crucial, and how should considerations drawn from different contexts (and various levels of context) be weighed against one another. Trials mean little without an appreciation of their social location. Comparative methodologies cannot work outside this. Having said this, social location requires refinement for the purpose of analysis. In looking at trials, we choose to emphasize decision-making as the particularity of process and decision sites, of social location.

The contextual model developed for this project has been designed to exploit this potential by facilitating the adoption of descriptions and evaluations of process within context at the legal, organizational and interactive levels of analysis. As we suggest, *evaluation in context* involves utilizing discrete methodologies directed by the contextual model's focus on particular evaluative paradigms (decisions) designed to comprehend particular social interactions in the trial process (Henham and Findlay 2001b). The adoption of mixed methodologies within the approach permits the identification and interpretation of relationships between trial variables at the macro and micro level, an example being the relationship between policy and judicial discretionary power (see Chapter 6). In this example, discretion is the nature of the decision, the mechanism for decision-making and reveals the influences which constrain decision-making. The success of contextual analysis largely depends on the extent to which it reveals subjective consensus regarding the function and meaning of trial process.

Levels of comparison

In order to appreciate the trial beyond its localized manifestations methodology for contextual analysis will be comparative at many levels. For instance, trial decisions will be interrogated (internally and bi-laterally) in terms of the procedures that require them, the participants that are responsible for them, the interactions which produce them, and their outcomes. Depending on the levels of analysis employed will be the richness and complexity of the comparative method, and its potential. For example, narrative analysis may be useful in appreciating the role of the judge across trials in a discreet jurisdiction. Once the research ventures into other jurisdictions (with different narrative form and content), the inclusion of some other method such as non-participant observation might be instructive to establish comparable standards of meaning.

The internationalization of criminal trials (the focus of the wider comparative research endeavour for this project), to start with, suggests several dualities. Initially the comparison might be within context (e.g. the trial as an essential institutional feature of traditions of criminal justice within nominated legal cultures, and particularly so internationally). At the same time the comparison of context with context (e.g. jurisdiction to jurisdiction, or to region) is possible. And these comparisons focus on particular decision relationships, judge and victim as an example.

To achieve its fullest potential within the theme of internationalization, comparative research methodology should concentrate:

- within a nominated cultural context;
- across two or more contexts within the same culture;
- across time and space within a culture in transition;
- culture to culture; and (not or)
- simultaneously at the local and global levels (Findlay 1999a: vii).

Within this understanding lies a fundamental paradox which we identify as the relative nature of justice simultaneously representing factors arguing for unity and the generalization of justice provision. As Nelken (1997b) points out, there is consequently a need to appreciate the variation in what each culture takes to be the phenomenon and, more specifically, to examine the way particular cultural definitions and debates about discretion *interact* with actual decision-making.[15] Hence, contextual analysis must 'resonate' with the culture in context, whilst at the same time exploring common institutions and processes. If the common process, as with the trial, is decision-making at particular sites and relationships determined by the institution, in order to recognize difference in cultural forms, we suggest a focus on relationships rather than boundaries (normative, procedural or otherwise) which constrain and determine processes of interaction and transition. Particularly, it is more productive for this analysis to see how trial decisions evolve through the process of agency in preference to a more removed examination of principle and procedural tradition.

As Figure 3.1 suggests, the challenge for comparativism is to recognize that objectivity can only exist through the identification of criteria which trial participants across different jurisdictions subjectively recognize as representing a distinct aspect of social reality.

This degree of subjective agreement implicitly acknowledges that process also arises from structures of collective behaviour which may operate at both the macro and micro level (Casanovas 1999). Methodologically, however, the holy grail of objectivity may prove illusory through analytical and/or institutional distortion. Although our expectations for comparativism acknowledge such limitations, we argue that the adoption of mixed methodologies within the theoretical framework provided by our interpretation of structuration theory allows significant insights into the recursive patterning of social

---

15 Even a cursory examination of different trial styles will suggest that reliance on discretion is not constant or common. Whilst discretion in some form or another is a feature of all criminal trial decision-making, the nature and influence of different pre-trial investigation practices, for instance, may fetter the discretion of advocates and judges in the presentation and use of evidence within the trial.

behaviour in the trial context (see Chapter 1; Henham and Findlay 2001a).

Figure 3.1 Contextual modelling

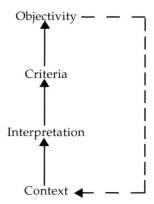

Subjectivity and universality

CCA offers the potential to reconcile *an acute sensitivity to the peculiarities of the local* with the *universalizing imperative*. The novelty in this approach to comparative analysis is not the rediscovery of context. Rather it is in the multi-levelled applications which context invites.

The trial as a social fact within nominated legal and social cultures becomes a universal object for research. It is the context of the trial and its representation, which gives these 'universals' their reality. Social context (and its relevance for analysis) lies behind the discussion of particular connections between sites for decision-making within a selected trial and across a range of comparable trial contexts. Each principal sub-theme (or evaluator of context) structuring the form of trial to be examined is a tool for revealing the social context of trial procedure through an understanding of actual and active contexts, and their interconnection. For instance, the social context may be one where participation in decision-making is a feature. The trial process within that context may emphasize the involvement of lay players in verdict delivery. The actual influence of community participation may be a platform for critiquing the social context, its trial process and the integration of one with the other as evidence of participation. It may also be a test for the real application of normative frameworks (such as rights represented through access to justice).

It is not unique to this consideration of methodology that the contest between cultural specificity and universality must be confronted. It is at the heart of the 'fact–value debate' essential in conventional social science research. And it is from these general traditions which we can draw movements for reconciliation in the opposing modes of thought. Case-study analysis (developed in Chapters 4 and 5) provides the opportunity for reconciling the relative with the general.

Whilst universal and relativist perspectives need distinction when comparatively researching trial processes, there is a next stage in their reconciliation. For instance, with the consideration of evidence and its production in several jurisdictions, the separate prevailing rules and procedural styles will produce different sources and significance of evidence. But within the trial evidence is evidence. It is the facts that the trial is designed to test and on which verdicts rest. However, as a consequence of the manner in which oral evidence is presented in the trial in particular, it could not be said that this evidence is value free. Quite the contrary, because the cross-examination of witnesses is designed to question, qualify and refine the evidence from the witness, even to the point where two versions of the facts may be competing for resolution in the minds of judge or jury. The relationships between trial players which produce decisions amounting to 'evidence' are therefore essential to the understanding of the subjective nature of that evidence, while the process of fact-finding is a universal for all trials.[16]

Fact-finding leads on to the purpose of truth distillation. This is another level at which value confronts fact. The trial to some extent as a search for truth (see Findlay and Duff 1988: chap. 1) is an important domain for our further analysis of new justice paradigms wherein the purpose of the trial is expanded to include the restoration of the victim with rights protected (see Chapter 6 and 7).

A process of producing fact in the trial inevitably adds value and meaning to the opinions or recall of the witness, or to a lesser extent to the contents of the dossier. The testimony is a subjective account that, through comparison with other subjectivities, approaches a more universal fact status by a process of adding value. The fact/value question here is collapsed by compiling these subjectivities or reflections, and adding value to the facts emerging for consideration by the verdict deliverers. This is a process of subjectifying the objective

16 This universal trial function prevails despite the differences in procedural styles where most evidence is settled and presented from pre-trial documents, and those styles that rely on the oral production of evidence within the trial process.

that in the trial context is a natural consequence of the determination of evidence through oral and written testimony.

The application of context, crucial in the reconciliation of subjective and objective knowledge here 'has rendered the distinction problematic through our recognition that we inevitably see the world (the facts) from within a situated, tradition infused (value laden) perspective' (Tamanaha 1997: 50). Where the fact/value distinction is drawn in this research we do so as Tamanaha suggests 'standing on the ground', in context and not proposing a perspective-free versus a perspective-bound contrast. It is argued that one cannot view the world beyond context (perspective), and that a fact/value distinction only has relevance within the researcher's actions in a real world, where values and facts are naturalistically conceived as functionally separate aspects of experience. The distinction, therefore, is drawn in commonsense terms, within the action of participants, and their integration through the process of the trial.

Comparative forms

The trial as a process provides a variety of internal analytical levels for analysis, influenced and interconnected as they are by discretion:

- personalities, players, their status and their interaction;
- sites for decision-making and the rules and conventions which predetermine these sites;
- decisions produced through such interaction and the degrees and forms of discretion enabling such decisions; and
- the pathways of influence that characterize the decisions and decision-making.

Levels such as these are interactive, involving people with predetermined tasks, in a climate of discretion. They will be influenced by discourse and narrative and will in turn produce discourse and narrative to be examined. At more formal levels trials can be comparatively investigated in terms of normative concerns such as:

- the legislation, rules and procedures which govern their institutions and processes; and
- the institutional outcomes they are required to produce.

Yet as we have said, this approach suffers from a narrow engagement with process and people.

These and other obvious normative indicators provide material measures against which the trial process itself can be gauged, but only text against text from which practice can be abstracted. Observational/visual methods of analysis, on the other hand, might cover such institutional features as:

- the spatial environment of the courtroom and the manner in which it recognizes status and predetermines communication;
- the dress and demeanour of the participants, their language and the manner in which they choose to (or not to) interact;
- communication and barriers to communication; and
- the 'theatre' of the court and the power relations it suggests.

When considering fields or levels for comparatively analysing trials (or their component parts) issues of structure, function, symbol and process tend to interact and thereby enrich the understanding of process. This realization significantly affects the construction of analytical methodologies able to engage comparatively dynamic process. Also, the preferred level of analysis will suggest the application of particular methodologies over others (e.g. non-participant observation when examining the courtroom environment) or a combination of methodologies. When discovering process and the interaction which is trial decision-making, a commitment to one method alone will reduce the potential to take the analysis from one level to another.[17] This is obvious if we accept that the enduring universal about the trial across all contexts is its dynamic and multifaceted decision-making process.

Interactive analysis

In regard to broad social science research traditions, the nature of the trial process is well suited to interactive analysis and supportive methodologies. Particularly those methodologies with an interest in the negotiation of social meaning (which is an essential function of the trial) will lend themselves to the comparative endeavour. Theoretical traditions including

---

17 The methodology so heavily reliant on narrative analysis which we have been required to adopt in Part II of this book might be criticized in just these terms. However, it is an integrated methodology to some extent in that the narrative is elaborated through expert commentary and trial practice experience. In addition, normative understandings inform the examination of process revealed through narrative.

- symbolic interaction,
- phenomenology,
- conflict, and
- opportunity

offer both stimulus and constraint over the creation of an agenda for appropriate methodologies.

Interactive analysis requires at the very least that no form or level of analysis is tackled in a static or isolated fashion. It also deconstructs the dynamics of structure/agency interaction in formal and informal social settings. The social context paradigm for the research will necessitate a dynamic methodology comfortable with explaining change and transition as well as any individual period or field in the process. This may appear to be a statement of the obvious but it is worth emphasizing in that analysing interaction through interactive analysis presents some challenges for conventional sociolegal research methods.

CCA gives empirical analysis deep and transitional social location, wherein people play a role in decision-making through established relationships, the influence of which can be charted. In this sense the data are not representative of model behaviours but rather they identify action and interaction, forming measurable and comparable process.

Trial process – context and object for analysis

The trial is an interactive context and as a research object or event, a process of interaction. Therefore, interaction (so crucial for the comparative research endeavour) is our methodological paradigm for the trial, and our model of trial process as decision-making.

Structures and functions

Conventional analyses of the trial tend to focus on issues of structure and function. For instance, note the research into juries and verdict delivery. In this there is a tendency to accept that the function of the verdict is the province of an institutional component of the trial and from there to interrogate the structures and functions of the jury primarily in terms of the verdict. This research profoundly ignores that in many jurisdictions with criminal trial juries the 'function of the jury is ideological' (Bankowski and Mungham 1980) Overall its principal purpose, and the justification for its existence, may not be verdict delivery alone.

While structure and function are credible concerns for trial studies they provoke a rather static approach to any such analysis. Considering the trial in structural terms, in particular, is likely to produce research that accepts as a given the ideologies within which trial institutions exist and operate, or criticizes these structures against wider process notions of efficiency and effectiveness. It is difficult in such research to appreciate structure as a fluid thing, or an object more interesting in the relationships and forces causing it to adapt and interact. Also, a simplistic analysis that sees uncontested connections between structure and function in the trial will overlook those functions that are externally dependent and constructed, such as those reliant on symbolism.

When employing interactive analysis to understand the process of the trial, structure and function must become part of the context and not the context itself. Issues of structure or function may be important in any particular context (such as the institution of the judge and the delivery of sentence) but they must be informed by considerations of decision-making that rely more on relationships than on institutions and outcomes (see Henham and Findlay 2001c).

Procedural traditions

Another conventional paradigm for the analysis of the trial is through the comparison of procedural traditions. This usually takes the form of looking for similarity and difference between historical or model procedures. More recently this has been incorporated into the debate about reforming trial procedure.

Again, while procedural traditions are significant in the construction of trial context there lies a danger in their over-simplification. It would seem for our purposes that there is no longer any uniform or model application of civil law or common law criminal procedure. The most influential jurisdictions operating from either tradition have created procedural hybrids exhibiting features of several procedural sources. This confounds comparison at the level of procedure alone. The foundation of the international tribunals in the history of military justice would make any analysis which simply considered the merging of civil and common law traditions unbalanced and inadequate (see Cockayne 2001).

Despite the relativity of procedural traditions they still form a useful influence over a context for trial comparison. Procedural frameworks for the operation of the trial in any particular social context pre-determine the nature of that context and are important for constructing the boundaries which determine pathways of influence in decision-making. At the comparative level, procedural traditions are not an effective context for comparison alone. Work that starts from this point tends to be overly static, model and dichotomous. In order that their analytical potential is maximized as a framework for comparison, these traditions need, however, to be conceptualized in a more dynamic, subjective and problematic fashion. A way of doing this is to look at the procedural histories of a trial context as creating a procedural *style*.

Procedural styles are conceptualized as multifaceted (i.e. they consider history, normative and structural boundaries, and process) and in this way sit well with methodologies designed to support a multi-levelled analysis. Focusing on procedural styles goes beyond abstract models of common law and civil law trial procedure. Styles represent the heterogeneity of contemporary trial procedures, not assuming that these logically emerge from single jurisprudential traditions. When looking at the development of ICJ a plurality of influences and a compromise of procedural styles might prove closer to the mark (see Delmas-Marty 2003).

The concept of *style* is carefully chosen because it elicits contemporary and individualized notions whilst being built on traditions, dynamic whilst possessing common components, and influential while being susceptible to influence.

By adopting style rather than tradition as a way to describe the influential legal/procedural foundations of the trial processes under analysis, resultant methodologies can encompass derivations and hybrids. These may claim their origins in a particular style, yet manifest a style of their own or a significant recasting of the style in question.

Style suggests a way of doing things as much as the thing itself. It tolerates contrary interpretations and tastes. It is not omnipotent or neutral. But above everything else it is a living concept, as will be those trials that are encountered.

Rules and practice

The trial is a process, and trial practice an interpretation of legal/procedural style. Trial practice is discretionary wherein decisions are made primarily by the professional participants and constrained by formal procedures, rules and practice conventions. The rules and practice conventions, whilst remaining formal, are sufficiently flexible and interpretative to give life to trial procedures.

Utilizing rules and practice conventions within a comparative methodology is to apply a more amenable context for trial analysis.

However, discretion is, in greater or lesser degree,[18] crucial for compliance with rules and practice conventions in a trial. Therefore, it is unwise to rely here on a methodology simply concerned with the normative status of rules and practice conventions. To understand their impact over trial process it is necessary to make the connection with the trial participants (and their interaction) through which the rules are kept, stretched or disregarded.

The dynamic of this context is the manner in which, through their discretionary application, rules and practice conventions are developed to suit new contextual challenges.

Personalities and discretion

Discretion as it operates within criminal justice is the principal characteristic of decision-making, the style employed to make decisions and the designation of where the responsibility for decision-making resides. Discretion is the province of individual participants in the trial, those who hold professional office and those who represent institutions. The analysis of the trial goes beyond an understanding of the status and offices of participants and the manner in which rules, procedures and conventions predetermine their decision-making. Opportunities for, and outcomes of, the exercise of discretion need examination.

The exercise of discretion is usually influenced by other decision-making sites and occurrences within and beyond the trial process. For instance, the status accorded participants in the trial, which is often both internally and externally sourced, will designate the pathway of influence for a particular decision encounter, and determine the boundaries for exercising discretion as part of the decision process.

Discretion is the fuel for the nature of decision-making in all trials.[19]

Sites for decision-making

The trial as a process comprises points at which decisions are made. These 'sites' are designated by:

---

18 Dependent on the particular procedural style out of which the rules and practice conventions emerge.
19 Obviously this will vary from procedural style to style and throughout different trial practices depending on the way in which potentials for discretion are constrained and discretion is fettered.

- legislation, rules and practice conventions;
- prevailing ideologies and their influence over trial progress (e.g. the way the presumption of innocence determines the onus and burden of proof);
- institutional precedent;
- the office held by professional participants;
- previous and following decision sites;
- the nature of, and relationship between, those covered by the decision; and
- political governance and other constraints on the exercise of discretion including bureaucratic/administrative/organizational constraints.

The comparative context of our methodology directed at these sites is worked through by ensuring that the model in Figure 3.2 is applied to each participating jurisdiction in respect of key issues for each decision site. From this we will reflect on the model for action (decisions) within each site in order to see how the process of the trial at its most constituent and interactive level is played out. The important aspect of this is that by focusing on common procedural sites and the decisions (actions) within these, the consideration of similarity or difference will emerge and be contextualized, as will broader opportunities for the critical evaluation of accommodation between various procedural styles.

Figure 3.2 Trial decision site

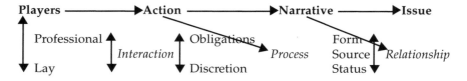

To identify which trial decision sites are relevant for particular jurisdictions we suggest that even without the benefit of detailed CCA of total trial process, certain general assumptions hold about which decision sites are common to most jurisdictions. There are a number of principal sites common to most jurisdictions, whether adversarial, inquisitorial or hybrid (i.e. those which have crucial connections with verdict delivery in whatever form). Some of these include the following:

- Pre-trial hearings – committals, magistrates' investigations, disclosures, agreed facts;
- Prosecutorial decisions – settling of the charge and plea bargaining, nature and ordering of witnesses, disclosure, address on sentence;
- Defence decisions – plea, no case, special defences, nature and ordering of witnesses including the accused, calling on due process, disclosure;
- Witness decisions – reliance on protections, compliance and hostility, specific involvement of victims;
- Judicial decisions – intervention in evidence and protections, legal rulings and explanations, summing up, declared reasoning;
- Verdict delivery – lay participation, reasons;
- Sentencing – principles and guidelines, reasoning, integration of influences, compensation; and
- Appeal.

Trial data

A central aspiration for most empirical research is the production and analysis of verifiable data. Recognizing as we do that in our model of the trial process as decision-making, data about the trial centre on its decisions, then the project is focused on what structures trial decision-making, how these decisions are produced, the relationships which produce them and their influence, and their outcomes. Apart from being personally involved in the decisions of each trial researched, the empirical representations of trial decision-making are limited, often partial and always removed. That is why in describing data sources we need to appreciate their subjectivities, the manner in which value might be added to them and their potential to be universalized.

Rules and norms governing practice

Trial practice in each procedural style will be determined by rules and norms. In most jurisdictions procedural codes (in the form of legislation) lay down formal frameworks for what is to be discussed in the trial, by whom, how it gets there and what may be drawn from it. The roles of participants are in varying degrees of detail legislated for,[20] and the manner in which they will interact is set out. The situations

---

20 Elaboration on these roles may also depend on professional status, commercial relationships, competitive mandates, etc.

with lay participants and their differential influence over trial decisions are good examples of the way codes, rules and practice conventions combine to produce trial action through the construction of decision relationships and the discretion they employ.

Procedural codes exhibit in a written form the principal features of any procedural style within which the trial operates. This legislation may connect with wider instruments of constitutional legality to designate the rights and duties of participants, and echo the way in which the trial is to embody justice and sit within the mechanisms of democratic government.

Most codes have subsidiary legislation attached such as rules and regulations that give more detail on the operational consequences of the code. In addition, and particularly where criminal procedures are not codified, legislative detail on issues such as investigation practice, sentencing, evidence presentation, etc., may arise in purpose-designed policing, evidence or sentencing Acts.

Rules concerning trial practice may also emanate from the professions in the trial. Judges declare rules of practice, principles for the application of sentencing and guidelines as to judgements. These will have varying impact in governing future judicial practice. In some jurisdictions, judges pronounce practice directions specifically designed to regulate what other judges and lawyers do in future trials. Lawyers, and their professional bodies, issue rules of practice and on ethics which are intended to determine the action of advocates in court and their relationship with their clients and other trial participants.

Practice conventions develop as these more formal rules are confronted and adapted to the requirements of the trial. For instance, the ordering of the presentation of evidence in the trial may be reliant, in some jurisdictions, on conventional practice in accord with more fundamental principles such as the presumption of innocence.

Any or all of these data will be dependent on their level of formality for the narrative in which they reside (Findlay and Henham 2001b). For instance, legislation should exist in a common form.[21] Practice directions and conventions, on the other hand, may not be written or, if they are, may have limited circulation.

It would be misguided to assume that simply because some of these data appear in legislative form that they have more than normative significance. Legislation and rules on criminal procedure and evidence, after all, are a statement of how governments or courts want to see

---

21 Access to legislation differs widely depending on its procedural traditions, language of drafting and its existence on the Internet.

things done. This is not to say things are done this way. Further, normative statements in procedure codes are usually quite general and may rely on degrees of discretion for their activation. What makes this data source more complicated to employ is the requirement for interactive reading; that several sources and forms of procedures and rules may need to be considered together in order to get the full impact.

Narrative – sources

Trial transcripts are at the heart of available narrative. In their most complete form[22] these may include:

- a record of pre-trial hearings such as committals;
- witness statements and exhibits;
- indictments;
- agreed facts;
- a record of pre-trial investigation (e.g. records of interview, statements of the accused);
- the advocate's opening and closing addresses;
- an examination and cross-examination of witnesses (record of oral testimony);
- instructions to the jury (where relevant);
- the judge's summing-up;
- the judgement; and
- sentencing remarks.

This is the record that may be available of first instance trials, the focus of this research.[23] Obviously, the prevalence of any particular component will depend on the nature of the trial and its procedural style.

Access to transcripts presents particular problems. First instance trials rarely if ever appear in official court report series. These mainly consist of appeal court arguments and judgements.[24] A first instance trial record is produced primarily for trial participants and in some jurisdictions access to it will also be so circumscribed.

---

22 This obviously does not hold for those jurisdictions and procedural styles where the 'minutes' of the trial may be little more than a declaration by the judge of guilt and/or sentence with limited justification.

23 The transcript for appeal court hearings will differ in its weighting towards questions of law and against oral or pre-trial testimony.

24 Particularly this is the case in those jurisdictions where appeal court decisions are employed as precedent.

In those jurisdictions where court reporting is the centralized responsibility of the state and courts administration then the location of transcript and its consistency in style and content are better ensured. In England, where court reporting is largely regionalized and in private hands, the diversity and inconsistency of transcript narrative are a major problem for review. More recent standardization has been driven by developments in information technology and access expectations.

Then there is the issue of what type of narrative is valued and is influenced in differing trial jurisdictions. In those procedural styles where the pre-trial dossier has a powerful impact as evidence in the trial, what status as trial narrative does it possess and how can it be usefully employed alongside trial transcript? Is it all down to questions of whom the narrative is between and at what stage the communication is affected?

The interrogation of narrative also leaves the researcher with a real dilemma concerning the types and degrees of meaning to be distilled from the words on the page. We are all aware of how written reasons and explanations can sometimes be designed to justify and conceal. How should this be exposed and understood? The answer to this should be measured by the influence of pre-trial record over actual trial decisions. There can be no doubt that such a record distinctly constructs trial context and the creation of evidence in particular.

Outcomes

One way of addressing the interpretive limitations of trial transcript as data is to see the narrative as the enunciation of decision-making; an imperfect and partial record of trial decisions. This then would tie the narrative and its content to a range of anticipated and actual outcomes: decisions and their consequences. It might also form a foundation for criticizing the limitations of these outcomes in light of the legitimate expectations of key players (see Chapter 7).

As with narrative, decisions are produced by parties in the trial. They are essentially interactive. They are the product of identifiable, traceable relationships (or the absence of these). Therefore, on the way to tying narrative to measurable outcomes, we should be able to plot the decision-making process by reflecting on the parties involved, their connections and interaction. Narrative has the capacity to portray all this.

The consideration of outcomes along with decision-making paths and the narrative record should also enable a connection between narrative and normative frameworks in the trial. Narrative is a partial description of how certain decisions were reached, based on which sources, and how particular outcomes were selected. It gives some usually bi-lateral conversation about the particular pathway of influence for that decision. Where outcomes are essential to the framework of justice and fairness in trials then a narrative record of a process to their achievement should also reveal crucial normative considerations. However, there may be scant evidence to contextualize the decision.

Observation

An important complement to trial narrative analysis is observation. Despite the barriers confronting this methodology[25] it has proven an important device for adding meaning to narrative through drawing closer to the emotions of the speaker, the situation of the conversation and the impact of the words employed.

With observation, arises the question to what extent does the observer become involved in the scene and its narrative? Despite the acceptance of non-participant observation as a legitimate research technique there is really no situation where the observer does not at least invest the scene with individual meaning. To this extent the observer becomes the significant 'other' in the construction of meaning. The reason for demeanour and inflection will be speculated upon as part of the process of adding value to the narrative.

Perhaps the distinction is best drawn around degrees of participation and the motive attached. Is the observer simply injecting meaning as the narrative is produced, or is there an attempt to engage in and influence the narrative?

In many ways this is back to the fact/value distinction in the sense of observations being actions in context. As Tamanaha suggests, both the fact of legal institutions and the perspective from which they are viewed will be grounded in research methodology that appreciates fact and value as part of the same scene and its interpretation: 'it is clear that a sharp distinction between factual observations and normative judgments cannot be maintained. What we see and hear is filtered and interpreted within a cognitive framework that is constructed largely from our own individual temperament and prior experience' (Wells

---

25 Such as privacy and closed access rules governing the observation and recording of many trials, components of those trials, or reporting on participants and trial decision-making such as verdict delivery.

1990: 143). The relationship between fact/value in context can be observed in the pragmatic and commonsense processes of jury trial and its outcomes. In this example fact is often modified or reinterpreted through non-legal popular wisdom (values) that produce decisions not essentially reconcilable to the evidence presented at trial. Judges as fact-finders and verdict deliverers may also introduce 'non-fact', or prefer one fact to another, in their search for truth. What takes fact to truth in the trial will be influenced by interactive and interpretive values. The relationship between fact and value in the production of trial decisions is part of what comprises pathways of influence.

Questionnaire

Narrative begs the questions how and why did the speakers say what they have said? Their voices will be governed within procedural environments, along with the spatial and temporal determinants of the trial context. Yet there may be many personal as well as structural and institutional reasons why people in the trial say what they do. This may not be revealed within the narrative plain and proper.

Take, for instance, verdict delivery by a jury. The members of the jury are anticipated to come to a collective decision through reasoned deliberation on the evidence. In many cases we know this not to be the case but only because we have questioned jurors about how decisions were reached, what they understood and what were their motivations for action (Findlay 1994a). The brief narrative of the verdict, or a normative exploration of the decision-making process and its outcome, would not reveal why jurors decided the way they did, and whether the decision was just and fair. To get to this level of understanding it is necessary to go behind the narrative, the norms and the decision outcome. Seeking the opinions and reflections of trial decision participants will at least enable the research to see one side of a decision relationship and how the relationship is interpreted from that perspective. Narrative justifications or the description of process will not allow any such subjective interpretation.

Questionnaire methodology suggests the importance of an omnibus approach to comparative contextual research method. Investigating the narrative (such as questions by jurors of the judge) may indicate qualifications on an examination of outcomes (the verdict). Employing observation techniques will reveal insights into status and deference, which might govern the relationship between jurors and the judge that would in turn inform the answers to questions asked of jurors concerning the influence of the judge and his or her narrative.

In order to appreciate the potency of each of these data sources, and their individual methodologies, their peculiar features need reviewing in more depth (Findlay and Henham 2001). We will endeavour in what follows to indicate the manner in which the best and most applicable features of these methodologies lend themselves to the analysis of trial decision-making in comparative contexts.

Procedural traditions

The style of procedure (legal culture) wherein a trial decision or process may be located, provides at least a normative location for the more removed and normative levels of comparative analysis. As we suggest in Chapter 6 this is a foundation of, but insufficient field for, comparative analysis. Much of comparative legal scholarship is stuck at this level.

Relationship between trial procedure and context

As with the earlier discussion of context, trials exist within broad procedural traditions. These are simultaneously normative and real in their impact. Conventional comparative legal analysis has been distracted by the normative proscriptions of either main procedural style in Western legal traditions, and analysis has been largely left to argue ideal types, or discretion when it comes to trial decision-making. The bi-lateral nature of this comparative endeavour tends to deny the dynamic reality of internationalism, so crucial as a context for moving on to critical considerations of ICJ.

Traditions, hybrids or dynamic?

The actual influence of procedural styles over the operation of the trial will depend on the site for decision-making selected for investigation and the decision to be determined therein. However, it is important when reflecting on procedural styles for the purpose of structural comparison that there is no longer model civil law or common law styles, but usually hybrids and their influences (Delmas-Marty 2003) None of these styles are static and therefore can be the subject of trend analysis.

Synthesis, difference and compromise

Particularly in the context of international tribunal trials the enterprise

95

to blend procedural traditions has produced an atmosphere of practical accommodation and compromise. The different influences of procedural traditions, and their impact in practice, is not so much a story of rational synthesis or even rapprochement. Therefore, any concentration on difference and synthesis for their own sake when seeking to employ procedures and rules as a framework for comparison may be illusory, without recognizing the importance of discretion and compromise. What is difference within one context may be common across contexts. In any case, difference context to context may arise from more uniform decision sites and relationships. International and regional procedural influences may be present in trial practice and vice versa but more likely as a result of process reasons requiring compromise well beyond a normative theory of procedural harmony.

Wider international and regional influence

International and regional procedural developments are a story of autonomy and dependence. The case of the European Union demonstrates the way in which a largely autonomous human rights jurisdiction has permeated through the criminal procedure frameworks of member jurisdictions to produce lines of dependence that strengthen the representation of victims' interests, for instance. With internationalization a largely autonomous jurisdiction operates out of a practical dependence on professional legal cultures from a variety of procedural styles. Tracing these pathways of influence is essential for a deeper comparative understanding of trial decision-making in terms of process and the relationships which comprise it. In addition, as they show a historical inheritance, ICJ institutions are influenced by regional conventions.

Influence of procedure on practice

The procedural level of analysis never strays far from the normative. This is a factor of the form and purpose of statutory injunctions such as procedural codes, as they are translated down into practice through rules and conventions. A rule of thumb might be that the further the analysis moves from legislative narrative, the closer it comes to trial action.

Narrative analysis

The foundation methodology for the proposed comparative project in the remainder of the book is narrative analysis, with trial transcript forming the centrepiece and suggesting some limited commonality in trial representation and recording.

Relationship between narrative and context

Again, if context is the perspective in which both subjective and objective sense is to be made of narrative then the circumstances within which narrative is produced, negotiated and recorded, and where it is given meaning, become as important to understand as the detail and structure of the narrative itself.

Obligations for narrative

The procedural level may provide hints as to the obligations for narrative to be produced and in what form. More than this is the obligation derived from the trial as a process for decision-making, the sites of decision-making as the trial progresses, the relationships which generate these decisions and their pathways of influence, and the obligations flowing from trial decisions and their outcomes.

Form and content

The form and content of trial narrative are dependent on the decision site out of which they emerge, and the decision they represent. A principal common theme is the importance of discretion as the activator of decisions and their consequences. Form and content are not simply a question of narrative components, such as oral evidence. They also represent the written record of relationships and interaction between participants in the trial. The authority generated by trial narrative will be a factor of form and content.

Location – sites for decision-making

The trial is a series of interconnected sites for decision-making. The procedural formalities of the trial designate the process through certain such sites and their climax in decisions which may determine the nature and task of the site to follow. The analysis from the perspective of these sites for decision-making should be viewed as an interconnected process, even when one particular site is selected for review. The sites themselves may be predetermined but, due to the nature of the decisions called upon and variation in the parties involved, the decision outcomes may differ widely, as will the nature and significance of the resultant narrative.

Decisions as narrative

Trial transcript is largely a record of decisions taken either in the form of sources for the decision (such as oral evidence), participants in the decision (advocates and witnesses), reasons for the decision (judgements) and commentaries on other decisions (rulings on admissibility). As records of decisions they should share some authority; argument; deliberations; findings; record of conversations, summaries, determinations of competing facts; statements; and reasoning.

Interactive narrative

The manner in which sites for decision-making in the trial are interdependent suggests that the decisions they produce will be interactive and dependent. That most trial decisions involve several participants acting in a normative framework and employing contested facts implies an interactive decision-making process. This clearly has an important temporal dimension where trial decisions may be influenced by precedent or administrative guidelines and are required to comply with overarching conventions of practice. The interactive nature of the narrative suggests that it can be rarely read on its own for an understanding of process.

Limitations of language and transcript form relative to trial context

Language as an issue of trial narrative goes beyond differences in the national language of any jurisdiction. Legal language is recognized as an exclusive form of communication and system of meaning that has grown over the centuries to protect lawyers' monopoly over their specialist knowledge. Within trial language, rule-bound components such as expert evidence increase challenges to comparability and comprehension.

Meanings and hidden meanings

The trial, particularly in its adversarial guise, is a process where meaning is mediated. In some respects it is a contest over versions of truth or fact. Therefore, even where meanings are revealed through the narrative they may be problematic, transitional or conditional, depending on the stage in the trial at which the narrative appears. Then there are the further challenges of inference and implication. Particularly within the formal discourse of judicial narrative may run layers of meaning not immediately apparent on the face of the narrative alone.

Access and language

Access to trial narrative is dependent on the nature, ownership and publication of transcripts. The trial in most jurisdictions is not a consistently public event and its narrative product is sometimes considered to be the property of its participants. Besides the general translation and comprehension barriers to comparative narrative analysis, trial transcript presents difficulties with locating and reproducing text.

Comparability

This may be the most significant impediment to the comparative analysis of trial transcript in its different form, content and constitution, jurisdiction to jurisdiction and across different procedural styles. This is to some extent a product of varying trial structures; different roles and status for professional participants; different conventions concerning lay participation; different forms, sources and content of evidence; different obligations and sites for decision-making; different boundaries around discretion; different requirements for reasoning and justification; and different appeal conventions. With these in mind successful access to and application of transcript is not only an issue about the comparability of narrative content but also, due to variations in the context of its production, of the comparability of its authority as an official account. The fact that trial transcripts are a product of interactive human processes and differing and relative narrative models compounds the problems of comparison. The different purposes for creating narrative will also have a bearing on convincing comparison.

Observation

As a process of action in which narrative may not betray all meanings, and in which personal interaction is crucial for the production of narrative, observational techniques offer another way of decoding the trial. As the second primary research methodology, observation will also reveal alternative or competing meanings to enrich the cognitive dimension of the comparative project.

Context of the trial as an event

We have determined the trial to be a process of decision-making; an event and a series of interconnected events at the one time. As a dynamic object for research it will not be completely or accurately understood by consulting written narrative which after all is a static representation of an active event. Even within narrative as conversation or interrogation there will not be a sufficient sense of the dynamic to record trial interaction successfully. Therefore, it is necessary to add an observational component to the methodology to ensure a sense of immediacy and dynamism, as well as to add value to the discovery of meaning offered out by an interrogation of narrative.[26] Accepting this, the question then arises how, if at all and to what extent, should the observation process participate in the trial and participate in its outcome? In its most removed form observation might be conceived of more universally as the commentary of local experts who have a contextual familiarity with the operation of trials being researched.

Lay/professional participation

It has been said of the criminal trial that it is a ritual display, largely for the benefit of legal professionals, in which the accused, the victim and civilian witnesses are largely excluded (Carlen 1976). In many trial procedures, lay participants have little voice, and what they do have is often re-routed through the mouths of professional advocates. Legal language and protocol are foreign to non-lawyers and tend further to exclude meaningful conversation and communication from the lay participant. Even the environment of the court and the placing of participants have a consequence of putting the professional in the centre and the lay participant on the periphery of communication. This leads to a structure of status instrumental in the pathways of influence which contextualize each trial decision. Even though this is crucial to understanding structures of influence in the decision relationship this would be difficult to tease out of the written narrative whilst it becomes immediately apparent through observation.

Also, the relationship between lay and professional players is crucial for understanding the activation of rights within the trial. And this may pose a dilemma for narrow methodologies. For instance, evidence of professional legal representation might be seen from the narrative as

---

26 In our case, due to the fact that we relied on data from the narrative of trials past, concurrent observation was not possible as a methodology. Therefore, an inferior style of 'observation' was sought out – the general experience of expert commentators in the jurisdiction concerned, who had observed similar trial process.

evidence of fair trial. Detailed observation of that narrative might reveal the flaws in that representation and the reality that it acted as an impediment to the voice of the accused being heard.

Decision as outcome

The dynamics of trial decisions may be concealed in the narrative, particularly where decisions are made by others not being party to the narrative. In some cases this is not even exposed through observation (such as the anonymous deliberations of a jury). The emotional impact and relative significance of certain trial decisions (such as the delivery of the verdict) can only be appreciated through observation. The silent influence of third parties shows up in the observable reactions of those directly party to the decisions.

Observation and recording

The recording of observations in the closed environment of the trial is problematic. If audio or video technologies are applied then they present the opportunity for secondary interpretation, but this has its own difficulties where the immediacy and drama of the trial action may be repackaged through the medium. The angle of filming, the lighting, and any commentary added can each distort observed meanings. If we are to rely on the reflections of observers as another level of narrative then what additional impediments does this place in the way of 'seeing' trial action, and how do we control against observer bias? Multiple observations of the one event present a technique where bias is generalized and meaning negotiated.

Value-added narrative

For this project, observation is an ancillary, or at least a complementary method to that of narrative analysis, recognizing the importance of a primary medium being verifiable, recorded, and as universal as possible. To this extent the motivation for observation is not necessarily a competing reality to narrative. It is to add meaning to the narrative at levels not available to, or revealed through, written transcript. This can be achieved at minimum by engaging the critical opinions of the narrative from expert commentators who have observed these types of trials long and hard.

Degrees of participation

While the distinction is drawn between participant and non-participant observational methodologies, with something like the observation of a small and confined event such as the trial, it is impossible for the observation to go unnoticed and therefore not have an impact. What tends to happen, at least with random observations, is that the professional trial participants in particular augment or qualify their performance to complement the expectations of the viewer. Another difficulty even with the most remote observation is the protection of privacy and the evidentiary consequences depending on this.

Meanings and hidden meanings

Accepting that observation techniques offer a way into new understandings of the trial, what are these and are they consciously concealed? Being an active process and one wherein the professional and the lay participant come into a unique, emotion-charged context then it is to be expected that things will not always be as they seem or as they are recorded. Nor will they necessarily be interpreted as such. With this in mind sensitive observation technologies will need to identify those decision-making sites, interactions and encounters most likely to be subject to innuendo. Also, what features of the trial hierarchy, both personal and communication-wise, require analysis to reveal where hidden meaning is most likely to reside and why? The status of participants in trial decision relationships may suggest who has the capacity to determine (or even conceal) meaning, and whose job it might be to interpret such issues.

Access, language and innuendo

These are each issues that highlight the need for observation to clarify rather than confuse the meaning of trial action. Because of the immediacy of observation as a method there is less opportunity for critical reflection in order to understand what is actually being seen. This is another reason why single methodology research into dynamic decision processes such as the trial is never sufficient, and only indicative of further research paths.

Integration with narrative analysis

As mentioned earlier, observation is just one component of an omnibus methodology designed to add meaning to a largely comparable written narrative. The application of multiple methodologies will not only depend on access to resources, but also on compatibility and com-plementarity of results.

Comparability

So as best to ensure comparability using observational method in distinctly different trial contexts, the techniques employed must be as constant and quantified as possible. In saying this we do not reject the importance of qualitative interpretation, which after all is required for narrative analysis to have any depth. This is employed through the careful use of primary and secondary source commentary, and the advice of experts in the field, as a background to significant points of analysis in Chapters 4 and 5.

It has not been possible in what follows to employ our preferred integrated methodology, particularly for detailed observations and interviews. We have supplemented this with the supportive experience of those in the jurisdictions compared who have deep experiential knowledge of the trial on which we are concentrating. To appreciate better in practice the comparability of what appears from normative structures and the narrative to be common we utilize the reflections of expert contributors who have observed many trial situations in their jurisdictions. Where trial observation in the future is possible, similar sites for decision-making may be the focus of each observation. Observational perspective, recall and bias control are required to be held as constant as possible. The way in which observation data are integrated with the written narrative must be common and consistent.

Questionnaires

The personalities in the trial making decisions have reasons for doing so not governed by procedure, justified through transcript or revealed through observation. Asking the different trial personalities why particular trial decisions arose offers a third comparative frame of meaning.

Relationship between participants, their opinions and context

In order to understand the reasons why things in the trial appear and sound the way they do one may have to ask why. The opinions of the principal players need to be sought out. This should inform the research about expectations for trial decisions and outcomes, expectations which may compete, and conflict, and require reconciliation against observational data and transcript. It should be remembered, however, that answers to questions might be no more factual or objectifiable data than any other source and have the capacity to present the world as the respondent wishes it to be seen. This can be controlled for (on the basis of roles, status, hierarchy, interaction, integration, investment in outcomes, etc.) so as to enable the responses to contribute richly to a new level of motivational and justificatory meaning.

Status of opinion as data

If the questionnaire technique is to be selectively employed as a complementary methodology it is unlikely that total or representative sampling will be possible. There is little use for this rigour considering the limited number of trials to be analysed in detail and therefore the relatively small number of trial participants directly associated with these trials, who may be questioned. The methodology founded on detailed narrative interrogation is not in the business of representative sampling and significance. It is about extracting from complex and interactive case studies the themes which tend to suggest process models and their application. In this context the unstructured questionnaire format may give more meat to the case study, as quantifiable response forms are not needed to be coded back into empirical variables for cross-tabulation.

Conflict with narrative and observation

Where there appears to be an irreconcilable difference between the transcript and observational record it may be necessary to go behind either form of data. For instance, a judge may remain impassive and yet his or her sentencing remarks may read as volatile. What was he or she feeling at the time of delivering judgement and what weight should be given to this narrative in light of his or her more general sentencing practice? More important it would be to have the judge declare what were the actual rather than normative and even presentational influences over his or her eventual decision. The influence of the victim in the sentencing relationship in particular requires this level of analysis if it is to be understood in a practical sense (see Chapter 6).

Access

Accessibility for the purposes of survey will depend on the trial participant surveyed. Interestingly, in the context of the trial, professional participants may be easier to access for this purpose and more willing to participate than will lay people. If this is true then a balanced appreciation of decision relationships involving lay and professional players is unlikely. The inducements to participate are distinctly different for both groups and their identification and availability will determine whether uniform surveying is realistic. It would be unbalanced, however, to concentrate on one side of a trial interaction, due to accessibility, if the questionnaire technique is meant to reveal what lies behind the interaction and its record in a balanced fashion.

Comparability

It is possible to pose common questions within the survey instrument, and if unstructured interviews are employed then to utilize similar subjects and general themes for inquiry.

Developing the methodological approach

This methodology fits with our observations on modelling (see Chapter 2; Henham and Findlay 2001c, 2002). A contextual model is constructed through the identification of core or common themes which emerge from watching different trials in context. What derives is a model of:

- the trial (as decision-making);
- sites for decision-making (in terms of common participants, interactions and outcomes);
- crucial decision relationships and the power and authority levels and forms on which these are based;
- pathways of influence revealing the process of how these relationships and their decision outputs are negotiated; and
- trial decisions, where relativity and difference is at its most apparent and interesting despite the decisions being grounded in a largely common process.

This is also both inductive and deductive modelling, down and back up the levels of analysis. The modelling process becomes part of the exercise in reconciling relativity and universalism, one in which grounding in the common contexts of process and action is crucial. To some extent the modelling endeavour in eventual policy terms may play a part in the realization of transformed international justice practice.

The analysis to follow is staged and designated in terms of the manner in which the process of trial decision-making actually unfolds in any particular context. The concentration on sites for decision-making allows for a consideration of these as relative and common. The CCA of procedural sites within trials depends on establishing the principal points of decision-making (decision sites) and identifying the players involved. Figure 3.2 shows (*inter alia*) how the relationship between action and narrative may be envisaged within the context of the trial decision site. Although this framework provides a clear conceptual link between the trial players and issues in the trial process, it does not help us to identify which trial decision sites might be relevant or exemplary as pathways of influence, nor the issues we might hope to elucidate as the contest for influence in decision-making.

In examining the particulars of trial decision-making it is useful to focus down this model and investigate the trial as law in action. The action component (in Figure 3.2) presupposes a model of decision-making crucial for the investigation of the trial as a process of decision sites. In so doing, the discretionary as well as the more formalized (normative) levels of analysis require investigation in the context of actual trial decisions. What makes these decisions comparable are the parties involved, their relationships and the structures of influence at work on discretion.

Grounding a model of trial decision-making

What makes contextual modelling referred to earlier unique is its essential connection to the evaluators of context comprising each different contextual situation. Through this device modelling may be reconciled to the subjective considerations of comparative contextual analysis.

Our modelling relevant for this methodology is three tiered. The model we employ for the trial as a whole is not unique as a process of decision-making. Within that process are identifiable sites for decision-making. These sites are considered (in Figure 3.2) to involve:

- players in the trial (professional and lay) interacting together;
- actions (decisions) where discretion is qualified by obligations and responsibilities, and where the decisions progress the trial process;
- narrative as a record of the decisions made and determined by form, source and status; and

- resultant issues which may in turn drive new decision-making.

This is multi-level modelling where players, their actions, the narrative they produce, and the issues they address do not travel on a single course or involve one direction of progress. The essence of interaction in trial decision-making requires that a model to describe the existence and activity of a trial decision-making site needs to contemplate layers of influence, representative of how these decisions are made. This is even before a comparison across sites within and without the trial is contemplated.

The first stage of CCA is, therefore, the interrogation of layers of meaning and process within an individual context. Because of the multi-layered nature of these models which deal with transactional decision-making, their graphic representation is difficult and in some instances not instructive.

A lower, applied and more focused stage of trial modelling is to address the action within decision-making sites; the decisions and the atmosphere of influence within which they are constructed. This fundamental and elementary modelling exercise derives from the consideration of decisions in trial contexts, the evaluators of such context, and the next context in which they might be applied.

By concentrating on action as the essence of the model it seems to confound the 'snapshot' approach inherent in most model representations. Even so, by focusing on very specific and integral issues in discretionary decision-making (wherever it occurs in the trial process) and from whatever method we employ to disclose it, we have endeavoured to identify certain common features or concerns which are likely to emerge out of an interrogation of trial decisions.

Discretion is the lubricant of the model, and it is issues-driven, as are the sites in the trial which its decisions represent. The boundaries of decision-making are the factors (such as status) which construct discretion and its application. As we discuss later in Chapter 6, by identifying the nature and boundaries of discretion in trial decision-making contexts the possibility emerges to release the instrumental potential for discretion and thereby transform the trial.

Our model is contextual and sensitive to context. In this respect it might appear to act differently from conventional social science models (i.e. not being used to test any particular evaluators of context). Rather this model of trial decisions is designed to interrogate trial record (e.g. narrative, observation, informed recall). Such record is of interactions in the trial producing decisions and providing some opportunity for targeted evaluation. Modelling here takes on the purpose of *evaluation in context* which in itself produces a contextual model for comparative analysis. Figure 3.2 suggests that the decision (action) context invites consideration from the levels of discretion and normative obligation (codes, procedures) in order to appreciate the competing motivations in the trial process. This implies a move from more formal to less formal modes of interactive decision-making in which the contextual issues or evaluators such as trial participants, styles of decision-making, sources of record, visual environments and outcomes are amongst the features

Figure 3.3   Model of trial decisions

EVALUATORS   FEATURES

1   Structural/legal levels of analysis
(Institutional and jurisdictional contexts)
(Rules/resources)

* *Courtroom environment*   * *Spatial and temporal determinants*
* *Information structures*   * *Legal imperatives and discretionary*
* *Power and social control*   *choices*
* *Allocative/authoritative resources* * *Fair trial variables*
                                       * *Principles and justifications*

Enabled outcomes? ▶

2   System/organizational levels of analysis
(Process context)
(Reproducible social practices)

* *Interactive process*   * *Communication structures*
* *Integration of trial process*   * *Relevance of pre- and post-phases*
* *Power and social control*   * *Agency interaction and power*

3   Discretionary/interactive levels of analysis
(Local context)
(Application of structured properties by social actors – structuration)

* *Participant status*   * *Lay/professional involvement*
* *Judicial style*   * *Conduct of proceedings*
* *Collective nature of decision-making* * *Emergence of pragmatic solutions/*
                                         accommodation

Actual outcomes?

that individualize each trial decision. These need to be factored into a tolerant model of trial decisions. It must also be recognized that none of these levels of analysis are discrete and of necessity there will be much overlap and interaction.

Such concerns are consistent with our interrogation of theory (see Chapter 1; Henham and Findlay 2001a). We have earlier suggested a theoretical framework which recognizes legal, organizational and interactive dimensions. Each of these is resonant in the context of trial decision-making. More particularly, the progression through local contexts (trial participants and their actions), institutional contexts (communication structures, managerial/bureaucratic variables) and jurisdictional contexts (legislation, case law, discretionary principles) is implicit in this model.

In an attempt to ground a contextual model[27] within a trial decision-making site which is action-oriented, discretion-driven and issues based, the model of trial decisions as shown in Figure 3.3 is proposed.

Conclusion – applying the methodology

Anti-dualism is essential to our image of comparative analysis. By embracing the widest levels of analysis this comparative research will go beyond a spectator conception of knowledge. The trial is adopted as an object of inquiry because it is process and action. Hence our analysis of the trial will be an operative experience, not shy to take control of the nature and experience compared. We agree that:

> Knowledge is obtained through experience gained in the course of working in the world to achieve our projects. Knowing for the experimentally conducted sciences means a certain kind of intelligently conducted doing ... Intelligently conducted doing takes place within a material environment and a context that involves both pre-existing ways of doing (knowing) and a community of doers; it takes place within practices ... inquiry is a cooperative human action within an environment; and both aspects, the active intervention, the active manipulation of the

27 The employment of this model may be seen as a progression into relativity. It is not intended as a *post hoc*, justificatory technique for verifying trial decision-making. Through its application researchers may suggest rather than settle the meaning of particular decisions and this is particularly so where discretion is most active and volatile.

environment and the cooperation with other human beings are vital (Tamanaha 1997: 28–9).

The research which follows (in the second part) is concerned to evaluate the methodology elaborated in this chapter through the detailed contextual analysis of sentencing as a trial decision site in English and Italian trials. The method options will be tested and the integration of modelling and theoretical underpinnings explored. The selection of research objects even at this stage is not aimless or random. The chosen trials offer a purposeful opportunity to inquire into the meaning of trial decision-making, and particularly at the pilot stage, difficulties with such meaning.

The theory of methodology prevailing is holistic and integrated. Throughout our comparisons the trial as decision-making will receive selective attention governed by the belief that it is a vital component in the realization of ICJ. Therefore, our social analysis of trials working in various contexts will attempt to keep open diverse paths of inquiry so that social thought and action may be evaluated as instruments to valued human goals such as the internationalization of justice rather than as ends in themselves.

Italian and English transcript analysis

Within a manageable research framework, an application of narrative analysis is now appropriate in order to test the foundation methodology. At this point it is not possible to introduce additional methodologies, such as observational analysis, beyond the expert advice and commentary of contributors within the selected jurisdictions. In any case, by concentrating on narrative analysis with an awareness of the potential of additional research technologies, the occasions where such additions to the methodology may be apparent and appropriate can be highlighted as part of the comparative study.

The data we will employ in narrative analysis are trial transcripts. None of the material is on the public record and for each jurisdiction we have had to rely on legal professionals with access to the documentation either due to their participation in the trial or because they have been given approval to access these documents. Access, therefore, was one of the first impediments to the early research, and will complicate comparable narrative trial analysis on a wider scale.

Due to the data available for the analysis to follow there are several comments to be made about the potential and process of the work.

Not comparison full transcript to full transcript

Resulting from our interest in decision-making sites within the trial as a focus for analysing trial process it is not considered essential that we compare complete trial transcripts with complete trial transcripts.[28] In fact, the structure of trials and their transcripts in Italy and England are very different and therefore what is a comparative 'complete' trial may be problematic.

Not comparison full professional role to full professional role

The focus on decision sites also means that we will not be engaging in complete, or representative, but rather transactional comparisons of professional roles and participant action throughout the trial. This would only be a possibility when a number of more representative trials were to be reviewed and trends in professional practice identified. However, from an analysis of decision sites where the narrative involves significant interaction between professionals then speculation on lay/professional involvement and professional roles will be possible. Also, the concentration on sentencing in our major transcripts focuses speculation about the manner in which judges in particular manage their discretion.[29] It also provides a keen example of how a pathway of influence is signified and operates to produce a critical and common decision outcome in the trial process. Focusing on sites of interaction and tracing pathways of influence also gets over the problem of relativity as reflected in narrative since it establishes clear boundaries for access and evaluation.

Not comparison legal tradition to legal tradition

Again, with such a limited analysis of the narrative, generalization on synthesis and difference between legal procedural styles would be

---

28 It might be said that a concentration on certain formal sites for decision-making such as sentence delivery may, if not accompanied by an examination of other less formal and interactive decision sites, limit the possibility of generalizing the central issues in that context.

29 This is particularly important for our analysis of the reality of the fact/law distinction and the importance of discretion over structure and system in its comparative evaluation.

inappropriate. Even so, issues around which such a comparison might later be sought should be anticipated. This is particularly so when, in the case of any selected jurisdiction, there has been recent significant procedural reform and the analysis is on notice of this.[30] In the case of victim impact, the procedural comparison detailed in Chapter 6 is an example of how this level of contextual analysis provides a critical platform for comparing how an important decision relationship (judge/victim) might be anticipated to function. At this level the normative preconditions for the relationship become a narrative background to process analysis and the exercise of discretion. Differences in the nature and style of the narrative may receive some limited explanation in this way.

More than any normative comparison, the analysis is designed through its interest first in context and then comparison to offer an opportunity to progress from the local to the international. Having sought out common trial motivations, it then provides a foundation for considering the place of other justice paradigms now outside the trial.

Comparison of insights into sites for decision-making

With decision sites nominated as the location for comparative analysis in the comparative study, and where limited modelling might be carried out, insights should be gained even from fragments of transcript at different stages of the trial (Italian) with understandings of similar situations in common law trial experience (English). Focus for the analysis will therefore lie on the processes of decision-making as revealed through narrative. The site of sentencing in both jurisdictions enables particular comparative insights into judicial discretion, and its impact on lay participants in the constitution and exercise of crucial decision relationships. In Chapter 6 we will extrapolate more fully on the significance of these relationships for knowing the future of ICJ, with the trial at its heart.

Some of the central interactive process issues which will focus the narrative analysis in Chapters 3 and 4 include:

- examination and cross-examination with limited judicial involvement;
- the role of prosecutor and defence advocates in the presentation of evidence;

---

30 Using Italy as a context for normative/procedural analysis is interesting in this regard due to its recent attempts to inject adversarial elements into an inquisitorial tradition.

- judicial intervention at this stage;
- protection of witnesses' rights;
- the reliance of lay verdict deliverers on judicial instruction;
- the interactive process of verdict delivery, etc.;
- the importance of fact-finding in the search for truth; and
- the significance of the lay/professional relationship in crucial decision sites.

These reflect on the pathways of influence common to the trial process in each context, and more generally. These are all canvassed in the models proposed in Figures 3.2 and 3.3, providing a framework for the detailed narrative analysis of the relationships they develop and exercise, to follow in Chapters 4 and 5.

Part II

Chapter 4

Trials in transition

Introduction

The second part of the book is introduced by exploring comparative case studies in two jurisdictions, England and Italy. It is not presented in any way as the definitive individual analysis of trial processes from the chosen jurisdictions. To attempt or even to represent this would distort the significance of these jurisdictions as a foundation for comparative contextual analysis (CCA) preceding projections on the transformation of international criminal justice (ICJ). Nor (as we say in Chapter 3) are the narrative data held out as being sufficient for a total comparative analysis of trial process in context (jurisdiction to jurisdiction, local to global). Rather, this is an opportunity to suggest from limited but no less provocative research terrain, the extent to which satisfying comparison is possible, and to develop insights for internationalization.

This is a selective, thematic analysis of process comprising personal relationships and the pathways of influence which produce trial decisions at crucial points. The interest in process is thereby dynamic. It is concerned in particular to explore evidentiary and declaratory relationships in the trials selected and to extrapolate on the pathways of influence which engage them and over which they have some presence and authority, contested and conflictual as this sometimes will be. For instance, the theme of lay/professional interaction in the trial process, and its significance in ensuring fair trial, is identified. Such relationships are the context for pathways of influence in trial decisions like guilt and sentence. We will generalize from these in order to draw out common themes from local/comparative to international trial contexts.[1] In particular, the example of victim/judge interaction is detailed in order both to explain one pathway of influence and to identify a common relationship for comparative application. Later in the book (Chapter 6) we detail how this particular pathway of influence will reveal the need for a wider trial transformation, and the normative and discretionary developments this will require for the evolution of this decision-making relationship.

In this chapter a complete murder trial transcript, and a number of vignettes of examination in other Italian trials, suggests the dynamics between lay and professional participants. They also reveal clues for a more specific investigation of the relationship between judges and victims, and its limitations when transported as a feature of emergent ICJ (see Chapter 7). The Italian jurisdiction is chosen because, as a consequence of recent procedural reform at least, it is a trial style experiencing fundamental change from inquisitorial to adversarial emphasis.[2] Expert commentary by Italian scholars and justice professionals concerning the context of these trials (and the Italian criminal procedure more generally) gives a place to locate our sporadic trial analysis.

A selective, conceptual interpretation is important in addressing the limitations of narrative analysis. Inter-related themes such as the influence of a rights paradigm, novel presentations of evidence, the role of the judge as mediator, the importance of pre-trial interrogation, and the tone and significance of narrative forms are set out. From these the contextual model is applied and tested setting the agenda for the next chapter. The ground is prepared for examining the significance of decision-making relationships (lay/professional) and extracting the influences formulating these relationships and their decision-making outcomes. The importance of discretion is suggested, picked up and then developed in Chapter 6 to deconstruct this important pathway of influence for sentencing decisions.

A particular feature of this chapter is the identification of themes supporting the later contention that the trial can be transformed to engage with and complement wider international justice paradigms. For instance, the importance of evidence production and fact-finding is

---

1 Obviously this progress in analysis is not without its problematic assumptions. In Findlay (2001a) we speculate on its potential in more detail.

2 Simplistically this could be represented as an inquisitorial criminal procedure, code based, transformed more recently by American adversarial influences and presently in a process of modifying the nature of this change.

revealed through a close examination of the relationships in the process which provide 'facts'. The connection between facts and 'truth' (moral or otherwise) seems important for both retributive and restorative justice processes (as developed in Chapter 7). If so then this aspiration, common within both paradigms will form an important point of incorporation in international trials better to serve the interests of victim communities (see Chapters 7 and 8). The argument that the trial is uniquely and universally well suited to produce facts is reflected upon. If confirmed through comparative analysis, then this may be one of other themes to support the mutuality of retribution and restoration as outcomes for international trials.

Chapters 4–6 provide the empirical backbone for the text. The methodology applied in this and the following chapter involves the identification, description and analysis of communication structures and interactive process in trial narrative through contextual analysis.[3] To understand the context of the narrative better it is supported by contextual commentary.[4] Although narrative itself records dimensions of formal process it does not permit us to understand how each player in the trial subjectively interprets any aspect of that process. A narrative simply records the ways in which formal requirements are interpreted (acted upon) as external processes. In addition, we have noted previously (Henham and Findlay 2001a: 23), how the meaning or value of trial narrative as a record of what is said and done may be distorted by interpretative methodologies (Sarantakos 1993), and the need for our narrative method to remain sensitive to phenomenological description in providing accounts of the reality of trial process at the symbolic and ideological level.[5] Notwithstanding, there are legitimate ways of adding interpretative value to narrative. In so doing, problems of cultural bias may be countered effectively through the ongoing critical evaluation of contextual analysis provided by expert commentators and subsequent interpretations of their accounts through translation. The commentary from those who know will add value without distracting from the empirical integrity of the narrative.

The analysis in this chapter is driven by the need to understand a trial context preceding thematic comparison. Even in the single

---

3 As the model for analysing trial decisions later indicates, interaction is of such a nature as to allow for levels of analysis including normative, institutional and discretionary environments.
4 When the methodology is applied to prospective trials it may be supplemented by various ethnographic approaches, including direct observation (participant or otherwise) and interviewing.
5 See, for example, Sudnow (1965).

jurisdictional setting internal thematic comparison provides a *locus* for testing and facilitating the emergence of various (possibly competing) versions of what constitutes the process of discretionary decision-making in the criminal trial within and across jurisdictional boundaries.

To achieve this, the research identifies common themes in trial practice (which may connect with essential and universal outcomes for the trial) and make these relative to the trial settings under analysis by then identifying difference in the contextual application of these themes. For instance, all trials are directed towards the verdict. This decision will arise out of an eventual site for decision-making (be it a judge, judicial chamber, judge assisted by lay assessors or a jury). The decision is worded in the common language of guilt or innocence but may be conditional or accompanied by reasons or questions unique to the practice of a particular trial type. The verdict will be informed by evidence which achieves particular levels of probative (factual) value. However, the sources and nature of evidence will differ across trial types.

CCA, therefore, involves both inductive and deductive pathways. We will need to look at several trials (or selected parts of trials) as well as consult normative materials on trial styles before the central issues or themes around trial decision-making are identified. What follows is the search for these themes in other trials in other jurisdictions to confirm their commonality and to explore the differences in their contextual application. The features of each relative context will help explain these different applications.

Italian transcripts

The transcript material of Italian trials involves extracts from a murder trial (*CL & O for the murder of SB, Court of P, 20***), extracts from a kidnapping (*concerning CC, Court of P, 19***) and the sentencing and judgement transcript of the murder trial (*CL & O for the murder of SB, Court of P, 20***). The general description of the transcripts is as follows.

Kidnapping of 'CC'

In the first narrative fragment, the prosecution introduces numbered pieces of evidence including written and verbal witness statements. The defence advocate has the opportunity to challenge the admission of this evidence and does so with various justifications. For example, the admission of the accused's prior criminal history is objected to on the basis of relevance, and evidence referring to surveys conducted by Criminalpol on the basis of reliability. Regarding the remaining pieces of evidence the defence concedes their admissibility with the proviso that opportunity be given to examine the witness deponents in person in order to clarify the material on the record.

The second extract of transcript is the examination of the victim CC. The prosecution refers to the testimony that the victim had previously provided (written record) and applies the written evidence to the task of examination in chief through clarifying the facts in the earlier written record by oral questioning. The prosecutor's questions concentrate on the first days of the kidnapping, the manner in which it occurred, where it occurred and what the early period of captivity was like for the victim. CC had described this previously in the written record and the present examination in chief seems designed to build upon and clarify the story in that earlier record. The victim's oral testimony recounts that he was abducted by three men in a car, blindfolded, and driven to a certain point where the three men alighted from the vehicle and were replaced by two men who drove the car to the garage where he spent the next two weeks in the car with these men. For the first few days CC was drugged with tranquillizers and kept blindfolded. The oral evidence of the victim proceeds with a description of the two captors, although this is patchy as a consequence of the constant blindfold suffered by the victim. He says that one of the men was hairy, and he could tell that they were of southern Italian extraction from their dialects. At times CC's oral evidence conflicts with that given in his earlier written record. On these matters the prosecutor points out the discrepancy and invites him to declare which version is correct. CC makes some concluding remarks about how he came to be released from captivity.

The defence advocate is then invited to cross-examine the victim, and attempt to use CC's prior written statement made to the police shortly after his release.[6] The prosecution objects on the basis that the record of interview is unsigned by the deponent and as such is inadmissible as evidence. The prosecution also alleges that the statement is merely an incomplete record of interview (statement) and that it was not known who was present during the taking of the record by

---

6 From a procedural point of view the role of the defence in introducing or challenging the evidence put by the prosecution is particularly revealing. Recall that it was only as a result of the relatively recent procedural reforms of the Italian trial that the defence are invited to adopt an active adversarial involvement.

the police, besides the victim. The President of the court rules that defence counsel is not to take direct quotations from the earlier record when putting questions to the witness, but can form generic questions which have reference to the content of the statement. This settled, the defence question the victim regarding the type of gate through which the car was driven in order to get to the garage. In addition, the defence asks about the type of car in which the victim was confined, whether it had electric or manual windows, where the victim was seated in the car, how big was the garage and so on. At times the President of the court intervenes with direct questions of the witness. The transcript concludes at the end of the victim's cross-examination.

CL & O (pre-verdict)

The excerpt of the transcript begins at a point in the trial where the prosecution and the defence are debating the extent of the 'right to silence' (and protections against self-incrimination). The prosecution argues the difficulty in complying with the right to silence, while satisfying the constitutional obligation on the prosecutor to ascertain the truth of the evidence in the trial. The prosecution advances a procedural solution that where the witness refuses to answer, their previously recorded testimony may only be used as evidence regarding their own actions and not those of third parties unless they consent to its use. The prosecution suggests that this approach to admissibility would be in keeping with Art. 11 of the Italian Constitution which states that 'guilt shall not be established on the basis of statements made by anyone who has freely chosen not to submit to questioning by the defendant or the defendant's counsel'.[7] The President contributes substantially to the debate and the prosecutor's submission is eventually accepted.

The next part of the transcript involves the cross-examination of three witnesses. It appears that the witnesses have been led by the defence, but the prosecution has the first opportunity to examine them.[8] On each occasion the questions are initially met by the witnesses claiming their right to silence. Despite this the prosecutor poses

---

7   Art. 111 *Official Gazette, Constitution of the Italian Republic*, n. 289, 27 December 1947. Effective on 1 January 1948 (*Costituzione della Repubblica Italiana*, in *Gazzetta Ufficiale*, n. 289, 27 Dicembre 1947, *entrata in vigore il primo Gennaio*, 1948).

8   This may be consistent with the constitutional requirement that the public prosecutor is responsible for the exercise of criminal proceedings (Art. 112).

questions and puts allegations to the witnesses. In so doing the prosecutor refers to previous written statements by the witnesses in order to formulate his questioning. In most instances the prosecutor puts questions to the witnesses having been asked and answered in the previous written statements. For example, at one point the prosecutor says 'I would like to know if you knew and when and where you first met X'. When the witness replies 'I am using my right to silence', the prosecutor reads from the witness's previous recorded statement 'At Christmas time in 1997 I went to Breme and there I met a girl called X'. In this manner the evidence is placed on the court record despite the claim of a right to silence. The extract ends when the court rises for lunch.

Sentence and judgement in CL & O for the murder of SB, Court of P, 20**

The transcript consists of a number of parts. First, the document sets out for what the accused and co-accused are being tried with reference to the facts of the case. For example, one of the charges against the accused and others is the kidnapping of 'SB' (the victim). The transcript reads: 'Del delitto in cui agli artt. 110,605,61 nn. 1, 2 e 4 C.P. perche' in concorso tra loro, mediante violenza fisica e minacce, privavano SB della liberta' personale ...'[9] It is interesting to note that one of the charges is 'omissione di soccorso' which is the failure to come to the aid of the victim. This charge is made against the co-accused and not the accused held primarily responsible for the murder.[10]

The transcript notes the requests of il Pubblico Ministero's (equivalent to Crown Prosecutor) as to how each individual should be sentenced and what their sentence should be using facts to support his argument. The transcript then refers to the defence response.

Procedural background

This part of the narrative describes the framework in which the accused and co-accused have been tried. It provides that other individuals involved in the kidnapping and murder of the victim were tried in a different court but gives no reason as to why this is so. It also indicates the types of information that the court has used to form its final decision such as witness statements given before the court and expert testimony.

---

9   'They are charged under Art. 110 because with physical violence and threats, they deprived SB of her personal freedom' (p. 4).
10 This seems to be a different approach from the common law system where there is, prima facie, no duty on a citizen to come to the aid of those in need.

Factual background (summing-up)
This section gives some factual background into the events following the discovery of the victim's body. It sets out the injuries suffered by the victim and the medical expert's opinion (which has been accepted by the court) as to the cause of death. It also sets out the findings of police investigations as to the victim's movements in the days preceding her death. The court describes how the accused and some of the co-accused were subsequently arrested and the content of their preliminary statements to police.

Probative value of the evidence
This part sets out the material that the court has found to have probative value and why. It is interesting to note that the court refers to the fact that legislative changes have rendered the court's task more laborious in making a final decision:

> I sussulti riformatori di questi ultimi anni e l'ansia legislativa di rendere sempre piu' giusto il processo hanno inciso in maniera sensibile sulla faticosa vicenda processuale che ha condotto alla emanazione di una prima sentenza ... della Corte di Assise di P in diversa composizione.[11]

The court emphasizes that, because of time constraints, it must be sure only to examine evidence of probative value. It then outlines which evidence is, according to the court, of probative value.[12]

In terms of evidence, the court deals first with the principal accused's statement that one of the co-accused suffocated the victim causing death. Using evidence given by the two doctors who examined the victim, *post mortem*, to support its view, the court rejects the accused's argument.

The court then explains its findings regarding the whereabouts of the victim and what happened to her in the days before death. The narrative is prose-like, it is as if the court is telling the victim's story and where necessary, facts are referenced to a witness statement. For example: 'era comparsa un sabato o una domenica pomeriggio con l'abbigliamento tipico della prostituta, ben diverso da quello dimesso

---

11 The reforms of these last years and legislative angst to make the (trial) process more and more 'just' (or 'fair') have cut into the already laborious process of issuing a first sentence in the *Corte di Assise di P.*

12 Perhaps the court is making the point that the tradeoff to ensuring that every part of the trial is 'fair' is that the amount of evidence that can be examined by the court is limited.

con cui era stata vista di solito sul punto di veda la testimonianza di "GC" ...'[13]

The court outlines what it has decided are indisputable facts (rendered from witness statements) as to what happened shortly before SB was killed.

The principal accused's involvement in the kidnapping and murder of SB
In this section the court examines the credibility of the accused as a witness and finds that he is not credible. The court declares inadmissible a psychiatric assessment of the accused. Based on the evidence the court determines that the accused did not intend to murder the victim but to inflict on her such injuries that she would be unable to retaliate. The court finds that the accused would have realized the seriousness and danger to the victim in thrashing her such that he accepted the risk that it would result in the death of the victim. This seems parallel to what is known in the common law system as reckless indifference.

The court accepts the evidence as to the character of the principal accused presented by 'AA'. AA gave further evidence as to what happened the night SB was killed. This evidence is also accepted by the court. The testimony of the co-accused 'SO' is used. SO witnessed the beating of the victim. The court reproduces a great amount of this testimony without explaining specifically why it and not other evidence has been accepted by the court as being the truth.

Having established that the accused was responsible for the murder of the victim, the court examines what his sentence should be. Factors taken into account are the maliciousness of the crime, the fact that the accused lied throughout his examination and that he implicated someone else as having killed the victim.

The court deals briefly with the principal accused's argument that another person murdered the victim by suffocating her. The court is unwilling to excuse the accused on the basis of an impaired psychological state, advanced by the defence.

The court also briefly addresses the kidnapping charge against the accused. The court finds that there is insufficient evidence to prove that the accused kidnapped the victim. In coming to its conclusion the court examines the evidence given by some of the co-accused and other witnesses.

---

13 'She [the victim] appeared one Saturday or Sunday afternoon wearing clothes typical of a prostitute, very different from how she usually looked [according to the testimony of GC ...]' (p. 21).

The co-accused 'EL'

EL is charged with disposing of the victim's body and failing to come to the victim's aid. Since EL has confessed to disposing of the victim's body and the court accepts that the confession was made voluntarily, the court does not deal further with that charge. EL is also charged with failing to come to the victim's aid. The proof of this charge is made out because: 'essendo evidente che il EL trovo' la SB ferita ed in stato di incapacita' di provvedere a se stessa ed omise di avvisare in qualche modo l'autorita' affinche' fosse prestato alla vittima il necessario soccorso ...'[14]

The court outlines the requirements of this particular charge. The malice essential for this offence is described by the court as generic – that is, what is needed is foresight and volition of the omission to help. Therefore, the actual awareness of the danger to the life of the victim and/or the acceptance of the risk of death becomes irrelevant. So this seems to suggest that if it has been shown that EL foresaw that he would have to help the victim and decided at that point that he would not help that he is guilty of this offence.

EL argued that he was not able to help because of the risk to himself. The court found that where the danger of retaliation is avoidable, this defence of necessity cannot be used.

'GF'

GF is charged with disposing of the body and of failing to come to the victim's aid. There is insufficient proof for the former charge but the latter is found by the court to be substantiated. Again the 'generic' test is used and it is sufficient if it is shown that he was under the influence of C (another of the co-accused but tried in different proceedings) and went along with all of C's suggestions before finding the victim.

'AR'

AR is charged with profiting from the prostitution of both SB and another woman, PH. It is interesting that the charge concerning the latter is dealt with in the case since it really is a case about the victim SB. AR is acquitted of both charges on the basis of lack of evidence.

'GC'

GC is charged with failing to come to the aid of SB. GC is acquitted

---

14 'It is evident that EL found SB injured and in a state where she could not look after herself, and he failed to advise the authorities and he himself could have offered the minimum assistance to the victim ...' (p. 63).

because the evidence is not sufficient to prove either that GC was at the scene where SB was beaten or that he knew what was going on.

'SO' and 'VS'

They are both charged with failing to go to the aid of the victim. They are found guilty of this charge. It is interesting how SO's testimony was relied on heavily to prove that the accused was guilty of murder yet the testimony was SO's own downfall. She stated that she was there when the victim was being beaten and that she was too frightened to intervene, thereby implicating the accused in the commission of the crime but also herself for failing to help.

Costs/damages

The sixteenth part of the sentencing narrative deals with the costs the accused and co-accused are required to satisfy. The co-accused and accused must pay for the court costs and the principal accused must also pay the costs of living in prison. Those charged with the less serious offences will not have these offences mentioned on their criminal record.

The accused and co-accused are also ordered to pay compensation to the civil authorities (*le costituite parti civili*). The accused is ordered to pay 'ES' thirty million lira for moral damages. We are not told elsewhere in the transcript who ES is. The accused and co-accused are also ordered to pay for the cost of representation by their lawyers.

Sentencing

The final part of the transcript is the court's sentencing (i.e. of what each offender is guilty or innocent and, if guilty, their sentence).

Nature of the transcript

This document seems to be the published judgement.[15] It is also interesting to note that the judgement is structured according to factual headings like 'Coinvolgimento di CL nell'omicidio e nel sequestro …' ('The Involvement of CL in the murder and kidnapping …') rather than separating the judgement according to points of law, as is often the case in common law judgements. The structure of the judgement is more prose-like than a common law judgement would be. It is rich with adjectives and emotive words.

---

15 'La Corte di Assise di P … ha pronunciato e pubblicato mediante lettura' ('The Court of Assise of P … has pronounced and published by written judgement …') (p. 1).

The reproduction of large parts of original transcript is useful in understanding the evidence put before the court but there is not much analysis of this evidence directly used in the sentencing remarks.[16]

Having very generally described the contents of the Italian transcripts it is valuable to examine these in terms of some broad, anticipated narrative themes. These are grouped around important sites for trial decision-making and enable speculation about the way that decision relationships set out to achieve common functions through significant and sometimes contested pathways of influence.

The importance of pre-existing written evidence (records of interview)

Italian criminal procedure has its roots in civil law traditions where the written record of pre-trial investigations is of crucial importance to the consolidation of evidence in the trial. Recent reforms in Italian criminal procedure have tended to emphasize a more adversarial approach to the trial, and a greater reliance on the presentation and testing of oral evidence.

Even so, as the Italian transcripts reveal, previously recorded evidence and in particular that which emerges from pre-trial investigation is important in the construction of trial questioning, and is a crucial concern in debates about admissibility and procedural protections for the accused.

Flaws in the pre-trial record, such as a failure by police to have records of interview signed as required, also leads to challenges to admissibility and the need for judicial officers to rule on the matter.

It seems from the transcripts that advocates in the Italian trial remain concentrated on having previous written testimony read on to the trial record as evidence, to the detriment of the significance of oral testimony. In the sentencing transcript the court refers to previous written record which was introduced into the trial through oral evidence. This enhances the probative value of the secondary transcript.

---

16 Perhaps in the Italian court system, once evidence is accepted by the court as having probative value and as being reliable, the court allows it to speak for itself without further analysis.

Language and tone of transcript – what does it say about the nature of professional interaction?

The formal nomenclature adopted when advocates address one another in some jurisdictions is not present in the Italian trial transcripts. The language between advocates seems relatively informal with no specific attempt made to address each other by name or title.

As regards the manner in which objections to admissibility are posed, it too is relatively informal and unstructured. For instance, at one point where defence counsel appears to be talking with a witness rather than asking a question, the prosecutor intervenes with 'Just ask the question'.

The procedure in relation to the examination of witnesses is somewhat unstructured. At times, counsel for the defence and the prosecution degenerate into heated argument with each other. At one point in the kidnapping case the judge, the advocates and the witness are all interrupting each other.

The distinction between adversarial and inquisitorial trial styles should not be overplayed as a predictor of language and tone in trial proceedings. In trials where oral evidence is presented and tested in common climates of proof then variations in narrative style may say more about professional/lay interaction than it does about procedural nuance.

In terms of examination and cross-examination the extract from *CL* demonstrates some interesting limitations on professional interaction. The prosecution examines three witnesses and there is no examination by defence counsel. All the witnesses continually claim their right to silence and refuse to answer, leaving the interrogation consisting of little more than the prosecutor reading out verbatim previous recorded statements.

In the sentencing transcript there is little professional interaction portrayed beyond the direct quotations from the exchanges in the trial during the oral examination of witnesses. These tend to confirm the more conversational and colloquial interchanges between advocates and judge.

The application of rules such as the rules of evidence

In the kidnapping trial witnesses make certain statements which might be challenged in other jurisdictions as hearsay. For example, the victim tells of his captors' conversations with each other: 'They talked about weapons, they recounted stories like "I killed a person" and "I did such and such" and "if someone says something I don't like, I kill them"'. The court also allows the victim to comment on the character of his captors: 'They have a criminal attitude that's for sure. Criminal and Mafia, I'd say.'

With the judge in the Italian trial having responsibility for verdict delivery there is not much debate about admissibility at that stage. The judge tends to assume the law on these points and concentrates on the probative value of different forms of evidence.

The role of the judge (lay and professional)

The role of *il Presidente* (the President of the court) is interactive as evidenced in the transcripts. He also takes on the task of *master of ceremonies* in deciding the progress of the trial and calling witnesses.[17]

Regarding the trial chamber, in the kidnapping trial it is held in *il Tribunale*, consisting of three professional judges including the President.[18] Here the President interacts with trial advocates, witnesses and fellow judges. He intercepts the examination of prosecution and defence lawyers by posing questions of his own to the witness. It appears that a desire to uncover the truth rather than a strategic contest of advocacy prevails in this more interactive interrogation.

It would also seem in the kidnapping case that the President acts to remedy deficiencies in the cases of the prosecution and the defence. For instance, at one point the President assists the defence advocate in formulating a question that might be otherwise inadmissible. After reformulating the question the President puts it to the witness himself.

The murder trial against *CL* and others was heard in the *Corte di Assise* and the bench consisted of eight judges: the President (a judge of the court of appeal), another judge (of the Tribunale), and six lay persons selected from citizens aged between 35 and 65 years.[19] The transcript of this trial also demonstrates the interactive nature of the

---

17 This reflects the constitutional obligation on the judge to ensure that all the evidence is before the court, which in common law is not so.

18 *Il Tribunale* has a criminal jurisdiction outside the ambit of the Pretore and the *Corte d'assise* (the remaining Italian criminal courts) and has exclusive jurisdiction over crimes such as financial crimes and criminal libel.

19 It is necessary for selection that these individuals be of good moral character and have at least obtained a basic secondary school education.

President's role. Interestingly the interchanges between the judge and the advocate do not identify any clear deference to hierarchy.

Again, a particular feature of the judge's role revealed through the Italian transcripts is verdict delivery. Without a jury, the manner in which the admissibility of evidence is argued should, one would assume, differ significantly from common law jury trial. Even in the Italian courts where lay judges are empanelled the court does not require their retirement during arguments over admissibility. Also it would appear that no particular instructions are provided by the professional judges to the lay judges regarding their decisions as to admissibility or otherwise.[20]

The Italian judge is the verdict deliverer and sentencer. As such his summarizing of the facts and his deliberations as to their probative value locate him close to the verdict. The judge is comfortable with incorporating the influence of victims into the sentencing process. In addition, he is not afraid to be critical of the restriction of judicial discretion through recent procedural law reforms.

The nature of professional interaction – examination of witnesses

It is a habit of advocates in the Italian transcripts to read out on to the record large sections of previously recorded witness statements and testimony, as part of the interrogation process. This will be followed by questions of the witness to comment on or clarify what has been read out. The questions themselves, which form the oral examination of witnesses, are lengthy, counterbalanced by a language not distinctly legal and more colloquial.

Again it is common in the Italian transcripts to read leading questions even during examination in chief. In the kidnapping trial the prosecution also employs this method when attempting to deal with discrepancies between the earlier recorded testimony and the oral evidence of the victim. For example, the prosecutor prompts the victim to recall what the kidnappers had done to him besides his recollection of being drugged: 'They gave something else to you, didn't they, they

---

20   This may be explained by the fact that, in theory at least, the career and lay judges for a unitary bench are in a position of parity when it comes to the exercise of judicial power. Further, they are considered to be the masters of law and fact, satisfying the constitutional requirement that all judicial decisions must be reasoned.

put something in your ears, didn't they?' On one such occasion the defence advocate objects to this line of questioning, but instead of presenting a formal objection for deliberation by the judge, it is directed to opposing counsel: 'Let him (the victim) answer the question', to which the prosecutor replies, 'This evidence has already been admitted in a previous statement'.

What other narrative forms are suggested and available?

In the extracts of transcript dealing with the examination of witnesses both prosecution and defence tend to rely heavily on the prior recorded statements of witnesses. Although it is not always apparent from the trial narrative what form these take, some at least are records of interview taken down by police as part of their investigation process. The sentencing transcript also considers expert evidence and police records of interview.

These themes arising from the Italian transcript narrative offer some initial understandings about the significant sites of decision-making in the trial and their operation. The methodology for comparison which will be applied once the English trial transcripts have received similar interrogation requires some expansion following the Italian narrative analysis.

Sites for decision-making

It is necessary to approach the comparative analysis of trial transcript attempted in this and the following chapter from a more developed model of sites for decision-making (Figure 3.2, Chapter 3) representative as it should be of the trial process. In this comparative analysis the application of the model will be from meta-sites of trial process down through those more discrete sites crucial for the larger decision-making process. This will enable the deconstruction of trial decision-making as a process reduced to the most specific and individual decisions.

At any point in the analysis which applies the 'decision site' model it should be possible also to focus on particular decisions (Figure 3.3, Chapter 3). This would enable the analysis of trial outcomes (rather than processes) at comparative levels (internal and external) of structure, system, and discretion.

A combination of both approaches, issues-driven as they are, will continue to locate the analysis in actual trial practice, despite the conscious application of prevailing theoretical models (see Findlay and Henham 2003a). This is as a result of the context of process and of outcome (sites for decision-making, and the decisions which they produce). It will also offer any depth of analysis, depending on the nature of the available data, and as a result a wide range of possibilities when it comes to the search for common features of process and outcome.[21]

In the transcripts examined from the Italian trials (as will be the case with the English transcripts to follow) at least four general sites for decision-making can be identified, despite their tendency to overlap:

1 Examination and cross-examination (decisions as to the refinement of facts).
2 Contests of law concerning admissibility (decisions regarding what evidence goes on to the record).
3 Verdict delivery (decisions about whether the prosecution has established its case).
4 Sentencing (decisions on appropriate penalty).

These general sites, however, do not operate on their own, but rather the trial process is an integration of decisions and relationships of influence, meta to micro (see Figure 4.1).

Within this process exist individual decision sites and relationships requiring detailed examination in context before any attempt at comparison through a search for uniform pathways of influence. Figure 4.2 identifies four major decision sites in the trial, where crucial relationships develop and wherein pathways of influence are in operation. These are not the only sites worthy of analysis, but they do represent different relationships at work through different levels of interaction. This is the first crucial stage in comparative contextual analysis.

Due to the nature of the transcripts before us some of these sites can be compared closely narrative to narrative, across jurisdictions (such as verdict delivery and sentencing). Others may be analysed in their

---

21 In the pilot analysis to follow, for instance, there may only be several applications of Figure 3.2 attempted, and only broad decision outcomes exposed to Figure 3.3. This is a realistic consequence of the limited comparative data and the danger of drawing too much in terms of uniformity from its analysis.

context and compared with broad observational and participatory experience of what is common in other jurisdictions or contexts (witness examination, challenges of evidence) etc.

Figure 4.1 Integrated analysis

PROCESS   OUTCOME

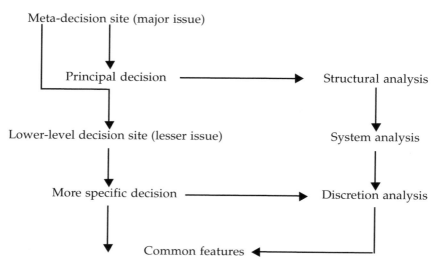

Each site requires individual analysis in the contexts of sites for decision-making, and the content of the decisions produced therein. To facilitate this the comparative employment of modeling is instructive (see Henham and Findlay 2002). Drawing on Figure 3.2 in Chapter 3 the conceptualization of each decision-making site prior to its interrogation through the narrative is possible and provides a map for the investigation of the decision relationships operating therein. If the features of each context were applied in context prior to comparison, they might look something like this.

In the case of the Italian kidnapping narrative where witnesses were examined (site 1), the players are the advocate and the victim witness. Their dialogue is question-and-answer, constructed around recorded prior testimony. In each of these question-and-answer sessions the advocate is endeavouring to elicit from the witness sufficient information to stand as fact and to strengthen or weaken a particular argument. The exercise of the advocate's discretion is individual, as is the witness' discretion to respond, although the questions and answers are constructed within the history of previous investigations and the actual situation of interrogation in the

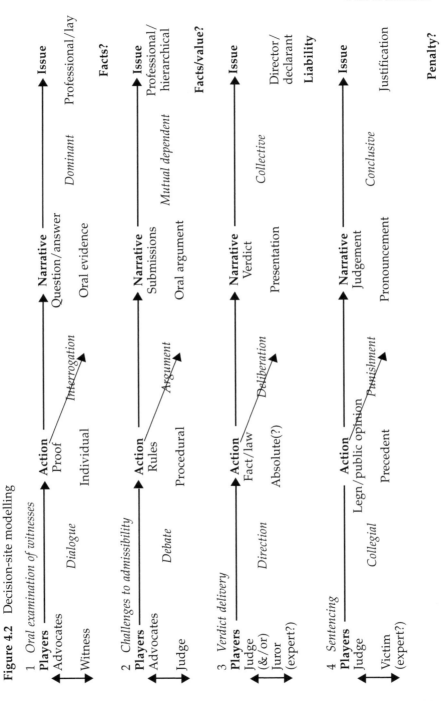

Figure 4.2 Decision-site modelling

trial. The action is conversational and interactive through a structured process of interrogation. The narrative produced is a record of oral evidence, in places constructed around pre-existing narrative of earlier interrogation. The status between advocate and witness is one of domination. The issue is that through professional/lay oral interaction 'facts' are produced on which other decision-making sites might rely. The decision to be produced from this site is, what are the facts?

There are peculiar features in this context which will make specific this encounter beyond its model representation. These include:

- the heavy reliance on previously recorded written record in the construction and intent of the questioning;
- the regular use of leading questions; and
- the application of generic information arising out of previously recorded interrogation for the cross-examination.

As for the second decision-site and the examination of witnesses in the Italian murder trial: the players are the prosecution and defence advocates, and the judge. They are in debate over the actuality of a constitutional right to silence and the way that its protection can be ensured without defeating the prosecution's obligation to lead evidence and ascertain the truth. The action is the proposing of arguments and the making of submissions concluding in a judge's ruling. The nature of the submissions and the manner in which the argument is presented depends on the rules of evidence and the procedural restrictions over the exercise of individual discretion by the debaters and the adjudicator. The narrative takes the form of oral argument and submissions in the form of debate and pronouncement. The status of the contestants is more equally defined by their professional status and yet depends on the decision of the judge. Within a professional and hierarchical environment of formal debate and adjudication the struggle is over the value of what is alleged as fact, and whether these facts would be available for consideration by verdict deliverers.

Again, there were individual features of the context in which the model is applied which would require recognition prior to comparison:

- The nature of the right to silence claimed and its constitutional foundations.
- The obligations on the prosecutor and his or her role to produce evidence.

- The pathways for objecting to the prosecution's submission.
- The possibility for compromise solutions to the clash between accused's rights and the prosecutor's duty.
- The discretion of the judge to admit evidence.

These then are open for comparison with similar decision-sites contextually analysed in other trial jurisdictions. An examination of the verdict delivery or sentencing sites in England and Italy offer such a possibility. This will be attempted in detail as part of our CCA in Chapter 5.

When addressing the contextual analysis of selected sites for decision-making, prior to the comparative endeavour, it is necessary to investigate the purpose of the enterprise. Consistent with our conceptualization of the trial we wish to know more about its significant sites for decision-making. This could be approached in several ways:

- Through the examination of outcomes of decision-making sites (the decisions produced).

- Through tracing the emergence of anticipated themes or issues out of the decision-making process, and their interconnection.

- Through exploring the decision-making structures of a particular site.

- Through a deductive process where the dynamics of the decision-making site (or its contextual evaluators) are searched against some common external paradigm (such as fair trial as enunciated in Art. 6 of the European Convention).

- Through contrast with a process matrix externally devised in order to identify contextual features which correspond with the matrix and for such to receive an empirical value.

- Through the application of specific decision-making models (based on our original site-model concept) and gradually making these more focused as we proceed down towards individual decisions or specific outcomes (peeling the onion).

- Through a measure of satisfaction for crucial constituents in the trial (and the wider justice process) such as victims and victim communities.[22]

---

22 Inadequacy at this level of analysis we argue leads to a wider critique of the trial and arguments for its transformation in contexts such as ICJ where such is possible and appropriate.

The application of both deductive and inductive analysis is favoured in a methodology for comparative analysis which recognizes the significance of context. These parallel pathways of thought are (Figure 4.3) also important in any research endeavour which aspires for pragmatic realism and emphasizes the need to ground understandings of dynamic social process such as the trial (and its social meaning) within the commonsense of trial practice.

Figure 4.3   Inductive and deductive parallels

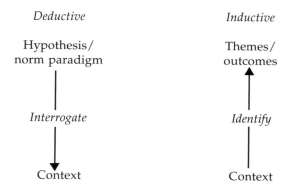

Whichever of these analytical approaches is preferred will depend on asking why we are involved in this analysis in the first place. Is it to:

- Test hypotheses regarding law, procedure and policy?

- Apply a normative paradigm as the preferred ideological framework for 'knowing' the trial?

- Provide some validation for preconceived notions about the trial?

- Make meaningful comparative generalizations about the process of the trial (and thereby explore differences in different processes)?

- Impose some objectivity onto the consideration of more subjective (or value-oriented) evaluators of trial context?

- Move from higher to lower levels of abstraction, getting closer to individual decisions in order to understand the inclusive levels of decision-making within the site, their different contexts and outcomes?

- Argue for trial transformation and a broadening of justice of inclusion in higher justice forms?

The application of the decision site model to decreasing levels of decision-making generality in each trial transcript should provide the capacity to juxtapose contextualized meanings using a variety of methodologies and from there lay the groundwork for meaningful comparative generalizations (however limited). A pragmatic (yet principled) approach to the deconstruction of trial transcript permits the penetration of the internal aspects of fact/value within trial decision-making. For instance, by reducing decisions on penalty down through the manner in which the judge's discretion is influenced by the harm to the victim and the mitigation of the accused's liability. In this context what lies behind the negotiation of justice through sentencing should be more apparent. At the same time, the decision-site model will show how these understandings enable us to appreciate the meaning of process in all its complexity.

In choosing the final two purposes and analytical approaches listed above we are not putting aside the search for generality and the testing of objectivity, particularly in the comparative phase of the work. Rather we are returning to our reliance on context (as we did when we discussed modelling in Chapter 2) in order to fulfil the aspirations of our simple narrative comparative exercise. These relate directly to the exploration of narrative as a methodological field for the analysis of trial decision-making. In so doing we would be blind not to anticipate some limitations of narrative and to expect an outcome that argues for complementary and integrated methodologies enabling both inductive and deductive dimensions to our analysis.[23]

Even with the limited narrative analysis in this and the next chapter, the form and content of the narrative to be analysed vary widely as between comparative contexts. This is compounded by the acceptance that the analysis will bring to the enterprise one's own preconceptions about the meaning of what appears in context. In this atmosphere of subjectivity, is meaningful generalization possible? We are not troubled to confront such a question at the contextual phase, relying on the expectation that as a matter of degree generalization will work on a continuum from the subjective to the universal and await empirical validation depending on whatever scientific measures are employed. At this stage, whilst generalization is meaningful and to be sought after, it will require the comparative endeavour and the application of further methodologies in addition to the narrative in order to prove

---

23 We suggest that these are crucially inter-related. Whilst we can apply one and the other dimension, in the comparative phase one cannot be inductive without also being deductive.

convincing. At this stage we should be satisfied with learning more about each site for decision-making.

Issues for methodology

As with the review of substantive decision-making, the consideration of research methodology appropriate for the interrogation of trial decision sites and their component at various levels of justice delivery requires conclusion in terms of general issues and broad themes. This concluding part will take the form of a consideration of the way in which the two important supplementary methodologies might complement narrative analysis as applied in this and the following chapter. This is then followed by a brief summary of the principal issues of methodology which have emerged from the narrative analysis carried out on its own.

Potential for observations and questionnaires

More has been said in the section on refining the research methodology (Chapter 3) regarding the potentials and limitations we have identified through the rather narrow application of narrative analysis. However, following the interrogation of transcript it is useful to pose several brief examples of where questionnaires and observation would have provided crucial supplementary methodologies.

Knowing more about the lay/professional relationship

It is possible to speculate from the narrative that influential relationships exist between lay and professional participants in the trial process. Yet, with the narrative voice being largely that of the judge, the dynamics of this relationship may be skewed in favour of the influence of the professional. In addition, certain structural and systemic realities, such as the anonymity of the jury, prevent the lay voice emerging.

Conventional research into juries (Duff and Findlay 1997) is replete with examples of where surveys of jurors have indicated what tends to influence their comprehension and deliberations. Even judges have been surveyed about what they think of juries and whether they would normally agree with their verdicts (Baldwin and McConville 1979). Because of the nature of the relationship between judges and jurors in the structure of trial decision-making these insights might only be discovered with the benefit of administering questionnaires outside the context of the trial.

As we have discovered in other research contexts, however, a questionnaire on its own will not tell all about how jurors were influenced and by whom (see Findlay 1991). In many settings it is the professional lawyer rather than the witness or the nature of the evidence which impacts on a jury's decisions. Paramount amongst professional influence is that of the judge (Findlay 1994a). But the high expression of influence (and approval) from jurors talking of judges will also be a factor of status and deference. Jurors have indicated that because of the prestige of the judge within the trial he or she should be seen as influential and judicial pronouncements accorded respect. Whether this is the same as jurors being specifically influenced by what the judge actually instructs may not be the same thing.

It seems clear that more needs to be known about how in the Italian trial setting the professional judges influence the impressions and decisions of their lay colleagues on the collective bench. The pathways of decision-making which influence judicial determinations will give insight here. The judicial voice in our narrative was of the professional President. It is not clear on whose behalf the voice speaks. If it is a collective pronouncement then how is the common view settled and to what extent does the specialist knowledge of the professional tone the fact/law division? Are the constitutional declarations of equality amongst judges translated into collegiate decision-making and, if so, how?

Here, perhaps, the most inclusive methodology for gaining these insights would be active participation in the lay/professional process of verdict delivery and deliberation. Structural and systemic prohibitions make this largely impossible. Therefore, the employment of survey techniques once the decision has been made is the next best option.

Knowing more about witnesses and examination

The Italian transcript makes much of the judges' attitude to certain witnesses and their character. In the case of the principal defendant in the murder trial one could assume from the tone of the narrative that the witness's untrustworthy demeanour did as much in the eyes of the judges to confirm his guilt, as did material facts and other testimony. However, due to the one-eyed interpretative direction of the narrative we are required to take on trust the judicial interpretation of demeanour as fact. From this point we can then comment on the comparative influence of character. This is not sufficient for a critical analysis reliant on judicial reinterpretation of the significance of evidence.

If the methodology had allowed for some observation of the witness in question and a consequent evaluation of demeanour, a superficial correlation of character and outcome might be tested. More importantly would have been the opportunity to speculate on judicial attitude to a witness when the observer disagrees with the judge's take on things. If judicial interpretation of character was not supported by independent observation, or not the same significance was placed on it, then why did the judge employ character to justify other conclusions on fact?

Because the professional is comfortable with the trial environment, and lay participants are not, then this disparity may be used by the professional for his or her own decision-making means. While the dominance by the professional may be apparent from the narrative, the nuances of this, and its application is better understood through observation.

The examination of witnesses is said to be representative of particular trial traditions. In the USA for instance, lawyers can physically intimidate witnesses as they pose questions and react to responses. In the English court settings counsel are restricted to remain behind the bar table during witness examination. None of this would be revealed without observation. The visual clues that professionals convey particularly to lay participants in order to formulate their impression of testimony may not translate into narrative and yet may be as influential for lay participants as the words of the testimony.

At the structural level of analysis we have employed the background of recent legislative reforms of Italian criminal procedure to suggest the application of a more adversarial trial style. The narrative demonstrates activity on behalf of the prosecution and defence lawyers in examining witnesses and testing oral evidence. Even so this appears by comparison with common law trial *lawyering* to be rather formal and at times ritualistic. The reality of such an impression and the extent to which useful conclusions can be drawn about emerging trial practice would depend on observation to complement narrative.

Themes for methodology regarding sites for decision-making

Continuing with the task of issue identification, we advance the following as general themes to inform the creation of an integrated method for comparing contexts of trial analysis.

Utility of narrative as record of decision-making – what it says and implies about decision-making

Even with such a small number of trials and in only two jurisdictions we were blessed with a rich array of data and experience in the narrative before us. We have not ventured into semiotics as a paradigm for analysis but even so the narrative reveals many and considerable opportunities for comparative analysis. Problems with access and translation aside, there is in narrative analysis enough, in combination with a normative framework of understanding, to allow for some unique insights into both the applicability of trial modelling and the critical evaluation of trial practice. The narrative analysis was no doubt enriched by a theoretical foundation tolerant of various methodologies and flexible modelling which could address the structures and processes for decision-making as well as decision outcomes.[24]

The utility of narrative analysis for exploring trial decision-making in particular is ensured through its compatibility as reflective of official normative requirements, as an externalization of reasons for action and an interpretation of language contingent on decisions.

Nature of interaction as decision-making – what informs decision-making and how can it be viewed and interpreted?

It might be argued that the narrative is static and therefore not well suited as a technique for revealing the nature of interactive decision-making. We did not always find this to be the case. If interaction itself is examined against players, action and outcomes, narrative is a material connection or pathway between. In trial decision-making the integration of different players in different action settings, producing various outcomes, can be charted through narrative even if the integration so revealed is recursive. As we suggest below, temporal and spatial sequence can be given new directions through the application of associated methodologies in order to enhance the dynamic suggestions of narrative.

External influences over decision-making – fair trial obligations, rules, and documents as boundaries for discretion

Obviously the use of normative frameworks (procedures, rules and practice directions) is a standard transformative mechanism for the interpretation of trial transcript as narrative.

---

24 For instance, our work is suggestive and does not in any way seek to be empirically representative.

The fact/value distinction, grounded as it should be and transitional (see Chapter 3), provides a criterion for managing subjective and objective meanings in the narrative and its analysis. Such meanings out of the narrative are instantaneous yet can reflect back on rules/ structures and the application of discretion in a more generalized and systematic fashion. The narrative provides a static snapshot of the transformation of rules and structures through human agency. The narrative reflects an interpretation of that process and how other interpretations might be mediated through interaction and conversation.

Outcomes to influence further decisions – nature of the trial process

The narrative talks constantly about alternative outcomes and then provides a charter of enabled and actual outcomes. In this respect a single narrative should not be analysed on its own but rather as a stage in the process preceding the trial, what is diverted from the trial and what follows from it. In this respect a 'tree' of narratives might be employed around the trial to explain why certain decision sites operate as they do and produce what they do.

Refining the research methodology

The experience of narrative analysis within a comparative project, examining trials as dynamic processes, was always going to point out the limitations of the methodology. Perhaps what has surprised us as a consequence of the analysis of transcripts in only two jurisdictions is the richness of narrative analysis when incorporated even with most static additional methodologies. For instance, the incorporations of an evaluation of normative instruments (legislation, rules, practice conventions) with the narrative analysis enabled a fuller appreciation of why trial decision-making took certain forms in different contexts (see Chapter 6).

The narrative analysis also enabled researchers to view situations where other methodologies would provide broader and deeper understandings. We have already commented on the possibilities for the application of narrative analysis along with observations and questionnaires.

The addition of methodologies to the mix, however, will create new challenges and change the dimensions of the research exercise. With narrative analysis we are largely operating an *ex-post facto* methodology. The narrative is a record of what has happened and what was said. In this sense it is a more manageable methodology than those which are more instantaneous. The narrative is also frozen in time, even though the issues that precede, and the consequences of the narrative voice, are constantly resonant.

To introduce observations would require the ability to be present at the trial. More than this one would need to be forewarned about the features of the trial required for frames of comparative reference.[25] In addition to the usual difficulties posed by observational methodology,[26] the time frame of the data collection is clearly enlarged if it is then incorporated with narrative analysis.

The temporal sequence problems posed by an incorporated methodology are not only generated through observations. If limited and specific questionnaire surveys are administered, research experience suggests that with trial players these need to be administered as soon after the delivery of the verdict as possible so as to maximize response rates and recall.

With most decision sites in the trial it would be advantageous to employ an integrated methodology. Such a methodology possesses the potential to reveal different layers of meaning, as well as a greater depth of understanding regarding sites for decision-making and their outcomes.

Another reason for an integrated methodology with this type of comparative research project is to confront the challenge of subjective and objective insights. We have earlier expressed our conviction that the comparative project needs to be able to engage subjective detail about trial process in any context whilst at the same time disclosing more universal or generalized findings which could claim objective status (see Chapter 3). In order that this could be possible, the research is grounded in trial practice from which position universal themes can be seen as adding depth and permanence (value) to more subjective social facts. The methodology needs several dimensions, and in particular different temporal and spatial parameters, so as to enhance the detail of the present, immediate and intimate data, as well as confirming more uniform realities through comparison and over time and space.

---

25 Measures of comparability include trial length, charges, number and nature of accused, disclosure, pre-trial documentation, expert evidence, contested issues of procedure, judicial intervention, role of the accused, frameworks for decision-making and outcome.

26 These difficulties obviously are exacerbated by the reality of comparing different trial systems at different times across different jurisdictions.

The 'best practice' integrated methodology proposed is to:

1 examine normative frameworks such as legislation, rules and practice conventions;

2 out of this, reflect on the structures and systems of jury processes in various contexts;

3 construct and test a theory of decision-making which incorporates structure, system and integration;

4 create contextual models of trial decision-making and decisions;

5 interrogate primary and secondary trial transcript narrative;

6 contrast this with selected non-participant observation of trial decision sites recorded in the narrative. Then to investigate the narrative of what was observed;

7 administer survey instruments to lay and professional trial participants in order to understand better the dynamic influences of integrated decision-making;

8 examine trial outcomes in the light of the other methodologies;

9 apply this integrated methodology within and across comparative trial context; and

10 analyse the data using CCA.

Chapter 5 presents the second narrative context and explores the potential for comparative research, context to context. This enabled the thematic examination of one significant pathway of influence, the judge/victim decision relationship in sentencing, to be explored in Chapter 6.

Chapter 5

Another trial style?

Introduction

Through the interrogation of common law trial transcripts similar in form and content to those reviewed in Chapter 4, we take the comparative investigation of trial decisions one context further. The common law referent is selected as the other major procedural influence on the internationalization of criminal justice.[1] Reflecting on the issues emerging from the Italian experience (and the application of our analytical model), this chapter employs structural and integrated process levels[2] of analysis in order to speculate on crucial components and variants trial process to trial process, and within each trial context. These themes have emerged in Chapter 4 and will be compared with the decision-making narrative declared through English judgements. The model of trial decision-making is also tested to see if there are some common levels of significance in the apparent pathways of influence described or suggested in the narrative.

An analysis such as this then allows for the identification and manipulation of those contextual elements common to trial decision-making in order to produce universal themes ripe for testing in regional and international justice contexts. Preparatory to this we will also

---

1   For a critique of the bifurcated procedural tradition position, see Cavadino and Dignan (1997).
2   This is particularly relevant for the later application of these data to our consideration of integrated sentencing decisions involving judges and victims.

reflect on fair trial influences in both procedural paradigms discussed in this and the preceding chapter. The 'rights' paradigm for trial decision-making is important in regional and international trial processes. Particularly as fair trial relies on access to justice and protective normative frameworks, we explore trial decision-making relationships as they represent and endorse human rights at the centre of criminal justice. A consideration of trial rights also presents a common language when, in our concluding part, we propose a transformed trial model to support dynamic international criminal justice (ICJ). The argument in Chapter 7 for including restorative justice considerations within international criminal trial processes is just that the trial is an institution for the protection of participant's rights, and not for their violation or compromise.

Common law transcript

Two transcript extracts chosen from English trials focus on verdict delivery and sentencing. Along with some associated material the narrative here is produced from the judge's summing-up of the evidence and his instructions to the jury concerning the law to be applied in considering their verdict. Once the verdict has been delivered then pleas in mitigation are made and the narrative concludes with the sentencing remarks and the passing of sentence.

The core of these transcripts is the summing-up by the judge and the verdict. The primary source of narrative is the judge's remarks which are structured around directions on the law and a summary of the most significant elements of the evidence.[3] In the latter the reader will discover segments of oral testimony (produced through examination and cross-examination), written record such as defence submissions, expert evidence and the reports on which it might be based, prior written dossier such as police records of interview, and judicial commentary on any or all these. Therefore, we gain, through this narrative, second-hand insights into lay/professional and professional interaction. Also, the judge may comment on the demeanour of witnesses and may pass inferences on external matters such as the legitimacy of legislation.

---

3   Unlike the situation with Italian procedure and the judicial narrative which results there from, the judge's voice here is tempered by the need to communicate with a lay jury for the purposes of verdict delivery.

R v. Stephen Victor Fountain

The extracts of transcript here include the judge's summing-up and verdict, the speech in mitigation on behalf of the accused and the sentencing remarks.

The summing-up can be conveniently divided into two parts: the directions on law to the jury and a summary of principal evidence. As the issue of diminished responsibility is at the heart of the defence case the judge spends time explaining the mental element of murder and the manner in which abnormality of the mind has to be dealt with. Here the judge cautions on the impact of an admission by the co-accused. At one stage of his remarks he distributes to the jury a written direction from him regarding the proof requirements for diminished responsibility.

Reference is made to doctors' reports regarding the assertion of diminished responsibility. Later the judge is to quote from or to refer back to five such reports. Segments of these reports are highlighted by the judge, either in the manner they support or deny diminished responsibility.

The judge comments on the accused's criminal antecedents. Usually these would not be put before the jury but here it appears that they have been advanced by the defence to support the suggestion of diminished responsibility.

The judge invites the jury to consider conflicting interpretations of the accused's motives for the attacks. One would support the conclusion that he was suffering at the time from an abnormality of the mind. The other would not. The judge then proceeds to summarize the facts by largely concentrating on the defence case.

To advance the summary the judge physically requires the jury to read sections of records of interview between the police and the accused, taken prior to the trial. The judge concedes to the jury that his references are 'extremely selective' and that in reviewing these records, he may be 'trespassing on your territory'. In addition the judge contextualizes these records as 'only forming part of a total of many, many hours of questioning as you know, but they are the only ones that are relevant'. What follows is ten pages of narrative introduced into the narrative: the questions of the police and the answers of the accused. The judge seeks some assistance from prosecution counsel in helping the jury follow the transcripts to which he refers.

The judge recites from a form put before the court by the defence detailing the prior criminal history of the accused. Added to this are submissions made by the defence to explain this history and to connect medical advice.

The summary then moves to the oral evidence presented by the defence in rebuttal of the crown case. Again the judge reminds the jury that his selective review only 'serves to illuminate the issue – you have to decide'.

The defence case relies primarily on the oral testimony given by the accused. This appears to consist of a statement that was then expanded through questions from the accused's counsel, and then cross-examined by the prosecution. The accused acknowledges the Crown case that he attacked and killed the victim but puts forward a psychiatric explanation for his actions. This is then elaborated on by the reports and oral testimonies of doctor witnesses.

The jury is instructed on the manner in which they are to return their verdict and then told to retire. During the period of their deliberation, the judge and counsel discuss luncheon arrangements. In addition, the judge wants to know that if an alternative verdict to murder is returned whether defence counsel will be minded to seek a hospital order. Defence counsel talks about the report of one doctor, a report which the judge has not seen 'for reasons as to which your lordship can draw the appropriate inferences'. The advocate will seek an adjournment for further advice if that is the outcome.

The jury returns and admits not to having reached a unanimous verdict. The judge then instructs them to work to return a majority verdict 'upon which at least ten of you are agreed'. Once the jury retires a second time the prosecution addresses the judge on what arrangements should be made to allow the jury to deliberate over to the following day. In so doing the judge is referred to a practice note on the point. The judge says he is not willing to follow that course and that he will have the jury back and if they are unable to reach a majority verdict he will discharge them. The foreman of the jury conveys the information that they have not reached a majority verdict. The judge thanks the jury and discharges them. The judge then asks the prosecutor 'where does this leave us?' The prosecutor says that in light of the medical evidence before the court, the narrowness of the issue before the court and the cost of a retrial 'that it would not be a legitimate expenditure of public money to proceed to a retrial'. The judge agrees and indicates to the defence counsel that he is minded to impose an indeterminate sentence on the alternative charge, and that he would take his submissions on it. The defence stated that they would not be opposing such an outcome.

The judge then explains 'so that there is no risk in the jury's mind' that whatever the accused stands convicted (murder or manslaughter) effectively he will receive the same sentence, life imprisonment. The prosecution reminds the judge that his position is conditional on the accused pleading guilty to the alternative charge and the judge confirms with counsel for the accused. The defence lawyers physically approach the accused to explain the situation to him. The defendant then pleads not guilty to murder but guilty to manslaughter, on the basis of diminished responsibility. The prosecutor accepts this position. The judge then indicates that he will sentence the accused along with his co-defendant tomorrow morning.

The next extract in the sentencing process is the address in mitigation by counsel for the defence. It commences in recognizing that the judge must take into account the seriousness of the offence by reference to its nature and the combination of offences associated with it. Counsel concedes that they have advised his client consistently throughout that applying such a test a sentence of life would be inevitable. The accused, therefore, entered his plea in full knowledge of this outcome. Reference is made to a doctor's report which says that the accused is presently untreatable. This view was given in relation to the judge's earlier expressed interest in a hospital order.

In terms of the issues submitted to be taken into account by the judge when sentencing, these included the youthfulness of the offender and the full admissions that he made (these should be balanced against his not-guilty plea). The judge commends defence counsel for all he has done for the accused.

The sentencing remarks recognise the accused's admissions and go on to chronicle the 'terrible' history of his criminal past. The judge declares that in coming to a penalty calculation he has employed the 'principle of totality' where multiple offences are concerned. The expert evidence confirms his view of the accused as 'exceptionally dangerous', with thirteen offences being taken into account. The judge is reminded by the prosecution (having consulted with the defence) that he should comply with legislation requiring that a minimum period to be served should be stipulated.

The principles of sentencing nominated by the judge are punishment, specific and general deterrence and community safety (risk). The judge asks counsel to explain the terms of the sentence to his client no matter how 'distressing the encounter'.

R v. Ian Turner

The extracts here are of the same type as in the *Fountain* case, with the addition of a pre-sentence report referred to in the sentencing remarks as well as the offender's prior criminal history. The trial proper consisted of evidence from eight prosecution witnesses and a written statement in support of the accused.

The summing-up from the judge commences with directions in law, the first regarding the onus of proof. On what constitutes proof the judge instructs that if the prosecution convinces the jury of the defendant's guilt then that is proof of the offence. Regarding the elements of the offence charged these need to be put against the defendant's assertion that he was acting in self-defence. The intent seriously to injure the victim must be proved by the prosecution to have been unlawful. The defendant does not have to prove that he was acting in lawful self-defence. For self-defence to stand the accused must believe that it was necessary for him to defend himself, and the amount of force he used in so doing was reasonable. The judge then proceeds to discuss in detail and in practice how such decisions might be made.

The next direction relates to possible alternative charges. These revolved around whether or not the jury was satisfied that an intention to cause really serious harm had been established. The judge is meticulous in setting out the prosecution's obligation of proof.

Finally, the judge instructs on the status of the written statement presented for the defence. The witness had not been available for oral testimony and whilst this put the prosecution at a disadvantage equally the defence did not have the use of a possibly convincing oral witness.

The judge commences his summary of the evidence with a warning that none of it is conclusive. He highlights the actions and conversations between the accused and the victim, and points to matters which are unclear or in contest. The description of events from the victim and some of his witnesses differs markedly from the version advanced by the accused.

The record of interview taken by the police from the defendant is made available to the jury. The judge chooses not to refer to this. He instructs the jury to select a foreperson, not to concern themselves about the majority verdict and to retire for their deliberations under no pressure. The judge reiterates that if the jury is not convinced about the proof of intent they can go on to the alternative verdict of simple wounding. There seems implicit in this final suggestion a reservation on behalf of the judge about the matter. After the jury retires the judge confirms this concern by suggesting to the prosecution that it might have been preferable if they had added the alternative charge to the indictment.

After lunch the jury send a question to the judge for clarification. It relates to intention and self-defence. The judge seeks the view of the advocates from both sides prior to passing his answer back to the jury.

The judge emphasizes the need not only to prove intention but, outside self-defence, to prove that it was unlawful. A guilty verdict is returned by the jury.

In mitigation counsel for the defence relies on character references from the community which take the form of a petition. Reference is also made to community support identified in the pre-sentence report. The advocate identifies the tactical decision not taken to introduce such character evidence during the trial particularly as it related to the accused's prior criminal history. His antecedents are now examined in light of the fact that strong community support for the accused existed irrespective of this.

The mitigation proceeds by discussing the relationship between the victim and the accused, and the nature of the encounter. The purpose of the mitigation is to persuade the judge that, despite his statutory obligations not to impose a life sentence, and if a custodial sentence is considered, then for as short a period as possible. The judge reminds counsel that he also does not have the benefit of a guilty plea in exercising his discretion.

The advocate identifies the legislative constraint on discretion as a controversial piece of legislation and backs this up with a critical article by a well regarded academic. The restriction may be avoided, the judge is reminded, if he finds any of the circumstances of the first or second violent offences extraordinary. He concedes that the case law does not allow the age of the offender at the first offence or the intervening period between offences to be considered extraordinary. Even so, counsel says that there are other facts in the offence which would qualify for that epithet. The nature of the first offence and the relatively lenient sentence it drew are submitted as being exceptional. In the present case it was the attack by the victim (despite the failure of self-defence) which is put as being exceptional. The advocate seems to imply that, despite the verdict, even facts that would support a charge of wounding with intent and deny self-defence may also support an exceptional attack by the victim which was perhaps excessively responded to by the accused. The injuries to the accused endorse this view. It is the sequence of events leading to the wounding of the victim which are argued as being exceptional. The judge responds with some circumspection and reminds counsel that in sentencing he must put into effect the decision of the jury even if his own decision would have been different. There ensues an exchange between the judge and defence counsel as to whether in drawing the conclusion submitted one would need to challenge the jury's verdict or not. The judge asks counsel if he thinks it is a particularly harsh verdict in the circumstances and he says that it is not for him to say. The judge retorts that it is not for him to say as well. The defence continues that this is the fine line between self-defence and the excessive use of force. The accused's assault was an act of passion and submitted to be as such exceptional.

The public support for the accused is said also to be exceptional and the fact that the accused is not alleged to be a risk to community safety should in the defence advocate's way of thinking, avoid the need to impose a life sentence as the legislation requires. The judge returns to legal authority tending to deny that the legislation is limited to accused persons' posing a risk.

In addition, the history of the case and its many adjournments are submitted by counsel as exceptional. The defendant is also proposed as exceptional, as is his community rehabilitation.

The judge is invited to impose a suspended sentence. He then apologizes for having to do something he 'does not like doing in this very difficult matter'.

In his sentencing remarks there is a clear implication that the judge is required to accept the verdict of the jury which he might otherwise have found difficult to reconcile. The judge then touches on the previous offence of manslaughter and observes that in the circumstances the outcome was 'largely a matter of luck'. Next the judge discusses legislation requiring the imposition of an indeterminate sentence in these circumstances unless the offender or the offence is deemed exceptional. Of this the judge observes: 'The question of justice is not a luxury in which I can wallow … justice apparently Parliament did not give judges the right to consider.' The judge concedes that the accused is not dangerous and that the victim may also have been violent.

The judge concurs with academic criticism of the legislation restricting the exercise of his discretion in this instance. Unfortunately for the judge he cannot, in light of precedent, find anything exceptional in the offence or the offender. He returns to the comparative harshness of the jury verdict and holds that it is irrelevant. He is constitutionally obliged to put into practice what the jury has found, as he is constitutionally bound to comply with even bad legislation. Despite struggling over the issue the judge cannot in conscience or in his interpretation of the law find exceptional circumstances which would overcome the obligation to impose a life sentence. He returns the obligation back to the community 'to wonder if this is the kind of statute they really want in a civilised society'. The judge reflects on the faces of the jury when they were told of the consequences of their verdict.

Context analysis

Again, following the description of the sentencing transcripts, collation against some narrative themes is useful. These themes have an interesting relationship with those drawn from the analysis of the Italian transcripts. They move from questions of form to the relationships and influences identified in the narrative. This then provides an opportunity in the comparative phase to reflect on more than methodology, and on to issues of trial process.

Differences in form, content and accessibility of transcript

The English sentencing transcript material is the product of private firms of commercial court reporters. Even so, it takes a consistent form of direct transcription of the words spoken by judges and lawyers.

The language used in the narrative is very formal, respectful of hierarchy, and deferential to the separation of powers between professional players. The progress of the narrative reflects both real and imagined ideologies of judicial independence and the separate role of the jury as fact-finder. For instance, the judge constantly defers to the jury's role in determining the facts and yet is at pains to present to them his version of the facts as he summarizes them.

The style of the narrative is heavily dependent on the role of the players and their obligations in any particular decision site. The jury, which is absolute in its verdict and private in its deliberations, is silent in the narrative except for the formal presentation of questions to the judge. In answering such questions the judge invites the views of those who have an interest in the outcome and then formally instructs the jury, pronouncement rather than dialogue. Regarding sentence delivery, the advocates submit to the judge in order to interpret those issues which will impact on his discretion along with those features of the case which should influence his determination of penalty. This can sometimes take the form of dialogue but it is more likely to be formal submissions. The judge then pronounces judgement in an atmosphere of justification and limited explanation.

Conventions of lay/professional interaction, judicial intervention

While the sentencing transcripts provide little in the way of lay/professional interaction, when compared with witness examination, the English material in particular demonstrates the unspoken influence of the judge over the jury. This is a very mannered and formal relationship and one in which the narrative is a limited form of revelation. Being only representative of what the judge says to the jury, the trial transcript would benefit from observational data which identified the manner in which jurors deferred to the judge and received judicial direction. In addition, questionnaires would assist in discovering the jurors' attitude to the judge and judicial influence. Even on the basis of the narrative, however, this appears to be a relationship pregnant with many levels of meaning and opportunities for inference and interpretation.

Professional interaction is a feature of the sentencing narrative particularly as it relates to the treatment of submissions. In the English transcript material these submissions take the form of pleas in mitigation, and particularly in *Turner* there are several occasions where the judge and the defence advocate converse (in polite and deferential tones) about the nature and limits of this influence on sentencing discretion. The debate is measured and inferential, designed to distil the outcome of the sentencer's deliberations.

Other examples within the narrative of professional interaction are found in the manner in which judge and legal counsel address medical reports and academic opinion.

Reliance on rules, use of pre-existing documentary evidence

In terms of the English sentencing transcripts there are levels of normative and procedural regulation which impact on verdict delivery and sentencing. Particularly in relation to sentencing, recent legislative reforms have created a range of regulations which introduce concerns beyond the dynamics of the individual case. For instance, in *Turner* the judge is required to impose a life sentence (well beyond the penalty range that the offence in question requires) because of the accused's prior criminal history.

The higher level of regulation relates to the separation of powers and constitutional legality. The jury's verdict binds the judge. Legislative enactment controls judicial discretion. Both these may significantly interfere with the judge's independent ability to bring about justice. In *Turner* the judge says as much.

Practice conventions require that the judge hear the defence in mitigation and give weight to pre-sentence reports from welfare professionals. These produce ancillary narrative around the exercise of sentencing.

The construction of the indictment and the charges at the heart of the jury's decision-making emerge from a hierarchy of penalty needing reflection through the sentencing process. The more normative rules or principles of sentencing contextualize and justify sentence calculation, within legislative parameters. Judicial interpretation of these principles, and the manner of their use, further circumscribe sentencing.

Secondary source narrative is most apparent in the judge's reinterpretation of the trial, the summing-up. This is a unique example of where the narrative, because of the hierarchical position of the judge, is used to emphasize, authorize, question and add meaning to the presentation of oral and written evidence. The judge employs the summing-up to categorize different forms of evidence and to influence indirectly the verdict deliverer. Another way in which the judge manipulates secondary narrative is through the inter-pretations of law and the exercise of judicial direction in the face of its constraint.

Significance of discretion in decision-making?

In both sets of English sentencing transcript material there is specific debate about the exercise of judicial discretion. The *Fountain* case presents questions about whether expert medical evidence would enable the judge to impose a secure hospital order rather than a sentence of imprisonment. This depends on the efficacy of the sentencing principle of treatment, which in this case was not supported by expert medical projections. In addition, while the accused's admissions may mitigate sentence in his favour, the totality of the offences under consideration outweighed any such impact.

In the *Turner* case the address in mitigation represents a valiant attempt not only to argue for lenient sentencing but also to influence the mind of the judge away from being compelled by legislation to impose an indeterminate sentence. This becomes a debate about whether in the face of prior case-law interpretations the situation of the accused was sufficient to be deemed exceptional.

The judge in *Turner* saw himself as bound by:

- a jury verdict which he may not have come to;
- legislation with which he did not agree; and
- judicial precedent which constrained his choices.

This then meant that the more regular influences on judicial discretion in sentencing, such as submissions on mitigation, the advice contained in the pre-sentence report and the threat posed to community safety by the accused are marginalized by more intrusive external restrictions on the exercise of sentencing independence. The particular issues of the case, which might have formulated a just outcome, were overtaken by broader and less flexible constitutional constraints.

Comparative contextual analysis of trial data

The comparative dimension of the narrative analysis presented so far is constrained by the nature of the transcript available. Our intention is that however the comparative endeavour is directed it should grow from detailed contextual analysis as that summarized in the preceding section. In order to draw out from the contextual analysis themes of similarity and difference the first phase of comparison is within each contextual trial situation against models for the action of decision-making sites and the decisions which eventuate (see Figures 3.2 and 3.3, Chapter 3).

The simple and initial analytical endeavour relates specifically to developing our understanding of how criminal trial processes and practices are constructed and negotiated in diverse jurisdictions, and how they relate to one another. The methodology is designed to facilitate the deconstruction of process where competing models of criminal justice and procedure operate,[4] and, ultimately, permit the identification of strategies for positive change in criminal justice policy, through trial transformation.

Our preliminary comparative analysis of trial decision-making in England and Italy necessarily focuses on the interpretation of discourse recorded in official accounts of the interaction which took place within these different, and perhaps unrepresentative, trial settings. In attempting to describe the rationale and operation of trial decision-making process we, therefore, acknowledge the limitations of narrative, whilst seeking to demonstrate that the analysis of narrative in context provides an important basis for comparative analysis.

The comparative focus is directed by the theoretical and modelling assumptions which underpin the adoption of this methodology (see further Henham and Findlay 2001b, 2002). Beyond the modelling exercise and its impact through contextual comparison, the data provide us with three further possibilities for comparison:

---

4 Namely, conventional adversarial or inquisitorial, or, as in Italy, a hybrid jurisdiction where trial process is in transition.

1 Similar decision sites in the same jurisdictions (sites 1 and 2 in the pre-sentence Italian transcripts).

2 Decision sites with practice knowledge of similar decision sites across two jurisdictions (sites 1 and 2 in the pre-sentence Italian transcripts compared with English trial practice relating to the oral examination of witnesses, and *vior dires*).

3 Similar decision sites across two jurisdictions and in different trials (sites 3 and 4 in Italian and English transcripts).

Any of these comparative directions will not exist outside their procedural (normative/structural) context. This is the implicit legal atmosphere within which the system of the trial operates and the discretion of its players is allowed. If the normative traditions of the trial sites are structurally different this should, one would assume, designate an initial terrain for comparison which the narrative should demonstrate. That this is not necessarily so, is one of the unique insights of the research. It represents a critical confirmation of the predominant and common influence of discretion/interaction rather than structure and system when it comes to trial decision-making.[5]

Narrative analysis

When confronting trial narrative the most immediate consideration is the voice. In the transcript with which we are dealing it is a judicial voice, but differing for whom it might speak.[6] Even from the narrative of the judicial voice there is evidence of interaction between players in the trial and it is possible to appreciate their relative significance.

---

5 Space precludes detailed description of the procedural traditions of England and Italy. As indicated earlier, it would be simplistic to take a normative comparison of the criminal procedure operating in the Italian and English courts as demonstrating some stark contrast between adversarial and inquisitorial traditions. In fact, the Italian legislature's express decision to favour an accusatorial model makes the hybrid and transitional state of Italian criminal procedure particularly attractive for comparative study. For detailed analysis of the Italian jurisdictional context, see Fassler (1991), Pizzi and Marafioti (1992), Freccero (1994), Zappala (1997), Gobert and Mugnai (2002), Henham and Mannozzi (2003), Mannozzi (2002b, 2003). For England, see Ashworth (1998, 2000a), McEwan (2000).

6 The single English judge or the representative of the Italian mixed bench.

Trial narrative here has at least two sources:

1 Primary source (trial transcript), wherein the obligations of the players are evident from the narrative, whether it comes from oral testimony or its interpretation.[7] The structural construction of the narrative should also be evident in this form, as the construction of rationales, and the significance of these rationales for the issues on trial and their conclusions (sites and outcomes).

2 Secondary sources (records of earlier investigations, preliminary hearings, reports). The contextualization of these sources within the trial narrative will add to the creative impact of the primary narrative and the manner with which it deals with the principal issues.

Having explored the participants in the narrative and its form, output considerations are pressing. At a structural/legal level description and determination of outcomes are possible, as they are in the context of the system/organization of the trial.[8] Structural and systemic levels of analysis should reveal the narrative as detailing enabled and actual trial outcomes, as well as the manner in which these were reached (see Figure 3.3, Chapter 3). The emphasis in the analysis below more commonly will be on process-type descriptions, actor relationships and judicial style, each being formative in the delivery of outcomes (decisions) from the perspective of discretion and interaction.

In order to test the utility and potential of trial narrative in the comparative endeavour we will focus on the sentencing transcripts, Italian and English. These we will broadly break down into verdict delivery and sentencing as sites for decision-making. Having identified the broad component of these sites in terms of our model we will move through the sites in our analysis towards the most specific and grounded decisions which go to make up these broader functions. The pathways of influence crucial to the production of verdict and sentence are suggested through the relationships referred to and depicted in the narrative.

---

7   Here even the narrative can move through layers of intimacy, representing conversations as they were in the trial, discussions of other narrative forms and summaries of interpretation (a narrative on the narrative).

8   In the trial contexts in question, these outcomes are constrained within a retributive justice paradigm.

Verdict delivery

In the English Crown Courts from which our two sentencing transcripts emerged, verdicts are delivered by a jury of twelve lay persons, randomly selected for the trial, and instructed on matters of law by the judge (Duff and Findlay 1982). The English common law tradition is that the jury is master of the facts while the judge determines and instructs on the law. This is also said therefore to differentiate responsibility for verdict delivery and sentencing. Even so, critics of this distinction between fact and law in the trial point to the judge's role in summing-up the facts to the jury and the emphasis placed in this process.

The *Corte d'assize* which delivered the Italian sentence transcript is composed of eight judges and is Italy's version of the European mixed tribunal. Two of the judges are professional judicial officers, one acting as an appellate judge and the President of this court and the other being a judge from the *Tribunale*. The remaining six 'judges' are lay people who participate in all aspects of the judicial process as *giudici poplari*. These popular judges are chosen randomly by the judicial council from the local electoral roll and serve for specified periods. Whilst it is said that both the lay and professional judges act as a unitary bench exercising equal and common judicial authority, it is the professional judge who delivers the sentence and no doubt has province over the law.

A distinct difference one might expect in the transcripts emanating from either court setting is the manner in which the judge deals with the evidence. Conventionally the English trial judge will exercise some energy in summarizing for the jury what he or she believes to be the material facts. This is not so common in trials where the judge may sit without a jury. It might be assumed that the summing-up is also not so detailed before the mixed tribunal. However, it seems that the Italian transcript reveals considerable application by the professional judges in their summing-up no doubt directed towards the popular judges exercising their fact-finding function.

As mentioned earlier, in the English jury trial it is said that the distinction between fact and law is clear and that the jury is the master of the facts, whilst the judge is of the law. Even here the distinction in practice is not quite so neat. The judge in his summing-up often gives preferred emphasis to certain 'facts' whilst commenting on the character of particular witnesses and the status of their evidence. The Italian judges appear to do the same. The jury, on the other hand, seeks of the judge explanations of the law which they then must interpret and apply in order to come to its verdict. No doubt the popular judges in Italy defer to the professional knowledge of the career judges in applying the law to their verdict deliberations as part of the bench, under the supervision of the President of the court.

The Italian mixed tribunal is responsible for both verdict delivery and the determination of sentence. In contrast with the jury's general verdict, *the Court d'assise* is constitutionally obliged to explain any decision it reaches, and both its factual premises and legal interpretations may be the subjects of appeal.[9]

The deliberative phase of the Italian trial is regulated by the code. The verdict is arrived at through a process of 'free conviction' or 'persuasion' of the individual judges (*libero convincimento del giudice*) based on 'weighty, accurate and concordant evidence'.[10] The judges may only consider evidence pertaining to the charges and the determination of sentence and such evidence must have been acquired legally and have been formally adduced at the trial.[11]

The bench is required to commence deliberations on verdict immediately that the trial is concluded. The deliberations are collegial with the President directing the discussion. First, any preliminary procedural matters which remain unsettled need to be determined. Each judge states his or her opinion on all major issues of fact or law, as well as appropriate sentences, and these are settled by a vote.[12] Decisions are on the basis of simple majority and, regarding penalty, if the bench is equally divided then the outcome most favourable to the accused prevails.

---

9   Article 111 of the Constitution requires that any dispositive judicial decision must be reasoned. The reasons must be explicit so that they can be scrutinized by public opinion or by an appellate court.

10   *CPP*, Art. 192.

11   *CPP*, Arts 187, 1912, 526.

12   Article 527 *CPP* (*Codice di Procedura Penale*) *Official Gazette, Code of Penal Procedure*. President of the Republic decree, 22 September 1988, n. 447, in ordinary supplement n. 1, general series, n. 250, 24 October 1988 (*Codice di procedurea penale*, Decreto del Presidente della Repubblica, 22 settembre 1988, n. 447, in supplemento ordinario n. 1, alla *Gazzetta Ufficiale*, serie generale, n. 250, 24 ottobre 1988).

Sentencing narrative as it reveals verdict delivery decision-making

The Italian trial transcript has the President announcing the verdict as a conclusion of their detailed reasoning. The tone is as a conclusion justified by a brief reference to motive and volition. The discussion of aggravating circumstances which precedes sentence continues the justification for the verdict against a range of evidentiary inter-pretations which impugn, for example, the accused's motives, character and credibility. The finding of innocence regarding the kidnapping in the Italian murder trial is the conclusion of an argument about the insufficiency of evidence. The only reference by the President to the influence of submissions by counsel for the defence involves the following:

- The dismissal of the principal accused's attempt to claim an abnormal mind as unsustainable, and his claim that a co-accused had carried out the murder as substantiating a charge of criminal liable.

- The dismissal of a claim by a co-accused that he failed to provide assistance to the victim out of 'necessity'. The elements of the defence were not substantiated.

Due to the English convention of jury trial in serious criminal cases, the pronouncement of verdict within the sentencing transcripts is recounted second-hand from the foreperson of the jury or the court reporter. No direct discussion or justification is presented on why they came to their verdict. In *Turner*, however, the judge seemed so unhappy about the sentencing consequences of the jury's decision he speculated that had they been aware of these they may have come to a different view.[13] A clue as to why the jury came to their decision might be found in the question they asked of the judge (during the deliberations) demonstrating a fundamental confusion about the mental state required to satisfy the elements of the offence. The judge's tone in passing sentence is constructed as if a jury's verdict cannot be impugned, but that is exactly what his narrative implies (incredulity).

---

13   'I cannot know on what basis they found [the accused] guilty ... but they did find you guilty, and we shall have to accept the verdict of the jury ... whether or not the sentencer agrees with the verdict of the jury, or sensed that the verdict of the jury was a harsh one, judging them against other juries is irrelevant ... I noticed the faces on the jurors when they were told that [the accused was] ... now subject to be sentenced to life imprisonment ...'

Perhaps the judge took some responsibility for the unhappy outcome as revealed in his discussion with counsel for the defence, after the jury retired, regarding the appropriateness of an alternative count (charge) in the indictment.[14] In *Fountain* the jury was unable to reach unanimous agreement, following which the judge sent them away again in search of a majority. After the judge was satisfied that 'this jury have had abundant time in which at least ten of them could arrive at a verdict in this case' he recalled them from their deliberations. The jury's representative declared them to be unable to decide a verdict, and as a result the judge (with his thanks) discharged the jury. In so doing he gave the suggestion that it may have been the question they had been asked which defied an easy answer.[15]

In the English and Italian transcripts, however, the process of verdict delivery is not directly recounted. The deliberations of the juries and of the bench of judges are not documented. Therefore, within the sentencing transcripts, the voices of those responsible for decisions on verdict are not directly heard.

Even so, the decision is declared and, significantly, if one is to assume that these decisions are informed by some logic born out of the trial, the matters most important to these deliberations are summarized. They involve:

1 the material evidence which is accepted as having bearing on guilt or innocence (and the reasons for its predominance); and

2 the interpretations of the law which are said to influence such things as the credibility of any defence raised.[16]

With these in mind the decision-site analysis of verdict delivery moves immediately down from the silent decision as verdict to the more apparent decisions which inform the verdict.

Decisions on material evidence

Employing our model in Figure 3.2 (Chapter 3) we can anticipate that the players (as demonstrated by the voice of the transcript) are the judges and, where appropriate, the recipient jurors. Even in the Italian

---

14 'It does not help. That is my fault. I am sorry I should have taken the initiative.'
15 'We recognise that the question, although I hope simply and clearly posed, is not one which necessarily for that reason admits of an easy answer and at least ten of you have been unable to reach a conclusion about it.'
16 Note the later critique of the place of the fact/law distinction within comparative trial narrative.

trial there is lay/professional interaction within the action of inter-pretation and reinterpretation. The nature and form of the normative constraints (procedural obligations) over lay/professional partici-pation, and whether this produces different atmospheres of interaction, may be at issue here.[17] Obviously, the exercise of judicial discretion by the judicial voice in the narrative is crucial to the process of interaction and influence. That voice of the narrative comes from the dominant judicial officer who, through the summing-up has control over levels of interpretation. For whom does the voice speak and what is its tone? Does the source of the narrative revert to judicial authority, or something essential to the process of lay/professional participation in the decision process here? The nature of, and reasons behind, these interpretations (and thus the exercise of discretion) will be significant to record. Whilst the overarching issue at this site relates to the way in which evidence is given materiality, lesser (but no less important) issues arise from the nature of the relationship between the lay and professional players.

Resulting from this consideration of process we should then be in a position to analyse decisions regarding materiality from several dif-ferent levels (see Figure 3.3, Chapter 3) and across trial contexts.

With the Italian sentencing transcript the parties to the decision about materiality[18] is the mixed bench of judges (two professional and six lay). Despite the normative ascription to the equality of the bench and its decision-making, the reality of deference to the professional means that the views of the career judges on what evidence was most useable would hold sway. This is emphasized through the voice of the narrative being that of the President of the bench, the senior career judge. No other voice (besides those quoted from examination in the trial) is heard. The voice is said to speak for the bench as if it is of one mind, up until the time that verdict and sentence are passed.

Normative (procedural) obligations regarding the admissibility of evidence recur throughout the transcript. For instance, the code provision that only documentary evidence which is available for oral interrogation will be admitted, is referred to during the discussion of what evidence is useable. In other instances reference is made to the need for the consent of the parties in order to introduce testimony from preliminary proceedings.

---

17   As our conclusions reveal concerning the fact/law distinction, this may have less significance than the exercise of discretion by trial professionals in their interaction with lay participants in decision-making.

18   The Italian trial narrative uses the terms supporting evidence or 'useable material'.

Another example of the influence of normative obligations is where certain evidence (such as police investigations) may be considered to be unnecessary because corroboration has been otherwise established.

The manner in which the President summarizes the facts (what he includes, excludes and emphasizes) will have an impact on decisions as to utility. Associated with this is the logical tone used to present the summary or 'case history', wherein what comes before is digested in a manner which tends to support the next stage as a logical step forward in the argument.[19]

The structural and narrative elements of the transcript become difficult to separate. For instance, an observation may be introduced by the declaration, 'It cannot be doubted that …' Structural tools are used to support the conclusions reached and to provide the momentum for the eventual justification of conclusions drawn.[20]

The transcript makes constant reference to what statements and what evidence can be used or linked to prove which aspects of the case. This, presumably, recognizes a detailed procedural framework within which such decisions are informed, though in the narrative this tends rarely to be made specific.

Another technique is to graduate the evidence of various witnesses in terms of its value. On several occasions the narrative voice comments that 'valuable information' was supplied, say, by third-party witnesses. In contrast the judge might observe that the testimony of another witness was 'unreliable'. The status of the witness as an expert will also imbue the evidence with an assumed and relative level of credibility.

The credibility of the witness, or lack of it, is advanced as another qualifier of the utility of his or her evidence. For instance, the principal accused is deemed to have craftily constructed a false alibi, this arguing against the need to test his psychological capacity, as well as enabling adverse inference to be drawn over his testimony. In addition, he is actually charged with slandering a co-accused and this tends further to taint his testimony.

Associated with this is the tendency to praise the contributions of certain professional participants in the trial. Thus the meticulousness of the public prosecutor is highlighted on more than one occasion.

---

19   Since this component of the transcript is quite lengthy this gives the impression of the solidity of the arguments it uses. Moreover, since the Italian sentences are often quite convoluted, this tone imbues the summary with a stylistic cohesion.

20   'As will be shown later on, the conclusions reached by the forensic experts regarding the cause of … death are an indispensable point of departure for the evaluation of the guilt of the principal defendant.'

The theories of the President are given the status of fact on certain occasions, perhaps due to the convincing nature of circumstantial evidence. 'It is perfectly reasonable to hypothesize' is the introduction to a conclusion about the location of other criminal activity not covered by the charges in hand. In other instances the style and tone of the narrative become stronger in order to support conjecture.[21]

The transcript moves from comments on case history to a more conventional form of summing-up. This is where the scene setting begins. The narrative takes on a more descriptive tone. It is a subtle but effective effort to describe the cynical and exploitative criminal network, and in particular when prostitution is referred to it is 'exploitative'. There is an occasional digression into almost journalistic account.[22] It also sounds in part conjectural as if the judges are thinking and the listener is invited to participate with them in coming to logical conclusions. The implication here is intimate.

Another narrative technique tending to reinterpret the evidence is the judge's juxtaposition of the victim as tragic and the accused as clear-headed and calculating. The tone and content of the summing-up when referring to the victim in particular serve to emphasize the image of exploiting the weak and vulnerable. This is coupled with recurrent references to the principal defendant changing his story[23] in order to blame a co-defendant, and the court's decision to deny him a psychiatric assessment:[24] '[His] unreliability can also be seen in relation to his attempt to lay the entire responsibility for the murder on [the co-accused] …'. This then is immediately followed by reference to the criminal slander charge against the principal accused. The court describes his efforts at challenging certain times and events expressed in the testimony of others as 'ridiculous'.

Tone takes on another significance when sarcasm is employed to diminish the defence. The President backs up his conclusion that the accused must have been aware of the dangerous consequences of their actions: 'It doesn't take a doctor or any specific medical knowledge to

---

21   'This would seemingly be inexplicable unless …'
22   'But there is more.'
23   'In order to limit or deny his own role in the offences [the accused] did not hesitate to blame his co-defendants for the crimes of which he was accused and to claim a sequence of movements even when this was clearly contradicted by documentary evidence.'
24   This tends to emphasize the continuing inferior position of the defence when set against the deliberative power of the judge. In common law trials, in contrast, the accused would present psychiatric evidence on his own part without seeking the authority or approval of the court.

see ...' This is accompanied with a more ordinary, matter-of-fact linguistic register.

The importance of secondary transcript such as police records of interview, whilst now conditional on certain procedural requirements, prevails throughout the narrative. Such transcript appears crucial to the construction of oral examination later referred to. In addition, it is used by the judge also to draw conclusions concerning the veracity of particular testimony. For instance, the statements of a female witness are accorded standing through the implication that it was very difficult for her to respond to the prosecutor because of the conflicting pressures she faced in giving evidence.[25] Beyond the testimony of the witness itself reference is made to her psychological state during questioning. The resultant evidence is contextualized in order to emphasize its reliability. The evidence of another female witness is deemed 'perfectly coherent and reliable' and admissible because it was corroborated by the statements of experts at the preliminary hearing.

The demeanour of witnesses is also juxtaposed against the substance of their defence so as to damage their character and hence the reliability of their testimony: 'The lucidity – or rather, the artfulness [*slyness, cunning*] – with which [the principal accused] handled his trial contrasts patently with his defence, which maintains his total or partial incapacity to understand events.' The narrative reflects on those witnesses in preliminary hearings or those interrogated by police whose evidence was inadmissible at the trial because it was unavailable for cross-examination. Obviously in an effort to recognize normative obligations as to admissibility the court reminds itself that the 'evaluation of guilt' should not only depend on 'testimony given and technical investigations' but also on the oral accusations made by some of the co-defendants.

A significant component of the summing-up is direct reference to the examination of two female witnesses, both of whom have been characterized in the narrative as credible and providing useful testimony. These large blocks of direct oral testimony are introduced as being of 'particular interest' and being 'particularly useful'.

Taken as a process, the decisions on the materiality of evidence revealed in the Italian sentencing transcript have the voice of the President of the court speaking on behalf of the bench and at the same time revealing the instances of influence that the career judges will have

---

25   'She was torn between the need to defend her uncle and the difficulty of rebutting the specific contentions of the public prosecutor who was questioning her.'

over their lay brethren. The narrative has the interaction between the lay and professional judges implicit in the process of reinterpreting in detail the evidence from the trial. This reinterpretation is particular and personalized beyond just the needs of a general audience. The action is about summarizing, prioritizing, regarding and disregarding contested evidence. It is to fill with meaning what may be problematic. It is to draw inferences from the connection of attitude, behaviour and intention, with pronouncement. The process is constrained by normative obligations but remains highly discretionary. The narrative gains its authority as the voice of the President and supposedly the collective mind of the bench. Its argument and justification are drawn from all levels of investigation and trial. The issue is both whether the evidence is enough as proof for the purposes of a verdict and whether it exposes matters which should influence sanction.

Moving the analysis across to output considerations it is compelling to examine more individual and specific decisions arising out of the materiality process. Take for instance the decision to reject the defence proposed by the principal accused that he was not responsible because the murder had been committed by the co-accused. How did this come about and how can it be explained? What then does it say about the trial process? At the structural/legal level:

- It was necessary for the principal accused to present oral evidence in addition to his previous testimony for the argument to be given standing in the trial narrative.

- The explanation therefore would have received a sympathetic introduction from the defence advocate and would have been critiqued (tested) by the prosecutor.

- The judicial voice doubted the explanation because the judge thought that it contradicted other accounts, and was inconsistent with the accused's attempt to pressure a co-defendant into supporting a false alibi for him.

- The demeanour of the principal accused as a witness, his artfulness and cunning are deemed to reduce his credibility.

- His relationship with the victim, and with co-accused, further impugns his character in the eyes of the judge.

- Finally his inconsistent claim that he required psychiatric assessment in the face of the manner in which he used the opportunity to implicate others in order to deny his guilt.

Justice (fair trial) requires that the accused be heard. Whilst the ideology of fair trial places the accused in a dominant position in the trial, the narrative reveals his impotence to respond to the judge's interpretation of his character and true intentions. With the narrative as a solo voice it is impossible to determine whether the judge's evaluation is fair or accurate and whether it represents the common opinion of each and all the judges who witnessed his trial.

The physical context or oral testimony in the trial, as well as its interpretation through the power and presence of the judge, give the defence a crucial if vulnerable place in the development of the verdict and sentence. It must be confronted by all the professional parties, and managed in favour of an eventual outcome.

The enabled outcome of a structural/legal analysis of the accused's defence is that it is neither substantiated nor true. As a consequence the infection of his remaining testimony is inevitable.

At a system/organizational level we must ask what was the interactive process which produced details of the defence, and in turn judicial opinion concerning its veracity. The procedural constraints of police interrogation, pre-trial and trial testimony create an atmosphere of inconsistency. The requirement that the accused deliver his defence in response to examination and cross-examination, before adjudication, makes for a stylized presentation. Then his version of the truth is placed against so many others; the stories of those with whom the narrative voice openly expresses more empathy and credibility. The professional interrogators have status and interests designed to colour and constrain the voice of the accused and ultimately his story is dependent on the interpretation of the judge in order to place it within (or exclude it from) the facts to influence verdict and sentence. By fitting the defendant's story within the social practice of oral testimony in the trial (against the background of other layers of pre-trial narrative) it has no independent existence. As with the accused himself, his defence depends on a managed series of reproducible social practices.

In terms of a discretionary/interactive analysis again the position of the accused *vis à vis* the professional players in the trial, and with other witnesses, is crucial to the ultimate decision on the credibility of the defence. In the case of the Italian sentencing narrative, the relationship between the principal defendant and the victim is particularly telling in terms of the reception by the judge of the victim's plight and the assumptions drawn concerning the accused's role in it. This seems almost enough to:

• credit certain testimony as truth;

- discredit the accused's contradiction of such evidence; and
- in turn, credit and discredit the witnesses against the accused and confirm the relative merit of unconnected testimony.

Judicial style is against the accused, ranging from quizzical to sarcastic and dismissive. Whilst the judge was compelled to tolerate the presentation of this false defence he took the opportunity to refuse psychiatric tests which might contribute towards it, or to explain away other features about which the judicial voice was critical. In discrediting the defence the judicial voice adopted structures and tones, as well as consciously drawing conclusions that would justify an adverse verdict and a heavy penalty. The destruction of the accused and his defence is crucial to this outcome.

The actual outcome of the decision-making process in the Italian murder trial was to dismiss the defence, but more than that, to damage the credibility of the accused as a wider witness and to advance the reliability of those whose testimony contradicted that of the principal accused.

To prepare the comparative contextual foundation, the same progress of analysis needs to be employed in the decision site of evidence materiality as revealed in the English sentencing transcripts. Take, for example, the sentencing decision in *Fountain*'s case. As with the convention in the English higher courts the judge's summing-up comprises two parts: directions to the jury regarding matters of law, and then a summary of the evidence which deals with oral testimony, written record and statements.

Despite the fact that the judge's voice here[26] is speaking to the jury[27] there is little or no interaction between the two functions, which share some responsibilities for fact and law. This is despite the fact the judge tends to apologize that when he reviews the facts he may trespass on the jury's territory: 'If I appear to express a view about those facts, then remember that it is your view that matters and not mine as you alone are the judges of the facts.'[28]

---

26   In these trials there is a single professional judge, sitting with a jury of twelve lay people who are responsible for the verdict.

27   For instance he commences: 'In this case, ladies and gentlemen, I am the judge of law and you twelve ladies and gentlemen and nobody else are the judges of fact.'

28   That the judge feels compelled to advance this instruction is evidence at least that he appreciates the potential influence that the judge's summing-up can have over the jury's deliberations, and the delicacy of the distinction between fact and law and the roles of judge and jury.

The judge sets the tone from the outset by referring to the 'distressing compass' of the facts and that they are 'nearly all agreed'. He then lays claim to determinations of the law.[29] Immediately he identifies where the law and the facts collide by indicating what they must decide: 'It is for the prosecution to prove [the accused's] guilt of the offence charged, to make you sure that he is guilty of the offence of murder.' This then requires that the elements of the offence be declared. In proceeding to this direction the judge refers to the jury having 'been correctly told what it is at least twice already'; a reference no doubt to the addresses of the prosecution and the defence. Linked to this direction is an issue which if unsuccessfully disproved by the prosecution, would diminish the offence from murder to manslaughter, and this is a central issue towards which the remaining evidence is adduced. In particular, the essential status of expert medical opinion is foreshadowed.

Early in his instructions the judge refers to a defence tactic regarding the admission of the accused's prior criminal history. Normally the defence is entitled to have this kept from the jury during the trial but here it was presented in order to help provide the context of his claim that he was suffering from some abnormality of the mind at the time of the attack. In relation to this abnormality, it rests with the defence to establish it at a reduced burden of proof than that borne by the prosecution.

For the defence of diminished responsibility, the judge decides to circulate to the jury a written direction. Therefore, the narrative takes on a dual form, both for credibility and clarity. The complexities of proof in relation to the defence of diminished responsibility tend to justify this additional form of narrative. The instruction on the law is detailed and unequivocal. The importance of expert medical testimony as part of the proof process is emphasized. The judge reminds the jury of 'the relevant parts' of such testimony but cautions that 'although medical evidence on both sides is important, you should consider not only the medical evidence, but the evidence as to the whole facts and circumstances of the case'.[30] The consensus of all the medical evidence from both sides will no doubt make it more influential.[31] Despite the medical consensus it is still for the jury to find that the identified

---

29 'The law ... you will take from me.'

30 This might be read as an attempt to tackle the disproportionate influence which scientific/professional testimony may have over other types of evidence.

31 'So you may think, although it remains a matter for you, because I have just directed that it is trial by you, the jury, not a trial by doctors, none the less, you may think, in fairness and justice you need not concern yourself much or at all with [the elements of the defence] because all the doctors are agreed about it.'

abnormality was sufficient to relieve the accused of criminal responsibility for murder. This appears to be the issue about which the jury could not produce agreement and hence a verdict.

Moving on to the summing-up of the evidence, the task is made less problematic for the judge because there is so little in contest. As part of this exercise the judge draws at length, but selectively, from the transcript of prior police records of interview. Again, the judge warns that whilst he is trespassing on the jury's domain over the facts it is still for them to determine within and outside his summary what is worthy of attention. The interviews are said only to form part of a total of many more hours of secondary narrative. The jury is given the benefit of consulting written text of the police interrogation whilst the judge takes them through it in summary. Part of the narrative then becomes the voice of the accused in answering questions. Narrative introduced into the narrative in this manner gives it immediacy and an intimacy which is telling. Through the process of introducing the secondary transcript to the jury the judge occasionally relies on the prosecutor for clarification.

Leaving the police records of interview the judge asks: 'What else is there in the prosecution case, members of the jury, which serves, you may think to illuminate the one issue you have to decide?' There is narrative cross-examination of a police officer who develops the prior criminal history of the accused in light of the assertion that he suffered from an abnormality of the mind. This was intended to correspond with the defence submission that the behaviour of the accused was consistent with 'an entrenched attitude of serious aggression and social irresponsibility'. The rebuttal of the charge of murder offered in oral evidence by the defence was then commented upon and in particular the evidence of the accused.

The judge commences on the issue of demeanour: 'You saw and heard [the accused]. You will make up your own mind about him.' The accused detailed his 'unhappy and deeply troubled life'. The judge mentions the accused's full acknowledgement of the attack which killed the victim.

Finally, the psychiatric evidence is returned to. Doctors' reports on the accused's relevant drug abuse are recounted in their oral form. Social service records are part of the narrative on which the report is based. Doctors' conclusions are presented without comment on their evidentiary status.

At the completion of the summing-up of evidence the judge directs on the return of unanimous and majority verdicts and the jury is instructed to retire.

Several hours later the jury returns with the news that no verdict has been reached. The judge instructs them on the process for achieving a majority verdict and they are retired a second time. Again in the absence of the jury the prosecution submits that because of the timing of the jury's retirement, and the intervention of lunch and the onset of the court's rising, that the judge should call them back tomorrow if they were still unable to reach a verdict at the close of the day. The prosecutor refers the judge to principles in support which are testily received. The submission is rejected preparing the way for the judge to dismiss the jury when it later returns unable to reach even a majority verdict. A reason for this might be the judge's view that the prosecution should be willing to accept the lesser verdict of manslaughter, and to which the defence was willing to plead. After all, this was the outcome about which the jury remained in doubt. In fact, the judge directly asks the prosecutor 'where does this leave us?' The prosecution concedes that a retrial would be inappropriate in the circumstances with which the judge 'entirely agrees'. The judge, as a consequence, indicates the sentence he is minded to give and suggests to counsel for the defence that he considers this in reflecting on his remarks in mitigation. In order that the jury is not confused (or perhaps frustrated at the consequences of their efforts) the judge indicates that his sentence resulting from a murder conviction or manslaughter on the basis of diminished responsibility would be the same. The accused is then called to plead guilty to manslaughter which he does.[32]

The manner in which the verdict arises in this case offers a unique opportunity for 'output analysis'. The interaction between the players is particularly revealing. The judge is at pains to direct the jurors that they are responsible for determining the facts, whilst at the same time admitting on several occasions that he 'trespasses' on this responsibility in his summary of the evidence and in particular with his management of the medical evidence. The judge also claims responsibility for interpreting the law but then offers to the jury the only issue in conflict being whether the accused at the time of the attack was suffering under an abnormality of the mind and if so whether this was sufficient to reduce his criminal liability. At least from the difficulty evidenced by the jurors in determining these issues, we could not say in the face of almost entirely consensual evidence before them that they were only wrestling with the facts. In reality it must have been the application

---

32 Interestingly, his lawyer asks the judge whether he might stand with his client at the time: 'It becomes a little bit complicated and I think there may be a need to prompt.' What does this say about the status of the accused in the trial and the lay/professional relationship? Who is actually making the decision on plea here?

of the law concerning abnormality and substantial impairment which confused their deliberations. And with the institutional (environmental) and structural (functional) barriers to free and open communication between the jury and the judge, the merging of their responsibilities in the deliberation process failed to produce a decision. It might also be said that this is evidence of the impracticality and irrationality of the fact/law distinction and the symbolic and functional demarcation of duties between the professional and lay players in the verdict delivery process. Due to the absence of a voice for the jury in the narrative, the only way we can appreciate the difficulties associated with verdict delivery here is to put the voice of the judge against the features of the outcome. This case is suited to this because of the following variables:

- The facts beyond the issue of diminished responsibility are not in contest.
- The judge is unequivocal about the responsibility of the jury.
- Unanimity of verdict is attempted and fails.
- Majority verdict is invited and fails.
- Except in the case of an acquittal, which was so unlikely as to be not a possible outcome, the decision on verdict would not have had an impact on the consequential sentencing outcome.

The obligations on lay and professional players in the verdict delivery site are clear from the transcript despite the absence of a voice for the jury. The status of the judge as dominant over all trial outcomes (even verdict) is demonstrated through his discharging of the jury and inviting the prosecution to accept a plea to a lesser charge. The terms for such a resolution were also foreshadowed by the judge, when he indicated that the sentence would not change as a consequence.

Insights into the professional roles of legal counsel are also apparent from the narrative, particularly as it relates to the interaction with the judge following the discharge of the jury. In his acquiescence to the new plea, rather than arguing for a retrial, the prosecutor identifies as influential over the exercise of his professional discretion (effecting his decision to what outcome he will argue for) the following:

- A structural issue (the sentencing powers of the judge).
- A systems issue (the narrowness of the issue in context).
- A discretionary issue (the nature and application of the psychiatric evidence).
- A systems/structure/discretion issue (cost of a retrial).

This is presented in the narrative as an answer to the judge's rhetoric 'what next'. It is clear from what follows that the judge has made up his mind in any case and the discretionary decision to discharge the jury when he did, precipitated this. In reality, what we have is bargaining amongst professionals, each with discretionary powers which impact on the other:

- The judge can discharge the jury without a verdict.
- The prosecutor can refrain from seeking a retrial.
- On the condition that the defence are willing to plead to the lesser charge.

So much of this, while precipitated by the jury's failure to agree, and the accused's agreement to accept the lesser charge, is not influenced by the lay participants. What clearly demonstrates this is the narrative conversation between the judge and counsel for the defence concerning the intentions of the accused. The prosecutor indicates his decision is conditional on the accused pleading guilty to manslaughter. The judge asks the defence whether 'this is in accordance with your position?' The judge interrupts the response by suggesting that one of the defence lawyers goes to the dock where the accused is standing in order to 'explain the implications' to the accused. This is followed by a 'set piece' in which the accused pleads 'not guilty but guilty to manslaughter'. The defence explain that this is on the basis of the diminished responsibility submission and the judge now anticipates this as agreeable in the circumstances to the prosecution, which it is.

In this case the outcome seems to have taken almost a secondary place to the structural obligations for its production, the systemic impediments to it and the discretionary interplay which brings it about outside the jury. The issue here is the manner in which through the dominant exercise of judicial discretion a resolution is achieved by professional compromise. Of subsidiary, but no less important, significance is the conditional reality of the fact/law distinction and its functional consequences for lay/professional interaction in verdict delivery.

Turner's case presents a different sentencing narrative in that whilst its form is similar to *Fountain* its substance is (as with the Italian sentencing transcript) much more focused on the materiality of disputed evidence. As a sentencing transcript the judicial voice reflects (similar to *Fountain*) concerns regarding the consequences of a guilty verdict when normative, legislative structures directed towards offence seriousness are in place.

The transcript again divides into directions and summing-up. The jury is enjoined to:

> ... bear in mind that when I [the judge] turn to [summarize the evidence] I am very much on your ground because you are the judges of fact. That means members of the jury, you decide who you believe and to what extent you believe them. You determine what facts you can be sure of and what proper inferences you can draw from those facts. That is all your province and you must jealously regard it.

The judge indicates that the jury may detect his 'point of view' in summing up. If the jury shares that view, so be it, but if not 'it is your duty to disagree and bring that disagreement out in your determination'. In fact, the outcome of the verdict decision site in this trial suggests that this in fact occurred.

The judicial voice talks of the requirements of proof which should satisfy the verdict deliverer. The standard instructions are given but, in particular here, because the accused took the unusual step of giving oral evidence in the trial, jurors are reminded that 'he does not by going into the witness box and giving evidence take upon himself any burden ... he does not have to prove that he was defending himself.' The judge then confronts the problem of what is meant by proof. His explanation reveals the difficulty in translating legal obligations and norms into a narrative which may be understood and applied by lay participants such as jurors:

> If at the end of the day the Crown [prosecutors] have made you sure that the defendant is guilty of the offence as defined by me then they will have proved the case and if you are sure it will be your duty to find him guilty. If you are less than sure, even if you think it is more likely than not that he is guilty but you are less than sure, it is equally your duty to find him not guilty.

In explaining the elements of the offence the judge observes the 'old-fashioned' language employed in the charge.[33] Even so the legal issues are said to be simple: was there an unlawful wounding of the victim by the accused and, if so, was it committed with an intention to inflict really serious harm? It is the issue of intent which seems to exercise the

---

33   Interestingly, the judge is insistent that each juror be provided with a copy of the indictment for the purposes of their deliberations.

mind of the judge and of the jury. This is particularly so when the intent must be unlawful (i.e. the accused would be justified if the attack had been intentional for the purposes of self-defence). As self-defence has been argued at trial by the accused the judge instructs the jury on what the prosecution must do to disprove the assertion.

Regarding self-defence, this is the principal area of contest in the facts. The accused argued at trial that he was doing no more than to ward of the attack of the victim. The jury needs to consider this and also whether in retaliating he acted unreasonably. There are a number of factual decisions necessary in the face of conflicting stories which require resolution in order to conclude on the larger issue of self-defence. To get to this point the jury will have to examine the evidence, as to form and substance, in favour and against such a contention.

The judicial voice insinuates a view concerning the more appropriate charge in this case. The judge invites the jury that if they are not persuaded on self-defence then they could consider a lesser form of assault (i.e. unlawful wounding without the intent to injure seriously).

The only other matter requiring judicial direction is the status of a prior statement from a defence witness, read out in the trial and where the deponent was not available for cross-examination. As this was the only witness supporting the defendant the testimony takes on particular significance. The judge suggests two matters on which the jury should reflect when considering the evidence. First that they 'have not seen the person in the witness box'. The judge opines that to see the witness sometimes 'helps you come to a conclusion about whether a person is telling the truth or not if you can see them and see the way they react'. This is a clear admission that more than the narrative is accepted as being influential over fact-finding. The second issue is that because the witness was not available for oral testimony the prosecution could not test his evidence through cross-examination but nor could the defence have the visual and oral benefit of a witness who may otherwise have been very good for the defence. The judge opens his summing-up with the observation that the evidence contained in the statement is not conclusive about anything, in his view, but might provide an insight into the defendant's character if it were accepted.

The summing-up comprises a review of the course of events which culminated in the assault, highlighting the points at which the prosecution evidence and the contentions of the accused differ. These principally relate to the verbal and physical exchanges which occurred at the home of the victim and how these were to be reasonably interpreted in light of the accused's allegation that he was acting in self-defence. The rest of the evidence is described by the judge as being of a rather formal nature, including medical and forensic reports. The secondary narrative in the form of police records of interview is made available to the jury to 'read at your hearts' content'.[34]

The summing-up is concluded by reviewing the limited evidence for the accused, along with a reiteration of what the defence is not required to prove. The jury is then invited to retire to consider its verdict with the reassurance that they were under no pressure to do so.[35] Specifically they are enjoined to come to a decision on whether the charge of unlawful wounding with intent has been proved.

During the jury's retirement the judge admits some reservation in not having the alternative verdict arising from a lesser charge of wounding made more available by being on the indictment. He takes responsibility for this and apologizes to counsel for the defence who responds that he is content that the jury are aware of all matters.[36]

The jury return with a question regarding the elements of the offence, in particular when intent must exist in order for the charge to be proved. Interestingly the narrative does not recite the jury's question and it becomes necessary to take inference from what the judge says to counsel he intends for the jury to ask themselves. In this way it might be said that the interrogatory is dealt with by another interrogatory. The judge then recalls the jury and as agreed with counsel instructs them on the coincidence of intention and the assault as well as the consequence of the intention being to cause really serious injury: 'In judging intention you have to look at all the surrounding circumstances.' The second part of the direction reiterates the reservations that intention here can exist and still be lawful if the prosecution is unable to disprove the accused's assertion of acting in self-defence. The jury returns a guilty verdict a short time later.

The verdict is met by some dismay from the judge to which we have referred in an earlier section. In passing sentence the judge cannot say on what basis the jury found guilt and he alludes to the fact that he may not agree with the jury. He even implies that some might see it as a

---

34 This seems to suggest some flippancy on the part of the judge when dealing with the detail of the evidence. It might be explained by what appears to be the judge's predetermined view of the merits of the case as requiring an obvious outcome.

35 Note the light-hearted way the judge apologizes that they cannot take their lunch in the sunshine and that their food may not be Egon Ronay but it will be something.

36 It is as if the judge now suspects that the jury may convict on the more serious charge and he is looking for someone else to blame.

harsh verdict but there was nothing he could do about it, nor the sentencing consequences it provokes of which he is directly critical. The injustice and the harshness of the verdict appear to be expressed in the faces of the jurors when they hear that a life sentence is to result. The judge says it is up to the civilized society rather than him to remedy the injustice.

In this we have a clear critique of the consequences of verdict delivery in normative and structural terms, one which cannot be remedied by discretion and interaction. The judicial personality and the status of the judge have failed to see justice done. The decision of the lay participants in the context of constitutional legality has produced injustice from the view of the narrative.

This might be understood as evidence that structural/systemic features of trial decision-making have predominated over the discretionary influences flowing in professional/lay interaction. The judge appears to have been unable to govern the outcome through implication and trespassing into the facts. It is, however, the treatment of this determination in the judge's narrative which strengthens the view that such influence commonly predicts the outcome to the satisfaction of the judge and it is this contradictory result which stands in such contrast to this decision-making custom.

Decisions on legal interpretation

At the pre-sentence stage, the issues concerning legal interpretation focus either on specific instructions about the law (reiterating the fact/law distinction) or on occasions where the elements of the offence are tested against the evidence. In reference to the latter, one section of the Italian sentencing transcript is entitled 'material and psychological factors of the offence of murder'. The court makes an early finding that it does not believe the principal aim for kidnapping the victim was to kill her. Even so, and in keeping with the mental state required for murder, the court went on to hold that the accused despite being: 'well aware of the seriousness of the situation and the danger that the victim was in, the defendants carried on inflicting cruelty on the poor thing in a kind of group frenzy.'[37]

It is when legal proofs are compared with the available evidence that sufficiency of evidence to satisfy the burden of proof is emphasized.

---

37 In the Italian this implies a loss of control and even pleasure. This ties in with later suggestions that the accused were subject to a kind of group psychology where each was encouraged by the behaviour of the rest.

Conjecture or circumstantial evidence are not sufficient.[38] Having said this the Italian sentencing transcript goes on to suggest that the existence of probable (consequential) intent could, in the circumstances, be deduced from the defendants' actions, without the need to apply the law regarding possible consequences.

What seems to be coming out of this feature of the transcript is that the distinction between the letter of the law, the oral evidence which may support or challenge it, and more intangible considerations such as the demeanour and credibility of the principal accused have become impossible to disentangle. So we have suggested to the reader that the accused should have thought in a particular way for not to would make no sense against other circumstances of the case. Such a conflation of the fact/law distinction may not only question the objective reality of oral evidence narrative, but also introduces innuendo into the construction of legal interpretation and reality. Does this mean that the discretionary/interactive levels of analysis (suggested in Chapter 3) would prevail in a consideration of the connection between law and fact in verdict delivery? Are the status of the players, the judicial style and the nature of interactive decision-making more likely to reveal the fact/law distinction for what it is worth rather than an examination of normative principles, or systemic stages? Perhaps this is where a consideration of the difference between enabled outcomes and actual outcomes is helpful.[39]

Such challenges to the fact/law distinction may take on structural and systemic resonance in trial procedures wherein a clearer institutional line is drawn between fact-finding and legal direction. Or do they? In the review of the English transcript material we have already identified a number of occasions where the judicial voice celebrates the fact/law distinction, whilst the summing-up trespasses the divide. In decision-making terms, and the relationship between lay and professional players in particular, how much does this reveal about where fact is determined, and how its objective reality once settled (if this can be said) influences verdict delivery?

---

38 'It is certainly a sign of a precise and wilful intention to kill, the mental state for murder, if one has seen evidence that the victim's life is in danger and yet continues to beat her. But the proceedings have not been able to prove this.'

39 For instance, in jury trials the symbolic distinction between the provinces of fact and law enables the jury to claim its legitimate presence and some might say the judge to avoid the consequences of sentencing. The actual outcome of verdict delivery, however, is only to be understood in terms of a Figure 3.2 analysis if the interaction between lay and professional players is viewed beyond the simple narrative of fact/law distinctions.

In both English sentencing transcripts the jury appears to appreciate the judicial ordering of, and emphasis on, the facts. They rely on judicial interpretation of law as the context within which to apply the facts to the legal and moral questions of guilt and innocence. In so doing they seem never to be free of judicial influence over fact and law, despite the distinction. Yet is there an essential and logical connection between decisions on fact (verdict) and those of law (sentence)? The Italian trial narrative suggests otherwise.

In one of the English transcripts the verdict proves to be largely irrelevant to the eventual sentence and sanction. In the other, the judge seems dismayed that his influence did not bring about another verdict despite his recitation that the responsibility for verdict delivery was with the jury alone.

It might be assumed that the fact/law distinction would be less rigid in the Italian trial context where both in structural and systemic terms the fact-finding and law-determining roles rest with the collegiate bench. However, the reality of the distinction appears to lie more in the division between the lay and professional participants in verdict delivery, and their differential purchase on the meaning of the law. The maintenance of the fact/law divide is more likely to be a product of deferential participant status, judicial style and the real nature of collective decision-making, than as some consequence of different decision-making structures or systems for determining fact. In their sentencing remarks the Italian judges constantly return to their version of the facts in justification. Again, the application of fact to law seems to rest more on discretionary connections between issues such as demeanour, credit, blame and sanction, than on structural and system divisions in decision-making such as verdict and sentence delivery.

The status of the judge and the exercise of judicial discretion appear both to reinforce the fact/law divide whilst traversing it as part of pragmatic accommodations in verdict delivery.

It might also be assumed that coming from an inquisitorial tradition with more interventionist judicial action in the trial the impact of judicial discretion in professional/lay interaction within Italian trials would be more marked than that evidenced in the English transcripts. Despite the constant reference by the English judicial voice to respecting the independence of the jury, and the procedural restrictions on juror/judge communication, the direction of the English sentencing narrative (pre-verdict) is entirely judge to jury. The judge is saying, interpreting, directing and implicating all to the jury. He is the master of the action.

A way to test the relative superiority of a discretionary/interactive analysis of trial decision-making in favour of structures or systems is revealed through a comparison of how the Italian and English courts treat the facts and instruct on the law. If structure and systems were supreme then enabled and actual outcomes in the two trial styles should differ.

Sentencing

In the Italian criminal trial procedure the court announces its judgement (*sentenza*) after its deliberations on verdict and sentence. In the case of an acquittal the court will differentiate between the various factual and legal grounds essential to the decision. In case of a conviction the court deals with matters of aggravation and mitigation as part of its justification of sentence. It will then specify sanctions and penalty. The court will also, where required, issue orders for the disposition of any properly constituted civil action attached to the trial.

A radical innovation in the new Italian penal code is a form of negotiated sentence or 'application of the penalty on the request of the parties'.[40] The defendant may enter into an agreement or a bargain to forgo a full trial in return for a reduction of up to one third of the possible sentence for the charge so long as the resulting sentence does not exceed two years' imprisonment. This agreement may be entered into at any time right up to the presentation of the opening statements in the trial. The agreement is then presented before a judge for verification.

English sentencing procedure involves three distinct phases. Following verdict delivery the judge may either decide to proceed immediately to the determination of sentence or, more commonly (obligatory where imprisonment is a possibility), adjourn the proceedings so that pre-sentence reports on the offender can be prepared. Essentially, the procedure before sentence involves the following:

- Establishing the facts of the offence for the purpose of sentence.

---

40 Arts 444–448 *CPP* (*Codice di Procedura Penale*) *Official Gazette, Code of Penal Procedure.* President of the Republic decree, 22 September 1988, n. 447, in ordinary supplement n. 1, general series, n. 250, 24 October 1988 (*Codice di procedurea penale*, Decreto del Presidente della Repubblica, 22 settembre 1988, n. 447, in supplemento ordinario n. 1, alla *Gazzetta Ufficiale*, serie generale, n. 250, 24 ottobre 1988).

- Establishing the defendant's previous criminal record and its significance.
- Receiving reports about the offender's background and mental state.
- Hearing submissions in mitigation from the defence.

The judicial determination of sentence is primarily concerned with the assessment of offence seriousness for desert purposes, and the individualization of the sentence. Subsidiary sentencing objectives such as rehabilitation may be satisfied within the over-riding deserts framework.[41] Hence, the following are generally taken into account:

- Report recommendations;
- Aggravating and mitigating circumstances;
- The need for public protection; and
- Victim factors.

Mitigation might include, for instance, the need to determine an appropriate sentence discount[42] where the offender has made a timely guilty plea. As indicated earlier, there is nothing approximating the form of 'negotiated sentence' available in English sentencing law but, in any event, the fact that the Italian system is based on mandatory prosecution means that that the rationale underlying such sentence bargains is quite different. As Mannozzi (1999) points out, the Italian prosecutor has nothing to gain from any sentence reduction since the sentence discount does not amount to a reward – it is not exchanged for a guilty plea. Although a punishment, the sentence that concludes the trial does not amount to the equivalent of an admission of guilt on the part of the accused. The only prosecutorial advantage is that gained through not having to proceed further with the prosecution and curtailing any additional gathering of evidence.[43] In the English trial the accused may negotiate over counts on the indictment, in which case the

---

41   Most obviously through satisfying the criteria for sentences such as community service and probation orders.
42   Normally, one third.
43   However, the pre-trial summary trial procedure available under Art. 442 *CPP* is not dissimilar to the English 'plea before venue procedure', whereby if an offender pleads guilty before the magistrates' court, the court may (provided certain conditions are met) proceed directly to sentence. The efficacy of this procedure in terms of dissuading defendants from proceeding to Crown Court trial depends on their being some tangible difference, i.e. a discount on sentence available for pleading before the magistrates. However, no research has ever been conducted to discover whether this is in fact the case.

judge is usually asked to express his or her view as to the suitability of the arrangement before the hearing commences. Under the statutory sentence discount system the accused is essentially rewarded for an early indication of guilt.

The pronouncement of sentence in an English trial is governed by numerous legislative and practice requirements as to form and transparency. In addition to having both legal and policy significance, the sentencing remarks made by the judge may (but need not) allude to the particular objectives it is hoped will be achieved by the sentence, and relate these to wider communitarian concerns, such as deterrence. The most obvious requirement for transparency now comes from art. 6 of the ECHR but, notwithstanding, the reasons articulated by the judge at this stage have added significance in the case of an appeal.[44] In cases of preventative detention, judges also have the unenviable task of determining the future dangerousness of offenders as a justification for extended sentences and supervision. In such cases, judges may seek deliberately to dissipate the responsibility for their decisions through explanations provided in their sentencing remarks.

The Italian sentencing narrative is unique. The sentencing process begins when the court has already reached its decision (para. 5.24). The announcement of the verdict and the process of sentencing are portrayed as one continuous component of the trial. However, at this point it is evident that the narrative has moved abruptly from the presentation and evaluation of witness testimony to the sentencing stage. The judges will have reached their decisions on verdict immediately after close of the trial[45] following collegial deliberations *in camera* directed by the President of the court.[46] The obligation on the court is then to announce its judgement (*sentenza*) and give reasons for its decisions. Where a conviction has resulted, the court is obliged to consider relevant aggravating and mitigating circumstances,[47] before detailing the sanctions to be imposed.[48] Any associated civil action order is also determined and announced at this stage.[49] The President

---

44 Although there is no (as yet) prosecution right of appeal, this would undoubtedly increase the need for a more careful articulation of the purposes of punishment in any particular case.

45 *CPP*, Art. 525.

46 *CPP*, Art. 527.

47 It is significant that aggravating and mitigating factors relating to the determination of both crime severity and sentence severity are classified in the Italian *Criminal Code* (*Codice Rocco* enacted in 1930).

48 *CPP*, Arts 533–537.

49 *CPP*, Arts 538–543.

delivers his remarks to the body of the court and there is no record in the narrative[50] of any interaction (procedural or otherwise) with anyone present therein at this point.

The construction of the narrative reflects the summary nature of this particular stage of the trial. The President moves swiftly through a consideration of factors which are regarded as aggravating circumstances of CL's murder of SB. The language is contemptuous of CL in every respect, and especially to re-enforce the baseness of his character. Brief references to previous trial testimony relating to motive and character are emphasized to serve as implicit justifications for penalty. The narrative does not provide us with a comprehensive discourse relating to sentencing justification beyond retributive penalty, and the emphasis is very much on individualism and the denunciation of the offender within that context. There are no allusions whatsoever to consequentialist sentencing objectives such as rehabilitation[51] and reparation (beyond the terms of the civil action). In this sense, the narrative is symbolic as public theatre; it serves to demonize the accused's character and provide a setting for his condemnation and reprobation.

This pattern is repeated in relation to the charges of slander and kidnapping[52] against CL. As regards the former, forensic reports are employed in order to demonstrate the 'intrinsic absurdity' of CL's putative defence, whilst the court continues to maintain any psychological motive for the slander as irrelevant. The psychological element does not appear to refer, as earlier, to any mitigating circumstances involving CL's mental state or well-being. It is not a defence. Rather, it appears to relate to the way the defendant's guilt can be inferred from the perceptions imputed at the time of the offence. An interesting structural element of these few paragraphs is that the evidence or the falsity of CL's accusation is presented in order of increasing strength. The best, that is the forensic reports, are saved until the last. This has an important narrative effect, adding to the impression of concreteness and soundness of judgement.

The narrative then covers offences charged against the remaining defendants, dealing with each respectively by utilizing the same

---

50   This does not, of course, mean that no formal or informal interaction took place. Observations of the manner, direction and tone of delivery might suggest particular emphasis and relevance. The further significance of any such observations could be explored by additional research methodologies.

51   This despite the fact that punishment of convicted persons must promote their rehabilitation (*CPP* Art. 27).

52   CL is acquitted of the charge of participating in the first kidnap of SB.

analytical formula. Where appropriate the President deconstructs the legal components of the offence and relates the relevant aspects to the eventual penalty as justificatory. Thus, where in relation to the criminal failure of EL to provide the required help to SB he had unsuccessfully pleaded the defence of necessity, the court related this failure as an aggravating factor relevant to sentence. Overall, the tone of this later discourse is less condemnatory than that directed to the principal defendant, CL, but similar in the sense that any allusions to sentence justification are merely declaratory of the court's considered view without further elaboration. For example, in one case, the President simply declares the penalty as justified on the basis that 'it seems fair, given the seriousness of the offence'. Hence, 'fairness' or 'justice' are equated with the proper exercise of judicial discretion within the constraints imposed by the *Criminal Code* (CC) and its jurisprudence.

The final section of the judgement narrative deals with consequential matters such as costs and the outcome of the civil claim in a fairly perfunctory manner, before the final stage dealing with the nature of the sanctions to be imposed. Here, the narrative adopts a declaratory tone according to the formula prescribed by the *Code of Criminal Procedure* (CPP).[53]

The narrative recording the court's reasons, judgements and decisions on sentence provides an important opportunity to evaluate the current Italian sentencing paradigm from several perspectives. At the legal/structural level, it reflects on the role of judicial discretion in sentencing decisions following the introduction of the new CCP in 1989. However, it is important to note that the current sentencing model derives not from the 1989 procedural revisions, but from Arts. 132 and 133[54] of the 1930 CC, which established the principle that the judge both determines the sentence and sets the punishment (Mannozzi 1999).

---

53   *CPP*, Arts 533 and 535.
54   Article 132. Discretionary power of the judge in applying the sentence. Within the limits set by law, the judge must apply the sentence discretionaly; it must indicate the reasons that justify the use of such discretionary power. In increasing or reducing the sentence the limits set for each type of sentence must not be exceeded excepting where otherwise specified by law.

Article 133. Gravity of the crime: evaluation for fixing the sentence. In the exercise of his or her discretionary powers indicated in the preceding article, the judge must take into consideration the gravity of the crime deduced from:

1 the nature, the type, the means, the object, the times, the place and each and every other modality of action;
2 the gravity of damage or danger caused by the person hurt by the crime; and
3 the intensity of the *mens rea* and the degree of guilt.

Article 132, in particular, provides that judicial discretion must be exercised within the legally permissible penalty range, and imposes an obligation to justify the sentence by relating the facts to the severity and nature of the punishment. The model is, therefore, essentially retributive in character, and operationalized through Art. 133, which lays down the criteria that guide judges in exercising their discretionary powers under Art. 132. The fundamental guiding criteria are:

1 the gravity of the behaviour; and
2 the offender's propensity to commit crime.

The first criterion is derived from an evaluation of objective and subjective factors, whilst the second is implicitly concerned to formulate a predictive judgement regarding the offender's likely recidivism.

This analytical framework is referred to by the President in para. 5.241 of the sentencing narrative in CL, and although the narrative alludes briefly to matters relevant to the criteria in Art. 133, it is, as noted previously, mainly significant for its failure to elaborate on the justification for punishment beyond mere retribution and denunciation.[55] The mechanical rigidity of the legislative formula, and the absence of any jurisprudential guidance[56] to develop sentencing practice, is reflected in the absence of any reference to similar judicial

---

The judge must also take into consideration the capacity of the offender to commit crimes, derived from:

1 the reasons for committing the crime and the character of the offender;
2 previous criminal record and generally the behaviour and life of the offender, before the fact;
3 the conduct of the offender during or successive to the crime; and
4 the lifestyle of the offender, his or her family and social environment.

55 As Mannozzi (1999: 3) points out, this reflects the lack of any indications in the code regarding the objectives of punishment, and has led to an inability to exercise control over the exercise of judicial discretionary powers in sentencing, and more or less hidden forms of sentencing disparity.

56 It should be noted that the Italian Constitution (Art. 27) explicitly mentions the rehabilitative ideal, and decisions of the Constitutional Court have consistently emphasized the 'polyfunctional' concept of punishment, whereby judges may determine the correct degree of punishment in the light of the characteristics of each case against retributive, rehabilitative and deterrent criteria. Mannozzi (1999: 4) suggests that the so-called polyfunctional theory is 'nothing more than

practice or concerns relating to the proper grading of punishment for the crime.[57]

Nevertheless, the court's obligations are further circumscribed by the constitutional requirement that any dispositive judicial decision must be 'reasoned', and that this reasoning must be explicit so that the basis of the decision can be scrutinized by public opinion, or by an appellate court.[58] The narrative, however, illustrates how, despite the 1989 criminal procedure reforms, the pre-existing discretionary model of retributive sentencing has failed to develop in the context of adversarialism which now pervades the Italian criminal trial process. This is evidenced by the absence of any apparent requirement to relate the reasoning for sentence to anything beyond the criteria specified in Art. 133 of the *CC*. With the emphasis on outcome, the adversarial nature of criminal process continues through verdict to sentence, where counsel, through mitigation and interaction, are directly interventionist and influential on sentence. The CL narrative, although alluding to mitigating circumstances indirectly through the application of the Art. 133 criteria as they relate to the capacity of the offender, is devoid of any substantive debate or deliberation amongst the legal participants. The reasoning is, therefore, constrained and declaratory. The President's language displays the incongruity of legal form and retributive accounting with the passionate detail of the trial facts. Just enough emotion is conveyed to illustrate contempt for the defendant and denounce him.[59]

In its application of Art. 133, and in the general exercise of its discretionary power under Art. 132 of the *CC*, the narrative reveals several instances of a lack of transparency in the court's deliberations.

---

an attempt to give the "ideological vagueness" afflicting those who drafted Art. 133 CC [*Official Gazette, Penal Code* (supplement), n. 253, 28 October 1930, effective on 1 July 1931 (*Gazzetta Ufficiale*, supplemento), *Codice Penale*, n. 253, 28 ottobre 1930, entrato in vigore il primo luglio 1931] some kind of coherence.'

57   The crime of murder is punishable by a sentence of no less than 21 years' imprisonment (*CC*, Art. 575). However, if more than one mitigating circumstance pertains, the term of imprisonment may be reduced to five years and six months. A variety of aggravating circumstances specified in the code may permit a sentence of life imprisonment (i.e. premeditation, parental murder or infanticide).

58   Italian Constitution, Art. 111 and see Certoma (1985: 223).

59   CL's (and the other defendant's) motives are described as 'futile and contemptible', his behaviour during the trial as 'artful'. Such language is emotive, as the word 'Scaltro' meaning 'crafty' or 'sly', reveals. The transcript deliberately paints a bleak, not unclichéd picture of CL's criminal character.

For instance, in sentencing EL and GF, the court seems somewhat vague and restrictive in its elaboration of extenuating circumstances which include, in EL's case, his apparent 'good conduct during the trial'.[60] Again, later, when the sentences of EL, GF and SO are conditionally suspended, it is based 'on the presumption that the defendants will not reoffend and due to lack of reasons to the contrary'. Finally, where, in the case of EL and GF, the basic sentence is first reduced,[61] and then, in EL's case extended,[62] there is no clearly comprehensible explanation for the lay participants involved in the trial. Again, the process seems designed to satisfy the strictures of legal formalism and addresses a legal audience.[63]

The legal/structural level of narrative analysis is, therefore, typified by legal formalism and particular procedural constraints on the information deemed relevant to discretionary decisions and its appropriation in sentencing. The restrictive and underdeveloped ideology of the Italian sentencing paradigm consequently delimits the terrain in terms of due process and restorative justice beyond any communitarian purposes attributed to the ritualism of denunciation. Thus, at the system/organizational level, the context of the sentencing stage of the trial is symbolic rather than interactive, and sits uncomfortably with the adversarial requirements imposed on the trial proper by the 1989 criminal procedure reforms. Sentencing is not an integrated process despite the conceptual link made between the determination of crime and sentence severity through the provisions of the CC. Delivery of verdict and sentence remains firmly in judicial hands. At the interactive level, judicial style is typified by its authoritarian approach reflective of the hierarchical status of the President and the solemn process of the sentencing ritual. Here, the emphasis is on public delivery without deference to principle (legal or otherwise) or to wider communitarian concerns. The enabled outcome of the structural constraints on sentencing revealed by the narrative is a formalized, mechanistic sentencing process which conceals the exercise of significant judicial discretionary power, delivered with minimum justification and maximum rhetorical force.

---

60   This is an interesting, and seemingly isolated, reference to the character and behaviour of EL. The court evidently looks favourably on him in the light of this. It is in marked contrast to the court's view of CL.

61   In accordance with CC, Art. 62(a).

62   Under CC, Art. 593.

63   The tone and the clarity of the text seem to change here. Sentence structure is complex and full of legal references.

The sentencing narrative reflects very clearly on the distinctly different nature nature of the sentencing stage in the English Crown Court trial. The preceding procedure will have resolved matters relating to the factual basis for sentence and the content and status of the defendant's previous criminal record, the relevance of medical and pre-sentence reports, and facilitated the presentation of defence mitigation. The predominant players involved include the judge, lawyers, the accused and the community (as silent recipient), and the range of related narrative is considerable.[64] The sentencing stage is quite different since, with the exception of legally relevant materials, the sole narrative is the written record of the judge's sentencing remarks which are directed to the body of the court, and the convicted person, in particular.

The construction of the sentencing narrative in *Turner* follows a familiar, though unstipulated, format.[65] The judge, therefore, by convention, concentrates his remarks on the provision of a short summary of the salient facts which have led to the conviction of the accused, culminating in confirmation of the jury verdict. Even at this stage, it is possible to interpret the judge's remarks as designed to weaken the perception of Turner's culpability, since the language used appears to diminish the seriousness of his past and present conduct. For example, the judge's almost resentful reference to the differing version of events constituting the present offence and, further, his statement that: 'I cannot know exactly on what basis they [the jury] found you guilty … But they did find you guilty, and we all have to accept the verdict of a Jury.' These remarks are a prelude to the remainder of the narrative which, both in its tenor and manner of delivery, is directed towards expressing forcefully the judge's extreme displeasure at the consequences of the legislative constraints on sentence choice placed upon him. Indeed, in his processual account it soon becomes evident that the judge is addressing his remarks to an audience beyond the courtroom, most especially by availing himself of every opportunity to berate the unfortunate legislative provision in the strongest possible terms. Towards the narrative's conclusion, the judge equates directly the expression of his frustration and disapproval with

---

64   These include oral remarks reduced to writing, medical and pre-sentence reports, police records, legislative and case-law materials.

65   In the sense that there is no legislative requirement that the sentencing remarks should follow a specific sequential pattern, although there are normative obligations as to content and transparency. Those relating to content are concerned with establishing offence seriousness for desert purposes and balancing individual mitigating factors and the need for public protection.

his perception of the public's disposition towards this irksome legislation, which has restricted his ability to do justice through the exercise of discretion in sentencing.[66] The implication is that discretion is a vital link between judicial and public perceptions of justice and not, simply, abstract notions of justice, but justice which is reflective of a communitarian view in which judge and community are at one.[67]

The final section of the narrative is chiefly concerned with articulating the reasons which satisfy the technical/legal requirements for transparency and fixing the appropriate sentence length to be served by Turner within the constraints of the mandatory sentence imposed upon him. Until the conclusion of the narrative, the judge continues to emphasize factors that minimize the defendant's culpability, and concludes his remarks with a short statement pregnant with irony and resignation: 'I think perhaps I had better say no more.'[68]

The reasons for the judge's condemnatory tone reflect upon the wider moves to restrict judicial discretionary power in sentencing referred to earlier and are especially striking. More specifically, they relate to the introduction of automatic life sentences under s. 109 of the *Powers of Criminal Courts (Sentencing) Act* 2000[69] (formerly s. 2 of the *Crime (Sentences) Act* 1997) for offenders who commit a second 'serious offence'.[70] The only permitted escape route is provided by a proviso to s. 109 (3) (formerly s. 2(2) of the 1997 Act), which allows the court not to impose a life sentence if it is 'of the opinion that there are 'exceptional circumstances' relating either to the offences or to the offender which justify its not doing so'.

The facts of *Turner* relevant to this discussion are relatively straightforward in so far as the defendant was found guilty of one count of wounding with intent to cause grievous bodily harm that 'triggered' the automatic life-sentence provision in s. 109. However, the previous 'serious offence' was a conviction for manslaughter committed in 1967 when he was 22, and for which he was sentenced to three years' imprisonment. As we have noted, in mitigation it was suggested

---

66 For example, 'those [the public] nearer the reality may find it unjust and hard'.

67 This is entirely consistent with the view that sentencing is an art in which the desire to do justice in each individual case predominates.

68 The further implication here is that matter should be determined by the Court of Appeal. In fact, the defendant's subsequent appeal against sentence was rejected (Thomas 2000; *The Times* 2000).

69 This consolidating statute came into force on the 25 August 2000.

70 See s. 109(5) for a definition. Although automatic life sentences were repealed by the *Criminal Justice Act* 2003 at the time of writing they remain relevant to offences committed before the new regime comes into force.

that there were facts relating to both offences that were probably 'exceptional' by themselves although not likely to be accepted as such according to existing case law.[71] For example, the three-year sentence for manslaughter was 'a very modest sentence' which the judge agreed reflected that the victim's death had been largely a matter of luck resulting from an assault. Similarly, the second offence resulted from a verbal argument in which the material point appears to have been the use of excessive force by the deceased. Additionally, it was accepted that the defendant was not 'dangerous', and there was no evidence that he was likely to reoffend; that he was 'effectively of good character', a 'popular' and 'decent' man; and that the victim in the case had earlier (and far more recently) been convicted of a serious offence. Previously, in mitigation, defence counsel had submitted that the defendant himself was 'exceptional': 'He is a man who was hitherto, to all intents and purposes, rehabilitated into society, and that was demonstrated not by a year or two but by thirty odd years of law-abiding life in which he acquired great loyalty from a very large number of people.' Nevertheless, the judge recognized that the length of time between offences could not be 'exceptional', anymore than the fact that the defendant was not a danger to the public. Accordingly in his sentencing remarks the learned judge expresses his frustration thus:

> I have struggled, but can in conscience and in my attempt to interpret the law, see no way that I can find that there are in the circumstances of this case, or in your circumstances,[72] exceptional circumstances to justify me not imposing a life sentence. You are a popular man. That may give cause to the public, certainly where you live, to wonder if this kind of statute is the kind of statute they really want in a civilised society.[73]

---

71   It should be noted that the need for strained interpretations of the 'exceptional circumstances' exception was firmly dispelled by Lord Woolf CJ in the important case of *R* v. *Offen* [2001] 2 All ER 154.

72   It is somewhat ironic that the pre-sentence report had been unequivocal in suggesting that a form of community service was an eminently suitable disposal for the offender.

73   Commenting in the Court of Appeal, Rougier J stated: 'Faced with this manifest distinction between successive sections in an Act of Parliament, it is difficult, if not impossible, to avoid the conclusion that Parliament must have realised, and even intended that a judge might be compelled by the terms of s. 2 to pass a sentence which would offend his sense of justice'; *R* v. *Turner* (2000) All England Official Transcripts, available on Butterworths LexisNexis, para. 9.

In terms of actions, the judge's statement is unequivocally one of revulsion that relates specifically in the narrative to issues of contrition, impact upon and characteristics of the accused and community impact. The judge's observations are made *ex-proprio motu* in the sense that the legislative provision confers no discretion except as to the decision whether 'exceptional circumstances' exist. The narrative is, therefore, steeped in symbolism and rhetoric, deliberately couched in terms designed to challenge what the judge perceives as legislative and executive repression of his proper role in sentencing. The connections between players, actions and outcomes as revealed through the narrative relate to the judge and the wider community, and concern issues of dangerousness, morality and the legitimacy of legislation. These themes are consciously developed by the judge in the construction of his condemnatory argument.

The legal/structural constraints on discretion operate to delimit the procedural context recorded in the sentencing narrative. A further example relates to the explanation given by the judge of how the sentence is calculated, and is concerned directly with the impact of legislative requirements and practice directions when pronouncing sentence. This is because, by s. 28 of the *Crime (Sentences) Act* 1997, the sentencing court must, when imposing an automatic life sentence under s.2, articulate what determinate sentence would have been appropriate if a life sentence had not been imposed, and then fix the specified period at one half of that notional term.[74] However, such constraints go far beyond the context of legal formalism; they relate specifically to processual context, since they determine the structures of communication and relevant information in the sentencing phase as reproducible social practices, and have particular institutional significance for post-trial phases (such as review and appeal).

Nevertheless, it is at the local discretionary/interactive level where the implications of the narrative record in *Turner* are most evident. Clearly the formal sentencing narrative reflects principally upon judicial ideology, authority and style and how, in particular, legislative norms have been transformed through *process* into justifications for sentence. But, as we have seen, this transformation in its local context

---

74 A further reason for seeking to diminish the defendant's culpability for the second offence. It is also arguable that the judge's explanation should be compatible with the expressed wishes of the Court of Appeal regarding transparency contained in the *Practice Direction on Custodial Sentences* (1998), which applies, *inter alia*, to discretionary life sentences.

involves the subversion of these norms at the level of the offender, victim and the community to facilitate the emergence of what the judge perceives as a way of legitimizing his own position. The facts and their exposure through *process* (as recorded in narrative) are reworked by the judge to develop themes and justifications for his argument at levels of the specific and ideological. Hence, the facts are evaluated to satisfy different purposes simultaneously. This finding tends to confirm our speculation that understanding the nature of interactive decision-making involves an appreciation of the dynamic(s) which determines the fluidity of fact and value within process,[75] and that which crystallizes meaning.

The narrative in the sentencing remarks from the *Fountain* case is notable for its condemnation of the defendant and its denunciatory tone. The judge begins with a short recollection of the principal facts designed to emphasize its seriousness and the defendant's dangerousness for the purposes of establishing the appropriateness of a discretionary life sentence. The procedure follows the familiar combination of adherence to legal form and rhetoric designed to communicate justification and process to a wider audience. In this respect the course of sentencing is ritualistic, the demeanour of the judge authoritarian and the process replete with symbolism.

The interaction is limited to judge and defendant, but the discourse carefully crafted to satisfy its purpose of wider communication. In recounting its salient facts, the heinous nature of the defendant's crime is reconstructed. For example, the judge focuses on the pitiless and remorseless nature of the fatal attack on S, especially the fact that the defendant showed no remorse, admitting that his claimed 'abnormality of mind'[76] was, in part, attributable to intoxication.[77] This is taken as evidence, substantiated by the medical reports (as authoritative secondary narrative),[78] of the defendant's present and prognostic dangerousness: 'The overall and clear message … is that if at liberty you will, for the foreseeable future, represent a very serious risk of very serious harm to the public and your condition is unfortunately presently untreatable.' The defendant is singled out for further censure

---

75   In other words, how degrees of meaning are arrived at.
76   The prosecution eventually accepts the defendant's plea of guilty to manslaughter on the basis of diminished responsibility.
77   The defendant had acknowledged that this exacerbated his condition.
78   The evidence is regarded by the judge as unequivocal.

because, although the younger of the two defendants,[79] the judge is satisfied as to his dominant role in the attack on one of the two victims.

The impact of legal norms on the process of sentencing the defendant as recorded in the narrative, is considerable. In terms of the most serious offence of manslaughter, the maximum discretionary sentence of life imprisonment should only be imposed on offenders whose history suggests that they are at risk of serious offending for an indefinite time.[80] The judge does not refer explicitly to his sentencing powers, but does concentrate on matters necessary in order to fulfil the criteria imposed by legislation and case law, particularly the dangerousness issue. He is also reminded politely by prosecution

---

79   The defendant's Trial Record Sheet (Form 5089) records the following five counts and outcomes:

1   Robbery – pleaded guilty – four years' detention under s. 53(2) *Children and Young Persons Act* 1933 concurrent.
2   Causing grievous bodily harm with intent to do grievous bodily harm – pleaded guilty – eight years' detention under s. 53(2) *CYPA* 1933.
3   Attempted murder – not guilty – count ordered to remain on file; not to be proceeded with without leave of the court or Court of Appeal.
4   Causing grievous bodily harm with intent to do grievous bodily harm – pleaded guilty – four years' detention under s. 53(2) *CYPA* 1933 consecutive.
5   Murder – pleaded guilty to lesser offence of manslaughter – detention under s. 53(2) *CYPA* 1933 for life. Guilty to manslaughter by reason of diminished responsibility – *Crime Sentences Act* – thirteen years' recommendation. Directed that the defendant must not apply for parole before January 2006.

The defendant also had thirteen other offences taken into account. His co-defendant was sentenced to four years' detention on count 1, seven years' detention on count 2 concurrent, and custody for life on count 5, having pleaded guilty to murder.

80   For offenders aged under 21, custody for life is the equivalent for young adults (18–21), and for juveniles (under 18) detention for life under s. 53(2) *Children and Young Persons Act* 1933.

The *Criminal Justice Act* 1991 requires a court, before imposing a life sentence, to be satisfied that the criteria in s. 2(2)(b) are complied with. This allows an extended sentence on public protection grounds where a violent or sexual offence (as defined) has been committed. However, the criteria for the imposition of discretionary life sentences were established far earlier in *R v. Hodgson* (1967) 52 Cr. App. R. 113. This case established that a life sentence may only be imposed:

1   where the offence or offences are in themselves grave enough to require a very long sentence; and
2   where it appears from the nature of the offences or from the defendant's history that he is a person of unstable character likely to commit such offences in future; and
3   where if such offences are committed the consequences to others may be specially injurious, as in the case of sexual offences or crimes of violence.

counsel[81] of his failure to avert to one particular legislative provision concerned with indicating what should be the appropriate term for the offender to serve under s. 28 of the *Crime (Sentences) Act* 1997.[82] This failure is significant procedurally, because the judge thereby also omits to allow defence counsel an opportunity to address the court on the appropriate length of the relevant part.[83] However, in other respects, the judge has already considered matters relevant to the decision under s. 28, without apparently being aware of their relevance. One of these is the sentencing principle known as the 'totality principle'. As the judge correctly explains: 'I must bear in mind that whatever individual sentence would be appropriate for each single offence, I must ensure that in total the sentences do not exceed the overall justice of the case.'

Since s. 28 refers to the need to take into account (*inter alia*) the seriousness of the offence or the combination of the offence and other offences associated with it, it has been held that the totality principle is entirely relevant, for example, as to the issue (present in the instant case) of whether sentences for associated offences should be consecutive or concurrent.[84] It is also interesting that, in acknowledging his own responsibility to address s. 28, the judge refers to a requirement that the specified period should reflect the need to:

Determining the proper relationship between s. 2(2)(b) and the criteria for life imprisonment has been problematic, particularly the correct balance between the seriousness of the offending behaviour and the propensity to dangerousness. Nevertheless, the position seems to be that the discretionary life sentence is really most suited to cases where the offender is likely to remain a serious danger to the public for an indefinite time (as in the instant case). The other significant factor satisfied in the present case is the untreatable nature of the defendant's mental condition (criterion 2 in *Hodgson*). Note that whilst these measures were consolidated in the *Powers of Criminal Courts (Sentencing) Act* 2000, new provisions for sentencing dangerous offenders are to be found in Chapter 5 of the *Criminal Justice Act* 2003. See Thomas (2004).

81   As part of his general obligation under the Bar's Code of Conduct.

82   According to this section the court must specify the 'tariff period', i.e. the number of years which the offender should serve before he may be considered for release by the Parole Board. The latter then makes a recommendation based on considerations of risk to the public which is subject to the Home Secretary's approval. In *R* v. *M* [1999] 1 WLR 485 the Court of Appeal confirmed that sentencers must state what the appropriate determinate sentence would have been had a life sentence not been passed and then fix the specified (or tariff) period at one half of that notional term (see now s. 82A of the *Powers of Criminal Courts (Sentencing) Act* 2000).

83   *Practice Direction (Crime: Life Sentences)* [1993] 1 WLR 223.

84   See *R* v. *Lundberg* (1995) 16 Cr App R (S) 948.

... punish him [the defendant] as well as to deter him and others from the like sort of conduct and that is, of course, *as I make plain for the record*,[85] wholly apart from the question of risk and that means the time I set by no means necessarily reflects the period for which Fountain will ultimately be detained (emphasis added).

The main reason for interest concerns the introduction of individual and general deterrent justifications for setting the appropriate specified period. Although significant judicial inroads have been made into the just deserts penalty of the *Criminal Justice Act* 1991,[86] individual and general deterrent justifications have been held[87] as relevant only in so far as they are achievable through the imposition of a commensurate sentence. The judge's remarks appear somewhat bizarre, therefore, given that the predominant determinant of the defendant's behaviour is his admittedly 'untreatable' psychological condition. Clearly the judge is not adding an extra element to the commensurate part in order to achieve some speculated consequentialist objective, but, on the other hand, it is not at all clear that the deterrent effect of the retributive penalty ascribed for the purpose of s. 28 can be conveniently detached in the way envisaged by the Court of Appeal. Again, it is unclear from the narrative whether the nuances of this provision have been anticipated by the judge. We can, however, speculate that this is unlikely to be the case given the fact that the provision was brought to the judge's attention at the last minute, and his comments to this were more or less spontaneous.

The narrative record of the interaction between the judge and the defendant's counsel is also instructive at this point. After having been reminded of his failure to address s. 28 by prosecution counsel, the judge then turns to defence counsel and, in an uncharacteristic[88] utterance, declares that the defendant should be informed by counsel of the result 'without the inhumanity of bringing him back', later instructing counsel: 'No doubt ... you would be at pains, however distressing the encounter, to convey that [the result] to your client.'

---

85   This implies that the judge feels that what he is doing is to satisfy the legislative requirement, not necessarily that he believes in the import of his words.

86   See ss. 80(1) and (2) of the *Powers of Criminal Courts (Sentencing) Act* 2000.

87   *R v. Cunningham* [1993] 1 WLR 183. This case also established that offence prevalence was a valid consideration in determining sentence length under these provisions.

88   In so far as the manner of expression is wholly uncharacteristic of the remainder of the narrative record.

The judge's apparent concern at this point, and the abrupt change in his manner of address, may be attributable to his awareness of a particular desire for transparency in the procedure for the pronouncement of sentence expressed by the Court of Appeal.[89] In the event, the judge is able to comply with the explanatory requirement, but not in the presence of the defendant.[90]

Another important sentencing consideration for the judge concerns the voluntariness and significance of the defendant's guilty pleas. This is drawn specifically to the judge's attention by defence counsel in mitigation who states:

> We would invite your Lordship to say the fact that a trial took place on a very limited issue within the very limited context of diminished responsibility should not deprive the defendant of the mitigation that he pleaded guilty and, indeed, indicated those pleas at the earliest possible opportunity.

Indeed, the judge alludes to his obligation to take account of both defendants' pleas of guilty,[91] and further indicates that, in Fountain's case, he had always shown a willingness to plead guilty to manslaughter. Nevertheless, the context of the defendant's guilty plea is particularly relevant for the structural reasons already advanced in our discussion of verdict delivery.[92] Consequently, given the circumstances

---

89 See *Practice Direction: Custodial Sentences*, 22 January 1998: 'It is desirable that when sentence is passed the practical effect of the sentence should be understood by the defendant, any victim and any member of the public who is present in court or reads a full report of the proceedings. In future, whenever a custodial sentence is imposed on an offender, the court should explain the practical effect of the sentence in addition to complying with existing statutory requirements. This will be no more than an explanation; the sentence will be that pronounced by the court.'

90 Apart from this, it is not possible to determine whether the remaining victim, his relatives (if any) or any members of the public are present during the sentencing phase of the trial.

91 There exists a statutory obligation under s. 48 of the *Criminal Justice and Public Order Act* 1994 (currently s. 152 *Powers of Criminal Courts (Sentencing) Act* (2000) but to become s. 144 of the *Criminal Justice Act* 2003) to take account of the stage in the proceedings when the guilty plea was entered, and any attendant circumstances. If, as a result of this, the sentencer allows a sentence discount, this has to be stated in open court. Note that a discount allowed in any other circumstances does not have to be so stated.

92 A combination of judicial manipulation and prosecutorial discretion conspired to produce the guilty plea to manslaughter following the failure of the jury to reach a majority verdict on the count of murder.

in which the plea is eventually advanced, there exists no obligation to go beyond the simple declaration that the plea has been advanced. As with the mitigating effect of the defendant's age, its eventual role as a determinant of sentence is not explained, let alone quantified.

There is no doubt that this case illustrates the significant role of legal/structural constraints as determinants of process. In addition to shaping the progress of the sentencing phase, these constraints influence judicial demeanour and provide the procedural context for the exercise of judicial discretion. However, the paradoxical nature of judicial regulation facilitates the clear expression of judicial justification, as reflected throughout the sentencing narrative. These explanations have strong ideological significance since they effectively re-enforce the function of the punishment process.

Of particular procedural and symbolic significance are conventional references in the narrative, such as where the judge, at first, directs the defendants to 'stand up' for the formal pronouncement of sentence, and then, following the imposition of custodial sentences, utters the familiar words: 'you may both go down.' In the theatre of the courtroom it is at this point in the trial process where the judge completely dominates the process, and the defendant is formally subjugated to state punishment. The condescending judicial language clearly reflects this reality. Therefore, in terms of the systems/organizational level of analysis, the emphasis is clearly on the interactive dimensions of symbolism and discourse. The process record confirms how the finality of the sentencing phase presents the judge with an opportunity, unparalleled in any other aspect of the trial process, to exploit discretionary power to the full. In drawing together the justifications for punishment as public theatre, the judge dramatizes and uniquely crafts the sentencing discourse for each trial. Although legal structure and form is reflected as a determinant of discourse, the transformation of legal rules into conduct norms is achieved by the judge acting as moral arbiter.

The actual pronouncement of sentence, particularly its denunciatory and dangerousness aspects, provides a showcase for the exercise of judicial authority and power. The sentence emerges idiosyncratically.[93] The judicial style is authoritarian and confrontational – hence, its ideological significance as reflective of the trial as an essential mechanism of social control.

In order to draw the narrative analysis to a conclusion in this pilot phase, it is useful to continue the detailed evaluation of sentencing

---

93 Or, 'eclectically'; see Walker (1985).

narrative in particular, in order to illustrate the way comparative contextual analysis (CCA) provides a mechanism for incorporating theory, modelling and the multi-levelled comparison of trial decision-making.

CCA of sentencing narrative: England and Italy

Legal/structural variables

Procedure before sentence
The English and Italian sentencing narratives reflect the fundamental differences of procedure between the two jurisdictions regarding verdict delivery and sentence pronouncement. As noted, verdict deliberations in the Italian *Corte d'assise* are judicial, collegiate and secret, with the result subsequently announced by the President of the court who directs the deliberations. This is in marked contrast to the often-protracted nature of English jury trial.

Notwithstanding, the narrative illustrates how, in both jurisdictions, the beginning of the sentencing phase signifies a new procedural context. Thus, the subsequent discourse discloses the fact that decisions of fundamental relevance to the sentencing decision-making process have already taken place.[94] This is evident, not only from the language content but also its tenor and the manner of its delivery. In each case, the judges begin to construct discourses which are designed to validate substantive procedural requirements, yet they are distinguished by emotive and symbolic language which transcends form and structure, investing each process with a distinctive (usually denunciatory) quality. It is this interplay, reflective of form, structure and interaction, which is absent from conventional comparative accounts. It is also arguable that it is a phenomenon largely attributable to the peculiarly wide sentencing discretion available to judges in both common law and civil law jurisdictions.

A brief example from each jurisdiction suffices to convey the point. The President in CL begins with only a cursory reference to form before

---

94   These involve:

- establishing the facts of the offence for the purpose of sentencing;
- establishing the defendant's previous record and its significance; and
- receiving reports about the defendant's background and mental state by oral and/or written evidence.

The formal mitigation of sentence is peculiar to the English tradition.

embarking on a litany of condemnatory adjectives that foreshadow the inevitable sentence of life imprisonment. The motives and character of the defendant are denigrated, the former being described as 'futile and contemptible',[95] and the latter as distinguished by its deviousness and artfulness. Similarly, in the English *Fountain* case, the judge immediately begins to construct an image of the defendant as callous, remorseless and uncontrollably violent. In both (and similar) cases, although conscious of legal form, the rhetoric is designed[96] to assuage retributive concerns and connect with the wider audience beyond the courtroom.

Framework for sentence delivery

The similarities in the tenor and dramatic symbolism of the discourse observed in the English and Italian narratives belie a complexity of normative obligations and conventions imposed on the respective judiciary. An appreciation of the legal and policy context of each narrative not only provides clarity to the framework for delivery, but also context to the phenomenology of action. The intention here, therefore, is to provide a guide to the form and substance of discourse, not a definitive comparative analysis of legal praxis in positivist terms. This intention is necessarily circumscribed by the nature of the narrative method.

The role of the constitution (meta-normative framework)

The wide judicial discretion enjoyed by English Crown Court judges in sentencing arises from a constitutional convention which has sustained and protected the independence of the judiciary from executive interference. This independence has effectively enabled the Court of Appeal to control the implementation of executive policy initiatives in sentencing through the guidance it provides to judges. In recent years its ability to so dictate the direction of sentencing policy has been circumscribed by the imposed just deserts framework of the *Criminal Justice Act* 1991 and mandatory minimum sentences, such as the automatic life sentence in *Turner*. Constitutional convention does not, therefore, provide accepted principles or rationales for English sentencing, nor any mechanisms to support or interpret them, such as a constitutional court. As described, the policy context of the judge's manifest displeasure with the mandatory regime imposed upon him

---

95   There seems to be no logical reason why a futile motive should necessarily be
      regarded as contemptible.
96   And would certainly appear so to any lay observer.

displayed in *Turner* is in part attributable to the sustained erosion of this perceived[97] constitutional justification for unfettered judicial discretion in sentencing decision-making.

The Italian Constitution,[98] by contrast, actually provides for rehabilitation as the main goal of punishment.[99] However, as is evident from the CL transcript, this seems to exercise little effect on the determination of the criteria for sentencing. The Constitutional Court[100] has effectively permitted the judiciary to select justifications for sentences from a broad range of aims that include retribution, rehabilitation and deterrence, and in establishing the length of imprisonment in each individual case. However, as Mannozzi (1999) has noted, Italian judges rarely provide detailed justification(s) for the chosen punishment, especially when the length of imprisonment is close to the legal minimum.[101] Furthermore, the range of penalty available for the crime of murder[102] (and other serious crimes) reflects the enormous discretionary power Italian judges still possess when sentencing.[103] In CL's case, it was the combination of aggravating factors which resulted in the sentence of life imprisonment.

The role of the courts and judiciary (institutional framework)

The position of the courts regarding issues of status, precedent and consistency is closely related to the constitutional context in the regulation of sentencing discretion. In English sentencing, the principles and guidance located in Appeal Court sentencing judgements are not binding, but of persuasive authority. Unjustified

---

97   Leading commentators have frequently asserted the absence of any legal constitutional basis for the convention. See, for example, Ashworth (1983).

98   *CC*, Art. 27, para. 3.

99   Most sentencing jurisprudence on punishment objectives deals with rehabilitation rather than retribution and general prevention.

100 *Corte Costituzionale*, judgement n. 107/1980.

101 Where justifications are scarce there is little opportunity for the Court of Appeal or the Court of Cassation to exercise any control over the measure of punishment imposed by the criminal courts.

102 See *CC*, Art. 575. This provision states that the crime of murder is punishable by a sentence of not less than 21 years' imprisonment.

103 The problem has been hugely exacerbated by the various forms of sentence bargaining introduced by the 1989 *CPP*. For murder, the 'virtual' punishment can range from 21 years to life, whereas the 'real' punishment may range from 3 years, 6 months' imprisonment to a life sentence. As Mannozzi (1999) further points out, a prison term may be modified either qualitatively or quantitatively by several judges (including the sentencing judge).

departures are, nevertheless, appellable[104] but the success of this mechanism in providing a degree of internal consistency largely depends on the range of offences covered,[105] and the extent to which the Court of Appeal is able (or willing) to combat the culture of judicial individualism.[106] In this respect it is interesting to note that the moral dilemma which confronted the judge in *Turner* was effectively circumvented by the Court of Appeal itself shortly thereafter.[107]

The absence of any discussion regarding the goals of punishment in CL is unexceptional for the reasons discussed. More typical would have been some deliberation on the decisions of the Court of Cassation concerned with the interpretation of the factual criteria for sentencing, if this had been considered appropriate.[108] Further, unlike their English counterparts, the Italian higher judiciary do not issue the equivalent of *practice directions* designed to persuade, guide or assist sentencers in exercising their discretion when sentencing.[109] The jurisprudence of the Court of Cassation is the only structural mechanism available, and this exercises more control over matters relating to substantive criminal law than it does regarding penality.

Sentence determination and pronouncement (discretionary framework)

There are considerable differences of approach between the English and Italian systems to establishing the criteria necessary to determine the seriousness of the offence for the purposes of sentencing. As described earlier, the English just deserts model has been interpreted liberally by the Court of Appeal to accommodate notions of penality beyond the bounds of limited retributivism. For the Italian judge, interpretation and guidance come mainly from the Court of Cassation

---

104   In the case of the prosecution, only on the basis of 'undue leniency'; s. 36 *Criminal Justice Act* 1988.

105   There is a serious lack of guidance for offences on the custodial/non-custodial boundary.

106   For the reasons discussed in the previous section, the Court of Appeal has proved itself unco-operative in supporting legislative incursions into judicial discretion in sentencing.

107   See *R* v. *Offen* [2001] 2 All ER 154.

108   See *CC*, Art. 133, and later in the text.

109   Whilst unsuccessful in restraining eclectic sentencing, this strategy has been used to greater effect more recently in attempts to foster transparency and consideration of victim impact in sentencing decisions. See the reference to transparency requirements in the analysis of sentencing in *Fountain*.

and relate specifically to the principles and criteria for sentence decision-making established by Arts 132 and 133 of the 1930 *CC*.[110]

In CL, the court adopts this general or 'pure' sentencing paradigm in the adversarial tradition, since there appears from the narrative to have been no sentence bargaining, or summary trial.[111] Hence, the narrative records the emphasis the President gives to facets of the defendant's crime and culpability according to the criteria for evaluation in Art. 133. Of particular interest is the nature of the second guiding criterion included in Art. 133. This lists a number of factors from which the judge must formulate a predictive judgement regarding the future criminal propensity of the defendant.[112] Normally, therefore, a certain amount of the punishment is linked to the objective seriousness of the crime, whilst any additional amount depends on the perceived dangerousness of the offender.[113] Unfortunately, since Italian judges rarely distinguish the two amounts of punishment in the sentence justification, it is frequently impossible to determine how (subjectively) they have exercised their discretionary power.

This is almost certainly the case in CL, where the focus of the President's remarks is directed towards an implicit evaluation of the defendant's dangerousness in the consideration of his attitude towards the commission of the crime (*capacita a delinquere*). It is notable that in an equivalent English case (such as *Fountain*), the principal criteria relating to the imposition of discretionary life sentences[114] do not relate the

---

110 As Mannozzi describes, these provisions establish a monophase sentencing model where verdict and sentence delivery are combined, but also guided discretion, similar to narrative guidelines is present. Appeals on the basis of merit, form and amount of punishment may be brought before a judge of appeal, and for reasons of unlawfulness, before the Court of Cassation.

111 The effect of these procedures introduced by the 1989 *CPP* are beyond the scope of this analysis but have been noted as extremely destructive to proportionality and consistency in Italian sentencing. See Mannozzi (1999).

112 Mannozzi (1999) suggests that the range of relevant factual criteria for Art. 133 is very wide since Italian criminal law doctrine designates that the term 'fact' should include all the elements that describe a particular crime.

113 The dangerousness of the offender may also be taken into account after the sentencing phase (*CC*, Arts 199–240). In this double-track system the punishment can be followed by the application of a so-called 'security measure' (*misura di sicurezza*). This measure is applicable only if the offender has served his or her punishment, and the offender has been assessed as 'socially dangerous' (*socialmente pericoloso*) by a special commission. Further, a recent Act (n. 66/1996) modified many sex-related crimes and their punishment ranges, instituting very severe sanctions justified with the intent of community protection.

114 See *R v. Hodgson* (1967) 52 Cr App R 113.

assessment of offence gravity for sentencing to substantive crime elements for the offence (as does the first Italian criterion in Art. 133), but refer simply to the fact that the offence must be *grave enough* to justify a very long sentence. Neither do the English principles refer (as does the second Italian criterion in Art. 133) directly to the relevance of the offender's conduct during or successive to the crime, as germane to the determination of dangerousness. However, there is no suggestion in CL (as is in *Fountain*) that the defendant is suffering from an untreatable mental condition which increases his dangerous propensity.[115]

It is also significant that the defendant in *Fountain* pleaded guilty to manslaughter by reason of diminished responsibility,[116] thus invoking a consideration of the principles applicable to discretionary life sentences whereas, in CL, such discretionary powers were relevant to the determination both of the appropriateness of the life sentence for murder and the determination of its length.[117] As discussed in the *Fountain* analysis,[118] the appropriate term to be served with respect to an English discretionary life sentence is determined by separate procedure in which the judge apportions the retributive element to be served before the defendant may be considered for release by the Parole Board.

Finally, the respective narratives reveal important differences in the legal norms regulating the presentation of information relevant to sentence in terms of transparency, and the form in which the sentence itself is formally delivered by the judge. The apparent evenness and open texture of the English sentencing narratives conceal the fact that judicial pragmatism in sentencing is illusory. Notwithstanding, the substantive rhetoric and hyperbole of the judges, particularly in *Turner*, seemingly distance the interaction from its normative structure to the extent that form becomes an incidental medium for the dramatization of punishment. The CL narrative is markedly more pedestrian in its development but, nevertheless, equally incisive in its condemnation of the defendant. In moving to the final stage[119] the tenor of the narrative clearly reflects its more formal procedural character. The Italian

---

115   Indeed, in CL, the court frequently imputes the defendant's guilt from its perception of his psychological state when the offence was committed.

116   Life imprisonment being mandatory for murder.

117   Article 132, *CC Codice Penale*, n. 253, 28 ottobre 1930 ([*entrato in vigore il primo luglio* 1931] *Official Gazette, Penal Code* (supplement), n. 253, 28 October 1930. Effective on 1 July 1931 (*Gazzetta Ufficiale* (supplemento)), *Codice Penale*, n. 253, 28 ottobre 1930, [*entrato in vigore il primo luglio* 1931]).

118   See s. 28 *Crime (Sentences) Act* 1997.

119   The formal procedural stage which follows the same format for each trial is headed P.Q.M., meaning *per questi motivi* (literally – *for these reasons*).

narrative further indicates that legal form appears to predominate over any requirements for transparency of process. The two English transcripts are both reflective of formal procedural norms relating to transparency, but these reflections do not expose the individual reasons for the allocation of punishment. As Tata (1997: 407) suggests, public declarations of reasoning do not necessarily explain the decision process, whereas intuitive accounts are required to deconstruct stereotypical examples of case representation.

System/organizational variables (process and procedural framework)

In this section we are concerned with the extent to which the English and Italian sentencing narratives are reflective of systemic and local patterns of interaction that exist as reproducible social practices.

Policy objectives

The extent to which it is possible to deduce in narrative the implementation of centralized or local sentencing policy initiatives through the operation of structures extending beyond legal form is limited in the pilot exercise.[120] Nevertheless, we are able to identify passages in the English narrative relating to *Turner* in which the judge severely criticizes structural attempts to restrain judicial discretion through mandatory sentencing. Similarly, both English and Italian transcripts reveal the routinization and interactive patterning of behaviour-implementing legal structures, relating to seriousness assessment and transparency.

Communication structures

The English and Italian sentencing transcripts exhibit important differences in the interactive structuring of decision-making. The most significant concerns the nature of the sentencing decision paradigm. Evidently, the English decision model is essentially individualistic and pragmatic although, paradoxically, the justificatory component is articulated publicly. By contrast, the Italian decision model requires collective behaviour with justifications (presumably) argued in private. The Italian discretionary decision-making paradigm established by Arts 132 and 133 of the CC has remained an obstacle to the development of justificatory aims for sentencing, thus permitting judges persistently to avoid public articulation and accountability for sentence justifications.

---

120   This is mainly due to the recursive nature of the variable under investigation.

In both jurisdictions the structuring and processing of information relevant to sentencing are largely completed by the sentencing stage itself. Legal constraints and protocol dictate the nature and context of information delivery. Information is subsequently filtered, juxtaposed and utilized by legal professionals to fulfil the categorizations necessary to enable sentencing to take place. The mode in which these structures are created and sustained is, therefore, a crucial determinant of judicial discretionary decision-making in sentencing.

In the English process the narratives reveal how the judge draws upon discrete information sources (such as pre-sentence reports and defence mitigation) to construct the legal justifications of seriousness and individualization. It is discretionary. The Italian narrative is more opaque in this respect. Information relevant to sentencing appears to be drawn more randomly from prior trial testimony or judicial inference. There is a tendency towards reiterated conclusions and the constant revalidation of previous value judgements throughout the trial narrative. The structural and narrative elements of the transcript seem intertwined in the narrative which precedes the sentencing phase, structural tools being used to support the conclusions reached, and provide the momentum for the justification of the sentence. A clear example of this continuing through to sentencing is the judicial rejection of any possible psychological justification for murder on CL's part, and the persistence of the court in its assertions that the defendant had the necessary *mens rea* for the offence.[121]

Integration of process
The Italian sentencing narrative is indicative of particular aspects in the integration of trial process.[122] This is evident in the exercise of the discretionary power of the judge under Art. 132 of the CC, which stipulates that the obligation to justify the sentence must be by reference to a reconstruction of the offence. Hence, Art. 133 provides indices of information designed to direct the exercise of discretion on seriousness (the first criterion). Although the process has the potential to promote proportionality as between offence and sentence (Ashworth 1999: 18–22), this is frustrated by an over-riding failure of the Italian system to rationalize the purposes of sentencing. Thus, judicial discretion operates in an ideological vacuum which appears incapable

---

121   The sentencing transcript refers to a 'decisive psychological element' in the case
      of CL. This is presumably an allusion to his undoubted guilt and the fact that
      throughout the narrative his actions are constantly related back to establish this.
122   In this we refer to the interconnectedness of process rather than style.

of promoting principles for the rational variation of cases. The English transcripts reflect the fact that offender culpability is dependent solely on the judicial interpretation and application of sentencing criteria procedurally unrelated to substantive offence requirements.[123]

Relevance of system factors

Undoubtedly, institutionalized systems of 'plea bargaining' have enormous significance for both the Italian and English sentencing systems.[124] Clearly, no narrative is likely to reveal the nature and context of pre-trial negotiations, unless acknowledged to form part of an officially recognized procedural mechanism, such as that provided

---

123 However, sentencing criteria will necessarily cause the same factual information to be reformulated and repositioned according to structure. The English approach tends to obfuscate the relationship between the relative seriousness of behaviour and the relative severity of sentence.

124 In England and Wales a clear distinction is drawn between charge, fact and plea bargaining, although all three are generally described as forms of 'plea bargaining'. Charge bargains occur where the prosecution agrees to drop a 'more serious' charge in return for a guilty plea to a lesser included offence or, in circumstances where the defendant faces two or more charges and intends pleading not guilty to all of them, the prosecution agrees to drop one or two charges provided the defendant pleads guilty to one of the charges. A fact bargain occurs where the prosecution agrees to present a particular (usually less serious) version of the facts in return for a guilty plea. Technically, a plea bargain occurs only where there is a change of plea from not guilty to guilty but no charge or fact bargain is involved. In such circumstances the 'bargain' relates to the defendant exchanging his or her right to trial and possible acquittal for the certainty of a lower sentence than he or she would otherwise have received upon conviction. There is no 'bargain' in the sense of negotiation and agreement with the judge on sentence. The institution of 'sentence bargaining' was superimposed on the unitary model of sentencing based on the 1930 CC by Art. 144 of the 1989 CCP. As Mannozzi (1999) suggests, the principle of mandatory prosecution means that only sentence rather than charge bargaining is possible in Italy. The prosecutor has virtually nothing to gain apart from system benefits such as shortening the trial and simplifying the gathering of evidence, since the reduction in sentence is not given in return for a guilty plea. The reduction in punishment requested by the defendant on the basis of Art. 144 CPP must be applied by the judge in practice, thereby placing the evaluation of what constitutes appropriate punishment firmly in the hands of the prosecutor. In England and Wales the expression 'sentence bargain' also normally refers to an agreement between judge and counsel whereby the former indicates the likely reduction in sentence if the defendant pleads guilty. The main difference with Italy, however, is that the practice is forbidden in principle following the decision in R v. Turner [1970] 2 WLR 1093.

by Art. 144 of the Italian *CCP*.[125] There is no evidence from the CL transcript of any such sentence bargain with regard to any defendant.[126] The English decision in *Fountain* does, however, reflect an important structural legal norm – the statutorily recognized practice of discounting the sentence in return for a guilty plea.[127] A significant aspect of this procedure in the present context is that, unlike the Italian mechanism based on the application of a sentence on request[128] under Art. 144 *CPP*, the English sentence discount mechanism is concerned with the negotiation of the defendant's plea, and is effectively a crime control process available (theoretically, but rarely in practice) until the moment the evidential part of the trial ceases. Notwithstanding, in *Fountain's case*, judicial discretion to accept a guilty plea to the lesser charge of manslaughter by reason of diminished responsibility was reached following the jury's failure to return a verdict on the murder charge. This illustrates that as a recursive mechanism the interpretation of the procedural norm relies entirely on judicial practice and discretionary power.

Discretionary/interactive variables (decision process framework)

This section is concerned to describe the extent to which the pilot sentencing narratives actually reflect the social reality of discretionary decision-making within the courtroom. It therefore explores the ways in which human agency (legal professionals) is involved in the application of structural properties (i.e. rules and resources) through process interaction and discretionary decision-making in sentencing.

Authority, power and status

Without doubt the authority and status of sentencing judges in both England and Italy are particularly evident in the sentencing phase of the trial. In CL we noted the apparent formality and solemnity of the process: its ritualistic nature. In such circumstances judicial interaction is negligible. Instead, the process is itself authoritarian and repressive, thereby providing the appropriate setting for the affirmation of judicial

---

125   Or, as in *Fountain*, where reference to a defendant's earlier willingness to tender a guilty plea to certain charges may be made.

126   If Art. 144 *CPP* applies, the judge must indicate that the agreed sentence derives from a request from both parties.

127   Under s. 48 of the *Criminal Justice and Public Order Act* 1994 (to become s. 144 of the *Criminal Justice Act* 2003).

128   'Applicazione della pena su richiesta.'

power and status, with judges acting as the ultimate arbiters of the state's penality.

Both *Fountain* and *Turner* provide ample similar evidence in the English context. However, there is much more of a sense of judicial detachment and independence from processural constraint in the English sentencing narrative. Perhaps because of the unique and idiosyncratic judicial sentencing tradition, judicial authority and control over the sentencing phase sanction its exploitation to serve wider judicial concerns, be they ideological or pragmatic.

Judicial style and the conduct of proceedings

These observations are similarly pertinent to what can be deduced from narrative in terms of interactive style, the legal professional context and the direction of the sentencing process. It is difficult to substantiate assertions made in the context of the conventional adversarial v. inquisitorial comparative paradigm, particularly since the Italian system is, in any event, a hybrid trial process. Nevertheless, that the more proactive and confrontational aspects of judicial behaviour typified by the adversarial paradigm are present in the English sentencing narratives. This is confirmed by the interaction with counsel and the directness of the sentencing homily. In CL, the emotive language of the Italian sentencing phase is couched in the narrative style of the discourse, whilst the English judicial discourse is characterized by its confrontational and pejorative quality. Further, this phenomenon is carried through to the more formal sentence pronouncement stage.[129] Additionally, the Italian discourse appears stilted, reactive and more consciously aware of procedural imperatives and bureaucratic form.

Symbolism and judicial rhetoric

It is the semantic deconstruction of discretionary decision-making which reveals the pivotal nature of *process* in comparative analysis. More particularly, the English narratives reflect the following:

* Sentencing as theatre (characterized by judicial denunciation, melodrama and homily).

---

129   The confrontational quality is markedly less evident in *Turner*, where the judge is clearly sympathetic to the defendant's plight and disapproving of the legislative provision he is forced to implement. Nevertheless, the discourse remains personally directed towards the defendant.

- The judge as moral arbiter (reaching beyond the courtroom audience to communicate in Durkheimian fashion a moral opprobrium which appears to resonate with a perceived common morality).

- The judge (and state) protecting the citizen (typified by the contrasting approaches in *Turner* and *Fountain*; in the former by the judge adopting the mantle of citizen protector in deprecating the state's dangerousness legislation; and in the latter, by the judge indirectly reinforcing executive sentencing policy through the application of sentencing principles relating to the imposition of discretionary life sentences).

- The judge connecting with victims (in *Turner*, the offender is so portrayed, as much as the real victim, whilst the appeal in *Fountain* is more emotive and concerned also with possible future victims).

The Italian transcript is distinguished by its more narrow representation of the wider symbolic force of judicial discretionary power, perhaps because of the conceptual and practical uncertainties which pervade the Italian sentencing system. The dynamics of interaction appear constrained by process to the extent that the symbolic aspects of sentencing relate to denunciatory and retributive themes. Beyond dramatization, there is no overt judicial attempt to connect with the wider audience beyond the courtroom, it being implicit that what is said and described by the judges is equally well reflected in the moral values held by the general public.[130] Thus, the theatrical and symbolic function of judicial sentencing remains controlled, emphatic and impassive yet, nevertheless, immensely powerful in its rhetorical impact.

Implications for CCA

The most important single outcome of this limited exercise for CCA of sentencing is its confirmation of the over-riding significance of *process* over form and structure. It is by deconstructing the objectivity of process that degrees of subjectivity are revealed, and exploring the capacity of judicial discretionary decision-making to add value to fact. As Tahamana (1997) contends, we are concerned here with the generic

---

130   It may be speculated that pressures for increased transparency and justification in the face of perceived public antagonism towards the judiciary and their sentencing practices are significant explanatory variables in this context.

process of decision-making, the extent to which the *internal judicial attitude* balances the dialectical requirements of rule orientation and instrumental rationality. As such, judicial discretionary decisions are relative and pragmatic, they involve appraisal and evaluative judgements based on preferred objectives.

Analysis of transcript material portrays the interactive process which records externalized reasons for actions. These externalized reasons arising from action collapse the fact/value distinction naturalistically drawn by subjective experience. The problematic issue remains the verification of what constitutes fact and, especially for comparativism, the language used for description.

In observing the dynamics of action *contextually*, the English and Italian sentencing transcripts reveal the instrumentality of judicial discretion as a crucial determinant of what recursively constitutes process. In so doing the interpretation of action is not objectified as with conventional comparative analyses. The analysis is projected beyond the *locus* of the narrow interpretative community of legal professionals, to the pluralistic modern state. The contextual analysis of sentencing practice, therefore, permits us to generalize about discretionary practices which are reflective of tensions between rule-governed behaviour and norms orientated towards justice and the individual-ization of sentences. This is precisely what is reflected in the *Turner* transcript by the judge who publicly articulates the inner tension triggered between what he perceives as justice and action forced upon him by mandatory legal norms. Similarly, in CL, it is instrumental rationality that drives the court to demonize the defendant's character with imputations of guilt at every available opportunity.

At the level of understanding sentencing process contextually, the pilot exercise has provided a methodology which undoubtedly adds value and meaning to narrative accounts. It has identified and elaborated crucial aspects of sentencing as a site of decision-making, such as the:

- role of judicial discretion;
- evidence relevant to sentence;
- dichotomy between verdict delivery and sentence;
- relationships between the judge and legal professionals;
- relevance of the victim;
- communitarian concerns in sentencing;
- transparency in sentencing;
- impact of legal principle and normative guidance; and
- processural abuse.

In general terms the analysis has allowed us to explore the comparative historical contexts of two contrasting procedural styles of sentence decision-making, and facilitated an understanding of the impact of procedural norms of sentencing. It has also provided insights into the respective pressures and common themes within these processes, particularly the unique problems posed by the developing hybrid jurisdiction in Italy. Finally, it has enabled us to sense particular issues which have significance across the two jurisdictions. This might allow limited observations and critiques at the jurisdictional level and speculations as to the appropriateness of fair trial paradigms.

Issues about trial decision-making emerging from CCA

The comparative analysis of different trial decision sites has been affected at various levels. These have included exploring:

1 particular decision sites in terms of different players, actions and narratives;

2 different decision sites in the same trial (at different moments of the process) in these terms;

3 similar decision sites across different trials within the same procedural style, in these terms;

4 similar decision sites across different trials, in different procedural styles, in these terms;

5 different decision sites across different trials, in different procedural styles, in these terms;

6 any and all of the above from the level of structure, system and discretion/integration; and

7 any or all of the above in terms of enabled and actual outcomes.

It was always anticipated that some central themes around the comparative endeavour (similarities, differences, harmony, accommodation) would arise. In fact, our earlier modelling endeavours were very much directed to distilling the issues which would emerge from the discovery of players, action and trial narrative (see Figure 3.2, Chapter 3). In this sense the issues become either those analytical universals which reappear throughout the comparative analysis of trial processes, as well as those discriminators which make the process different.

Issues in the trial process, whether it is local, regional or international, will, in our analysis, revolve around decision-making. This is not surprising when we have constructed the trial as a process of decision-making (concentrating on process and practice as well as structure and system). This is further endorsed through a methodology of narrative analysis which, after all, interrogated the written record of decision-making. What is interesting about this research, however, is that through the potential of comparative analysis, and the interactive analysis of decision-making, we have been able to accumulate insights about decision processes beyond the narrative, as well as about structures and systems of trial which foster or retard this interactive process. This then offers up the trial as much more than a symbol, structure or institution of justice, or of any particular justice tradition. With decision-making as the unifying context around which other issues are revealed, the comparative landscape of the trial is rich, multifaceted and dynamic.

If there is an essential theme to arise from the comparative analysis of trial narrative it is the significance of human agency over structure and system in the explanation of decision-making. Whilst the importance of discretion in trial decisions is well established, the comparative exercise takes it well beyond this.

Were one to look for similarity and difference in trial styles it makes sense first to approach the structures and systems of different trial contexts. This level of analysis will reveal common institutional and process features, as well as variation. But this may not tell us how and why certain similar or different decisions arise from different and similar decision sites. Progressing to a consideration of the players in the trial and their actions will open up the issues of integration and discretion. Decision sites are enlivened and decisions owned. The narrative suggests pathways of influence flowing from professional to lay players that are surprisingly similar in process and outcome despite clear differences in the structure and systems of decision sites. Associated with is the possibility to test uniform principles and presumptions (such as the fact/law distinction) operating in different decision sites but being manipulated in very similar ways through human agency.

The policy consequences of such a theme are powerful, particularly in the international context. Take, for example, the establishment debates surrounding the ICC. Much time and energy were spent arguing and reconciling structural and systems issues between procedural styles. Far less thought seems to have been put into the power of professional discretion and its influence over the limited and particular lay/professional integration in ICC trials. Why so? It may be that, because the verdict delivery and sentencing stages of the international tribunals are in the hands of the professionals, the planners assumed the importance of their influence would be generalized over a uniform professional context. Even if this were true, and it tends to ignore the relationships with the accused, the victim and civilian witnesses, it does not account for other hierarchies which exist within the professional context.[131]

Rogers and Erez (1999) are right to the extent that they see trial decision-making as a consequence of the subjective experience of trial professionals. We would add to this the observation that such an experience is also constructed out of their relationship with those they intend to persuade, whether this is lay participants or other professionals in the trial. The practical and symbolic references for their aspirations and efforts to influence and persuade may provide a degree of objectivity from within which individual relationships of influence in the trial operate.[132] This seems crucial to the construction of meaning and the generation of resultant individual and collective decisions. Therefore, it is interaction, rather than singular and subjective professional experience, which best explains trial decision-making.

Our impressions of professional influence in trial decision-making complement the views of Casanovas (1999) that legal decisions are produced through and by changing structures of collective behaviour which do not rely solely on the consciousness of individuals, but on the enacting power of networks that modulate their interactive and co-ordinated behaviour. Decisions are a result of collective reasoning. The nature of the collectivity may differ with trial structure and system. However, our analysis has suggested that variations in the 'collective situation' do not necessarily mean corresponding differences in the nature of decision-making interactions or the style of outcomes. The key may lie here in what Casanovas indicates are the 'pragmatic contexts': the cognitive result of patterning professional relationships. While the pattern of these relationships also suggest some universal

---

131 These might include such features as different procedural traditions from which the professionals may come and variations in professional experience.

132 It also appears true from our narrative analysis that even where these symbolic and practice-centred referents differ from trial to trial, the pathways of professional influence may be remarkably similar. So, even when the procedures for the admissibility of evidence at the trial differ, the lawyers and the judges still endeavour to persuade the lay participants about a preferred interpretation of the character of the witness and hence his or her credibility.

features of trial relationships, it is the process of interaction, pragmatic or otherwise, which tends to predominate over structural and system concerns. Our discussion about rationalizing the fact/law distinction in verdict delivery tends to support this in a comparative sense. The paradoxical 'reconstruction of reality' from a statement of principle, to the practice of the judge's summing-up needs, as Casanovas suggests, to be modelled at the micro-situational level so as to reveal the nature of human interaction and cognition in trial decision-making. He suggests this is asymmetrical. We conclude that it is essentially interactive and interdependent.

Common decision action, different pathways to decisions

Following on from these general observations concerning interactive trial decision-making and the potency of professional influence, narrative analysis confirms certain commonality in trial decision-making, whilst presenting different pathways to decision outcomes. Take, for instance, the discussion of evidence and materiality. In both trial traditions analysed, evidence is essential to substantiate trial decisions. Italy and England impose in their courts complex rules governing admissibility. Associated with this, the judicial voice, in its reinterpretative mode, speaks much about materiality: what facts are most useful and what they might be used for. The nature and styles of the different narratives reveal distinct similarities when it comes to the determination of materiality.

The manner in which materiality is derived, within each trial, trial to trial and across traditions, differs. Take, for instance, oral examination of the witness and the judge's summing-up. In the Italian kidnapping transcript the advocate faces a constant refusal by the witness to respond to versions of events submitted from prior written testimony. Materiality is claimed here not out of the answers to questions but rather from what was not said in response to the written record. As we commented earlier, during the judges' summing-up of evidence in the trial it seems often to matter little what the principal accused did or did not say in oral testimony. The demeanour of the accused and the credibility of his general defence become the material components of 'evidence' against him.

Common decision actions, different pathways. But in some instances these structural differences may prove superficial or only marginally influential. At the end of the day, through whatever process of distillation, the nature and status of the evidence are ruled upon by the judge and even lay verdict deliverers are not allowed to reflect on their relative weight without the particular instruction from the judicial voice.

In sentencing, the pronouncement is a form of justification. In the determination, through the exercise of qualified discretion, it is represented instrumental rationality which provides the reasoning for any enabled and actual outcomes (goal achievement).

Interaction of participants and directions of influence – lay/professional; advocate to advocate; intervention of the judge

To some extent we have already covered the theme of interactive decision-making. At this point it is useful to consider the nature of interaction in the trial. The narrative portrays the following forms of interaction:

- Pronouncement (judge to the immediate audience).
- Explanation and direction (judge to verdict deliverers).
- Conversation (judge to lawyers).
- Examination (lawyer/judge to witness).
- Impression and innuendo (professional to professional).

But such interaction is not simply a bilateral process. The judge, in his sentencing remarks, for instance, is addressing first the accused, and at the same time his lawyers, the other professionals, perhaps fellow judges and verdict deliverers, but also certainly the wider community. The complexity of the intended interaction here impacts on the narrative and its construction. It is not coincidental, for instance, or simply a consequence of legislative requirement that the judicial voice takes time to reason out the decisions it recounts.

The directions of influence in the trial narratives which we have consulted tend to mirror the professional/lay divide and the professional hierarchies which trial practice endorses. They do not, on the other hand, correspond with ideological and structural predominance such as that which is said to invest in juries their fact-finding function.

That trial decision-making relies on interaction is not surprising. Different trial structures and systems provide for this. That the interaction involves relationships of influence is also to be expected. The professionalization of the trial demands this. Where the narrative analysis tends to be revealing is in the rather uniform actions and predictable outcomes of influence in the human agency of the trial. Take, for example, where there can be little or no contest, in the trial transcript at least, over judicial determinations, however they may be arrived at. On the other hand, whilst the judge may say he can do little to avoid his constitutional obligations in responding to a verdict with which he or she may not agree, the judicial voice can critically contextualize these outcomes as unjust or extreme.

Nature and importance of taking oral evidence and materiality – protection of witnesses; nature and application of rules; styles of advocacy

All these issues have something to do with the eventual status of the evidence as a foundation for decision-making. That evidence is fundamental to trial decisions is universal in the trial styles analysed. What comprises 'evidence' may be where some interesting variation emerges.

Oral testimony, and the availability of the prosecution case to be openly tested by the accused, is now an accepted component of fair trial jurisprudence in all the major procedural traditions. It is not so much the form of evidence here which is at issue in the protection of the accused but, rather, its accessibility and the manner in which it is introduced into the trial narrative.

Materiality, as primarily within the determination of the judicial voice, is a constant and common theme for the narrative. In this, the witness as an active player in the trial appears to be more important in certain settings than the content of testimony. Demeanour, credibility and even inferences regarding the purposes and pressures behind testimony tend to colour judicial interpretations of materiality. In the Italian transcripts, where witness examination was available as narrative, it becomes obvious that the construction of oral testimony (as answers to questions rather than as statements) is also an important factor in the lay/professional relationship. The spoken word corresponds with the nature of the evidence introduced and its materiality.

Once again, it does not seem to be productive to focus analysis of the evidence (and its production) on differences in the professional role, the form of evidence or the stage at which it was produced, all features likely to generate difference at the level of structure and system, but perhaps not outcome. What is more significant is the interrogation of general themes such as admissibility and materiality, the climates of their debate, the decisions on their status and the outcomes that they produced.

In the nature and application of rules we see discretion reconciling the instrumental with limited creativity. The styles of advocacy operating within the 'rule environment' are supportive, non-participatory and deferential.

Reliance on pre-existing documentary evidence and secondary narrative – status as evidence and technique for testing oral evidence

One of the earliest assumptions that we had regarding differences in trial practice and hence trial narrative from one procedural style to another concerned the relative significance of written and oral evidence. Even within a hybrid procedure such as that presently operating in the Italian courts, we anticipated that there would be less reliance on oral evidence and a predominance of secondary narrative as pre-existing written record. This was supposed to be evidence of the difference between procedural traditions and hence produce different attitudes to evidence and perhaps different trial outcomes.

There are two ways of dealing with this. One is to go for proof of difference by a prevalence of different narrative forms. This could be established, although not in a conclusive manner at the level of structure or system, due to the small number of transcripts consulted. Once having identified the variance it was then the task to test the assumptions about different conceptualizations of evidence. We started down this path but soon became aware, again, that due to the significance of interactive and collective decision-making, it was an appreciation of the more common purposes for evidence which would lead to a better understanding of its relative place in the trial.

First, it is worth recalling that secondary narrative, particularly in the form of expert opinion, is important in any procedural style. Secondly, when it comes to the introduction of documents such as prior records of interview, they appear to be employed for similar purposes (i.e. to refresh the memory of the witness and to provide opportunities to critique previous and present testimony). Thirdly is the realization that irrespective of at what stage in the investigation the documentary evidence is produced, provided it confronts similar regimes for admissibility as might oral evidence, then the difference in form has less impact on outcome. Finally, and following on from this, if evidence is only as valuable for decision-making as is its measure of materiality, then it is the discrimination of the legal professional rather than the nature of evidence which becomes important.

The reliance on secondary narrative tends to take the static exposure of the narrative beyond the present. The relevance of earlier and later stages in the process also allows for the dissipation of responsibility.

Roles of professionals and their place in the construction of narrative – structure, system and discretion

Normative comparisons between the roles of trial professionals in inquisitorial and adversarial systems tend to dwell on the different parts played by the judge and by the advocates (prosecutor and defence). Even this rests on the fundamentally similar foundation that there are features of specialist knowledge and practice shared by the lawyers in the trial so as to support general claims to professionalism.

Much of this role differentiation in any case focuses on issues of structure and system. But even these can be reinterpreted into common concerns (see Figure 3.3, Chapter 3). Therefore, the structures for identifying, eliciting and communicating information, despite variations in who does what and with what resources, tend to employ fairly uniform legal imperatives and discretionary choices. The fair trial variables which govern the accumulation of information, as a consequence of regionalization, also impose an atmosphere which is predictable and replicable when it comes to contests for power and social control in the trial.

A simple comparative structural analysis of trial practice, by examining pre-trial and trial phases, might come up with different roles for counterpart professional participants which interestingly do not appear to mean radically varying decision outcomes. We would argue from the narrative analysis that this tends more to reveal the uniform theme of integration and interactive decision-making, rather than the influence of structural variance in the roles of professional players. It is more important to analyse, therefore, action and outcomes than structures and systems for the purpose of understanding how decisions emerge in a variety of different settings.[133]

The collective nature of decision-making can, from quite different professional foundations, produce profoundly common pragmatic solutions and accommodations. The exercise of sentencing responsibility across traditions is a case in point. This might be explained by the uniformly important position of judicial voice in trial narrative now to be integrated in the next chapter.

---

133   This is not to suggest that there is any neat split between structure and agency, system and action in so far as trial decision-making is concerned.

Chapter 6

Sentencing for what?

Introduction

Sentencing is the focal point of outcome where the decision-making pathways identified within the criminal trial process converge. It is also the context where the justification for punishment is (re)formulated for public consumption. In this chapter we examine these issues by reflecting on two particular (but inter-related) aspects of sentencing and their implications for international criminal justice (ICJ). First, we interrogate comparatively the relational contexts between victims and judicial officers in the construction of the sentence; the English and Italian trial models are chosen here to reflect the manner in which often rival interests are integrated to satisfy what appear to be competing sentencing principles within the common/civil/law process styles. Secondly, these relationships are examined against the 'fair trial' aspirations of ICJ institutions and the difficulties faced in their realization. Emphasis throughout is placed on the relationship between verdict delivery and sentencing, the evaluation of evidence relevant to sentencing within these contexts, and the importance of discretion in the relationship between lay and professional participants. Crucially, the importance of the 'rights' paradigm provokes consideration of whether, at the international level, the trial should be transformed to ensure wider aspirations for justice. These issues are elaborated further in the final chapter.

The victim/judge relationship exhibits contemporary thinking and political policy about appropriate purposes for justice. The trial therefore becomes an interesting comparative context in which the real and the symbolic significance of the victim in the construction of justice can be evaluated. It is the relationship between the victim and trial professionals (the judge in particular) which establishes a revealing pathway of influence in trial decision-making. This chapter analyses the expectations held out for that relationship, their achievement in comparative contexts and the manner in which this relates to the processes and purposes of ICJ. Our focus on evaluating victim participation against particular rights paradigms also invites an examination of procedural traditions which support the assertion of victims' rights in sentencing, rather than adopting conventional models which seek to protect the defendant in the pre-trial and trial phases of the criminal process. Since the latter generally suggest minimal guarantees of access to justice and fair trial for victims, our analysis is significant in the provision of information which could influence the future direction of the construction and harmonization of sentencing principles at the international level, particularly through the merging of dynamic trial motivations such as restoration and retribution. These motivations we argue are important and shared within global victim communities.

Pathways to sentencing

The notion that there are pathways or clearly identifiable routes which converge to produce a particular sentence (or outcome) recognizes the processual nature of decision-making within the criminal trial. This becomes especially significant if we begin to think of the actual (and proposed) roles of particular participants in the trial process, such as the victim. For example, the concept of integrated decision-making as it relates to sentencing acquires meaning in relation to the victim only if the trial (and pre-trial) process is evaluated against a rational process principle that advocates greater participation for the victim in the sentencing process.[1] Conceptually, therefore, this position recognizes that the sentencing decision should be conceived as an amalgam of relevant process decisions, rather than simply representing the processual climax of those decisions. It also acknowledges the fact that integration should encompass both lay and professional interests in trial decisions. Viewed like this, the concept of integrated sentencing is evidently concerned with evaluating different modalities of judicial discretion and intervention as regards the perception, evaluation and use of information about victims for sentencing purposes, and the

---

1   For an excellent discussion of these issues, see Sanders (2002e).

connections made between penal justifications, policy and decision-making.

More particularly, in conceptualizing sentencing in international criminal trials, a crucial integrative variable will be the extent to which the instrumental capacity of the sentencer is allowed to develop through the pursuit of creative and constructive penal resolutions. Thus, the relative distance between the ideology of the trial and the legitimacy of its outcomes as reflected in sentencing decisions can be seen as a measure of the degree of integration. Moreover, since relational contexts in the trial reflect tensions between officially endorsed moral justifications for penality and processual norms, an important purpose for comparative contextual analysis (CCA) is to understand how these tensions are resolved in different trial contexts and to suggest an agenda for their reconceptualization.

However, our conceptualization of pathways of influence in sentencing also moves beyond the notion of decision sites and their relative significance as process variables. The notion of pathways adds to that. If we focus on relationships (such as victim and judge), what we are adding is *context*. The context we are adding relates to the cultural origins of influence, its practical effect and significance for decision-making and its relative effects on sentencing outcomes as well as the status of parties involved. More specifically, we are examining the cultural context in which the influences of the judge and victim are created and merge to determine the exercise of discretionary power at significant decision sites for sentencing in the trial process. Yet such relationships (and their outcome) may be purely symbolic, each participant trying to achieve particular aims that do not necessarily coincide with policy or administrative imperatives. Clearly, the forms of influence for each decision site will also differ according to the individuals involved.[2] These may be predetermined by the political atmosphere constructing the status of participants at any one time. At the international level, the very nature of the victim (community), for instance, will be crucially politicized.

It is important to contrast this approach with Tamanaha's (1997: 237) concept of *instrumental rationality*. Tamanaha recognizes that the exercise of judicial discretion has an autonomous quality which goes beyond concern for rule orientation and procedural concerns towards the attainment of social purposes. The direction and control of this cognitive framework are crucial to the consistent and principled

---

2   It will also depend on social context and, more particularly, the rationalizations for criminal justice policy.

development of sentencing practice. However, the concept of 'pathways' acknowledges the creative potential claimed for instrumental legal reasoning and seeks to provide a conceptual tool for understanding its effect in the nature and outcome of process. As well it enables, crucial for a dynamic comparative endeavour, the understanding of what transforms the key components of influence depending on changes in context.

At the macro-theoretical level, we have shown that structuration seeks to explain how social processes exist over time and space, whilst it is the CCA of process that conveys to us the form it *actually* takes. Consequently, the adoption of a micro-paradigm (or contextual model) within this framework enables us to model the determinants of inclusion or exclusion (see Figure 6.1). Understanding pathways of influence in sentencing is, therefore, concerned with establishing the conditions for *selective inclusivity* – the form and reasons for influence depending on judge and court level. To explain the operation of this selectivity (the form and direction of influence) is to understand the forces that are at work in forging the relationship and how they relate to (or compete against) one another. It is also to comprehend and generalize their significance for outcome. Further, these parameters

Figure 6.1   Modelling victim inclusion/exclusion in trial process

Macro dimension – examining criminal process structures across time and space focusing on:

1   cultural origins of influence;
2   practical effects and significance for decision-making; and
3   relative effects on sentence outcome.

Micro dimension – examining the form process *actually* takes by establishing:

1   determinants of inclusion and exclusion;
2   conditions for selective inclusivity – reasons for influence; and
3   operation of selectivity – form and direction of influence.

Rights dimension – assessing rights against particular paradigms.

The macro/micro dimensions provide the parameters that permit us to speculate about the ideological and normative implications of particular rights paradigms for victims (e.g. reasons for inclusion/exclusion of victims in criminal justice policy).

provide the context for assessing the *social reality* of victims' rights and their evaluation against ideological prescriptions and normative paradigms. If the international trial is to retain a keynote in this then, we suggest in Chapter 7, it will need to be inclusive of wider justice principles essential to the interests of victim communities. This is not only because victims require consideration in any rational justice process, but also that criminal justice is not and should be more inclusive of all legitimate interests. All the more so in international contexts where there may be wide community and class interests in contest.

As far as fair trial and access to justice are concerned, we examine the issue of balance (justice) in the broader context of influence; namely, what rights are deemed worthy of protection (and are protected) within the process, or more specifically, within the decision site(s) where particular relationships pertain and why.[3] Our notion of pathways suggests a broad, dynamic model; one that explains differently each time it is applied – because the individuals and the pathways of influence produce different configurations of fact/value and, therefore, different understandings for process and outcome. However, as clarified earlier, these understandings can be generalized and theorized through CCA since our theoretical interpretation of structuration permits the accommodation and appreciation of what might constitute the objectivity of structure. It is, therefore, capable of generating speculation about particular ideologies and their normative implications for victims.[4]

As we described earlier, structuration theory provides a reflexive theoretical formulation for conceptualizing the sources and direction of information and their significance for structure and the recursivity of decision-making within the criminal trial process. More particularly, it allows us to identify and locate specific variables and speculate on their potential impact for process, decisions within a *dynamic* model which is validated through our analysis of context. Consequently, at each stage of the criminal trial process factors such as the courtroom environment, information structures, the nature of the decision-making process and legal and social constraints relate in discrete ways to the different levels of analysis implicit in structuration.

---

3   For a discussion of the social context of this normative issue, see Sanders (2002e: 205).

4   These could include a sociological analysis of the reasons for the inclusion/exclusion of victims in criminal justice policy. Contextual analysis tolerates election here in preference to inclusion, and the broadening of justice principle which this will invite.

These issues can be more easily located in terms of structuration theory by providing a brief illustration. Research carried out by Henham (1990) on the role of Appeal Court sentencing principles[5] in magistrates' sentencing behaviour in England and Wales involved investigating the communication of information about sentencing principles to magistrates through the medium of court clerks, and the use made of such information by magistrates in their sentence decision-making. In terms of structuration theory, the nature and function of the sentencing principles examined in the research were conceptualized as an aspect of the legal level of analysis, whilst the channels of communication of information on sentencing principles to magistrates (and the various agencies of communication such as court clerks and training officers) were conceived as part of system, existing as regular organized social practices, i.e. as modes of social interaction where structural properties are implemented. Finally, the social reality of decision-making within the courtroom was regarded as part of the process of application of structural properties by social actors through the mechanism of social institutions. Accordingly, this involved a consideration of relationships between sentencing behaviour and the social background characteristics of magistrates; sentencing objectives and sentencing behaviour; evaluation of the perceived effectiveness and appropriateness of certain sentences; the effect of alternative means of communication on sentencing behaviour, and an evaluation of the actual application of sentencing principles by magistrates in sentencing.

Thus, we argue that structuration theory provides the analytical framework for interrogating the different levels of analysis and meaning dictated by the nature of the research problem under investigation. Thus, for comparative sentencing, our analytical framework might look like that portrayed in Figure 6.2. Within this conceptualization we are able to speculate upon the principal relationships which determine the outcome of particular interactions and discretionary decisions within the course of the trial are crucial for informing rationalizations and determining sentence. Of these, the relationship between victims and the judiciary is pivotal in delineating the relative reality of victim integration across jurisdictions and internationally.

---

5   Sentencing principles are used in this context to describe juridical norms designed to guide sentencing practice rather than principles of distribution.

Figure 6.2 An analytical framework for the CCA of sentencing

Legal/structural (**rules and resources**) – **concerned with the nature and function of legal norms:**

- Procedure before sentence – the relationship between verdict delivery and sentence.
- Framework for sentence delivery:
  - constitutional issues (the separation of powers);
  - the role of the courts (issues of status and policy);
  - the role of the judiciary (the use of discretionary power);
  - the justifications for punishment (form and substance); and
  - the nature and effect of legal norms (establishing harm and culpability; aggravation and mitigation).

Organizational/system (**reproducible social practices**) – **concerned with the organization and systematic replication of modes of social interaction:**

- Policy objectives.
- Communication structures and interactive variables (impact of legal, bureaucratic and managerial variables on decision-making – e.g. negotiated justice).
- Integration variables (system requirements).

Interactive/discretionary (**application of structured properties**) – **concerned with the social reality of decision-making within the courtroom:**

- Authority, power and status (impact of relationships on decision-making).
- Judicial style and the conduct of proceedings.
- Symbolism and judicial rhetoric.
- Sentencing as theatre.
- Connecting with victims and the community.

In the first part of this chapter we use the contrasting sentencing paradigms of England and Italy to illustrate how the principal aspects of this relationship can be deconstructed at the legal, organizational and interactive levels of analysis, focusing particularly on verdict and sentence delivery and the role of discretion in decision-making. In the second part, we examine the victim/judge relationship and victim integration against the conceptualization of rights at the international level. Throughout, our discussion aims to explore the extent to which the nature, development and transformation of sentencing process at the domestic and international levels are inter-related and influenced by normative principles relating to fair trial and access to justice.[6] Access in particular, as a feature of fair trial, suggests a critical interrogation of the limited justice outcomes the trial provides for, and how these can be transformed to reflect victim interests.

The domestic context

The English and Italian jurisdictions are deliberately chosen here because they reflect different and innovative approaches to victim participation and the notion of integrated sentencing. More particularly, they demonstrate recent initiatives in victim involvement and peculiarities in judicial discretion and intervention in the sentencing process in the context of various procedural traditions (Findlay and Henham 2001). The following are especially noteworthy:

- Verdict deliberations in the Italian process are judicial, collegiate and secret, with the result subsequently announced by the court. This is in marked contrast to the often protracted nature of English jury trial.

- The sentencing phase of the English trial process (in contrast to Italy) is separate from that which determines guilt or innocence. Its form is determined by conventions, principles, relationships and inter-actions which differ from the main body of the trial.

- There are considerable differences of approach between the English and Italian systems in establishing the criteria necessary to determine the seriousness of the offence for the purposes of sentencing.

---

6   The specification of different analytical levels in our comparative account provides a critical context in which to reflect on manifestations of similar phenomena in international criminal trial fora. For example, our focus on evaluating victim participation against particular rights paradigms invites an examination of procedural traditions which supports the assertion of victims' rights in sentencing, rather than adopting conventional models which seek to protect the defendant in the pre-trial and trial phases of the criminal process. Since the latter generally suggest minimal guarantees of access to justice and fair trial for victims, our analysis is significant in the provision of information which could influence the future direction of the construction and harmonization of sentencing principles at the international level.

- The over-riding failure of the Italian system to rationalize the purposes of sentencing means that judicial discretion operates in an ideological vacuum which appears incapable of promoting principles for the rational variation of cases. In England, judicial ideology and instrumental rationality are grounded in a substantial body of sentencing principle.

- The more proactive and confrontational aspects of judicial behaviour typified by the adversarial paradigm are present in the English sentencing phase.

The instrumentality of judicial discretion when applied to recognize victim impact is significant in that it provides the means for directing our attention to the way in which the tensions between the ideologies of crime and social control are resolved within the criminal process structures provided for particular jurisdictions. An important aspect of this resolution concerns the balance between the symbolism and reality of victim participation and how this is realized as an ongoing routine judicial activity within jurisdictions which (as with England and Italy) have developed from different doctrinal roots, but have undergone varying degrees of substantive and procedural transformation to the criminal trial process.

It should also be borne in mind that the significance of the phenomenon of victim participation in sentencing and the instrumentality of relationships and discretionary decision-making all depend upon the extent to which CCA is successful in exposing *comparable* descriptions and evaluations of process (Nelken 2000).[7] In the instant case, therefore, contextualization demands analysis which reveals culturally meaningful descriptions[8] of the following conceptions and how they relate to the legal, organizational and interactive levels which constitute the social reality of trial process:

- The notion of victim.
- Participation and interaction.

---

7 Thus, Crawford (2000: 210) is explicit in cautioning that: 'whilst language and terminology have a specific cultural place, they are neither static nor impermeable but, rather, subject to challenge and change. The essential lesson for comparative criminology is to recognise the need simultaneously to be aware of the deeper sense of words and their ability to be transformed and take on external referents.'

8 These are provided through expert CCA of the legal and policy contexts of sentencing praxis in England and Italy (Henham and Mannozzi 2003). For an excellent account of the problems of comparative interpretation implicit in this type of research, see Brants and Field (2000: 78).

- Significance of process and outcome.
- Ideological and socio-historic context.
- Relationships in the judicial decision-making process.

In order to elucidate the contextual relationship between victims and judges and its effect on discretionary decision-making we restrict our description and evaluation to conceptions and modalities of process which can be located within the levels of analysis suggested by structuration theory. As stated, these are interrogated in terms of developing our understanding of the *context* of decision-making, and its actual (and symbolic) significance for the eventual sentence outcome. This is facilitated by concentrating our analysis on two variables which impact crucially on the nature of the judge/victim relationship and its significance in terms of process integration and sentence outcome; namely, the ideology informing the local sentencing paradigm and the effect of legal and procedural constraints.

Legal/structural

Sentencing models and structure[9]
The underlying rationalizations which inform process models are crucial factors in shaping the relationship between victims and the judiciary during the sentencing phase of the trial (Henham and Findlay 2001c). In this respect the English and Italian paradigms are significantly different in their socio-historic origins. Consequently, the focus of our comparative modelling is to deconstruct the relational context of victim and judge in decision-making over time and space, and evaluate its significance as an important pathway of influence for sentence outcomes.

The theoretical model which continues to inform Italian sentencing procedure and policy for adults, the 1930 *Criminal Code* (*CC*), is based on the liberal theory of criminal law which espouses a fundamental link between retributivism as a rational sentencing philosophy and its intrinsic moral legitimacy (Moore 1993). The structural implementation of liberal theory has been achieved through the adoption of a *partially flexible* rather than a *rigid* system. Mannozzi has explained why within this apparently flexible system the exercise of discretion in Italian sentencing remains both opaque and illusory:

---

9 These relate to the jurisdictional justifications for sentencing values and norms.

the transparent exercise of judicial discretion has been made arduous by the fact that the Italian Criminal Code sets very severe grades of mandatory punishment ... In more recent times judges have generally applied the minimum sentence, thus forgoing, in practice, their discretionary power. This widespread lowering of sentencing rates to their minimum by judges (made feasible by the adroit use of mitigating circumstances), has ended up by making the provision for the justification of the sentence superfluous. This is because each time the sentence is close to the mandatory minimum, the judge avoids enunciating the reasons that led him to apply the punishment in the first place (Mannozzi 2002b: 111).

From these comments it is evident that, despite the explicit nature of the Constitutional provision providing for rehabilitation as the principal aim of punishment (Art. 27, para. 3), and the Constitutional Court's continued emphasis on the so-called 'polyfunctional theory of punishment', there remains general obfuscation and irrationality in the articulation and implementation of the purposes for punishment.

The ideological context of English retributive-based sentencing model is similarly rooted in the liberalism of the Enlightenment (Radzinowicz and Hood 1979), but the nature and development of constitutional convention and the absence of any Constitutional Court (or other effective regulatory mechanisms) have all contributed towards a continual re-enforcement of the centrality of the judicial role and judicial discretion in trial proceedings. Whilst structural considerations are also crucially involved, it is apparent that an appreciation of the critical role of judicial discretion in sentencing provides the basis for understanding why contemporary English and Italian sentencing models differ, both in their conception and implementation.

Furthermore, as described earlier, instead of instituting a single rational system of punishment, the Italian sentencing system has more recently embarked on a series of structural reforms, which, to a greater or lesser degree, adopt, subvert or modify the neoliberal model established in the 1930 *CC*. In consequence, sentencing for adults, juveniles and corporations is modelled differently, yet there is still no coherent statement of how each of these variants is supposed to relate to the 1930 *CC* paradigm or to one another, either procedurally or in terms of the philosophical justifications for punishment. In addition, procedural reforms based on adversarial forms of criminal trial instituted by the 1989 *Code of Criminal Procedure* (CCP) have failed to impact on the development of the existing model for retributive sentencing.

The implications of these developments for victims are profound. As Dignan and Cavadino (1996: 157) suggest, the English position, as exemplified by Ashworth's (1993) narrow distinction between procedural and service rights for victims, tends to approximate a pure retributivist model, where the victim is marginalized and there is little acknowledgement of victims' needs beyond their status as witnesses, or limited recognition of their potential as participants in the sentencing process apart from some restricted form of victim impact statement. Whilst this restricted view of the victim's role is echoed in the Italian model for adult sentencing based on the 1930 *CC*, various forms of institutional structure now exist based upon restorative justice modelling. The English approach has been to endeavour to rationalize and accommodate alternative sentencing justifications within the overarching philosophy of limited retributivism and the proportionality demanded by just deserts, as creatively interpreted by judicial discretionary sentence decision-making.[10] The Italian retributive model, by contrast, has fragmented in the sense that the rationality of the 1930 reforms does not necessarily sustain any conceptual affinity with more recently introduced models. This may be a reflection of the debate between those who argue that restorative justice does require a paradigmatic shift away from retributive concerns (Zedner 1994), and others who envisage the possibility of conceptual links between retribution and restorative concerns, particularly through linking notions of communitarianism to retributive punishment by questioning its moral legitimacy (Cotterrell 1999a).

Notwithstanding these controversies, we would argue that, in the context of sentence modelling, it is the *instrumentality* of judicial discretion which distinguishes the English and Italian paradigms. In Italy, the neoclassical form of retributivism embodied in the framework for decision-making advocated for Arts. 132 and 133 has been judicially interpreted within a civil law, non-adversarial paradigm and jurisprudential tradition that regards the creativity and interpretative function of the judiciary with circumspection, whereas the opposite has been the case in England since the outset of the Enlightenment project in criminal law and justice.

Hence, the significance of comparative accounts relating to the role of judicial discretionary decision-making in sentencing relates to its instrumentality in the reproduction of particularized justifications for sentencing. In England, this instrumentality has been integral to

---

10   This has spawned an extensive resource of sentencing jurisprudence. See Thomas (1982).

maintaining the pre-eminence of the judiciary as lawmakers and *de facto* determiners of sentencing policy (or executive attempts to direct it). For example, the instrumentality of judicial reasoning in English sentencing is evidenced by the deliberate efforts of the judiciary to counteract the effects of the just deserts framework imposed by the Criminal Justice Act 1991, and the debacle surrounding various executive attempts to impose mandatory minimum sentences (Ashworth 2000a). In Italy, on the other hand, discretion has not been instrumental in determining process since, historically, this has not been a crucial determinant in the development of the judicial role. The emphasis on procedural form and the failure of legislative or juridical attempts to rationalize contemporary punishment justifications has been countered defensively by the Italian judiciary. It re-enforces, for example, a marked reluctance on the part of Italian judges to provide reasons for their decisions in public. Whilst their decisions are equally instrumental at the individual level, they are not predisposed to consider the development of guidelines which would set the pattern of sentencing in particular cases and help to encourage transparency and consistency. This phenomenon appears to have been exacerbated by the more recent adversarialization of the Italian trial process. It also provides an illustration of how the determinants of legal culture (particularly power variables) impact directly on the potential for pathways to influence sentencing outcomes.

Our conclusion that the concept of judicial discretion is a fundamental determinant of how fact and value are presented in sentencing is not surprising. What is significant is that our understanding of why this might be the case provides a critical perspective for evaluating the position of the victim in the criminal trial process. If, as we suppose, the context in which judicial discretion is exercised is the key independent variable in our contextual evaluation of sentence modelling, it becomes important to evaluate its operation and the implications for victims in the substantive and procedural practice of sentencing. A preliminary hypothesis would suggest that it could play a pivotal role in determining the impact of adversarial forms within a hybrid jurisdiction such as Italy.

Certainly, the instrumental capacity of judicial discretion to influence the rationalization and purposeful outcome of penalty is potentially of enormous significance for local and global justice forms. Discretion must be allowed to flourish creatively and constructively to produce outcomes that resonate and engage with victims and communitarian aspirations for justice. However, our analysis confirms that the symbolic and rhetorical repositioning of penalty is insufficient to bring this about. What we argue is the need for ideological realignment – for the morality which informs the ideology of justice to engage with the morally legitimate expectations of the victims of crime and the contexts of their criminality. This is a crucial imperative for justice (whether national, regional or international) which precedes normative prescription and the ascription of rights.

Nature of sentencing law and policy[11]

As suggested earlier, the so-called mono-phase or unitary sentencing model for adult sentencing in Italian criminal procedure is especially significant as a determinant of the boundaries of judicial discretion since there is effectively no distinction in processual terms made between the delivery of the verdict and the sentence. The effect of such a paradigm is potentially of great significance in terms of the factual basis for sentencing, since it is essentially trial norms and the forces that shape their implementation which determine what counts as fact rather than the rationale and normative framework for sentencing.

The judges reach their verdict immediately following the close of the trial (*CCP*, Art. 525) following collegial deliberations *in camera* directed by the President of the court (*CCP*, Art. 527). The obligation on the court is then to announce its judgement (*sentenza*) and give reasons for its decisions (usually within 30–90 days). Where a conviction results, the court is obliged to consider relevant aggravating and mitigating circumstances as specified in *CC*, Art. 133 before dealing with the sanctions to be imposed (*CCP*, Arts 533–537). Unlike the English adversarial form of jury trial, there is no independent procedural structure provided for sentencing and, therefore, no conceptual distinction made between the procedural contexts for receiving information relevant to sentence which might serve to differentiate the qualitative nature of the evidence for the purposes of either verdict or sentence.[12] The sentencing phase of the Italian trial is characterized by form (*CCP*, Arts 533 and 535), with any allusions to sentence justification being merely declaratory of the court's considered view without further justification. This suggests that the potential for contexts of influence to impact upon sentencing outcomes is constrained by the fact that the paradigm for decision-making is essentially governed by the requirements of the trial. Hence, the potential for flexibility and the constructive use of

---

11 This is concerned with both the conventional doctrinal analysis of sentencing law, practice and procedure, and its broader sociological context.

12 Note the significance of 'Newton' hearings in English sentencing law. See Ashworth (2000a: 307).

discretion is seriously limited. Furthermore, since the normative framework itself is chiefly concerned with form and regulation, this restricts the nature and extent of substantive evidence admitted to trial.

These apparent differences in structure and form between Italian and English sentencing are paradoxical for victims in the sense that Italian law imposes no substantive limits on the possible extent of victim participation in sentencing, whilst English sentencing law envisages no substantive rights at all, and has only recently succumbed to the notion of victim personal statements which contrive to satisfy purely procedural or 'service' rights. This paradox is more understandable if the force and motivation for political influence are taken into account in the context of the relationship between states, offenders and victims. As Garland (2001: 110) has argued, in most Western European domestic systems of penality, the state's claim to sovereignty in terms of crime control and punishment is a myth. Since it is politically unacceptable for the state to withdraw from the promise to protect its citizens this results in limited institutional reform together with adaptations taking the form of either politicized/pragmatic reactions to new threats, or what Garland calls 'expressive mode', (a sort of acting out of the anger and outrage that crime provokes. This scenario emphasizes the exclusory nature of the dialectical) connection between formal justice and popular justice; the fact that so-called rational formal law as a mechanism of organized social control is supportive of selected moral and political norms, whilst 'popular justice' is misrepresented as supporting the social and political interests of individual citizens and the rule of law (Norrie 1996b: 395). In the context of the status of victims in sentencing, the relative distance between formal and popular justice in England and Italy remains significant despite the fact that in both countries political rhetoric and penal policies have suggested that the state is connecting with the expectations of its citizens for justice in a much more inclusive way through various restorative justice initiatives. Such an approach to penal policy serves an important purpose as bifurcation since it allows states to maintain the myth that formal and popular justice forms draw closer, whilst in reality the responsibility for the protection of citizens is effectively abandoned in favour of policies targeted at specific groups of offenders or forms of criminality which are portrayed as threatening civil society.

Notwithstanding, it is the legal culture and the broader contextualization of process that have determined the response of the Italian courts to victim conceptualization. It is these factors which condition the circumspection with which victim evidence is received and treated by the Italian judiciary. As pointed out earlier, there are in fact no substantive legal reasons for excluding or restricting victim participation in decisions which inform the basis for sentencing under CC, Art. 133. The position is further complicated where a civil claim is also being simultaneously pursued by the injured party. Not only might this reinforce the potentially prejudicial nature of victim witness testimony for the judiciary, but it also sets *state* and *individual* interests at odds.

It is interesting to speculate further upon the processual implications of this apparent paradox. If, for example, we consider the English case of *R* v. *Turner* discussed earlier, it will be recalled that (at first instance) the judge overtly sides with the victim in order to reconcile what he perceives to be the correct response to the executive's unilateral imposition of automatic life sentences sentences; allying himself to the public's perception of the legislation as he perceives it to be, and putting himself in the position of representing their interests and, coincidentally, those of the victim:

I have struggled, but can in conscience and in my attempt to interpret the law, see no way that I can find that there are in the circumstances of this case, or in your circumstances, exceptional circumstances to justify me not imposing a life sentence. You are a popular man. That may give cause to the public, certainly where you live, to wonder if this kind of statute is the kind of statute they really want in a civilised society.

Herein lies an important aspect of the context of influence, since its effect depends entirely upon a cultural interpretation of these words. More specifically, it may be questioned whether this is pure symbolism or rhetoric – is the judge really using this case to make a point about the importance of the individualization of sentences and the injustices of mandatory sentencing, or is he in reality using it to highlight the (as he portrays it) crucial role of the judiciary as the defenders of a truly communitarian approach to the formulation of sentencing policy as contrasted with the partisan vagaries of political pragmatism? It could be argued that what the judge is *in fact* doing is using his influence in a *selectively inclusive* manner – invoking imagery that notionally draws together the victim and the community when it suits him in order to re-enforce the case for judicial discretionary power, but otherwise maintaining the exclusivity of the victim (Sanders 2002e: 206). In other words, continuing to give symbolic recognition and effect to victims' interests through the limited procedural mechanisms provided

237

by the law. This is highly significant because it provides an example of how the discretionary power of the judge can be utilized instrumentally to promote an inclusive context for the victim. It is not an argument for unfettered discretion; rather it sets a challenge for constructing rationales for penality which are flexible, allowing (and suggesting how and why) judges and victims to work together in achieving constructive solutions to criminality within an inclusive framework.

For an Italian perspective it is instructive to revisit the Italian case discussed in the previous chapter and reflect upon the dismissive way in which the offender and the credibility of his testimony was received by the presiding judge. It may be asked whether this phenomenon points to any particular aspects of Italian legal or social culture which might impact on the nature of the relationships Italian judges have with offenders or victims and the representation of their interests in the trial. Do Italian judges deliberately keep the offender and victim at arm's length and, if so, for what reasons?

As far as victims are concerned, Mannozzi (2003) confirms that the victim in the Italian penal system plays a minimal role as regards the phase that deals with decision-making on the length of punishment. However, the victim does not have a real interest in supplying relevant information spontaneously during the course of the trial. In his civil role the victim participates in the criminal trial as the "plaintiff", and possesses a limited capacity to protect his interest regarding damages. The plaintiff does not have an independent right to contest the accused's acquittal, and is excluded from the sentence bargaining procedure. Furthermore, the act of compensation through damages within the penal process arising from the offence is viewed as a possible source of distortion of the formal procedure, which is almost totally dominated by the *public* interest of punishing the guilty party and restoring social tranquillity, not the *private* interest of compensating an individual for economic damages.

During the Italian trial victims provide their account almost exclusively through oral testimony. Although the injured party has status as a witness, and as such is examined during the hearing, such a witness is regarded by the judiciary with particular circumspection as *substantially* different from other possible witnesses since the injured party is implicated in the criminal act (often dramatically so), and usually makes the accusation, or initiates the private prosecution. Mannozzi (2003) makes the point that such suspicion can be considered institutionalized since it derives from well entrenched judicial practice in Italy.

On the basis of these observations it arguable that the treatment of victims in the Italian trial process and its implications for the sentencing phase reflect the traditionally circumspect and formal way in which the inquisitorial trial has proceeded in the past – a culture which continues to pervade the approach of the Italian judiciary to victims' concerns. Further, as indicated earlier, Italian sentencing narrative tends towards a narrower representation of the wider symbolic force of judicial discretionary power, perhaps because of the conceptual and practical uncertainties which pervade the Italian sentencing system. The dynamics of interaction appear constrained by process to the extent that the symbolic aspects of sentencing relate more directly to the denunciatory and retributive themes evinced by the 1930 CC. Beyond dramatization, there is no overt judicial attempt to connect with the wider audience outside the courtroom, it being implicit that what is said and described by the judges is equally well reflected in the moral values held by the general public.

In legal/structural terms, therefore, Italian sentencing process appears typified by legal formalism and the restrictive judicial interpretation of particular procedural constraints as regards the appropriation of information that might be deemed relevant to victim participation in sentencing decisions. This narrow ideology consequently delimits the appropriate terrain for victim participation in sentencing in terms of due process. The potential for restorative justice themes to be developed beyond any communitarian function that might be attributed to denunciation as an aspect of retribution is so limited.

By contrast, in English sentencing, the principle of judicial independence has by convention placed the judiciary in the vanguard of determining the ambit of substantive and procedural sentencing law and the parameters of policy. Furthermore, the context in which this judicial discretion has been exercised has been one which supports and sustains the concept of individualization of sentences (Thomas 1979). Within this conceptual framework retributive considerations are balanced against utilitarian concerns such as deterrence, rehabilitation and reparation. Therein would seem to reside the potential for developing a sentencing jurisprudence devoted to restorative themes. However, this paradigm has failed to deliver any material benefits in terms of compelling the judiciary to take account of victims in sentencing. The main reason for this is that, particularly since the 1991 reforms, judicial discretion has been constrained by the proportionality requirements of an over-riding just deserts justification for sentencing. This effectively sought to reduce unfettered discretion, and failed to address the conceptual problem of determining how conflicting rationales for sentencing should be reconciled and, in consequence, the possible parameters for sentence individualization.[13]

English judicial discretion in sentencing (both at first instance and on appeal) has, therefore, been directed towards sustaining the primacy of judicial independence in matters of law and policy. Victim participation has been marginalized as a procedural issue and, as with many policy initiatives driven by political rhetoric and populism, there is a palpable sense in which the judicial reaction to further reform has been (and remains) one of deep scepticism. In effect, it appears as if the provision of some degree of transparency in the sentence decision-making process is perceived by the higher judiciary as a sufficient concession to the executive in its efforts to assuage alleged public demands for greater victim participation.[14]

Therefore, in both Italy and England we note that, for what appear to be entirely different reasons, the legal and political contexts relating to the exercise of judicial discretionary power have produced a narrow and partisan conceptualization of the victim, and restricted the extent to which victim participation in sentencing might otherwise be promoted. Thus, in structural terms, the cultural contexts for trial action in both jurisdictions have evolved to sustain the paradox between the symbolism and actuality of justice. Trial relationships are structured by processual norms that exclude victim participation and, consequently, restrict the opportunities for influences which support inclusivity in trial decision-making. Pursuing the analysis further, the following dichotomies can be postulated as characterizing the contexts of judicial discretionary behaviour across the two jurisdictions.

The distinction made between individualization and proportionality and legality in the general approach to sentencing in Table 6.1 is a function of distinct legal and political judicial cultures. In England, these are the contexts which sustain the principle of judicial independence, whilst, in Italy, the judiciary do not (and need not) exercise the same juridical and political power over the policy and development of sentencing.

Similarly, the dichotomy of process styles and the sentencing models for sentence are reflective of movements of significant socio-historical

---

13 This observation is derived from narrative analysis of Appeal Court judgements and expert comment (Newburn 2003).

14 The threat of direct political involvement in the formulation of sentencing guidance in the Criminal Justice Act 2003 goes far beyond the previously accepted boundaries for executive interference in the judicial implementation and development of sentencing policy (Ashworth 1983).

Table 6.1 Instrumental factors in judicial discretionary behaviour

England	Italy
Individualization	Proportionality and legality
Independence	Marginalization
Adversarial process	Hybrid process
Binary model	Unitary model
Pragmatism	Social contract theory

and political importance. In essence, the certainty, restraint and control of discretion demanded of neoclassicism continues to inform the culture in which Italian judicial discretion is exercised, whilst the norms governing English judicial discretionary behaviour remain rooted in the values of Victorian pragmatism.

Whilst Table 6.1 describes only the legal/structural variables involved in this comparative analysis, we can speculate on their policy implications in terms of synthesis and difference. From what we have described it is plausible to suggest that the imposition of forms of adversarial procedure and the adoption of penal pluralism in Italy have failed to impact substantially on the pre-existing discretionary model of retributive sentencing. The form of verdict and sentence delivery and the requirements of the reasoning and justificatory process remain firmly wedded to their neoclassical roots, so that the primary duty of the judiciary is as defenders of the principles established for the administration of justice embodied in the criminal code. This reflects the boundaries of the notional social contract between citizens and state; namely, the extent to which state structures and the agents of the state are permitted to interfere with the individual liberty of its citizens. In modified form, this reality sustains the synergy between legality and proportionality in sentencing.

However, the autonomy of the judiciary in sentencing and the realization of an integrated sentencing process for victims in adult sentencing have, as Mannozzi (2002b: 122) notes, been further threatened by the fragmentation of the unitary model of sentencing through the impact of summary proceedings and sentence bargaining. Although Mannozzi makes detailed proposals for reform, such as clarification of the justifications for punishment and their linkage to sentencing outcomes, our analysis also indicates a further need for similar restatement and clarification of the role of judicial discretion within this remodelling of Italian sentencing according to clearly established boundaries. As she suggests: 'It is thus vital that procedural rules regarding "non-adversary proceedings" should be made consistent with "substantive" rules on sentencing laid down by the criminal code' (Mannozzi 2002b: 123). In this injunction the parallels with English sentencing are clear in their implications for victim participation; that restorative justice paradigms necessitate evaluative judicial responses that sit uneasily with proportionality requirements, legislative sentencing guidelines or narrative criteria. If we are to draw lessons from analyses of the use of judicial discretion in sentencing, it must surely be that the relationship between the philosophical justifications for punishment and sentencing outcomes is complex and, more particularly, that the conception and representation of legalistic criteria have more symbolic than real significance for the choice of sentencing options. If this is true, then the co-ordination of philosophical justifications and procedural imperatives must be clarified for restorative justice. As Ashworth (2002b: 579–82) maintains, this should involve a reconceptualization of the state's role in the administration of justice and, with it, the concomitant responsibility to provide a framework that ensures consistency in the application of punishments and safeguards for victims.

However, the constraints of proportionality are difficult to reconcile with the different forms and demands suggested by restorative justice praxis and its potential to exploit more inclusive forms of penal resolution. The implications are that the role of judicial discretion would need to be redefined within philosophical parameters set for sentencing which reflect the state's obligations to pursue communitarian goals and set principled limits for their implementation within and beyond the conventional structures of penality. Without doubt both England and Italian sentencing law and policy currently fall well short of such a commitment to integrated sentencing.

Organizational/system

Significance of process and procedure[15]

We now turn our attention to describing the role of structural constraints in sentencing, and the extent to which they can be said to contribute to sentencing as a reproducible local practice – in other words, instrumental factors implicated in the recursivity of process. As

---

15 The emphasis here is on sentencing as a reproducible social practice so that the focus is on the nature and reasons for the existence of structural constraints on process.

Henham (2001a) has previously described, for sentencing, this implies an examination of the sources, inputs and channelling of information relevant to sentencing (i.e. communication structures) and the ways in which these impact on the operation and function of legal norms and the everyday reality of discretionary decision-making.

We have already alluded to the distinction between the collective nature of Italian trial decision-making as contrasted with the role of the single judge in the English adversarial form of jury trial. In the English process the judge draws upon discrete information sources (such as pre-sentence reports, medical reports) together with defence mitigation to construct the legal justifications of seriousness and individualization of the sentence. In Italy, not only are the collective deliberations of the judges relating to verdict and sentence held *in camera* and the pronouncement of the sentence and its justifications strictly formalized, but also evidence relevant to sentencing is inextricably linked to prior trial testimony and its judicial interpretation during the course of the trial phase. This is clearly not the case in England, since the factual basis for sentence is established independently from the trial proper and is governed by detailed procedural rules and case-law principles. Nevertheless, the existing English sentencing criteria based on *just deserts* necessarily cause the same factual information to be reformulated and repositioned according to structure; the English approach tends to obfuscate the relationship between the relative seriousness of behaviour and the relative seriousness of sentence. Thus, in terms of pathways of influence at the sentencing site, our analysis illustrates the degree to which structure is instrumental in delineating the contours of pathways of influence for decision-making which lead ultimately to outcomes. It also suggests how procedural norms are operationalized as constraints on decision-making. However, understanding instrumental behaviour depends on the CCA of social interaction as an ongoing recursive processual activity.

In terms of process integration and the potential for victims to participate in the trial, we have also observed that, for different reasons, both the Italian and the English systems have failed to develop rational justifications for sentencing which address reparative or restorative justice concerns, other than through reaching some accommodation with the predominant philosophy of limited retributivism and the framework of proportionality it imposes. The position of victims has therefore been weakened through the introduction of particular procedural reforms (some designed to further restorative concerns) within a penal context focused primarily on blame allocation, censure and proportionate punishment.

In Italy such reforms are exemplified by the introduction of summary trial and sentence bargaining described earlier.[16] The primary rationale for the special proceedings introduced by the 1989 *CPP* appears to have been bureaucratic and managerial efficiency, since it was envisaged that the movement towards a more adversarial form of trial would make greater demands on already scarce resources (Freccero 1994). The more radical innovation of sentence bargaining under *CCP*, Art. 444 envisaged a considerable role for judicial discretion in that the defendant and the prosecutor must present their negotiated sentence to the preliminary investigations judge who (in turn) must verify that the parties' determination of the applicable charge and penalty is correct. In an important decision of the Constitutional Court[17] it was held that the *CCP*'s plea bargaining provisions were unconstitutional as a violation of the constitutional presumption of innocence, to the extent that no provision exists for judicial review of the bargain to ensure proper balance between the crime and the bargained sentence. This decision effectively increased the judicial role in reviewing negotiated sentences in the special proceedings and, as Cockayne (2002) suggests, indicated an unwillingness to see sentencing discretion pass from the judge, as under the traditional inquisitorial system, to the parties themselves, under the new system.[18]

Significantly, under the Italian process of sentence bargaining, there is no requirement of an *express* acceptance of guilt; the defendant *implicitly* accepts guilt by requesting a negotiated sentence. Comparisons with the English practice of 'plea bargaining' reveal other significant differences; for example, the fact that the procedure is limited to offences which carry a maximum penalty of two years' imprisonment, and dissimilarities in the nature and exercise of prosecutorial discretion.

However, it is the similarities that are of greater comparative interest. For instance, in common with the English sentence discount procedure

---

16 The Italian possibility of reflecting reparative concerns during the enforcement phase of the sentence has no comparable process in England, where sentence enforcement is strictly an administrative function under executive control.

17 Judgment no. 313, 3 July 1990, *Corte cost.* 35, *Giurisprudenza constituzionale*, 1981 (1990).

18 This trend is exemplified by the reforms instituted on 28 August 2000 (effective from 2 January 2002) which awarded a new penal competence to the Justice of the Peace. However, in this case the shift in discretionary power is more towards the police and the accused, each exercising greater control over the acquisition and presentation of evidence in public, oral proceedings. Nevertheless, the conciliatory phase of this process represents a radical departure from the Italian tradition of penal prosecution governed by the principle of legality (Cockayne 2002a).

described earlier, the Italian judicial decision to accept the plea in return for a reduced sentence is made without the benefit of a full trial whereby evidence is subjected to rigorous appraisal and evaluation. Certainly, in neither jurisdiction does the victim have a right to participate in the decision-making process. Hence, as Fenwick (1997) points out, the victim's likely desire that the trial should proceed without the offer of a sentence discount may be ignored. Such a result may prove detrimental from the perspective of legitimacy since victims (actual or potential) clearly have an interest in seeing a true offender convicted. Further, some victims may prefer the ordeal of a court appearance to seeing the defendant receive a light sentence as a result of a sentence discount. Past support for plea discounts and the ideology of crime control, with its emphasis on financial expediency, speed and finality of conviction,[19] has been on the basis that it is broadly in the interests of victims. This is because it spares victims the ordeal of giving evidence whilst recognizing that some due process rights may be infringed and some innocent defendants may be induced to plead guilty.

Fenwick's (1997: 330) conclusion is surely apposite for both Italian and English sentencing – that the perceptions of victims towards these processes are extremely complex and that there is a substantive case for establishing rights of consultation and participation in these decisions, at least for victims of serious offences. This is a crucial observation for the development of structural norms of inclusivity because it highlights a failure by commentators to grasp the significance of *how* specific procedural norms (such as those which determine the acceptability and parameters of charge/sentence bargaining) operate to diminish aspirations which may have a valid claim for inclusion. In addition, the normative allocation of responsibility for decision-making also determines the extent to which relationships are exposed to decision-making contexts which might affect pathways of influence and inclusion.

An important structural judicial influence on the sentencing process in Italian trials which illustrates the last point is the judicial supervision and enforcement of sentences. As Mannozzi (2002b: 113) discusses, an offender who receives a sentence of imprisonment from the sentencing judge may have this modified either qualitatively or quantitatively, even by a different judge. The sentence can be changed *qualitatively*

---

19 It should be noted that the Italian *CCP* states that the application of the penalty is 'comparable' to a judgement of guilty, but is clearly not equivalent to a conviction which follows a guilty plea in English law.

either by the sentencing judge through the use of substitutive sanctions consisting of non-custodial or semi-custodial penalties for short periods of imprisonment of up to one year (e.g. a suspended sentence for up to two years; CC, Art. 162) or by the supervisory judge, who may substitute various alternative measures (such as house arrest; Act no. 354/1975, Art. 47). Further, quantitative changes to the prison term and its application may be ordered by the enforcement judge, who is the judge that had previously issued the sentence. Mannozzi illustrates how the availability of these procedures to avoid incaceration has contributed to the so-called crisis in the mono-phase (or unitary) model of sentencing, in effect helping to perpetuate a sentencing paradigm with endosystematic aims (i.e. internal to the system).

The significance of these observations for the present discussion turns not on the systemic weaknesses of the Italian sentencing process but, rather, on the concept of the supervisory or enforcement judge itself. Such a concept is entirely alien to English sentencing since, historically, the doctrine of the separation of powers has meant that sentence supervision and enforcement have been the preserve of executive agencies, albeit subject to judicial review, and, more recently, the jurisprudence of the European Convention on Human Rights. English judges are only called upon to vary or modify community sentences where there has been some legally specified breach of the original terms – the evidential requirements being satisfied by the supervisory executive agency. Naturally, there may be conflicting aims and rationales that operate where the criminal process is fragmented in this way. These are likely to be system rather than process concerns, in that the particular interests of offenders and victims may well be subsumed to the 'endosystematic aims' of particular agencies or functionaries.

The Italian experience shows us that the reasons for increasing penal obfuscation, and the 'labyrinthine' effect produced by the alternative effects of the supervisory and enforcement judges are intimately related to the problems inherent in the rationale and operation of the main sentencing provisions included in CC, Arts 132 and 133. In other words, these procedures exacerbated an already increasingly unworkable system lacking in rationality, coherence and transparency. Despite this, we would suggest that, where a sentencing system *is* capable of being rationalized and structured in such a way as to promote the notion of sentence integration, actual integration should normally include decision processes that occur *after* the formal pronouncement of sentence, and that, subject to appellate review, all phases of the criminal process where such discretion is exercised should be judicially supervised. The English and Italian experiences merely illustrate what can go wrong where structure and process are not directed by any overarching vision of which aims should determine their existence and function within an integrated criminal trial process.

Interactive/discretionary

Relationship between process and outcome[20]
The purpose of this section is to draw attention to the social reality of discretionary decision-making within the courtroom as it affects victim participation. As we have suggested, deconstructing this aspect of discretionary decision-making behaviour is crucial for exposing how relationships of influence operate to delineate the parameters of inclusion/exclusion and, more generally, provide a context where aspirations for more constructive solutions to penality may be explored. More specifically, we examine ways in which trial participants (lay and professional) are involved in the application of rules and resources through interaction and decision-making as a processual activity.

We begin with some observations regarding judicial style and the conduct of proceedings which have an important bearing on how victims are perceived and their evidence received. Earlier was described how the victim in an Italian criminal trial (despite having certain basic rights accorded by *CCP*, Art. 90)[21] is by convention treated with some circumspection and suspicion by the judge. This is because

---

20 This level analyses the nature and effects of the process of sentence decision-making on the eventual sentencing outcome. Essentially, it examines local context against variables relating to participant status, judicial style and the collective nature of decision-making.

21 According to a strict interpretation of existing law, the rights of the person injured by an offence (as set out in *CCP*, Art. 90) are basically threefold:

    (i)   the right to request a judge to commit the defendant for trial (in the case of crimes susceptible to 'private prosecution') and associated rights (principally the right to be advised in the event of a request for dismissal by the public prosecutor; the right to oppose a specific settlement of the proceedings by payment of a fine)

    (ii)   the right to present defence briefs to the public prosecutor and judge

    (iii) the right to present elements of evidence.

It should be noted that the law does not in any way circumscribe the nature and aims of participation in the trial by the injured party; the latter can take part personally in the preliminary hearing and discussion, and is not required to appoint a defence attorney to exercise his or her legal rights (*CCP*, Art. 101).

of his apparently incongruous position as a 'neutral' witness, seeking to serve the interests of justice and the state, when contrasted with that of the injured party 'involved' in the criminal act, and often pursuing compensation through a simultaneous civil action. It is arguable that the more adversarial paradigm and the special proceedings introduced by under the 1989 *CCP* reforms have exacerbated this tendency for victims on the basis that, at the interactive level, judicial style is still typified by an authoritarian approach reflective of the President's hierarchical status, solemnity, formality and adherence to ritual; the embodiment of the traditional inquisitorial style. Therefore, these conflicting contexts for interaction have re-enforced the negative potential already existing in Italian criminal procedure for down-grading the status and credibility of the defendant. It presents a peculiar paradox for Italian sentencing because, on the one hand (contrary to the adversarial paradigm) the victim has participative rights in the trial as civil complainant; clearly, an inclusive process. However, inclusion in this context results in negative effects in terms of the victim's participation in the criminal part of the trial because the form and substance of this procedure and the judicial role in it is governed by a restrictive judicial culture. The paradox is amplified through the introduction of adversarial reforms which demand more interaction, intervention and involvement for trial participants in trial proceedings, but which instead merely re-enforce the social patterning of relationships that existed hitherto.

The move towards a more adversarial trial procedure in Italy has had serious implications for trial process, and judicial culture in particular. For example, the principle of orality and the nature and order of permissible testimony resemble common law trials. Yet, significantly, inquisitorial elements remain; judges may direct the further exploration of issues on their own initiative (*CCP*, Art. 506(1)), intervene with their own questions during the examination of witnesses (*CCP*, Art. 506(2)), subpoena experts (*CCP*, Art. 508), and require the acquisition of further evidence where absolutely necessary (*CCP*, Art. 507). The principle of immediacy also means that the judge who collects the evidence is also the one who decides on the merits of the case, further pressure coming from the fact that the trial must be held within a reasonable time to permit clear recollection of the evidence at the time of its evaluation (Corso 1993). For these reasons, there may be even greater restraint on the part of victims to exercise their procedural rights under Art. 90, or expose themselves unduly to the rigours of adversarial evidential procedure and possible further questioning at the discretion of the judge. The potential to develop a relationship of inclusion between judge and victim remains circumscribed and critically weakened by the pre-existing inquisitorial culture of minimal involvement and adherence to form.

A comparison with the English judiciary is instructive at this level. Again, for reasons relating to the judicial culture of independence and its relationship to sentencing policy referred to, the English judge appears more detached and free from processural constraints than his Italian counterpart (Findlay and Henham 2001). Consequently, judicial style is more idiosyncratic with judicial authority and control over the sentencing phase of the trial also possibly serving wider ideological or pragmatic judicial concerns. Trial interaction is more judicially pro-active and confrontational, and (as described) through the sentencing homily, the judge may address specific victims' concerns, or express wider communitarian justifications for sentence. Certainly, as explained earlier, the relative reality of increasing political influence over judicial independence in both jurisdictions provides a cultural context for realizing the instrumental potential of discretion to influence outcomes, but it is not necessarily the only, or the most significant, determinant of inclusivity in actual decision-making. Hence, viewed comparatively, politics provides the formula for possible outcomes, but discretion provides outcomes which are reformulated for politics. Understanding how and why relationships of influence favour specific outcomes is an essential prerequisite before considering the repositioning of penality.

An unfettered adversarial paradigm *per se* is not, therefore, the issue that distinguishes Italian and English judicial practice in the exercise of any discretion relating to the extent of victim participation in ordinary criminal trials.[22] Generically, the crucial determinant is *the context which informs the instrumentality of judicial discretion*; in other words, the legal, social and political culture of the judiciary.[23] In terms of victims' interests and their reflection through victim/judge relationships in process decisions, this variable describes and explains:

---

22 The connection between adversarialism and victim participation is asserted here in the sense that the adversarial/common law tradition historically has provided a context for discretion, although varying in degrees of control. Where judicial discretion flourishes so does individualization in sentencing. Individualization is a context for decision-making that more readily accommodates and reconciles victims and offenders than tariff or just deserts approaches.

23 Namely, the variables that determine the ideology and pattern of judicial behaviour (praxis) (Bell 2001: 2).

1 the cultural meaning of inclusion and exclusion for trial participants;
2 the cultural conditions which promote *selective inclusivity* in judicial discretionary decisions; and
3 the *actual* form and direction of selectivity in decision-making.

The third factor provides the contextual motivation for our analysis, and the driver for our interrogation of the relationship between the judge and the victim. Its is highly significant as acknowledging that the pathway of influence here is in fact preconstructed by whoever has the power to include or exclude.

Our comparative study tends to confirm the view that the prospects for victim integration and the development of restorative justice strategies are not advanced within the constraints imposed by proportionality and deserts-based ideology. Further, the fragmentation of process through the introduction of discrete structures for dealing with particular forms of offender or offending behaviour understandably does little to advance the cause of integration, either in theory or practice. As the Italian experience suggests, changes in structure and form without a corresponding re-evaluation in the overall purposes of prosecution, trial and sentence (beyond a basic need to remedy procedural deficiency) produce penal structures whose philosophical justifications are impossible to reconcile within the existing stated aims of punishment and the legislative model which embodies them.

Hence, the simplified trial process introduced for the adjudication of crimes before the recently created Justice of the Peace procedure clearly represents a radical departure from the Italian tradition of penal prosecution as governed by the principle of legality. Instead, it not only challenges the notion of 'crime' and criminality for the penal process, but also culturally accepted notions of 'trial'. It does so by transferring the discretionary process of deciding how the violation of criminal norms should be resolved from the state to the parties directly involved. Such cultural shifts in penality and individual empowerment have taken place against the background of the 1989 reforms that challenged the conventionally accepted notion of inquisitorial 'trial' process for ordinary criminal proceedings as under the 1930 CC. This was achieved by introducing adversarial reforms which refocused attention on the trial rather than the pre-trial process as the mechanism for testing and verifying the evidence.

As regards the role of judicial discretion[24] and the prospects for process and victim integration, the 2000 reforms have in a sense

24 Acknowledging its potential as a vehicle for overcoming limitations of principle and procedure.

democratized the Italian criminal process by restoring aspects of penal resolution to citizens. Yet this weakening of judicial and state authority has been reversed by the pivotal role accorded to judicial discretion in ordinary criminal proceedings following the 1989 reforms. These reforms have gone far beyond those experienced in England, or in fact in the notion of victim participation evident in the norms and practices of international criminal tribunals, such as the International Criminal Court (ICC) (Henham 2003a).

The general effect of the Italian reforms is, of course, to reduce the overall significance of the new adversarial model through the introduction of alternative models which provide significant derogations from the accusatorial approach. For example, the novel penal jurisdiction of the Justice of the Peace[25] created a new sanctioning 'microcosm' (new sanctions and alternative mechanisms for resolving conflicts) that functions independently of the ordinary criminal justice system for adult offenders. Structurally, it is a mixed model that combines retributive and reparative aspects. The basic objectives of the reform were administrative and bureaucratic: to lighten the workload of the system of ordinary justice, thereby minimizing recourse to criminal sanctions, and favouring reparative conduct and reconciliation between the parties in a dispute. The implantation of this alternative paradigm was forced into the existing hybridized trial context without any attempt being made to rationalize the overall framework for penality. Consequently, the adversarial reforms designed (in part) to promote the adult trial as *the* context for determining truth, guilt and justice have been undermined by initiatives such as this designed to democratize justice by giving the power to victims to drive the process and have a definitive role in the determination of the sanction.

In England, the democratization of justice has featured as a regular theme for policy-makers since the early 1980s, but its rationale has been driven more by the administrative problems of prison overcrowding than the suspected failings of the criminal trial system as in Italy. This perception has now changed, so that criticisms of unfettered judicial discretion and policy initiatives for diversion or mediation and the generalized repackaging of custodial alternatives as punitive disposals are presented as part of a comprehensive programme to reposition the judiciary, their discretion and the role of the criminal trial in the public mind (Rex and Tonry 2002). This is evidenced by the recent

---

25 Although introduced on 28 August 2000 by law n. 274, the justice of the peace paradigm only became operative on 2 January 2002.

reformulation of the purposes for sentencing against a background of increasingly inflexible guideline mechanisms and provisions for transparency contained in the Criminal Justice Act 2003.

It is arguable that such reforms in English sentencing will do little to further the cause of victim integration in sentencing simply on the grounds, first, that they do not increase victims' procedural rights in any substantive sense; and, secondly, that they fail to address one of the main structural obstacles to the notion of integration, i.e. the strict separation of the trial/verdict and sentencing phases of the criminal process characteristic of adversarial trial forms. The reasons for arguing against the latter are not weakened by our observations of the Italian experience. In Italy we have suggested that attempts to adversarialize process and the way in which the judiciary use their discretion in ordinary proceedings following the 1989 *CCP* reforms have been hampered by the slowness of an inquisitorial judicial culture to adapt to change and exploit the potential for addressing victims' concerns within the existing philosophical framework imposed by the 1930 *CC*. Consequently, the advantages for victim integration in sentencing that might be derived from a process structure which combined the verdict and sentencing phases of the trial have not been fulfilled. In summary, these would include the ability to conceptualize the criminal process culminating in sentencing as an amalgam of process decisions informed by a unified rationale and co-ordinated policy aspirations.[26] In England, not only has the sentencing phase of the trial traditionally been where the principle of judicial independence has found its fullest expression, but it has also developed its own philosophical rationales, procedural rules, sentencing principles and policy. Further, notions of lay/professional participation in the process are grounded in these contexts rather than any overall integrated conception of the criminal trial.

However, these observations conceal some complex realities. The separation of verdict from sentence, whether as a unified or two-stage process, poses a significant structural question regarding the most appropriate processual context for nurturing and facilitating the constructive potential for discretion as an instrumental force for influencing praxis and thereby advancing the potential for restorative justice ideology to become integrated in trial decision-making as a recursive reality. Essentially, we argue that discretion is instrumental for reconciling retributive and restorative aspirations for justice in

---

26 For an excellent analysis of the theoretical and practical implications of such a suggestion, see Lacey (1987).

penality. We also argue that this must be achieved through the reconceptualization of penality within a given local or global context. Our analysis demonstrates that access and rights otherwise remain symbolic and rhetorical. Ideally, the integration of verdict and sentence phases in the trial should maximize the potential for outcomes that promote legitimate claims to access and rights. However, CCA recognizes that the notion of integration promoted through the fusion of process depends on cultural context and is distinguished by the significance it accords to different regimes of criminal process and procedure.

One of the most significant practical implications for victim integration, of the separation of verdict and sentence, concerns the need for evidence to be reconstructed to serve the purposes of the sentencing phase.[27] However, this phenomenon can also take place within any integrated model. In Italy, for example, specific criteria establish the boundaries for the exercise of discretionary power relevant to sentence, but it is witness testimony elicited during the trial phase that is evaluated against these legal constraints.[28] Similarly, the rights accorded to victims under *CCP*, Art. 90 are directed towards the trial (verdict and sentence) rather than to sentence. Such a model should also be integrated in the sense that the rationale, policy and procedure governing the exercise of judicial discretion for the purposes of verdict and sentence should reflect and relate to one another. For reasons we have explained, this has not occurred with Italian sentencing. In a sense, what has transpired in Italy reflects the fundamental tensions which occur in purely adversarial systems; that, ultimately, the ideology of traditional criminal law theory – certainty, predictability and consistency – are problematic for rationalizations of penality which envisage consequentialist justifications as primary rationales for the penal system. The failure of adversarial systems to integrate trial

---

27 In England, the difficulties caused by the need to establish the factual basis for sentencing are a direct result of the division of the trial into two distinct phases. In particular, evidence relevant to sentence (such as provocation) may not be sufficiently explored, even during a full trial. Where the offender pleads guilty these difficulties are exacerbated, since the prosecution and defence accounts of the facts may differ considerably.

28 Judicial deliberations follow immediately after the close of the trial and, after considering any unresolved preliminary matter and/or procedural issues, judges must consider each issue of fact or law, *as well as the proper sentence*. Needless to say, abbreviated proceedings and procedures that facilitate bargaining for sentence distort the extent to which the facts upon which sentence is based actually correspond with those that occurred.

philosophy and practice has meant that questions of procedural fairness and rights protection have assumed particular significance.

We have suggested that access to legitimacy (justice) depends on ideological and structural change in the contexts for trial discretionary decision-making. Rights are an important processual corollary to access – essential for any appreciation of inclusivity. Consequently, inclusion must operate within a framework where the rights of contested interests are recognized and accorded. Research suggests that a disjunction may exist between rights paradigms and their relative existence in different jurisdictional settings, whether local or global (Henham 2000c).

Indeed, it is arguable that the jurisprudence of international human rights norms will assume a disproportionate significance in the broader context of the internationalization of sentencing. More especially, it remains to be seen how conflicting interpretations of legal norms are resolved at the local level, and on what moral basis such instruments derive their legitimacy in these contexts (Henham 2000c). Although it may be suggested that human rights (and other) norms have impacted on the remodelling of criminal trial processes in European states, our analysis of the legal and policy contexts of English and Italian sentencing thus far indicates that our understanding of the complex inter-relationship of process variables operating at many different levels renders any such generalized conclusions overly simplistic, and of little practical utility for policy-makers. For example, we have noted how similar process results are achieved through different penal strategies in different jurisdictional settings because of the operational effects of legal culture. Similarly, notions of lateral and upward internationalization need to reflect what appear as realignments, convergence or dissimilarities in sentencing against an awareness of their wider sociopolitical significance.

Our consideration of integration as a processual paradigm for reconciling relative notions of access and rights has recognized the limitations imposed by differences of context. It also cautions that the main obstacle to real victim integration in postmodern penal strategies has more to do with political pragmatism than ideology. As Garland (1996) suggests, state/citizen relationships are continuously re-configured or remodelled in order to shift penal accountability. The centralization of penal authority in the state, the institutionalization of penality and restrictions on individual autonomy and participation have symbolic rather than moral legitimacy.[29] Within this context, the

---

29   Beyond any that may be attributed to retributivism.

manipulation and redistribution of judicial discretion within process models and the apparent empowerment of lay actors are merely a functional response rather than indicative of any meaningful increased democratization. This analysis is also consistent with the general willingness on the part of both civil and common law systems to institutionalize criminal processes which are unconstitutional, or otherwise in breach of human rights norms, on the grounds of managerial or bureaucratic efficiency. Such manifestations have little to do with notions of integration as models for penological change.

The international context[30]

It should be noted that the predominance of the retributive dynamic in international penality exists notwithstanding the fact that common law/civil law models of criminal procedure as reflected in international sentencing process have influenced the conceptualization and recognition of rights balanced between the accused and the victim. If we take as an illustration the presumption of innocence, as Chiavario (2002) notes, this is deeply entrenched in Western European judicial culture and, whilst its form and significance vary between countries, there is general recognition that its existence is related to the 'right to a judicial process' for the accused. The presumption of innocence is similarly enshrined in the ICC Statute (Art. 66). Overcoming the presumption is a necessary precondition for a non-arbitrary conviction. However, in both domestic and international jurisdictions, fundamental rights remain theoretical to the extent that they are readily sacrificed for procedural, managerial and bureaucratic advantage in the rush to convict. One way to reconcile these apparently competing forces is to suggest, as Tulkens (2002: 652) does, that for Western European systems of criminal procedure, negotiated justice represents a move away from notions of the universality of the criminal law towards a more civil law-oriented model that recognizes its facilitative function in the reconciliation of public/private interests. In ICJ terms this might be extended to address the contested rights of victim and offender communities.

There are interesting parallels here for internationalized justice and rights. Clearly, fundamental objections to the functionalist paradigm of consensual justice are inequality between the parties (particularly

---

30 For detailed analysis of victims' rights in the context of international sentencing, see Henham (2004).

when the lay participants may be generic), discriminatory practice and lack of transparency. These arguments tend to suggest that rights protection will increase if the normative practice of criminal procedure is more effectively regulated. However, such technical adjustments are unlikely to sever the link between ideology and praxis.[31] In particular, for international sentencing the ideology and structures of punishment are closely aligned to maintaining the economic and political integrity of Western liberal democracies. Conceptualizations of criminal law and procedure as facilitative of consensual forms of justice provision therefore fail to recognize cultural relativism and the predominantly authoritarian and undemocratic function of international criminal trials. This has crucial implications for understanding the significance of relative differences in status and rules of engagement for lay/professional players within the trial process.

Such a facilitative paradigm also ignores the different levels of influence which establish the conditions for *selective inclusivity* in the recognition of victims' rights through the exercise of judicial discretionary power in the international criminal tribunals.[32] At the macro level we might speculate that the reasons for differentiation and exclusion are, as Foucault (1977a) and Garland (2001) have argued in relation to shifts in penal culture during the eighteenth and nineteenth centuries, concerned with the manipulation and transformation of knowledge about crime in the international context, and the re-distribution and consolidation of punitive power in the hands of Western liberal democracies through the retributive penality of the international tribunals. At the micro level, the ideological and normative implications for victims in the international tribunals are played out in a context of significant judicial discretionary power. Here judges are drawn from a mixture of common law/civil law traditions, procedures predominantly based on compromises made between common law/civil law process styles and an absence of clarity as to which penal justifications might be appropriate to inform international sentencing practice.

Thus, international sentencing praxis provides the conditions and predisposition for the differentiation and repression of particular

---

31 As Frase (1998) suggests in another context: 'mere procedural guarantees are an inadequate safeguard against political and governmental oppression ... if human rights are to serve as an effective bulwark against government oppression, they must be extended beyond procedure.

32 It is important here to distinguish between normative/formalist inclusion and what happens in practice, since this distinction is essential for establishing pathways of influence.

ideologies, states and victims. In fact, the cultural context in which these issues are (re)defined as a matter of social reality is not the foundation instruments of international criminal tribunals and the broader contexts of their institutionalization, but rather in the decision-making practices of the courts themselves. The point is well illustrated by the ICTY case of *Furundzija*,[33] where the Trial Chamber referred to 'the infallibility of punishment [as] the tool for retribution, stigmatisation and deterrence', despite the fact that this assertion completely ignored the relativity of concepts such as justice and penality, and the contexts of their implementation.

Finally, it is important to note that, just as common law/civil law models of criminal procedure as reflected in international sentencing process (Cassese 1999: 484) are relevant to the conceptualization and recognition of rights (Findlay 2001a), so the development of these paradigms is likely to reflect back on domestic jurisdictions in their assessments of what constitutes acceptable trial practice. Here the distinction between what Ashworth describes as 'service rights' and 'participatory rights' for victims is equally relevant to the international context: namely, between those rights that allow for some form of participation by victims, and those that are tangible as a matter of social reality. Whilst Zappala (2003: 221) may be correct in asserting that 'in the ICC Statute an attempt has been made to increase the procedural rights for victims and expand them to the procedural dimension',[34] we would argue that this expansion has been symbolic rather than concrete in its effects and has had little (if any) impact in addressing the fundamental philosophical and structural weaknesses afflicting the penality of international sentencing. Similar conclusions are drawn from our analysis of sentencing praxis in England and Italy.

Further, for the ICC, as Roht-Arriaza (1999: 484) suggests, states may take more positive steps than in the past to ensure compatibility with internationally affirmed rights, and the principle of complementarity is also likely to provide a powerful incentive for compliance.

The foregoing analysis has drawn attention to the significance of lack of autonomy and global governance as major factors in the conceptualization of rights for international sentencing. It also identifies the essence of inclusion as a process confirming access to justice but reliant on rights protections for its reality. If we accept the premise that

---

33 *Prosecutor* v. *Furundzija* (Case no. IT-95-17/1-T), judgement, 10 December 1998, para. 290.
34 Zappala (2003: 232) does acknowledge certain practical drawbacks pertaining to the greater procedural participation possible for victims under the ICC regime.

the rationales adopted by states for the redistribution of economic and political risk are the true motivators for the reconfiguration of criminal justice, both domestically and internationally, then it follows that institutional structures for punishment are key symbolic mechanisms for sustaining these modalities of power and control. The recognition of motivators for power must, therefore, be confronted as significant obstacles to our ideological truth-finding mission for the trial (or, indeed, any form of process). The contribution of CCA in facilitating the reconciliation of relative understandings cannot, therefore, be underestimated.

Whilst the relative autonomy of citizens and the state in conventional liberal democracies is reflected domestically in recognized principles for the administration of justice, international penal processes and rights norms have to date claimed no direct involvement with citizens within victim communities. The obligations of the ICC Trial Chamber, for example, do not extend beyond immediate victims within the jurisdiction of the court and their families[35] to take on board the feelings and concerns of 'significant others' within victim communities. No attempt has been to provide mechanisms to address what these wider concerns might be and how the court might engage with them, or whether what is proposed has any sort of moral legitimacy in terms of the wider victim community. As with our English/Italian comparison, the concerns of victims and victim communities receive symbolic rather than actual attention; the conception and representation of legalistic criteria has more symbolic than real significance for the choice of sentencing options and their potential rationalization. The implications for inclusivity are significant since not only does symbolism serve to distance states and citizens in terms of ideology and legitimacy, but it also emphasizes the key role for process in the implementation of a trial rationale which embraces penality as a significant force for peace and reconciliation.

However, the perception remains that retributive punishment is the appropriate response for the commission of gross violations of human rights. Retributivism together with the rationale of prevention continue to determine the nature of the conceptual linkage between process norms and values rather than any relational context. In other words, the symbolism of international penality is instrumental in maintaining the relative distance between the ideology it represents and the concerns of victims and communities caught up in social conflict and war.

---

35   The fact that there were multiple victims may be taken into account as an aggravating factor in the determination of sentence; Rule 145(2)(b)(iv) of the ICC Rules of Procedure and Evidence.

These reflections also serve to emphasize the theoretical and methodological difficulties involved in providing measures of victim inclusivity for ICJ that are both contextually meaningful yet generalizable. These difficulties are compounded for understanding international process since there must be some comparable[36] definitions of what participants in the sentencing process understand by a particular event and its significance. If we return to our earlier example of the presumption of innocence, Chiavario (2002: 553) suggests its general connection to the 'right to a judicial process'. However, enshrined in the foundation instruments of international criminal tribunals this fundamental right falls to be interpreted in the context of novel hybridized processes which contain procedural imports and compromises, such as the procedure relating to the admission of guilt under Art. 65 of the ICC Statute. The relationship between theory and context is complex here because what is required of rights modelling is the capacity to appreciate how the subjective experience of process in domestic jurisdictions is connected to its objective existence in international criminal process. In this sense, modelling the objectivity of process recognizes the commonality of subjective experience.

Consequently, the objectivity of process exists to the extent that we are able to identify the criteria whereby relevant participants recognize external reality, i.e. the reality of objects, events or states. The connections between subjective experience and objectivity exist in so far as there are common definitions of process as objective reality. The interaction between normative principles such as the presumption of innocence and procedural rules relating to the admission of guilt will necessarily be conditioned by legal culture. However, although making provision for the admission of guilt on the part of the accused at some stage in the proceedings, the instruments of international criminal tribunals are generally silent regarding their effect. This is problematic because there is no way of knowing what such legal norms and their application might signify in terms of having drawn on local contexts. We cannot deduce their subjective significance (either locally or

---

36 Not only within but also across cultural traditions. As Ewald (1998) suggests: 'If one's aim is to understand the ideas that lie behind [the] foreign legal system ... what we want ... is a grasp, from the inside, of the conscious reasons and principles and conceptions that are employed by the foreign lawyers – a grasp of the styles of legal thought ... in interpreting a foreign legal system, "the law" is best understood as a style of conscious thought: that we should be seeking to understand is not law in books or in action but law in minds.'

globally) from the objective reality of their existence as international norms.

For the purposes of description and evaluation there needs to be some agreement regarding the nature of the issues against which we might wish to evaluate the relevance of existing fair trial and access to justice paradigms. Clearly, a general perception that the presumption of innocence implies some right to judicial process does not provide a method for contextual understanding at either the global or local level. If we take our comparative example, on the surface it seems perfectly obvious that the notion of a 'bargain' implies some sort of negotiation or agreement. Coupled with the common law notion of 'plea', the implication is that the defendant is exchanging his right to a trial (and possible acquittal) by bargaining for a lower sentence.[37] Yet, the English adversarial process fails to acknowledge the existence of any bargain since no negotiation or bargaining with the judge is officially permitted.[38] The so-called Italian procedural innovation in the form of a negotiated sentence ('application of the penalty upon the request of the parties') under *CCP*, Art. 444 is a sentence bargain in the sense that the Italian system is characterized by the principle of mandatory prosecution, so that any 'bargaining' can only exist in relation to the degree of punishment rather than the charge. Furthermore, under the Italian process, there is no formal express acceptance of guilt; the defendant implicitly accepts guilt by requesting a negotiated sentence and by virtue of Art. 445 the penalty is regarded as 'comparable to a judgement of guilty'.[39] In theory, since there is no actual plea, it remains open for the judge, after reviewing the record, to disapprove a sentence bargain under Art. 444 and find the defendant 'not guilty'.

The above example illustrates perfectly the need for CCA. As we suggested in Chapter 2, the comparative contextual model recognizes that meaningful accounts of processual activity as objectively verifiable phenomena are dependent on describing and appreciating the connections made between the subjectivity and objective reality of process. The significance of this dichotomy for comparativism is that our modelling allows us to explore common definitions of process (or objectivity), whilst also providing the means for deconstructing its subjectivity. Our focus on sites of discretionary decision-making within

37 Known as a 'sentence discount' in England and Wales. The statutory conditions governing their use are now contained in s. 144 of the Criminal Justice Act 2003.
38 *R v. Turner* [1970] 2 WLR 1093.
39 According to Pizzi and Marafioti (1992), the guilty plea requirement was omitted because the code's drafters feared an admission of guilt would undermine the presumption of innocence guaranteed to all defendants by the Italian Constitution.

the trial is crucial, since this is where the semantics of process as external/internal reality are created. Although our CCA of the English and Italian jurisdictions has so far been restricted to an exploration of the legal and policy context,[40] and did not go beyond the contextual analysis of trial narrative by employing methodologies designed to deconstruct the social interaction of trial decision-making, it nevertheless suggests how complex cultural understandings of legal/processual norms and their significance can be exposed through expert commentary.

More particularly, employing CCA has undoubtedly raised important issues concerning the interpretation and significance of victim inclusivity in the sentencing processes of England and Italy. We suggest that, despite the fact that they relate to two Western European jurisdictions, conclusions such as these do have an important bearing for the conceptualization of ICJ. First, as we have already argued, utilizing CCA provides culturally meaningful explanations of trial dynamics in different jurisdictional settings, and our understandings of these relationships and pathways of influence provide us with different modalities that can be used to model trial process in its local and global forms. Accepting this proposition means we can construct models containing evaluators drawn from comparative analyses that allow us to interrogate the processes that actually determine victim inclusion and exclusion. Based on our CCA of this issue in England and Italy we are already able to hypothesize about the following:

- Determinants of inclusion and exclusion.
- Conditions for selective inclusivity – the reasons for influence.
- Operations of pathways of selectivity – the form and direction of influence.

Such a model can be refined through the inclusion of additional evaluators of context, tested empirically and further modified as appropriate following the results obtained through utilizing deductive and inductive methodological techniques in different jurisdictional settings.

In terms of our work on international sentencing (for example),[41] comparative contextual research such as the English and Italian study

---

40 The legal/jurisdictional level of analysis in structuration terms.
41 To date our research has focused on the ICC and involved legal analysis of its foundation instruments, and speculation about the likely future direction of its sentencing practice. See Henham (2002b, 2003b, 2004: 27).

can be particularly significant. It influences the direction of future empirical research because it suggests certain propositions for modelling victim participation that may be relevant to understanding the nature and significance of victim inclusion/exclusion in international criminal trials. Ultimately, it may inform policy. Whilst neither it, nor any other methodology, can reconceptualize, rationalize or reposition the justifications for international sentencing decisions, what it can do is to explore the relative contexts of penality, thereby allowing informed speculation about the potential for achieving particular penal outcomes.

The important point to remember, however, is that the modelling derived from CCA is not simply setting out to test theoretical assumptions about the nature and operation of a particular normative context. What is provided through contextual modelling are interpretative categories for understanding the meaning of proccessual activity. They are interpretative in the sense that they represent certain understandings about the meaning of process that are being tested against realities other than those from which they were derived; they are categories because they are determined by analysing a specific contextual setting. It is the testing of contextual meanings against each other by commentators who can appreciate the significance of comparison and its implications for advancing understanding, that distinguishes the heuristic force of CCA from alternative approaches. Thus, CCA of victim participation in English and Italian trials helps us to understand why and how the perceptions of victims towards procedural similarities and differences and their actual significance are determined by legal and sociocultural context. For example, in procedural terms, both the English and Italian jurisdictions are characterized by the fact that victims do not have the right to participate in the negotiation of sentencing decisions; but what does this imply for the notion of negotiated justice in cultural terms? Does it mean that victims who do not testify are content for the criminal process to 'balance' their personal and communitarian interests as victims against ideological and system interests for speed, certainty and finality that are driven by economic and managerial agendas? In the international context the resolution of such issues is crucial for the pursuit of reparative and restorative goals in communities where socially harmful actions have been perpetrated on a catastrophically large scale.

Conventional ways of modelling process fail to appreciate the different levels of abstraction implicit in context and its global, regional and domestic dimensions. These understandings are crucial for appreciating the ideologies of justice employed by powerful nation-states and the legitimacy attached to them in different jurisdictional contexts. In addition to reflecting these factors, credible models and methodologies of the international criminal sentencing process must be capable of distinguishing and analysing the following:

1 *Proposed process values* – those values regarded as fundamental for the criminal process which international instruments are designed to protect.

2 *Proposed categories for rights* – those principles which are designed and incorporated into international criminal procedures to give effect to the values specified in (1).

3 *The reality of rights in practice* – the institutionalization of rights; the degree to which practice in international sentencing actually gives effect to the rights specified in international instruments.

4 *The nature of the process values attaching to rights in practice* – the degree to which the process values which reflect actual practice correspond to those which originally inspired the conceptualization of rights for the international process.

The shortcomings of conventional approaches are illustrated if we search for convincing accounts of the procedural practices relevant to international sentencing (such as plea bargaining). In relation to the ICC, for instance, Schabas states:

> There were difficulties in circumscribing the rules applicable to guilty pleas because of differing philosophical approaches to the matter in the main judicial systems of national law … Under the Rome Statute a 'healthy balance' has been struck between the two [common law/civil law] approaches (2001b: 124, words in square brackets added).

This analysis, although perfectly accurate as far as it goes, exemplifies the serious limitations of legal positivism as a methodology for supplying justifications for the legitimacy of process. In these statements Schabas concludes that the reconciliation of difference is legitimized through procedural rules, although his reading of context does not extend beyond this. In short, evaluative judgements about the balancing of different values implied by different procedural traditions once crystallized in legal form are invested with an appearance of procedural credibility and reality. This kind of analysis fails to consider that an examination of the social reality of process is required in order to appreciate what actually 'counts as facts' within a particular context by conflicting ideologies and political realities.

Hence, the modelling of values through to norms and back to values suggested by CCA is crucial from a theoretical and empirical perspective; theoretically, because such conceptualization reflects the recursive relationship between ideology and structure; and empirically, because it proposes an interpretative agenda for understanding and methodology. In other words, it identifies the different dimensions of context, engages with it and suggests methodologies of deconstruction which will in turn yield improvements in our understanding of process.

Conceptualizing access to justice and victims' rights

Tochilovsky (1998: 55, 59) acknowledges that many of the procedural rights made available to victims for trials conducted by the *ad hoc* tribunals are absent from the criminal procedures of those countries where the crimes charged were perpetrated. For as Findlay suggests:

> The consideration of access to justice as exemplified through trial participation has not much ventured outside the 'rights foundation' of international criminal procedure. This turn is primarily conceived as applying to the accused. For instance, little is said at the international level, about the access by victims to justice within the trial context, beyond peripheral concerns such as protection for victim witnesses and victim compensation (2002b: 253).

These observations raise fundamental issues concerning the conceptualization of access to justice and rights in international sentencing. Findlay's paradigm (2002b: 256) is instructive in this respect as it envisages access to trial justice at three distinct levels; namely, access to trial, access by those within the trial and access to the community by the trial. Findlay concludes by suggesting that the institutional features of trial access are best analysed against principal sites for decision-making such as sentencing where particular issues (including victims' procedural rights) may be identified and evaluated. This model therefore possesses the conceptual capacity to facilitate our understanding of the nature and significance of victims' rights within the international sentencing process and the wider local and regional contexts beyond the trial itself. Therefore, the capacity for such modelling to lead to a contextual understanding of points within the trial where pathways of interest are contested is a crucial precursor to developing meaningful notions of inclusivity.

As stressed earlier, an important aspect in conceptualizing the reality of access and the impact of normative controls such as rights for sentencing is to view sentence decision-making as reflective of a recursive process of discretionary decision-making (occurring through-out the trial process) that is determined primarily by lay/professional interaction. Consequently, it is important to emphasize in connection with the concept of integrated judicial decision-making as it relates to sentencing that all relevant actors should participate fully, and have a significant input in those decisions which impact on the sentencing process, as well as the sentencing decision itself. Further, for inter-national penality the notion of integration should not only encompass the integration of lay and professional interests in trial decisions, but also engage with local and regional contexts.

Access to justice and rights for victims in international sentencing processes can therefore be evaluated against the theme of integration in terms of the following paradigmatic factors:

Access to sentencing – pre-sentence factors which either preclude trial and sentence, or have a fundamental impact on sentence determination. For international trials these include:

- The ability of victims to determine or participate in pre-trial process (for example, regarding authorization to proceed with investi-gations; challenges to jurisdiction or admissibility; presence and participation at pre-trial chamber deliberations).

- Influence of the prosecutor; the significance of plea agreements (participation and relevance of guilty plea decisions for victims).

- The permissible extent of victim intervention and participation in Trial Chamber deliberations (for example, as witnesses).

- Mechanisms for establishing the facts which are relevant for sentence (separate sentence hearings).

Access to sentencing by those within the trial – victim participation in sentence determination. This includes:

- Victim impact statements (discretionary effect on sentence).

- Determining gravity/aggravating circumstances (possible submission of additional evidence).[42]

- Determining mitigating circumstances (expressions of remorse, effect of admission of guilt).

Access to the community through sentencing – factors which identify or connect with 'victims', 'communities', 'significant others':

- Punishment justifications (symbolism and reality).
- Relevance of existing sentencing practice.
- Significance of reparation and compensation.
- Specific units/trust funds for victims.

In addition to the existence of specific issues, the ICC Statute (Art. 68 (3)) contains a general injunction to take into account views and interests of victims throughout the trial and allow them to make representations at any time. Although Cassese (1999: 167) hails this as 'of great significance' and 'a great advance in international criminal procedure' because 'for the first time in international criminal proceedings the victims are allowed to take part in such proceedings by expounding in court their "views and concerns" … on matters relevant to the proceedings', it is questionable how real these effects are.

Elsewhere, Henham has argued that the need to obtain additional evidence in the *interests of justice* for victims, or take their views into account, may be largely over-ridden by crime control and system considerations:

> it cannot be stated with any degree of conviction that victims' rights in the ICC are likely to be a paramount consideration. A more realistic assessment suggests that the *interests of justice* are more likely to be equated with notions of retributive justice than victims' rights and reparation (Henham 2003a: 108).

Regrettably, the same sentiment applies to the other factors identified above in terms of their significance for victims' access to justice in international sentencing. There is no sense in which the integration of victims into the international criminal process can move beyond form

---

42 For example, the ICC must consider (*inter alia*) the extent of the damage caused, especially the harm suffered by victims and their families (Rule 145 1(c)).

to substance because the identification and degree of importance attached to victims' views are largely dependent upon judicial discretion exercised within the constraints imposed by ideology and power. What is needed is a reconceptualization of the purpose of the international criminal trial process itself.

In our view, victims' rights cannot simply be viewed against the provision of minimum procedural standards for each stage of the international sentencing process, or as guarantors that existing procedures are consistent with the symbolic purposes of international punishment articulated in the foundation instruments and sentencing practices of international criminal tribunals. Access to justice implies that the moral integrity of process can only be protected through rights that equate with fundamental and available notions of truth and justice.

We suggest that the parameters of access and effective rights protection are functions of trial ideology and how penality is conceptualized in terms of ICJ. As we argue in Chapter 7, the broadening of justice expectation through the recognition that justice is not rooted in a narrow focus for penality, is crucial. We go further (within the themes of access and inclusion) to see peace and governance as legitimate aspirations for ICJ (wherein penality and restoration have a place). As we have demonstrated, greater victim participation and access rights will not change the prevailing philosophical direction of justice, nor will it provide the essential context for trust and constructive resolution where discretion can be used as a positive force for peace and reconciliation.

Conclusion

This chapter has illustrated how victims' concerns and interests and our evaluation of them are driven by the ideological dynamics of the trial process: namely, the extent to which judicial decisions determine the context for the individualization of sentences and what that context *actually* signifies. This has led some commentators to question the appropriateness of the trial paradigm as a mechanism for negotiating links between ideology and legitimacy for victims and victim communities (Christodoulidis 2000).

By contrast, we argue that the CCA of trial relationships and how they impact on victim participation have significant implications for transforming the legitimate expectations for punishment of all trial participants. More specifically, we have suggested how the dynamic of the judge/victim relationship operates in different jurisdictional structures to produce particular pathways of influence. We have also analysed the manner in which international trial institutions and sentencing principles recognize the importance of the judge/victim relationship and its significance in terms of access to justice and rights, and drawn parallels between what has been revealed through our comparative trial analysis and international sentencing practice.

The conceptualization and description of the relative reality of trial process and victims' rights in local and global contexts illustrate how our understanding of the relationship between the instrumentality of legal reasoning and punishment through sentencing is dependent on the capacity to deconstruct comparative accounts of context and generalize about the conditions which determine the transformative capacity of law. By refining our ability to move from the contextuality of action to its generality we have been able to suggest reasons why relations of autonomy and dependence between trial participants exist and speculate as to their impact on the recursive patterns of social interaction which contribute to sentencing outcomes. Consequently, we have seen how the legal and social contexts of trial relationships (such as those between victims and the judiciary) and their influence on sentencing are concerned with understanding the negotiation of fact and value within criminal trial processes at the local and global level.

The challenge for CCA is to reflect upon our speculation that the victim's (community's) desire is for restoration and retribution. This involves identifying those common features of the judge/victim relationship that work towards restorative and retributive outcomes and the pathways of influence which support the legitimate expectations of victims and communities. It also suggests the need to challenge conventional understandings of trial ideology. The analyses presented in this chapter allow us to formulate some general pro-positions about the likely key variables in judge/victim relationships which are important for repositioning restorative and retributive justice within a more inclusive form of trial justice. These suggest the need to consider the following:

- *Ideological inclusivity* – repositioning the rationale of the trial for ICJ.
- *Structural inclusivity* – the legal and political contexts in which judicial discretion is exercised.
- *Symbolic inclusivity* – the relationship between the symbolism and legitimacy of discretionary decisions.
- *Instrumental inclusivity* – the instrumentality of judicial discretion – this is the autonomous and purposeful channelling of discretionary

power for perceived legitimate ends. It is within this discretionary framework that the judiciary are empowered to negotiate legitimacy.

Reconciling existing aims of access to legislative models can deliver paradox and as well as rights paradigms that operate within existing conceptualizations of trial justice. Delivering trial justice involves recognition of the duality of fact/value collapsed in decision-making. This means that for discretion to be exercised instrumentally (i.e. as a force for constructive outcomes) requires the synergy of trial decision-making with processual justifications based on legitimate expectations for trial participants. The trial and its participants are there in order to negotiate truth according to a prescribed set of norms. Determining norms for reconciliation in the context of judicial instrumentality means recognition of the judiciary as norm agents – as carriers of encoded values and agreed imperatives for behaviour.

The development of notions of inclusive justice which deliver restorative and retributive aspirations that are deemed legitimate for all trial participants implies (above all) a reconceptualization of the trial process as a mechanism for re-establishing relationships of trust and understanding. What comparative sentencing research tends to show is that the instrumental agents of social control (the judges) must themselves be trusted to develop the legitimate parameters for inclusivity appropriate for trial justice within a normative framework flexible enough to accommodate the legitimate expectations of civil society. We therefore argue that any new normative framework which recognizes access and inclusivity (through rights) as legitimate rationales for ICJ must be based on a reconceptualization of the trial context as a transformative structure for promoting peace and reconciliation.

In this chapter we have argued that the CCA of trial relationships (particularly that of victim and judge) provides the key to understanding the possibilities for promoting inclusivity for victims within the trial process and that the realization of this aspiration for ICJ depends on the extent to which relevant justice paradigms for victims and communities in post-conflict societies can influence the transformation of international trial process. We have seen how CCA of the trial provides a method for deconstructing the symbolism and reality of victim inclusivity and allows us to speculate about legitimate expectations for trial transformation. If we can understand how trial relationships are implicated in the creation and reproduction of pathways of influence which determine outcomes, we can identify and model how inclusivity may be capable of achieving the aspirations of victims and communities for justice.

Our analysis also suggests that the ideological commitment necessary to achieve trial transformation through utilizing the instrumentality of discretionary decision-making needs to be reflected in norms of access for victims which transcend symbolism and have tangible effects as social reality. Trial transformation must therefore be accompanied by normative accountability. In short, the corollary of those values mediated through the trial should be a social reality that has legitimacy as a just resolution to conflict. It is the enhancement of decision-making relationships within the transformed trial that will delineate the boundaries for accountability. Furthermore, accountability must be seen as a flexible medium for legitimizing the ideology of ICJ. Rights consciousness should be reflective of the legitimate aspirations for justice within post-conflict societies for rights to sustain the legitimacy of the trial process. In the following two chapters we argue for a communitarian vision of international trial ideology; one which repositions trial decision-making relationships and norms of accountability to provide resolutions for international criminal trials that are capable of reconciling the universality of ICJ with the relativity of local justice.

Part III

Chapter 7

Restorative international criminal justice and the place of the trial

Introduction

Retribution is currently recognized as a prime objective of criminal trials, and international criminal justice (ICJ) is no different in this regard. Perhaps now more so because the trial is crucial to the delivery of ICJ. However, the aspirations declared for ICJ involve both restoration *and* retribution (*Harvard Law Review*, 114 (2001): 1970). With this in mind can we anticipate that trial decision-making in the international context might also develop restorative commitments, provided the conditions for such a transformation of the trial process are right? Or are the trial and restorative justice (RJ) to continue as alien at the global level? This chapter will explore the case and the conditions necessary for this transformation.

RJ in local, regional and international manifestations demonstrates common process, themes and intentions.[1] These include the desire to get to the truth without requiring punishment as the motivation. Further, restoration rather than retribution provides for the empowerment and the inclusion of victims, which may not be presently guaranteed through professional justice, typifying modern trial process and often working against victim inclusion.[2] Irrespective of changes in

---

1 Later we will reveal the manner in which the context of ICJ requires a reinterpretation of RJ process and outcomes against new and challenging victim communities.

2 Recurrent throughout this chapter is the tension between exclusion through criminalization and retributive penalty, and inclusion through reintegration and restoration. Common ground is the requirement to establish responsibility for criminal harm. The challenge for the transformed trial lies in whether responsibility is the product of adversarial argument or of mediated agreement.

273

the community setting for RJ, these themes recur and can be traced (Findlay 2000a). Recurrent themes also support retribution and its representation in trials, local to global. Restorative and retributive justice paradigms now form ICJ alternatives.

To advocate that justice is to remain constant through context and different statements of principle, some common qualities of justice and its application should be identified as restorative and retributive, despite distinct differences in declared purpose. We propose that the international trial can be a potent context for processing these commonalities, without relegating RJ to the status of alternative to the trial, or challenging its integrity through harmonization.

Therefore, the trial as the carriage of ICJ, and its possible transformation to satisfy better community expectations for justice, requires argument in terms of the nature as well as the purposes of justice, and the legitimate functions of the trial. The analysis to follow is not merely a call for trial transformation better to reconcile competing justice motivations or outcomes. More than this we see the need to re-emphasize the trial as a search for truth contained within a principled, inclusive and accountable process.[3]

RJ principles have a place in ICJ, and the trial in particular. They can assist in the process of fact-finding, crucial for trial decision-making. They can provide a sense of satisfaction and closure for victims and victim communities, not available from the trial as it is. For victim interests, RJ principles in their broad application will help dismantle cultures of violence as can be seen from the experience in Rwanda where murder and violence prevailed for a decade and vast numbers of citizens were caught up as offenders and victims. Even within trial structures which are community-centred, victim communities are taking the initiative in the reconciliation process (Cockayne and Huckerby 2004).

The overall justification for the trial will be argued as a forum for reflecting and reconciling competing perceptions of truth.[4] Recognizing and valuing those whose versions of the truth count and why, are

---

3 In this respect we are approaching the trial as an ideal type, governed by an inclusive rights framework which advances the legitimate interests of lay participants. Divergence from this can be critiqued in our comparative contextual analysis of local, regional and international trials. See Part II.

4 We accept that the determination of truth, particularly in common-law jury trials, may not be the objective of the process. The importance of the proof of the prosecution case in these models will need to be redirected to a truth-finding enterprise. As is discussed later this may form part of the diminution of the prosecutorial emphasis of international criminal trials.

central to this rationale. The consequences for penality (or other appropriate trial outcomes prior to conviction and sentence) will be that trial processes are more legitimate (through the wider inclusion of lay participants) and trial outcomes are more appropriate for the parties whose rights are at issue.[5] Trial dispositions including punishment should focus on measures where the most productive and inclusive outcomes for all parties can be forged. Obviously competing interests will present this as a complex resolution for trial justice. These dispositions may canvass elements of retribution, denunciation and deterrence, but they should take account of all contesting interests in the trial, primarily to produce a more generally constructive and 'owned', rather than a symbolic outcome. Greater inclusion of victim community interests in particular, and the infusion of restorative and retributive themes, will allow trial participants to experience the actual and symbolic suffering inflicted through punishment, whilst offering trust and reconciliation delivered by restorative solutions worked through by the court prior to conviction and sentence.

The challenge is to adjust trial normative frameworks and processes to incorporate restoration, without totally deactivating retributive trial decision-making or diluting the integrity of RJ. Applying a model of process as decision-making to RJ and the trial process, should enable a theoretical framework for synergies between these two justice paradigms within the public entity of the international criminal trial (United Nations 2002). This assumes, correctly, that decision-making is essential to both restoration and trial justice, even if their forms may currently differ greatly. It is never enough for a dynamic understanding of ICJ to remain within normative proscriptions with an exclusive connection to one punitive principle of justice. In its current manifestations, and beyond the trial, ICJ seeks retribution and restoration for local and global communities.[6]

New notions of justice

Advocating a restorative paradigm for any system of criminal justice necessitates a reconsideration of justice at the outset (Braithwaite

---

5 This, of course, works on the assumption that an over-professionalization of the trial is not in the interests of lay participants and victims in particular. In saying this we do not wish to diminish the role of professional representation in the protection of legitimate trial rights. This is an argument in fact for why RJ should enjoy the protections of trial justice.
6 For a critique of the current trial process, see Chapter 3.

2002a). It requires consideration of to whom justice must be made accountable, and how competing and contested interests can be collaborated without sacrificing the fundamental rights of a range of participant communities. Within the context of ICJ, where the institutions of trial justice in particular stipulate conventional procedures of practice and principles of retributive sentencing as indicia of justice (Henham 2001a), the restorative project demands a fundamental rethinking of the context and objectives of that justice paradigm. This chapter charts such reconsideration.

RJ is fundamentally communitarian (Braithwaite 1989a). ICJ is said to service the global community. An effort to reconcile these two justice forms needs to engage with the notions of community they prefer in an effort to seek out some common constituency, and the characteristics of competing communities which might stand in the way of integration.

The case for RJ relies on its empirical success in preventing/reducing crime, but more than this in repositioning the aims and outcomes of justice. The international jurisdiction of criminal justice also seeks justification in punishing and perhaps controlling new forms of crime for the newly accredited victim, humanity. Therefore, a development and repositioning of RJ and ICJ should concentrate on outcomes in common purpose, as well as enabling new atmospheres of moral legitimacy.[7] All this is in the context of ICJ's legitimate commitments to retribution, and to their synthesis.

The justice/punishment corollary is presently crucial to the legitimacy of formal ICJ institutions (Henham 2003a). RJ, on the other hand, can seek to test this bond and claim new and more relevant motivations for justice in the face of transitional cultures (Braithwaite 2002a). Global cultures are such a context. This is due to the power of RJ to engage communities of victims, often where the trial has been a restricted justice domain to them (see Chapter 6).

Consistent with the tenets of comparative contextual analysis (CCA) (Findlay 1999a; Henham and Findlay 2003b) (our prevailing methodology) is the intention to construct universal themes for analysis beyond strained synthesis or unconvincing coincidence and generality. In the case of this analytical exercise we will suggest alternative aspirations for justice compatible with internationalization and global communities, which at the same time are comfortable for RJ paradigms. In arriving at this point it will be necessary to discuss and

---

7 These should involve a wider dimension for criminal justice beyond just deserts and retributive outcomes. Justice should be viewed as the production of peace and harmony alongside the identification of guilt and the desire for vengeance.

determine the global community and its potential as a communitarian foundation for RJ. Having achieved this we will challenge the justifications for ICJ, focusing as these do on penality, and just deserts in particular. This direction for analysis will interrogate a rights-based process model[8] for ICJ that often fails to recognize the potency of tolerance and regulation to the same degree it celebrates punishment. The chapter will conclude with an exploration of the aims for justice offered out by a restorative paradigm, having a special resonance in an international context. These include problem-solving, conflict resolution and peacemaking. Global RJ provides a novel conceptualization of criminal justice (see Braithwaite 2002a) as it internationalizes, empowers and mediates pathways of decision-making which best bring about such outcomes. Further to this, it requires decision relationships with a capacity for parity, mutuality, tolerance and, above all else, wider access and inclusion.

A case for synthesis?

Assuming its appropriateness (which will be interrogated more fully later) let us explore the possibility of incorporating RJ within international trial models. Any such achievement will enhance and expand the style and process of justice that can be delivered by this institutional framework. The legitimation potential here is both for the trial as a central symbol within ICJ, and for RJ as an equally significant justice paradigm, no longer relegated to alternative status by reference to institutional justice processes. If the harmonious development of restorative and retributive dimensions in ICJ can be achieved (without the diminution of either) and access and rights concerns are enhanced, this will also generate a significant force for legitimation in ICJ at large. In turn, this will increase the potency of justice as a driver of global governance.

The pressure for synthesis, however, should not ignore the common sense that RJ in the international setting should also continue to operate successfully outside the trial. There will remain many justice challenges for communities which neither merit nor require recourse to formal or institutional resolution. Rather, it should be that the potential for such transfer to a RJ paradigm is at the ready should the community, the

---

8 Which currently prefers the process of sentencing, and the mechanisms which lead to the determination of individual liability, rather than collective concerns of community justice promoted in a restorative context.

conflict or the consequences require. Within retributive justice, penality as an outcome may never be singularly satisfied through restorative process. The moral rigidity (normative location) of the trial and its reliance on guilt and sanction tend to deny the place of restorative imperatives in this retributive purpose. What we argue, however, is that through collaboration many justice determinations may be more appropriately implemented before the stage of punishment. In addition, what is required to establish a sanction might be assisted through restorative truths. Finally, restoration and retribution may sit together in a collaborative justice resolution.

Restorative and retributive synergies seem to fly in the face of current RJ requirements, and the manner in which conventional retributive trial justice can be distinguished from the restorative paradigm. The resolution of this dilemma is a crucial task for the analysis to follow.

Zehr has identified three main problems with dual justice systems (restorative and retributive):

1 The (formal) criminal justice system is by nature retributive and not restorative.

2 The criminal justice system is oriented to offenders and not victims.

3 When challenged, the instinct of the criminal justice system is towards self-preservation and thereby is resilient to change or pressure to reconfigure (1990: 233–5).

Being open and accepting of change is not a feature of formal criminal justice, as it presently operates (Llewellyn and Howse 1998). Crucial for an atmosphere of harmony is a freeing up of access by lay participants to the trial system. An essential consequence will be the increased recognition of victim interests which go beyond retribution. Along with this should be the enhancing of confidence in the consequences of voluntary participation. The fear of punishment in the retributive system and doubts about the genuineness of restoration concerns in the formal justice processes may encourage participation in one alternative system in preference to the other (Llewellyn and Howse 1998: 59). This has lead to apprehensions about the fairness of the trial in the mind of those who find it either difficult or unsatisfying to access.

The international trial at least needs to expand the motives for participation by non-professional interests in the decision-making process and this may extend as far as the supportive communities for lay participants. This in turn will enhance real choice between justice processes and outcomes through expanded access and increased trust.

The separation between alternative justice systems challenges consistency in justice practice, and claims for ICJ as a holistic entity. For instance, the restorative approach seeks a specific response to conflicting individual interests, whilst retributive justice masquerades consistency under the principle of *the punishment fits the crime*. Both approaches have their arbitrary dimensions (Llewellyn and Howse 1998: 59). In addition, determined by the nature of access and the 'language' of participation, trial justice is seen as states' justice, and the community is left to make the best of restorative processes.

The perpetuation of two parallel justice systems begs the question, who is it that decides where any matter is best assigned, and what criteria should be applied? Prosecutorial discretion is now a key feature in this determination process. RJ, for it to assume a part of trial reformulation, cannot remain the alternative to the status quo (Llewellyn and Howse 1998: 59–60). This is so because it requires the institutional legitimacy of the trial process, in order to be part of the dominant symbolic image of justice, and the normative consistency associated with the retributive context. Crucial in this reassignment of authority is the goodwill and eventual disestablishment of trial professionals. The problem with this may be that it is often these professionals and their representation which ensure that trial rights are respected. A step in the right direction is to enhance victim initiation of any justice process and this will promote inclusivity as well as access, with professional representation or not. The role for the professional then becomes facilitating access and inclusion for community interests.[9]

Common themes for restorative and retributive justice

Both justice paradigms require responsibility and shaming. Shaming is seen as part of the process of reintegration and, at the same time, the beginning and the end of punishment. Without shame, then, restoration will not balance against contrition and forgiveness. In the

---

9 There exists currently the opportunity in formal ICJ for victims to initiate process only through the endeavours of the prosecutor. In restorative models, however, victim initiation of process is allowed for more directly, through his or her acceptance of the accused's responsibility and his or her voice in the choice of outcome. With the integration of restorative processes within the trial the prosecutor will need to concede his or her monopoly over the governance of trial process.

case of punishment, shame even if only in the eyes of the community is what provides the moral glue for sentencing themes such as retribution and general deterrence.

Shaming is both a cost-effective and politically marketable method of punishment, as well as a crucial community framework for international restorative processes. Truth may precede reconciliation, but the path to confession and the emergence of truth relies heavily on amnesty from punishment and forgiveness, but not the avoidance of community approbation. This is particularly in tune with the trial being used symbolically to process the most obvious and notorious individual offenders.

Restoration well covers classes of criminals, whilst retribution is against the individual, but both are working in ICJ to minimize both state and non-state-sanctioned vengeance.

Shaming provides a common platform for moral condemnation to precede retribution and to construct restoration. Even so, through our suggested reference in the transformed trial for truth-finding, and accepting responsibility rather than contests over liability, restoration and retribution both tend to take for granted the conditionality and complexity of guilt. This is either as a result of the prevalence of one case over the other, or that the process itself will not go forward without contrition. The quest for truth in preference to the struggle over guilt or innocence will tend to reduce the significance of the retributive resolution in preference to mediated outcomes for justice.

To reconcile or not to reconcile?

Why reconcile two apparently opposed justice paradigms which are significant in an international context? It is in recognition of contemporary ICJ that retribution and restoration are prominent, if as yet institutionally distinct. More lives have been touched worldwide through searches for the truth rather than determinations of guilt, and by the workings of truth and reconciliation commissions (TRCs) than trials and tribunals and yet the retributive trial remains the exemplar of ICJ and the ICC, its pinnacle. Rather the form of their institutional delivery is quarantined in instances where the trial is kept for retributive outcomes with vindication or punishment as its alternatives. Where the conclusion cannot be so clear cut, and contesting realities need to be reconciled for communitarian utilities, a TRC is preferred.

The institutional manifestation of RJ internationally may in key respects resemble the trial, or they may not. None of the common procedural elements of the trial, except for decision-making and the status relationships on which it rests (crucial for the processing of retributive punishment), seem essential for restorative institutions. It is truth determination which is the common process function here. Fact-finding and evidence interrogation in some trial traditions and restorative forums are examples of common and supportive processes. However, many of them are compatible and supportive of both or either paradigm. Further, those processes designed to encourage the acceptance of responsibility in both paradigms may be similar. Guilt determinations in the trial and community responsibility in restoration are where the processes may diverge.

Harmonization of the two justice paradigms is possible from the perspective of RJ. This justice paradigm is flexible enough so that essential elements, processes and/or outcomes can be identified and incorporated into the trial. The trial structure, on the other hand, is more rigid and professionalized. Harmonization would have to involve a fundamental renegotiation of the notion of justice ('retributive' to 'retributive and restorative') from all those involved in the criminal justice system, academics, governments and the community (victim or otherwise). There is already strong support for RJ internationally as evidenced in the production by the UN of draft *basic principles of RJ* (United Nations 2002). The draft recognizes that the existing criminal justice system is flawed and can be improved. Yet even so it may complement an augmented restorative approach. Harmonization is desirable because it can in theory take the best from both systems and address flaws in each so as to create a system with principles, processes and outcomes from both. It is the process of merger without destroying the integrity of either paradigm where critics and advocates of harmonization divide. There are some who propose this enterprise is misconceived and that RJ is set apart from formal trial justice to address the incurable failures of the latter. Others are of the view that the dominance of formal justice would destroy the restorative perspective in any merger.

Harmonization will require state and community as agents from either paradigm to collaborate in an atmosphere of mutuality. The deficiencies in the system which they operate might provide the stimulus for this (Llewellyn and Howse 1998: 60). Governments can offer resources for the merger to ensure that all communities regardless of their economic situation are able to adequately attend to conflicts and to ensure that rights are protected in the various processes, merged or alternative (Llewellyn and Howse 1998: 60–1).

How to reconcile?[10]

The question can be posed: how does one reconcile (in theory or process) two approaches to justice delivery that differ in their fundamental purposes and their methods for achievement? Retributive justice works out of the distillation of 'truth' through the production and interrogation of evidence as 'facts'. Once this truth is established to acceptable levels of certainty (Maher 1988) it becomes the foundation for allocating guilt or innocence from which punishment must arise and be legitimated. The punishment outcome is proposed as a necessary consequence of the individual's proven liability, measured against a range of 'desert' criteria, harm to the victim (the community being only one). Parity in penalty is claimed in order to endorse the science of retributivism. RJ on the other hand, addresses harm but not through punishment, deserved or vengeful. Rather than thinking of proportional measures of punishment to re-establish social order, RJ asks: who are harmed (individual and community), what are their needs, and how can their needs be met (McCold and Wachtel 2003)?

To overcome problems with parallel systems for the delivery of ICJ, the trial institutions such as the ICC will, in part, need to shift the mindset away from prosecution to accountability and from retribution to restoration. The emphasis on international criminal law and its instruments will therefore require a reinterpretation of the connection between prosecution and the search for truth and responsibility, towards the holding of those responsible accountable.

Requirements of RJ in international trials

Finding the truth and acknowledging the past involves making individuals and communities accountable. Accountability complements the growing criticism of the use of amnesties on an international scale. Paradoxically, by encouraging individuals to come forward, amnesty can ensure accountability rather than always being seen as allowing offenders to get away with their crimes because they do not face the weight of liability. In many situations where amnesties are employed there may be no other source for the truth let alone the establishment of liability.

The work of the international criminal tribunals exhibits the duty to prosecute those who commit genocide and crimes against humanity, as

---

10 More detail on the policy and practice of trial transformation is to be found in Chapter 8.

enunciated in several human rights treaties and customary international law.[11] However, this duty is not absolute or demanded in all ICJ resolutions. A post-conflict state may be unable to prosecute those responsible for human rights violations due to corruption, a breakdown in the national justice system (Garkawe 2003: 342) or, if the end of hostilities has been negotiated, by a peace agreement which grants concessions to both sides; prosecution is likely to jeopardize relations between the parties and would be counterproductive to the stability of society. The circumstances under which peace exists and the goals of the society must also be taken into account (Orentlicher 1991). As such, the duty to prosecute is not unequivocal; rather, it is a method used to ensure accountability and justice.

Obtaining accountability and justice can help stabilize a transitional society after conflict but this need not be through prosecution. If this duty to prosecute were to become a duty to hold accountable then international criminal law could open up towards more restorative forms of justice such as truth commissions and other more flexible methods to achieve RJ.

Garkawe argues that the international obligation to prosecute is not absolute and does not necessarily apply in two particular circumstances: where the stability of a state would be threatened by the conduct of criminal trials; and where, owing to the condition of its criminal justice system, the state is 'objectively unable to prosecute those responsible for human rights violations' due to corruption of the judicial system or other dysfunctions of the criminal justice system in place (Van Zyl 2000).

It is obvious in terms of restorative expectations and outcomes that there is a need to balance prosecution against tolerance. There is a fine line between when prosecution should be pursued and when it should not (Orentlicher 1991; Villa-Vicencio 2000). At the international level, because of the nature of breaches of international criminal law (ICL), which may involve genocide and crimes against humanity, RJ approaches might be more appropriate than prosecution. At an international level, in many cases, large numbers of people are involved and the crimes may be as a result of the collectivity of victims, horrific. Communities of victims seek to become communities of justice (see Chapter 8). The kinds of crimes involved at this level affect whole communities and may have been carried out over a period of time

---

11 Following the Nuremberg precedent until the ICTY and ICTR, it has become part of customary international law to prosecute repeated or notorious instances of genocide and crimes against humanity.

against a large number of targeted groups. Further, different communities of victims may be interested in different justice outcomes. For
instance, retributive outcomes were determined as not useful or
productive for the new South Africa after apartheid, because
prosecution would have perpetuated antagonism and conflict rather
than promoted healing and reconciliation for the future. In this
instance, victims were encouraged to tell their stories to the TRC, and
offender participation gave these stories meaning. This is in contrast to
the minimal place accorded to RJ in the international criminal tribunals
(ICTs) where the focus is on prosecution of the individual rather than
the restoration of communities or the reintegration of victim and
(where appropriate) offenders.

Popovski argues (we think unconvincingly) that the ICC is a
synthesis of retributive and RJ. He states 'It is this attempt to reach a
balance between punishment of those who commit crimes and justice
for the victims of those crimes which gives the ICC purpose' (Popovski
2000: 27). However the ICC instruments do not appear to apply equally,
and to implement restorative and retributive justice techniques. The
main aim of the ICC remains to prosecute offenders. Indeed, if the goal
of the court is to hold offenders accountable through prosecution, then
it may not allow any other option to be pursued within the trial itself. RJ
approaches are relegated to the pre-trial or post-trial stage at the
international level.[12]

RJ is conceived in the ICC foundation instruments more clearly than
is the case for the ICTY/ICTR. Both Schabas (2001a) and Zappala (2003)
argue that the ICC represents a considerable step forward for victims'
rights (e.g. as declared through the reparation provisions and the Trust
Fund). In addition to post- and pre-trial rights of 'participation', there
are also rights of consultation/information in relation to trial issues,
and the right of legal representation for victims, etc., to advance their
interests throughout the trial. We would argue, however, that these
provisions are not (in reality) rights of participation at all – they are
merely symbolic; unconnected with the true needs of victims because
they may eventually prove ineffective and be perceived as less than
legitimate by those affected in post-conflict societies. They do not
represent a comprehensive attempt to incorporate RJ within the ICC
trial process but stand rather as selective and piecemeal reflections

---

12 Rules of Procedure and Evidence of the International Tribunal for the Prosecution of
Persons Responsible for Serious Violations of International Humanitarian Law
Committed in the Former Yugoslavia since 1991, UN doc. IT/32/ (14 March 1994),
rule 34.

of the real status of victim communities and their requirements outside the formal dimensions of international trial justice. The institutional focus of the ICC remains on the proof of guilt and the individualization of sanction rather than on truth-finding and potential mediation.[13]

ICJ might claim through the pre-eminent endorsement of public trial that community incorporation is achieved through the open display of trial justice. However, trial practice conventions such as professionalized trial language and rituals of exclusion affecting the defendant in particular make any real and universal community engagement with the trial as is more an aspiration than reality.

The processes and the outcomes of RJ may share similar intentions for individualized liability as those recurrent in retributive trials, but their paths for getting there and the consequences of the liability they settle are distinctly different. Most obviously, the trial produces findings of guilt or innocence, and with RJ the consequence of liability is collective in so far as reconciliation is possible, yet the individual offender is still required to express shame for his or her actions. Specific RJ outcomes include restitution, community service, victim support services, victim compensation programmes and rehabilitation programmes for offenders.

For RJ outcomes to be transferred to the trial process, this would involve much more than simply providing an expanded range of sentencing options to the judge. About this, Guest (1999) states: 'the real danger remains that reform in the area of RJ will be a simple repackaging and relabelling of the existing criminal justice system'. Transformation of ICJ institutions towards RJ will require reshuffling sites of power and authority between the parties involved in the process in particular, and commitment from the wider community. A dedication to RJ values from judges, support from victim groups, and co-operation from offenders would all need to feature in any such realignment (Van Ness 1998: 7). In addition, the trial focus would need to be satisfied in certain circumstances with findings about truth rather than the assignment of guilt. All this points to an emergence of collaborative justice in the trial context which is explained in detail later in Chapter 8.

---

13 However, it might be said that it is the individualization of responsibility through prosecution or confrontation which is common between restorative and retributive justice process. The communitarian context for requiring such responsibility in RJ currently sets it apart from retributive institutions such as the trial.

A discussion of the merging in the trial of restorative and retributive paradigms should not minimize the ideological and practical difficulties within any such project. For trial process to be repositioned (in whatever direction) requires a fundamental shift in trial ideology. This depends on political pragmatism. We therefore need to universalize the ideology of the repositioned trial (uniting retributive and restorative themes) so that its legitimacy may not only become a focus for universally accepted morality about the desired consequences for those who commit international crimes and what role the trial should play in post-conflict resolution, but also that this morality is seen as something which stands a realistic chance of being translated into action. In order to influence such a policy shift, we argue in Chapter 8 (in outline) the moral and sociological case for bringing change about, and the shift in normative framework which will support an enhanced legitimacy for international trial justice. Assuming as we do that communitarian interests can claim this justice hegemony, political reality requires a developed policy prospectus for an integrated international trial justice which recognizes the importance of victim communities and opens up access, inclusion and accountability. Collaborative justice can in its widest state form the basis for this omnibus policy. The collaboration is between:

- lay and professional interests;
- alternative justice paradigms;
- alternative justice procedures;
- different processes for establishing liability;
- different outcomes as a result of liability; and, above all,
- sometimes incompatible mechanisms of justice decision-making (e.g. adversarial and mediated).

Institutional manifestations of restorative ICJ

In developing restorative processes compatible with a transformed trial, perpetrators, victims/victims groups, representatives of the various communities, government officials, etc., will not simply be involved in the processes, but in their development and design (Llewellyn and Howse 1998: 61). In this respect the place of ICJ within a wider theory of restorative governance for international communities is important to interrogate (Miller and Schacter 2000). As we conclude in the next chapter, restorative governance in this sense incorporates appropriate criminal justice paradigms into a wide framework of international peace and good order to bind global civil society. To achieve this the foundations of legitimacy for ICJ must at least claim the constituency of the principal combatants (i.e. victim and offender communities).

A site for injecting RJ into state transition and reformation has been truth and reconciliation peacemaking. Here restoration has taken successful institutional form in order to provide one powerful foundation for community rebuilding after political crisis. TRCs are an instrumental and processual example of the fusion of accountability and restoration, within a formal tribunal framework such as that which exists in some trial models. Offenders are still held accountable to victims and their communities for their crimes by being required to make full (often public) disclosure of their involvement in the crimes concerned in order to receive amnesty. In the recent South African context, some were made accountable by being officially and publicly named, which is significant for the process of shaming, along with the allocation of individual and collective responsibilities. Others participated in the TRC for reconciliation, the involvement of respected community leaders in South Africa, for instance, being particularly relevant. The sense of closure and acknowledgment felt by victims is proof of the impact of accountability within this model (Garkawe 2003: 342). This reconciliation then became the communitarian foundation for state formation and political hegemony.

Truth commissions in El Salvador, Chile and South Africa (focused as they are on ICJ concerns like genocide and ethnic cleansing) have sought to produce justice through setting the historical record straight by uncovering the truth, and promoting reconciliation through restoration. Shriver (2001) indicates that such commissions can:

- fortify fledgling legal cultures by providing them with the time and context to create new institutions and processes free of the back-log and illegitimacy of the past;

- give priority attention and recognition to the interests and expectations of victims and victim communities;

- honour the feelings, experiences and personal stories of victimization whilst at the same time

- expand the bounds of public truth and community knowledge;

- bring communities, institutions and systems to moral judgement; and

- provide public education by seeking a truth that serves RJ without eliminating the potential for selective retribution.

Local village tribunals such as the *gacaca* in Rwanda were established by the Rwandese Transitional National Assembly in an attempt to satisfy the need for justice in Rwanda by incorporating restoration, some retributive institutionality and a realignment of the authority foundations for criminal justice. The process of *gacaca* is a community-based dispute resolution forum, whereby traditionally members of the *gacaca* sit on the grass to listen and consider matters before them. The emphasis on community involvement is paramount, yet the judicial division of labour is present. Respected community leaders are elected as 'judges' who attempt to involve the whole community in the process. The primary aims of *gacaca* are restitution and reconciliation (Tully 2003: 396). *Gacaca* attempts to achieve these aims by building and strengthening communities and empowering the population by requiring people within the communities to work together as voters, witnesses, tribunal personnel and jurors (Daly 2002: 376).

The *gacaca* trials have assisted with the process of reconciliation by individualizing responsibility for atrocities committed, whilst involving the community in the whole process and ensuring that it is local and visible. The *gacaca* trials are also empowered to determine appropriate punishments for convicted individuals. Punishments include being made to repair the damage that they caused, to carry out community service that is equivalent to the restitution owed, a combination sentence of prison time and community service or other public utility work or a sentence of between five and seven years (Tully 2003: 400). This range of sentencing options allows the 'judges' to prescribe the most appropriate punishment which fits the overall aims of restitution and reconciliation. It might be said that *gacaca* trials were ultimately a retributive process with a restorative aim. Criticisms of these community-centred inquisitions which claim that they lack due process, reveal that there may be insufficient protection of accused's rights, sacrificed in favour of victim communities, in certain informal justice mechanisms.

A restorative approach to crimes against humanity in Rwanda has been deemed by victim communities and new state authorities as more appropriate than by individual retribution, due to the nature of the conflict. Six decades of ethnic hatred were reinforced by collective violence. By putting individuals on trial at the ICTR, Maogoto (2001) argues, it may individualize liability but fails to confront the prevailing culture of violence or its crucial contextual determinants.

What outcomes came from the *gacaca* process? Unless it takes a more restorative approach, the ICTR risks the propagation of formal justice symbolism which is of little relevance to victim communities nor reflects political developments. An intense, creative and sustained intervention including a reinvigorated Rwandan government, civil society, justice participants, UN entities, international financial institutions and bi-lateral funding agencies has recently opened the way for involving a more inclusive style of ICJ into the restorative governance of Rwanda.

Daly argues that RJ can deliver a 'better' or 'more effective' kind of justice in diverse and unequal societies *if* it is tied to a political process and *if* it is well resourced (Daly 1998; see also *Law in Context*, 17 (1998): 173). With respect to racial-ethnic and cultural differences at the heart of many of the conflicts requiring ICJ intervention today, the potential exists in the openness of the emergent political process in newly transitional states for differing cultural sensibilities to be democratically and inclusively recognized by addressing relations of inequality (La Prairie 1995; see also *Law in Context*, 17 (1998): 183).

RJ can make the justice system more humane in getting lay participants together in more equitable contexts, and sharing around responsibility away from professionals and formal processes, towards fundamental justice resolutions. But that potential of this new justice paradigm cannot be assumed in the abstract or by passing new laws. Normative recognition alone is never enough. It needs to be part of a broader engagement of ICJ with the politics of race, class and culture (Daly 2002).

RJ locates within disparate communities and is not focused on the interests of the powerful or necessarily of authority as may be the case with more professionalized justice such as the trial exhibits in certain contexts.

Some RJ advocates say that it must be kept separate from the trial in order to retain its integrity. Eisnaugle, for instance, proposes an international truth commission to be established permanently, just like the ICC. He considers that a TRC promotes an end to conflict, cyclical violence and revenge through healing, forgiveness and understanding, whereas a retributive response is another step in a cycle of violence. In this regard retributive justice as the province of the state (on behalf of victims) visits punishment (often violent) on the offender, without the moderation of restorative obligations (Eisnaugle and Neibur 2003: 238). From this position Eisnaugle does not recognize the possibility of fusing retributive and restorative processes and outcomes and thus his analysis is limited.

Guest (1999) holds that the difference between the two systems is too great for the implementation of RJ principles to become fully effective as a criminal justice paradigm. The most appropriate place for RJ processes, he argues, remains within separate indigenous justice systems existing within local communities in order for it to be fully effective.

Newly emerged ICJ should serve 'indigenous' global communities. Victim communities internationally, in particular, give life to global communitarianism. They represent actual communities seeking international justice, which in turn suffer without global rights and responsibility concerns crucial to ICJ.

Our model of trial decision-making which we have advanced recognizes and employs a structure of status relationships and pathways of influence to explain trial process. It does not, however, bind itself to an inevitable connection between the state, authority and justice. Communitarian interests can equally claim the justice hegemony in the transformed trial of our argument, and require restorative and retributive outcomes for their benefit. In this situation the place of the victim, their inclusion, treatment and their recognition by professionals in the trial may each need to change, and possible victims' outcomes from the trial must diversify. Finally, repositioning the normative purposes and structural interaction of the trial will follow. Obviously, this will depend on the political place of the trial within that community context, and its global relevance.

Despite these considerations there will remain in the minds of many, and indeed our own, problems for the reconciliation of retributivism and RJ as general and complementary justifying aims for international penality. Therefore, recognition that penality may in the transformed trial continue to depend on retributive processes is practical, provided it does not exclude any complementary applications of RJ, particularly as it relates to truth-seeking and responsibility (see Chapter 8). Retribution provides both a justifying rationale and a principle for distributive justice. Principles of communitarian justice can only exist – restorative *justice* itself can only exist as reality – if its principles are legitimated. It cannot therefore exist as a universal rationale for distributive justice in the same way as retributivism. Nor can it exist as symbolism or rhetoric in the same way as retributivist penality because that would represent a contradiction, a denial of the subjectivity of 'truth'. In short, can RJ exist as a universal 'moral' principle? Perhaps that is its attraction as the gel for compromise in an expanded and integrated ICJ: not to be bound by unitarian moral frameworks.

Compromise can be achieved through operationalizing our concept of 'communities of justice'. Communities of justice (as explained in Chapter 8), can mitigate the effects of moral relativity through re-enforcing the moral value of community cohesion. This may not in reality universalize international justice but it provides ICJ with located contexts for the satisfaction of participant need. There is much moral value in this, currently lacking in formal ICJ processes.

RJ internationally

Most of the limited literature exploring the place of restoration within ICJ, presents justice models that are exclusive and exclusionary. The international trial is reserved for the most serious violators, and victim communities are bystanders only included to bear witness to liability. RJ processes, on the other hand, reject professional representation, judicial determination and contested liability in favour of selective community participation. We speculate that victim communities need exposure to the protection of professional adjudication and its account-ability as much as they do the flexibility of restorative outcomes. Those seeking or promoting justice for crimes against humanity are required to choose between a trial/punishment approach or one which allows for the identification of truth on the way to reconciliation (Roberts 2003: 115). Political imperatives will often predetermine the nature of that choice, as much as the appropriateness of either model for the communities involved. Also, the nature of the conflict contested, whether the conflict is ongoing, its cultural settings and the governments in power will be the political context in question (Geula 2000). These may impact on the bifurcation of the justice model, as well as access between them. We do not accept the inevitability or indeed the desirability of choice between these different outcomes, when they form part of the totality anticipated by those seeking ICJ. This is particularly so when the 'choice' is the domain of professionals, and may be beyond the direct interests of victim communities.

Within the international criminal tribunals, and the ICTR in particular, RJ is accepted outside the tribunal framework as the only realistic way of managing such massive challenges to justice and human rights, which the resources of the tribunal/trial could not cover. In both Rwanda and East Timor, the justice delivered by retributive tribunals has been distinctly rejected by large communities of interest which have chosen to empower and operate their own restorative mechanisms (see Carsten 2001; Daly 2002). This is not simply an inevitable consequence of selective and limited access to trial justice but is in recognition that this paradigm fails to offer processes and outcomes which are inclusive of wider victims' interests. Even if trial resources were available in these jurisdictions, the pressure for national healing will not be relieved by bulging prisons alone.

Alternative governance processes?

These alternative justice processes in both international and more local settings flourish as a prolonged period of human rights abuses draw to a close and civil unrest is replaced by fragile state peace. Even so, many of the institutional manifestations of the 'alternative' paradigm (such as TRC in South Africa and the *gacaca* in Rwanda) exhibit features of procedural formalism which resemble the trial, and indicate inevitable cross-fertilization from one paradigm to another in ICJ as it develops. To pursue an argument that formal and informal justice paradigms resist integration is effectively challenged by the operation and accommodation of village courts and truth commissions. RJ has found a home to some extent in institutionalization as part of state building.

The potential connection between RJ and emergent governance patterns in transitional states is clear. The reconciliation they offer complements the peace process, and the potential to defuse ethnic or cultural animosity through recognition of victim's interests is a foundation for peacemaking. Justice in a retributive sense may seem compromised through the culture of amnesty and tolerance essential to participation and the outreach of these alternatives. However, against a background where more formal agencies and processes of justice in the past had been part of the apparatus of oppression by the state against victim communities, a new approach to justice was required. This is not without its challenges to justice in any form, as the compromise at the heart of truth and reconciliation may be through avoiding guilt and punishment. The commissions and their mission for truth and reconciliation above any other purpose could be criticized for not adequately addressing the institutional and economic consequences of racism and ethnic exclusion. In South Africa, for instance, blacks were asked to be forgiving, reconcilable, conciliatory and forward-looking, whilst whites are to be apologetic, remorseful and willing inevitably to relinquish power (Horowitz 2003: 80). The South African TRC's *prima facie* race-neutral approach avoided addressing the inequity of apartheid and therefore did not always take an active role in reversing apartheid's legacy through restorative governance (Horowitz 2003).

The justification of what appears as a dangerous omission to confront and punish the courses of tyranny and state degeneration was the need to base alternative governance process on a justice paradigm which values truth and reconciliation above retribution and exclusion. Therefore, the emergent justice style (at least in phases of political transition) is predetermined by and supports the needs of post-conflict governance.

On the other hand, retributivists say of the ICC that its central justification is the denial of immunity to the corrupt and powerful. They argue that only after the punishment of the corrupt regime can the new regime flourish. The thrust of the court in this respect has to be retributive in that concessions over liability will not prevail against establishing any unactionable truth.[14] However, the significant energies invested by the court registry in protecting the interests of the victim

---

14 Preamble of Rome Statute:

The States Parties to this Statute, Conscious that all peoples are united by common bonds, their cultures pieced together in a shared heritage, and concerned that this delicate mosaic may be shattered at any time.

Mindful that during this century millions of children, women and men have been victims of unimaginable atrocities that deeply shock the conscience of humanity,

Recognising that such grave crimes threaten the peace, security and well-being of the world,

Affirming that the most serious crimes of concern to the international community as a whole must not go unpunished and that their most effective prosecution must be ensured by taking measures at the national level and by enhancing international cooperation,

Determined to put an end to impunity for the perpetrators of these crimes and thus to contribute to the prevention of such crimes,

Recalling that it is the duty of every State to exercise its criminal jurisdiction over those responsible for international crimes,

Reaffirming the Purposes and Principles of the Charter of the United Nations, and in particular that all States shall refrain from the threat or use of force against the territorial integrity or political independence of any State, or in any other manner inconsistent with the purposes of the United Nations,

Emphasising in this connection that noting in this Stature shall be taken as authorising any State Party to intervene in an armed conflict or in the internal affairs of any State,

Determined to these ends and for the sake of present and future generations, to establish an independent permanent International Criminal Court in relationship with the United Nations system, with jurisdiction over the most serious crimes of concern to the international community as a whole,

Emphasising that the International Criminal Court established under this Statute shall be complementary to national criminal jurisdictions,

Resolved to guarantee lasting respect for and the enforcement of international justice

Have agreed as follows

and the accused at least set the scene for considering more than retributive outcomes.[15]

What are the actual rather than intended long-term consequences of international criminal trials (Orentlicher 1991; Maogoto 2001; Eisnaugle and Neibur 2003)? The current experience of the ICTY in the trial of Milosēvic reveals that a belligerent defence and an uncertain prosecution will not allow smooth or swift progress to a retributive resolution. This case has and no doubt will present ample opportunities for restorative engagement and genuine restitution were the consequences of responsibility not only couched in adversarial conflict.

The case for the international trial as a place for RJ

Trials provide an institutional framework, established processes and procedures, guarantee internationally recognized rights of victims and offenders, and compulsory attendance and participation by the offender. As noted earlier, trial rights even as presently developed offer a foundation language and practice for the expansion of access and victim participation. They certainly offer a mechanism for accountability within which these rights may be tested.

At the international level, and across different procedural traditions, the trial is already well established as a mechanism through which justice (retributive) can be achieved. Outcomes at the trial are generally more acceptable to the state, equating with simplistic and politically palatable notions that the punishment fits the crime. RJ outcomes, on the other hand, may seem by comparison from a state or public opinion perspective either inadequate or disproportionate.

The international community, whilst seeming to endorse the pre-eminence of public trial as justice, has accepted both the trial and truth commissions as suitable forums in which justice can be achieved as evidenced by the existence and perpetuation of both ICTs and TRCs. However the power imbalance which we have identified as a feature of trial decision-making (see Chapter 3) militates against the interests of certain crucial participants in decision relationships (such as victims), by the manner in which their presence and influence are constrained at trial. The trial represents an institution in which decisions are made and where with increased access opportunities and a raising of the rights profiles of lay participants, inclusivity in ICJ might be advanced.

---

15 *Quare* is this any more than merely symbolic as there are the allusions to rehabilitation in both the foundation instruments of the ICTY and the ICTR.

The inequities of power and authority in trial decision relationships should be addressed before the trial can be proposed as a framework to the advantage of victim communities. Inequalities between the trial parties include (Groenhuijsen 1996):

- discrepancies in legal advice, representation and legal aid;
- the requirement to give evidence in court for victims versus the right to silence of offenders;
- the right to cross-examination by the defendant which does not have an equivalent on the part of the victim;
- mitigation – the accused may say whatever he or she wishes in an attempt to get a lenient sentence, whereas the victim does not have a right to dispute or to answer; and
- the right to appeal against the sentence, awarded to the convicted person but not to the victim.

Shriver's (2001: 21) criticism of the trial not only challenges its appropriateness as a home for RJ but at the same time suggests why such a development might be the only answer in addressing some of the deficiencies he identifies:

- Trials cannot prosecute the dead.
- It is not possible for sentencing truly to match punishments to crime when the crime at issue in the international context often consists of the murder of many victims.
- It is rare for the trial to put institutions and systems to the test, aided by general principles against self-incrimination and torture.
- Particularly where the presumption of innocence applies, trial practice rarely compels perpetrators to confess.
- Summary classes of offenders newly tagged as such do not need the mechanism of the trial or to engage in the ambiguities of *ex-post facto* prosecution.
- Diversion from trial avoids, in most societies, the skewing influence of money and power on the effectiveness of prosecution and defence.
- Trial dispositions attempt unconvincingly to implement distinctions between retribution and vengeance.

- Only the eventual sentence guarantees 'closure' or satisfaction among victims. Justice only seems to have been done once a perpetrator has been punished.

- Trials risk the adversarial abuse of victims, defendants and witnesses.

- Inherent in the adversarial trial system is that the courtroom will become a playing-field in which the most skilled, rather than the most truthful, side will win.

RJ in an international context is markedly different in its coverage and location from more local applications, if only because it represents large global victim communities and their interests across culture, time and space. The internationalization of RJ will necessarily require a re-formulation of processes if not outcomes, from local models where its inclusivity is very particular and often quite personal. The challenge is not to lose the sharp edge which the cultural embodiment and specific location of RJ has in its local manifestations, when broadened out into ICJ.

In our view the trial represents a framework for justice decision-making confirmed and prioritized in the international context. More important as a consequence of recent regional criminal justice traditions, the trial is a concrete and public process to uphold identified 'rights' requirements and, as such, through the confirmation of fair trial, should become an exemplar of rights priorities. Therefore, if the protection of human rights is an indicator of ICJ then the trial through its process should confirm this.

RJ, whilst being criticized for not demonstrating a balanced and equitable interest in rights protection,[16] has a mission to recognize the rights of those forgotten in trial justice. To incorporate this where possible into trial decision-making could only add to its rights dimension. The rigour of trial process may, on the other hand, go some way to addressing the alternative/selective recognition of rights in RJ. Having given one reason for the integration of the two justice paradigms within the trial, is it possible, or would such collaboration lead ultimately to compromise and confusion? Whose interests would such integration advance?

---

16 Some critics allege against juvenile conferencing in particular (and especially with indigenous accused) protecting the rights of the victim and the law-abiding community is to the detriment of any rights recognition of the accused.

Reconfiguring victim community interests

Victim and communitarian interests will be served if the victim/community have someone to represent their interests within the decision-process.[17] For the trial, it will need redefinition to accommodate another level of interest and representation[18] but this process has commenced in many jurisdictions with a growing voice being formally conferred on the victim and their representatives. It would not take much to develop this in the direction of restorative interests within a retributive representational framework, such as:

- Disestablishing the professional monopoly over trial communication.

- Deconstructing legal language to open up meaning to lay participants.

- Reframing judicial discretion to facilitate more flexible and spontaneous levels of trial conversation.

- Allowing the determination of truth to divert trial outcomes from the determination of individual liability through determinations of guilt.

- Staging trial outcomes where RJ can precede and perhaps defuse the need for findings of guilt, and sentence to follow.

- Softening the entry and exit stages in the trial and making the accountability of the process serve more than the satisfaction of professional participants.

In order to establish any of these possibilities, a full-scale comparative analysis of the trial and other alternatives is inevitable. This must involve a consideration of the possibilities for justice principles not normally associated with the retributive mission. In this enterprise, comparative research has a clear policy/reform potential covering themes such as truth-finding, diversion to the community prior to sentence and the graphic inclusion of interests beyond those of the immediate perpetrator and victim. To achieve this it is also important

---

17 Note the paradox of representation as a rights guarantee, but also a barrier to the lay voice, discussed more fully in Chapter 8.

18 This includes lawyers and other trial professionals, as well as other victim representatives who might speak on behalf of the victim community in particular.

for the trial not to lose its way as a decision-making process protected by a normative structure which works towards certainty. In the context of this argument, the analysis of the trial is to test the potential for transforming its central purpose, whilst exploring trial decision-making to find common and supportive contexts for any new justice paradigm such as restoration.

It will be said later (see Chapter 8) that the importance of the fact/law distinction, crucial to evidence decisions in the trial, and the discretion which informs the drawing of this distinction, is not only essential to trial decision-making at present, but also has relevance for the truth and reconciliation processes.[19] This works from the assumptions that:

- the trial is at least in part interested in truth and, therefore, evidence and fact-finding, while perhaps not representing truth may, in certain circumstances, facilitate its recovery; and

- RJ relies on truth-finding, and one way of revealing truth is to interrogate the stories of participants (evidence) and the details of events (facts). The trial can also provide a mechanism for this.

In a transformed trial process, access to the truth-finding potential of the trial is a challenge for efforts at expanding trial rights in the international context. The emphasis on truth and away from guilt and liability (as a natural consequence of fact-finding) will make less essential the adversarial approach to facts, in favour of a more consensual story-telling process.

Our interrogation of trial determinations in the forms of verdict delivery and sentence reveals where the interests of crucial parties such as the victim remain in part unsatisfied by retribution alone. In particular, the struggle for a voice beyond professional representation is a common frustration of victim communities despite the emergence of victim impact considerations in the sentencing process. Therefore the 'failure' of sentencing to address the legitimate interests of victim communities, and to enhance the victim/judge relationship as one of dynamic resolution and enhanced choice, suggests room for reconciliation in a common context. If the trial is to act as that context then a more flexible (while accountable) exercise of judicial discretion to

---

19 It is with the outcomes of the fact/law distinction that retributive trial processes, and truth and reconciliation, may divide.

promote inclusivity and victim participation, in particular, is envisaged (see Chapter 6).

The requirement will emerge from comparative trial analysis, to promote ICJ beyond a single or dominant paradigm. In turn, in order to narrow the gap between the symbolic and the applied significance of the trial there needs to be an expansion of the coverage, relevance and hence legitimacy of trial justice (see Chapter 8). A similar transformation was required when taking justice beyond national and axis interests in order to recognize internationalism and its justice requirements (Miller and Schacter 2000).

Trial transformation in ICJ – foundations for change

In seeking to transform the trial to accommodate wider ICJ outcomes it is useful to ask what is the trial for.[20] To:

- test competing versions of the truth;
- to pronounce guilt or innocence;
- act as a forum where power and influence are negotiated;
- stigmatize, shame or label others;
- vindicate ideology through symbolism;
- reinforce definitions of acceptable behaviour and liability;
- serve the needs of constituent communities through social control; and
- provide closure and compensation to victims.

Each of these can be analysed comparatively within our decision-making model (see Chapter 2) in order that the relevance of the trial to ICJ is effectively established and its essential presence constrained. The model approach (Findlay and Henham 2003a) is also attractive in that it allows for manipulation of the retributive and restorative variables within trial decision-making in order to plot their mutual influence and outcomes. These variables in large measure are the decision relationships (the settings of influence which end in decisions), explored in more detail later in the analysis. No doubt the introduction and advancement of RJ within international trials, even if advised, would necessitate fundamental changes in trial decision-making processes at all major sites we have identified (see Chapter 8). The model trial as decision-making (see Chapter 2) that at present is directed towards

---

20 See Chapter 8 for a more detailed discussion of the essence of the trial.

retributive resolutions will need to be made flexible for the inclusion of restorative passages.

More interestingly, these listed purposes (above) could commonly support retributive and restorative processes. How, then, could trial decision-making be developed for complementary processes, towards competing justice outcomes? Villa-Vicencio (2000), in his article, discusses the layers of justice (retributive, deterrent, compensatory, rehabilitative) as needing to affirm human dignity and provide justice as exoneration. The trial is set, in principle, to achieve this. The challenge is to address these layers in process terms within a transformed trial.

The progression from model to process should be possible and painless. Accepting that ICJ has (in theory at least) restorative and retributive aspirations, and the trial is the centre-piece of international justice, then it argues as a natural location for the achievement of these aspirations. It is the possibility and probity of this trial application which require analysis.

Our model of the trial as:

- sites of decision-making;
- crucial lay/professional relationships; and
- pathways of influence to produce decisions (Findlay and Henham 2003a)

tolerates the dynamics of both restorative and retributive justice processes (see Chapter 6). The sentencing decision site discussed in Chapter 6 and its essential victim/judge relationship reveal just how the retributive exercise leaves open the supplementation of restorative determinations to complement victim need, and the potential for judicial discretion. Recognising this we intend to form the framework for the co-operative engagement within international criminal trials that will offer a restorative/retributive collaboration.

Collaborative justice (Findlay 2000c), then, is the challenge for international trial justice which will enable it to cover more collective and contested crime scenarios where there are no simple measures of guilt or innocence, where perpetrator and victim merge, and individualized justice may be little more than a mechanism for the perpetuation of injustice. Collaboration will even-out the contest at trial over the desire to prosecute and award individual liability and the need to restore to the widest community of interests on the basis of truth and contrition rather than guilt and penalty.

As a foundation for harmonizing RJ with other international justice paradigms, through collaboration, it is crucial to investigate their important constituencies; for RJ this is 'community'. The concept is problematic at the best of times but where internationalism is added to the mix, the multiple meanings of community, and their symbolic significance, need to be set out.

Prospects for global communitarianism

Conceptualizing community

In his seminal book, *Visions of Social Control*, (1985) Stan Cohen interrogated the 'quest for community'. The story of the 1980s translates well into considerations for the reality of a 'global community'. Cohen suggests that nominated crime control (read justice) strategies owe their appeal to the rhetorical quest for community. The power of the community symbol as a legitimator for justice styles is obvious.

It would be difficult to exaggerate how this ideology (community) – or more accurately this single word – has come to dominate Western crime control discourse in the last few decades (Cohen 1985).

Why is this so? Cohen confessed the uncertainty surrounding community and in particular its powerful context for crime control. The community has become conceptually and actually blurred and Cohen posited that this ambiguity of symbolism is one of its attractions. Now almost anything can appear under the heading of community and almost anything can be justified if this prefix is applied. In the context of ICJ this is apparent through the manner in which certain communities are legitimated by association with Western pluralist and democratic traditions whilst others are alienated as antipathetic to these preferred ideologies.

At first glance Cohen's recursive and 'pastorale' exposure of community looks simple enough. Traditional 'values' are said to be enshrined in this notion of community as much as they are a feature of the way we reflect upon its conventional values. From this it is not difficult to seek justice for the community, because in so doing we are confirming these values and restoring the justice process through its contribution to their continuation. Beyond a non-specific pluralist interpretation of the dominant political and cultural traditions, none of this accepts the complex diversity of individual communities and their contested values. The homogenizing of community symbolism denies not only the reality of community diversity, but also alienates attempts to assert cultural independence outside the dominant internationalist political imperatives. It further reduces fluidity and needs-based solutions (United Nations 2002). The tendency to delegitimize difference is exacerbated through the language of the 'global community'. This is a language of inclusion and exclusion.[21] To be in the global community 'club', a community requires the approval of the dominant political culture, and consequent hegemony. In this respect the 'global community' is not democratic in its common political conceptualization, but exclusive and thereby not communitarian (Findlay 2003b, 2003c).

Why is the stereotyping of the global community a crucial issue for the determination of ICJ? It is recognition of ICJ as serving an identifiable community which gives it potency. Particularly where the justice model in force relies on a 'rights framework' (such as is claimed for the ICC and the international tribunals), victim's rights, and the generic rights of victim communities, require location. Without specificity regarding the communities served through ICJ, the operational influence of 'community' over the development of ICJ will be muted. This is a telling criticism where the international (global) community is so often invoked to justify the nature and direction of partial justice responses.

Communities, by their nature, are both inclusive and exclusive, depending on the context in question and the relationships to benefit or are at risk. One mechanism for inclusion and exclusion of communities and their members from the collective legitimacy is through the application of the criminal sanction. At the international level this is particularly significant where the strong justification against the impunity of the powerful is advanced by justice agencies on behalf of victim communities rather than national states.

We have earlier suggested the international possibility of criminal justice as a crucial component of restorative governance. Essential to governance, at least in a communitarian setting, is a sharp notion of citizenship. Civil society, and the reward of citizenship, requires clearly defined community obligations for inclusion and exclusion. These should transcend particular political alliances or positioning and refer

---

21 In employing these notions we are interested to explore the processes which bring them about, the influences which determine what is to be included/excluded, the nature of the communities which emerge from the process, and how the process tends to confirm a distorted framework of inclusivity. In addition, there are symbolic representations of community which prevail above this process in practice.

more to fundamental characteristics of humanity, which ICJ is expected to ensure. Criminal justice is part of this process because it relies on and confirms the differentiation of community members (and communities) around a highly politicized social artifact such as crime. Integral to this, in ideal at least, is an eventual return of the reformed citizen to the community of citizens which are the 'significant others', essential to the original process of differentiation, and to reintegration. The criminal sanction works throughout that process of exclusion/ inclusion as a crucial measure of signification/identification.

One reason for the importance of translating notions of global community from the ideal to the actual, and perhaps an explanation for the continuing failure to achieve this in international relations, is the challenge it poses to the role of the state and of the professional in the resolution of justice. These are intensified at an international level, as are the tensions they pose in a system so heavily reliant on the trial as its exemplar.

Even in a political age where the dominant economy, and prevailing political culture, rather than international organizations and agencies, are set to determine the parameters of the global community, the acceptance of pluralist community moralities coexisting with shared core values of communitarianism is vital for this translation process. Justice, particularly with its sights set on the rights of victim communities, needs to work within these core values. Even so, community moralities become the referent for legitimation of justice institutions. This is why the international tribunals are rejected by some victim communities in favour of their own justice priorities and processual empowerment.

The moral relativity of community justice is capable as a legitimator in recognizing the flexible and transforming concepts of justice at play. RJ mediates this relativity in terms of restorative core values, case to case, whilst endorsing universal core values. In addition, exclusion and inclusion are balanced through restorative practices which reproduce the importance of community cohesion as a justice outcome.

Local community notions of the moral legitimacy of justice should be mirrored in national, regional and international processes of justice (trial rituals in particular). This has not been universally achieved. In fact, as justice internationalizes there is increasing pressure from the two principal procedural styles to create a hybrid justice process with which their citizens, and those they influence, are at ease. We argue that a more representative and inclusive ICJ requires acceptance by the players in the restorative endeavour and by those interested in the retributive event.

Communities of justice

International victim community interests are dependent on moving from the symbolism of community to a transactional and transformative social/political entity. Real global community can be assisted in the short term through the establishment of *communities of justice.* These need to possess the specificity of the case, the harm, the retribution and eventually the restoration which trial after trial should concern. Within each community of justice there needs to evolve pathways of influence between lay and professional players where victim communities are given the benefit of more inclusive justice outcomes. As discussed in Chapter 8, this will require a refinement of discretion within the trial process so that professional authority may be strong to ensure access, and tolerant to allow for an emancipation of the victim's voice within trial decision-making. Communities of justice can also be endorsed through the restorative endeavour by the recognition of *communities of interest.* The studies of pathways of influence within specific trial decision sites such as sentencing (see Chapter 6) will help understand how legitimate communitarian interests can be better achieved.

The concept of communities of justice is at once tolerant of the subjective interests of the victim and of the state/formal institutions of justice. In our model of trial decision-making certain pathways of influence (or components within these) may be representative of these communities, or may exert influence on their behalf. Within the trial as presently conceived the opportunity for victim influence and inclusion is limited, particularly for communities of victims (see Chapter 6). A greater degree of inclusion for victims within trial decisions which bear greater relevance for themes will mean that the 'community of justice' concept takes on more relevance in the trial.

Conflict may be a feature of communities of justice (as it is in the early stages of RJ on the way to reintegration). As communities are diverse and justice determinations complex, it will be natural that competing interests will feature in communities of justice.

Translated into the trial context, pathways of influence wherein victim communities are involved naturally will be the product of contested influences within those communities, and the state. Where community interests for justice are harmonized around restoration or retribution then their impact as a pathway of influence over important trial decisions is heightened. To produce community compromise and mutuality regarding justice outcomes, the collective and generic community rights may transcend the individual 'rights focus' which predominates in trial process. RJ paradigms currently dominant in informal ICJ evidence this. They are problematic, however, because in order to achieve truth and reconciliation within these non-trial contexts, the rights of individuals may be compromised in favour of the communitarian solution. The challenge for a transformed trial process committed more to the influence of communities of justice is to ensure the respect of rights in competing manifestations. In this respect the trial, if it gives broader access to victim community interests, within the context of fairness and the respect of rights, can itself become a community of justice, at least in so far as it represents a framework for justice decision-making.

RJ and trial communities

As argued earlier in this chapter, RJ liberates the search for truth, taking it away from questions of right and wrong, guilt or innocence (which is the fact-finding focus of adversarial justice). RJ returns the search for truth to the ideal motivation of the adversarial system, through the proof of the accuser's case and thereby its truth or otherwise. Facts become the story which enables the victim to engage with the offender, and the community to set terms for their reintegration.

For RJ (and we suggest through its inclusion in the trial as well), the search for truth is not inextricably connected to penality, nor should it be. Its declaration need not progress to a contest over guilt, but rather a recognition of responsibility laying the foundation for generic reconciliation based on truth and the acceptance of individual and community responsibilities for exclusion and inclusion. Truth, on the other hand, when established within the trial through fact-finding and evidence, should be as capable of founding liability as the proof of the prosecution case. It may impose a higher burden but this can be augmented by changes in the rules of evidence to accommodate truth-finding.

The micro communities necessary to engage the processes of RJ in a global context can be envisaged as particular communities of justice drawn together to confirm (and resolve) specific problems for a just outcome. Each of these may require a different restorative/retributive mix, depending on the nature of the justice they seek. To gain that mix the citizen (victim) should negotiate, forestall or discriminate the just-deserts aspirations of justice, particularly through transmogrification in certain 'unjust' community justice settings. If the discriminatory access to formal justice institutions and processes is such a setting then the trial will require adjustment to that criticism in order that its preferred position within ICJ can be endorsed for victim communities.

ICJ and community expectation

RJ relies on communities of interest (for decision-making) and 'communities of care' (to endorse outcomes). The trial should be able to consolidate both (see Chapter 8). Internationally, such communities will differ in form and compass from their local counterparts. At the same time, ICJ is politically bound to the trial model, and many victims, whilst accepting the benefits of reconciliation, still seek retribution in the individual case. Are these mutually exclusive expectations? International criminal trials market retribution in a very symbolic sense. Underneath this demonstration of penal justice, we will argue, however, there is scope for restorative processes and resolutions. As we say in Chapter 8, the emphasis here is on a trial as a model for inclusive and symbolic aspirations of ICJ within a rights framework. Speculation on the place of trials in determining world agendas of crime and both punishment and restoration, and their translation into practice is, a grand challenge in this regard. Is there an international normative framework to assist this?

The UN *Basic Principles of Restorative Justice* do not stipulate how RJ initiatives should be employed (locally or globally). For instance, there is no clear demarcation between trial or truth commission institutional locations. They only refer to whether restorative principles should be considered. It is the recognition of RJ's international advancement through, and its applicability to, different jurisdictions around the world, for which the principles are significant. They create an implicit international context for a new and RJ paradigm for ICJ.

ICJ is accommodating a range of expectations dependent on the communities of justice involved and the contexts in which justice processes are played out. These include the following:

• *Just deserts* – retributive expectations emerging from a trial, operating a dispute and domination decision model with minimum community involvement. Punitive outcomes are an attraction for the community and determinations of innocence or guilt the purpose for fact-finding.

• *Human rights* – emerging from an individualized, institutional process context such as the trial within a due process and access-sensitive decision model. This may be contrary to justice paradigms more concerned with collective or 'third generation' rights.

- *Truth* – emerging from a reconciliation justice context within a disclosure and tolerance decision model. Truth distillation may be difficult in purpose and application than fact-finding which supports trial process, but there is no essential reason why truth and fact-finding could not be complementary, even in adversarial trial models.

- *Regulation* – emerging from a control context within a rules and compliance decision model. Regulation anticipates a justice paradigm closely aligned to law enforcement, wherein resolutions will allow for the continuation of nominated practices and relationships. The institutional form for regulation varies over a wide range of justice contexts (public and private).

- *Restoration* – emerging from a community inclusion and empowerment decision model, relying on institutional encounters which have wide opportunities for access and currently supplement retributive justice outcomes.

Each of these expectations is to some extent influenced by external, political and imposed rationales for justice, as well as by their appropriateness within given institutional settings (i.e. the trial). Conventionally the dominant expectation (in terms of sponsorship and location) will force other expectations into the role of alternatives to retributive systems. The establishment of truth and the verification of attendant community moralities may provide a universal and potentially collaborative justice platform from which more than one expectation may be forthcoming out of one institutional context like the trial.

The expectations for ICJ to date have been translated into the current ICJ process through:

- an institutional commitment to the trial and penality;

- an emphasis on rights and due process (now for offenders, victims and communities), but largely within pre-trial and trial environments;

- problems with the reconciliation of truth and justice. Is the search for truth only seen as outside and alternative to the adversarial contest of the trial?

- the employment of 'community' imagery in terms of victimization beyond the trial, rather than as a context for restoration. The trial can protect both interests particularly within the *communities of justice* notion of justice expectations.

Preconditions for enabling more of these expectations to coalesce within a collaborative approach to ICJ delivery include the following:

- The need to readdress rights in their community guise – trial as a foundation for truth – truth as a basis for tolerance – tolerance as a precondition for restoration, and restoration as a condition of peacemaking.

- The driving outcome for communities of justice is community justice and justice for the community.

- That the moral legitimacy of the process (trial or otherwise) relies on pathways for decision-making which advance community interests (both for the community of global citizens and humanity as the victim). The predominant outcome for justice will emerge therefore in community terms and the protection of humanity becomes the collective interest of justice.

Consequently RJ as a significant community expectation is removed from its current position in ICJ as the alternative choice or replacement for retributive justice. Reintegration and retribution have their position in emphasizing the actual rather than symbolic interests of the community in justice outcomes, particularly when moving from individual to communities of justice. There will also be occasions where that community interest is acutely retributive, and where the conditions for reintegration are neither apparent nor appropriate. Here, a collaborative approach will allow for a progression from one paradigm to the other as legitimate interests demand.

The importance of reintegration is not as an uncomfortable implant into retributive institutions, where it takes an inferior or diversionary role. Rather, it must influence the application of retributive outcomes and their appropriateness as well. Then, RJ has the potential to relieve retribution from those aspirations for ICJ that it cannot presently achieve except outside the formal institutional context.

Restorative pathways of decision-making and influence

Consistent with our theoretical interest in the trial as a decision-making process, the transformed trial will see process change at all major decision sites. Crucial to this transformation will be the manner in which pathways of influence are repositioned.

To present as an appropriate medium through which RJ processes and outcomes can be introduced into ICJ (and thereby remedy the deficiencies of trial justice particularly as they relate to the rights of lay participants), the transformed trial must entertain new contexts for communication. Victims in particular will need a voice beyond the legal representative. Within the necessary formality of the trial hearing, victim statements and opportunities to 'speak out' may take the form of conversation so far not envisaged in the practice of TRCs. Such conversations, whilst being governed broadly by the normative proscriptions of trial procedure and the rules of evidence, may require the loosening up of some such formalities through the exercise of judicial discretion. In so saying, these conversations may therefore take on a different legal significance from other forms of evidence tested against the formal protections of the accused.

A great challenge for our wider theoretical/comparative project on trial decision-making is to accommodate global aspirations for criminal justice within a transformational trial model, drawing on a:

- synthesis of procedural traditions;
- compromise of jurisdictional practice;
- harmonization of local authority with regional and international superventions;
- hybridizing of normative frameworks; and
- plurality of process (Delmas-Marty 2003).

Burke-White (2003b) argues for regionalization of ICJ as, with the incorporation of RJ techniques into ICJ, this may mean the customization to local and regional cultures and ethics of local communities that require restoration and justice.

Another significant challenge for incorporation is to introduce restorative agendas and mechanisms within the formal institutions of justice so as to enhance their moral legitimacy, but more so to facilitate the transformation of their decision-making and its objectives. In the case of the trial the moral legitimacy of transformed decision options and outcomes will depend heavily on improved access for the non-professional interests in the trial, to the decision process and at more decision sites. This then will depend on a reordering of influence in trial decisions, particularly between lay and professional players (see Chapter 6).

The status structures that demark pathways of decision-making in the trial and delineate lay/professional participation will naturally change through the new emphasis on the service of justice 'communities' and the increase in victim consciousness that this will invite.

Reintegration as an aim for international justice recognizes communitarian contexts. From here it seeks to break down the status divide which complicates communication between lay and professional players in the trial. The invigoration of the victim communities' interests into the trial demonstrates how this division can work against genuine integration (rather than alienating representation).

Not only are the pathways of decision-making influencing in the trial transformed through RJ, but also their processes and outcomes – a transformation of trial focus away from adversarial conflict and towards the mediation of interests. Such a shift will necessitate a reconsideration of the direction of the rights-based concept of fair trial, away from its procedural concentration on the accused primarily and towards contested rights between the accused and victim communities.

Policy for trial transformation will need to concentrate on remodelling the relationships of interest which govern decision pathways. We suggest in both Chapters 6 and 8 that a new interpretation of judicial discretion within and beyond the trial will be crucial to this commitment. However, to avoid the criticisms associated with the enhancement of professional discretion within criminal justice whilst at the same time looking for a more flexible and dynamic approach by professionals to their responsibilities, they will need to be governed by core values of moral legitimacy to stand as a crucial influence in the development of ICJ. This strengthened normative framework will provide the back-drop for a greater reliance on the accountable exercise of professional discretion and will recognize the power of trial institutions and processes to endorse a range of fundamental rights relationships.

In this regard, justice decision–making is informed by rationality rather than rationalized through the imposition of external rationales foreign to the local priorities for truth and restoration. The achievement of this will determine that instead of rationales for process being imposed or presumed, localized notions of moral legitimacy are mirrored in national and international structures.

If the trial is to achieve transformative expectations then its own dynamic transformation as a process is inevitable. Even adversarial process can transform into the mediation of opposing moralities. In the international sense the trial can become an arbiter over the moral relativity of truth and justice. Process mediates value conflict through decision-making and the trial has the operational certainty for this. Trials that work towards restoration as well as just deserts have a potential to satisfy community (rather than institutional) aspirations for justice.

Restorative outcomes for ICJ

Commentators (Bush and Fogler 1994: 84–5) suggest that restorative processes (such as victim-centred mediation) have the potential to transform conflict (which is at the centre of the adversarial trial, by design) through community empowerment and a recognition by civil society of the need to acknowledge and be responsive to the needs of others. In turn, the empathetic foundations of RJ will enhance the moral legitimacy of formal ICJ and its institutions, particularly in the eyes of those communities outside its current franchise for whatever reasons. Is it essentially that such legitimacy now needs to be accorded from within the global community rather than imposed from the political superstructure; a method which is failing both international organizations and post-conflict states. A broadening of the legitimacy of ICJ will then, we predict, reassert the significance of justice as a component within international governance.

Restorative motivation for justice decision-making promotes the equation of moral legitimacy and justice so that the accounts produced by the process can be regarded as truth rather than victory through contested fact. Here, therefore, legitimacy rests as much or even more in the process than the outcome. Guilt and penalty become just one of several possible and hopefully legitimate by-products of the search for truth. The questionable science of just deserts as the rationale for punishment no longer needs such reliance when truth will justify a range of negotiable outcomes, under a transparent normative framework.

As with all justice promotions, perceptions of the morality and legitimacy of ICJ are dependent on 'significant others'. If the significant other is located essentially within an inclusive community of justice, the restorative features will be required of moral justifications and for the legitimacy of justice outcomes. Penality is therefore transformed into a supportive (regulatory, declaratory, implemental) role where restorative outcomes can be empowered. The context for restoration may in fact operate under the influence of impending sanction. RJ in this context as the priority for ICJ (even within the trial) transforms the role of international penality to signifier rather than modifier.

Just deserts in a victim-focused ICJ?

The political potency of penality cannot be denied. The trial is the exclusive international justice forum for the imposition of justice-sanctioned punishment, even where it is particularly focused on victims' rights.

In terms of the trial process and sentencing in particular, the certainty and predictability of outcomes are a political attraction for retributive justice forms. Alternatively, the apparent ambiguity of truth outcomes and restorative process seems inferior to the superficial predictability of penality.

Whatever the justification for a transformed trial, it must be transparent. The public nature of international criminal trials has been a great attraction in its development. Justice being seen to be done, and all that! Restorative negotiations on the other hand have an element of privacy and transaction which will mean some adaptation if they are to operate within a transparent trial environment. The need to have the widest community framework to reflect and endorse a restorative outcome should be compatible with this requirement.

The conventional conceptualization of justice institutions (and trial process in particular) produces winners and losers (a zero-sum game). In the case of *victor's justice*, and compatible with war rhetoric preceding the current origins and calls for ICJ, retribution rather than restoration would accord. To readdress this conceptualization of justice which is somewhat ill-fitting with modern day prosecution and adjudication it will be necessary for ICJ to inject its interests into the political debate regarding the reality and legitimate expectations of a global community.

Professionalization of criminal justice and law enforcement, along with the popular culture of crime and control, does not currently sit well with RJ. In the transformation trial dynamic there will need to be some acceptance of the potential disjuncture between formal justice agency and professional interest in retributive justice, and thereby to move the trial towards community interest and restoration. The role of justice professionals in this is as a facilitator or impediment. It is up to them.

New aims for ICJ

We conclude this argument for a new ICJ through trial transformation by re-envisioning the trial as a process for truth rather than processing penality. In this respect trial decisions will be transformative and directed towards the restoration of the place of truth within justice as much as the restoration of the offender within the communities of justice and their victim communities.

Without this approach, ICJ and its institutions will fail the challenge of restoration and add to global division rather than reconciliation.

Trial transformation anticipates new processes and outcomes for communication and decision-making, which are discussed in detail in the chapter to follow. It is the harmonization of restorative and retributive aims for ICJ which will give the transformed trial its new and ongoing legitimacy.

Chapter 8

Transformed trials and new ICJ paradigms

Introduction

Having got to the position where the argument for transforming international criminal trials is set out, we now face the challenge of giving substance to this aspiration. So saying, this chapter does not pretend to be a comprehensive blueprint for a transformed international trial process. An attempt at this would be presumptuous against our contention that the trial is dynamic and, as the recent development of international criminal justice (ICJ) confirms, the form of any successful transformation will arise out of practice as much as from normative repositioning. In addition, whilst the chapter offers conceptual clarity regarding transformation, there necessarily will be generalization around universal notions like victim communities. These have been recognized (see Chapter 6) as vital stimulants for change, yet they will vary context to context and application to application. This variance will, in turn, feed back into the nature and consequences of the transformation process.

This concluding chapter has the purpose of materializing the process and outcomes of the transformed international trial, in so far as this can be achieved at the level of speculation and prediction. From the analysis in this part, selective policy projections and the frameworks that support them cannot but be addressed. Pre-emptive or not, the chapter charts the following:

- The essentials of the trial which will survive transformation in order to ensure the integrity of this decision process and its potential to offer order and certainty to other justice paradigms.

- The need for, and nature of trial change, building on the essence of the trial and adding value to its decision relationships, through enhancing expanded pathways of influence.

- The challenges confronting change and the achievement of the purposes proposed for trial transformation.

- The dimensions within which transformation might be anticipated, and the meta levels of context within which transformation can be measured.

- The principal process themes which emerge from the broad consideration both of expanded access and of the impediments to reform.

- The outcomes possible with the emergence of a new international trial process that realizes justice expectations, so far outside the trial tradition.

- The manner in which ICJ policy transformed through the new trial process and its potentials will impact on global governance through the influence of justice.

In an effort to assist those whose task it is to make sense of ICJ, and to operate international criminal trials in particular, we offer up a vision of the trial as it is, as it can be made to be, the difficulties in achieving transformation and the consequences for the effort. The discourse of this chapter reasserts our model of the trial as a process of decision-making up for change through the expansion and repositioning of currently under-recognized influence. We anticipate a new process will emerge, with some novel decision sites and relationships, and certainly renegotiated pathways of influence for new trial outcomes. Even so, if the trial is to retain its entity, one which we argue can protect the rights of a wider client access and improve the operation of alternative justice paradigms, then the transformation process must proceed mindful of what it is within the international trial process as we know it, that requires retention and enhancement. This also holds true for the alternative justice approaches which, as part of ICJ, determine to remain outside the influence of the trial.

The transformation of the trial to consider restoration as well as retribution, and to pick up those who want both, does not require the end of alternative paradigms. It will mean, however, that other justice forms may not operate without recognizing the choice within a protective environment like the transformed trial guarantees. To fail in this regard will result in the expansion of international criminal trial process at the expense of other paradigms not accommodating of rights contests and differential justice outcomes.

The need for a practical engagement with the nature of the transformed international criminal trial naturally follows on from the discussion in Chapter 7 of if, why and where change should occur. Transformation is seen as a remedy for the inadequacies of access and engagement in trial justice. How engagement is to be made more significant and access is to be enhanced for the benefit of trial communities are interrogated in detail in this chapter.

The thesis here expounded is that the operational relevance of the trial in ICJ needs to be transformed through the radical restructuring of access to justice, the nature of lay/professional decision-making, an expansion of justice processes and outcomes in the trial, and a transformation of the trial as vehicle for liability and punishment (now to include responsibility and restoration). Therefore, the motivations for transformation are as follows:

1 *Internal to the trial* – introduction of restorative as well as retributive processes and outcomes within a rights framework, supported by and consistent with an expansion of access for wider communities of justice.

2 *External to the trial* – increasing the legitimacy of the trial by enhancing its symbolic and operational relevance to a wider range of communities of justice.

3 *Integral to ICJ* – enhancing the significance of the trial within ICJ; increasing the relevance of ICJ; and, consequently, raising the influence of ICJ as a component of global governance.

The concept of legitimacy will be utilized as a binding theme. Legitimacy will be viewed from the perspective of a range of current and potential trial clients. The role of the professional player in particular will require reinvention through the pathways of influence in new trial decision-making. How can the trial enhance its legitimacy as an essential deliverer of ICJ through the integration of other justice forms and what are the critical consequences of these? What will emerge from this increased legitimacy when it comes to the influence of ICJ on governance at a global level?

In its concluding moments this chapter speculates on the role of ICJ, reinvigorated around the transformed trial, as a significant influence for good global governance. International organizations such as the UN have already employed the war crimes tribunal model as a post-conflict mechanism to seek justice as the outcome of war and social dislocation. Post-conflict communities themselves have resorted to truth and reconciliation commissions and local justice frameworks to prepare just foundations for social reconciliation and new democratic institutions. To date these attempts at directing criminal justice at peacekeeping and community rebuilding have not achieved all that might be hoped for after violent struggle has been contained. We argue that this in part results from the dichotomous development of retributive and restorative paradigms within ICJ. Reconciliation of these two powerful approaches in criminal justice, within an important justice symbol like the trial, will, we suggest, expand the legitimate potential to employ ICJ in a wider domain of governance and peacemaking.

To ensure this aspiration, the direction of ICJ cannot remain the province of international organizations, powerful states, dominant cultures or prevailing economies. Ownership of ICJ by global *communities of justice* is an essential prerequisite for the generation and maintenance of legitimacy which more democratic influences for governance determine and require.

The essence of the trial: essentialism and context

Distilling the essence of the criminal trial is not a conservative or regressive exercise, but one designed to produce a foundation from which transformation will have both flexibility and integrity. Implied is avoiding a concentration on structures and institutions in favour of agency and process. This emphasizes our stress on the potential of agency for changing outcomes through changing the dynamics of decision-making relationships within the context of the trial. Hence, while essentialism implies a reductive process or mode of testing the qualities of a thing, our reconstruction of the international criminal trial is driven by a desire to redefine its characteristics because its legitimacy has been found wanting (Henham 2003a). However, since judicial decision-making is made against contested facts and legal analysis, the notion of 'testing' a process of decision-making must be so flexibly interpreted as to allow for the enhancement of judicial discretion, which is the implicit force in the judicial role. This then orchestrates the exercise of discretion at all levels of the process.

The discretion which we have discussed essentially involves the structured and contextually informed resolution of social problems.[1] Trial discretion implies a capacity for individual flexibility in decision-making, whilst individual decision-making is a socio-psychological process which reflects social, demographic and psychological variables. Consequently, decisions may be seen as points where the totality of individual subjective experience categorizes and prioritizes items of information that have contextual significance. However, the decision-making capacity of individual actors is also influenced by the nature and impact of those relationships demanded by the adversarial context of the trial process.[2] Hence, the objectification of discretion in terms of the outcomes it produces reflects a compromise and negotiation of different contextual experiences. Transformation argues for a shift in the parameters of discretion as well as a broadening of potential outcomes.

The adversarial dynamic both characterizes the predominant influence that has forged the processual context for evidence, verdict delivery and sentence in international criminal trials and suggests a context for the communication, interrogation and evaluation of trial information. This context is essential to the trial model whether the processual paradigm is adversarial, inquisitorial or hybrid in form. Indeed, the observations made herein about discretion and its role in decision-making are equally pertinent to the inquisitorial paradigm. In this sense, therefore, the notion of adversarialism has little to do with trial style. On the contrary, it is concerned with highlighting the nature of adversarial ideology rather than praxis; an ideology which suggests that real truth and accountability must always be forged from contexts of disharmony, confrontation and antagonism. It presupposes a conflict model of social relations where ritualized conflict itself is seen as the panacea for fractured social relations. Thus, conflict and confrontation provide the essential ideological context for discretion in local and global trial forms. It is also worth noting that adversarialism is more amenable for operationalizing the ideology of retributivism throughout the criminal trial process and, as such, has been the subject of criticism in the structures and norms of international criminal justice (Drumbl 2000c; Henham 2003a).

---

1 Namely, that of giving legitimate expression to penality following periods of social conflict.
2 As illustrated in our discussion of victim/judge relationships in Chapter 6.

The transformed trial will recognize that the need for restorative mediation arises out of conflict. It is this which can be mediated rather than argued out in order to produce truth within a restorative as opposed to an adversarial context.

The manufacture of trial evidence is, therefore, currently conceptualized as interpretations of objective reality that are forged within decision-making contexts coloured by the need to play out the dynamics of the adversarial trial. Changing the ideology and dynamic of the context for producing such outcomes is a precondition for legitimizing and facilitating a changed decision-making environment wherein the process of objectification can be given due flexibility. Such basic reformulation is also necessary to maximize the creative force of individual subjective experience within discretionary decision-making relationships, rather than channelling it towards the manufacture of selective truth for adversarial consumption. Restorative justice breaks free of this by severing the link between truth-finding and penality.

The essence of discretionary decision-making within the adversarial paradigm prevalent in common law jurisdictions can be seen through the division of the trial into the stages of pre-trial, trial, verdict and sentence, each stage being predicated on the fundamental requirement to establish guilt. Since the trial is a legal and social construct, the social reality of decision-making within the trial is informed by its adversarial context; in other words, the ideology of adversarialism influences both structure and norm. Decisions as social reality represent transformative outcomes; they are transformative in the sense that they attribute moral status to ideologies. This means that they (and the decision-makers) provide the structure and agency for transformation. Adversarialism provides a distorting context for establishing truth since it is designed to establish criminal liability (responsibility) – this may coincide with establishing truth. Hence, the sites for decision-making within the adversarial paradigm are essential reference points for creating the liability and accountability conventionally accorded to a strictly positivist legal paradigm which envisions the law and legal process as the means of providing accountability and justice through officially structured sanctioning and punishment.

Deconstructing trial decision-making

In order to deconstruct trial decision-making and identify its essential mechanisms it is first necessary to isolate the components of trial decision sites where relationships operate. To use sentencing as an illustration, this can be conceptualized in three distinct phases:

1 *Procedure before sentence* – this concerns the way in which information is tested, filtered and accepted throughout the trial phase in order to establish its validity in the context of whether the defendant is guilty of substantive offences. Thus, the construction of this evidence is in terms of its relevance for criminal liability rather than punishment. To further the interests of legitimacy, why could that information not be interrogated in terms that facilitate the production of outcomes based on a broader and more flexible conception of the purposes of the trial?

2 *Determination of sentence* – this phase is where information is reconstructed to meet criteria which are sentence specific such as seriousness; reflecting gravity; reflecting mitigating and personal circumstances; and reflecting broader social aims. Again, it is legitimate to consider what purpose this serves. Essentially, it is done in order to meet the requirements of the sanctioning process. However, what if the process was not envisioned as one concerned with sanctioning but, rather, as one contributing to the production of positive legitimate outcomes for communities? The focus might then move towards extracting more positive factors from trial information rather than continuing to devote greatest effort in playing the trial game. Opposing trial professionals would be redirecting the focus for their discretion. They would be using and developing their relationships in order to test the possibilities and boundaries for positive outcomes instead of defending trial norms (supported by professional codes of conduct) designed to negate those aspects of trial information which do not support the discrete adversarialized versions of reality which they are endeavouring to create.

3 *Pronouncement of sentence* – if the first two stages are collapsed into what we might call an outcome phase then there would be no need on the part of judges in international criminal trials to reconstitute adversarial ideology for public consumption by disproportionately focusing on transparency, homily and accountability in terms which reflect and emphasize the pervading adversarial and retributive dynamics of the trial. Instead, the processes of discretionary decision-making determining outcome would be incrementally moving towards sentence as the natural outcome of processual deliberations. In other words, the theatre, symbolism and

denunciation implicit in publicly pronounced punishment would no longer be needed.

Deconstructing trial decision sites in this way allows us to identify the contexts for change. It enables us to describe the operation of processual and procedural norms as aspects of the social reality of discretionary decision-making created through the playing out of scripted relationship scenarios throughout the trial. For example, the capacity for victim impact in the evidential or sentencing phases is not simply structured through norms of access. It is operationalized by trial actors who exercise their normative responsibilities within the pragmatic contexts afforded by the individual case and the constraints of trial relationships, as evidenced, for example, in the limited opportunities presented to either the prosecution or the defence to address matters relevant to sentencing within the context of a mono-phase sentencing system such as the ICTY. Similarly, where facts for sentence are in dispute, it is important to know who can raise the issue and what mechanisms exists for its resolution. If evidence relating to previous convictions is permissible, what are the normative requirements as to timing and contents; when can such evidence be admitted during the course of the trial; who, and on what basis, can its admission and/or contents be challenged? The resolution of all such questions depends on ensuring that actions are linked by coherent strategies for the achievement of desired outcomes for the trial. Crucial to the success of strategic action is the recognition that relationships determine how discretion can influence outcomes. Our analysis therefore moves beyond the notion of decision sites and their relative significance as process variables and focuses on the trial context itself. More specifically, we stress the cultural contexts in which significant trial relationships are created and merge to determine the exercise of discretionary power at significant decision sites for sentencing in the trial process. For instance, the unique constitution of victim communities within ICJ argues for a particular connection to judicial discretion if their interests are to be sufficiently recognized within the trial as an active community of justice.

Reconstructing international criminal trial process

In this section we attempt to identify those decision relationships which we consider essential to the transformation of international trial justice, and suggest ways in which such relationships may be optimized in the

321

negotiation of pathways of influence that favour more integrated and legitimate outcomes for international criminal trials.

Clearly, trial relationships are contextualized through the complex interaction of ideology and norms. The predominant trial ideology of Western liberal democracies espouses the notion that the truth of past events (which may or may not be perceived as deviant) should be publicly determined and affirmed through state prosecution; the ascription of blame; the allocation of responsibility; and the punishment of perpetrators. This ideology also informs ICJ form and praxis with the notable difference that its justification, governance and accountability have explicitly global significance. Notwithstanding, the key players and relationships in this scenario involve the judge(s), prosecution and defence lawyers, victims and witnesses, the offender and (possibly) expert/agencies. These players act out the process through relationships formed and fostered as pathways of influence. These pathways are the avenues for change.

The context created for the operation of these relationships within the international trial is one that focuses on the testing and admissibility of evidence against the perceived requirements of legal conduct norms. Furthermore, relationships are mediated through the judiciary. The Trial Chamber is concerned with precedence; hierarchy; relationships with the prosecutor/defence advocate; obligations, examination and protection of witnesses and victims; issues of privilege and immunity; the integrity of evidence; and balancing the offender's rights. As discussed in Chapter 6, we consider that it is through mobilizing the discretionary power of the judiciary that trial relationships can be best directed towards the production of outcomes that further the search for truth and complement wider victim/community interests.

The essence of trial transformation following on from an ideological shift in justification could be achieved by considering how trial relationships can be reconsidered within a normative framework that facilitates change. Such a framework would reflect the rebalancing of victims' interests[3] and suggest the possibilities for mediation, diversion and multi-agency pathways to be developed within the trial process. These institutional reforms would provide victims with an active processual role in terms of initiation, negotiation and participation. Consequently, existing decision relationships, such as that between prosecutor and defence advocate, would be directed towards the

---

3   In particular the significance of victim communities as the legitimate initiators of ICJ should not be underestimated.

establishment of a different kind of evidential truth, whilst the formative and instrumental focus for the process, would be maintained by the judiciary.

At the evidential stage, for example, rules of admissibility would operate within such a transformed processual context to provide the material for a broader range of outcomes. We suggest that changing the context within which decision relationships influence the production of truth will alter trial practice and the justification for producing evidential material solely to reflect the exigencies of adversarial trial. Such a change in emphasis would, in consequence, render many of the criticisms currently levelled at the operation of evidential rules in adversarial trials as superfluous. A persistent problem highlighted by McEwan (1998), for example, concerns the unwillingness of interested parties to introduce facts which they may perceive as potentially prejudicial. In guiding the proceedings the judge in the adversarial mode of trial is more concerned with establishing the truth based on the material placed before the court rather than with seeking to establish a definitive form of objective truth; a function more akin to the adversarial form. However, to reposition trial rationality releases professional participants from the tactical games demanded by particular models of trial decision-making, whether they be adversarial, inquisitorial or hybrid. Hence, it is through the interpretation of substantive rules in the changed context for the trial that we see relationships as a liberating force for the achievement of a more objective, and perhaps more importantly, legitimate form of truth.

We suggest that the essential decision relationships of judge/ prosecution; judge/defence; judge/victim; prosecution/defence, may enhance the development of constructive trial outcomes by emphasizing aspects of these relationships can be to maximize the potential for trial pathways to influence such outcomes. To elaborate, the interactive context of any trial decision relationship consists of the following variables:

- Perceived goals (such as penalty, not restitution).
- Perception of social and normative constraints (such as language).
- Perceived relationship norms and interactive constraints (such as status).

Against this framework, we can speculate on how decision relationships might operate within the transformed trial at various essential decision sites. Prosecutorial decision-making, for example, instead of focusing largely on issues of charge and plea, might involve strategic negotiations with defence advocates and victims' representatives to determine how the trial process might best address their relative demands for justice. Within changed perceptions for justification, the conduct of trial professionals will become conditioned by the development of different perceptions and expectations for legal and social conduct norms. Consequently, divisions between pre-trial and trial; trial and verdict; verdict and sentence; sentence and outcome will merge in the transformation of a trial process where the participants are working towards a common objective rather than playing out the predetermined roles and expectations of adversarialism.

Similarly, sentence decision-making would also reflect notions of integration promoted through the fusion of process. This would cover the adequate representation for both lay and professional interests in trial decision-making, and different modalities of discretionary behaviour and intervention regarding the perception, evaluation and use of information for sentencing purposes. These factors would be reflected in the connections made between penal justifications, policy and decision-making. Consequently, trial relationships would change, develop and merge to determine the exercise of discretionary power at significant decision sites for sentencing within the transformed trial process.

Nevertheless, it is important to bear in mind that the processual essence of the trial in terms of the formulation of an indictment; disclosure of evidence; tendering of plea; reliance on defences; the calling and testing of witness testimony; judicial interventions, explanations and declarations on law and procedure; verdict delivery; and sentencing, will remain as crucial decision sites for the transformed trial. The important point is that these events will take on a different meaning within the context of the transformation so that they will be utilized by the participants in promoting new goals of restoration and reconciliation as well as conventional calls for retribution and deterrence. Further, diversion out of the adversarial process towards restorative outcomes needs to be available at crucial sites for trial decision-making. Consequently, strategic demands for collective justice will find expression through the development of new and changed relationship contexts under the ultimate direction of the judiciary.

The essence of change

This section identifies what is available, or appropriate within the trial, for change. Change is not proposed here for its own sake. All too often in justice policy, and particularly in context of modern international relations, change is put up as proof of development or progress.[4] Structural and institutional change is regularly presented as evidence of development and progress without there being a need to interrogate its genuine social impact.[5]

To protect against the distraction of change as a measure of integration or collaboration, later argued for as the indicators of true trial transformation, we downplay an initial interest in structure and institutions in favour of agency and decision-making.[6] In this spirit, what is nominated as appropriate for change are those pathways of influence which currently dominate the international trial model (see Chapters 3 and 6).

Another device to avoid change for change's sake is the preference for *transformation* as the dynamic. Transformation as employed here means a radical reordering of the way things are done and how outcomes are achieved. In identifying what should be transformed within the trial and what can be expected of that change, it is process and results which are in the frame.

Consistent with our interest in comparative contextual analysis (CCA) is a foundation concern with the conditions that make transformation possible. The context for trial transformation envisages fundamental and essential re-determinations of the purpose and possibility of the trial. These invite the suspicions of traditionalists in both alternative justice paradigms concerning the damage such transformation may inflict on the retributive focus of the trial, and on the integrity of restorative alternatives. The transformation context developed here requires an acceptance of the possibility of integration and collaboration within the trial and of the revolutionary consequences this can bring (see Chapter 7). The challenge as identified in the preceding section is to achieve transformation whilst retaining the features of the adversarial/retributive trial, which justify transformation and integration in the first place. It would be of little purpose to produce such a conceptually confused decision process, with hybrid

---

4 In fact, as Findlay (1999) suggests, for transitional cultures where custom remains dominant over modern criminal justice formalism, the introduction of institutional change may be counterproductive to crime control and social order.

5 The development of state-sponsored policing in certain indigenous cultures has had the impact of marginalizing the community, and victims in particular, from the securing of their own community peace and safety. See Findlay and Zvekic (1988), Findlay (2003b).

6 This obviously sits well with our model for the trial as a process of decision-making (see Chapter 3) and our theory of process as dependent on agency (see Chapter 1).

and reluctant agents, unable and unwilling to secure the protections of greater access to justice, fairer opportunities for different justice routes, and more satisfactory and inclusive outcomes than were present with the trial, and with the alternative justice paradigm untouched.

Having made these conditions clear, what are those features of process suitable for transformation? Again these involve the components of decision relationships, the dynamics of decision-making, as well as the activity and agency of pathways of influence.

Lay/professional relationships

An essential purpose for trial transformation is to reach new communities of justice (client communities) by expanding access to the trial. Access expansion will be achieved by opening up trial decisions to greater and wider participation whilst at the same time making the consequences of such participation more attractive. In terms of both these developments the lay/professional relationship in the trial will be profoundly affected. Quite simply there will be a greater component of trial business involving, incorporating and preferring lay participation. More citizens and communities will want to be part of trial decisions and to benefit from their outcomes.

Perhaps of more significance for the lay/professional decision relationships in the trial will be a shift in the nature of lay participation afforded through transformation. This will mean that the language of trial communication will have to change.[7] The status that comes with professional representation will be moderated if lay players can speak more for themselves and if it is the judge rather than the lawyers who govern communication with lay participants. As this occurs the trial lawyer will need to exhibit skills in mediation along with advocacy and forensic analysis.

Role of the judge as adjudicator

It is anticipated in our vision of trial transformation that the judge will become a more central, involved and powerful figure within the process. This is not only because more discretion over more varied process and determination options will be available. Also, the judge will be faced with new and challenging roles, accompanied by less rigidity in the application of the current judicial responsibilities. Here, some of the different functions of the judge in alternative trial traditions will be

---

7   In this respect Cotterrell's (1992) assertion that legal professionalism rests on the cordoning off of specialist knowledge (through elite professional language in particular) will need to be challenged.

merged more in order to enjoy and achieve the new possibilities for trial decision-making than in some attempt to conciliate competing traditions.[8] Such a new role for judges will change their relationships with the lawyers in the court as well as with lay participants. Depending on the way in which a judge were to activate and operate these new powers would be the consequence of breaking down or, in certain situations, reinforcing professional status structures.

ICJ presents a unique context for any such judicial reinvention. The recent (and some times uncomfortable) merging of judicial traditions in the operation of the international criminal tribunals offers fertile ground for the growth of new judicial interventions.[9] Yet there will be a pressing need to train judges from different procedural traditions to fully appreciate the discretion they possess within the present normative frameworks of ICJ in order to practise more than retributive discretionary interventions.

Place of the victim as justice recipient

The involvement of victims in international criminal trials has already been recognized. However, this is only in terms of administrative support for the victim, and the possibility that victims' interests may be enunciated as a legitimate influence over trial decision-making. The transformed trial will open its doors not simply to more victims and more vocal victim communities. It will view theses individuals and communities of victims as crucial recipients of justice dispensed. This will come as a natural consequence of repositioning trial authority and legitimacy from state and international organization authority, to the affirmation and ownership by the global community. As is the case with restorative justice alternative paradigms currently in ICJ, victims will become the predominant focus for the dispensation of trial justice. In this way the trial will develop into a domain for the realization of legitimate victim interests and victim communities will take ownership of its dispensations.

Nature of evidence as truth

The central commitments of trial decision-making are determinations about what comprises fact, what evidentiary status facts may have and

---

8   For instance, it will now be important for the judge to be active in eliciting the truth from lay participants rather than ruling over the advocates' attempts to do so.

9   This is despite recent attempts by the Sierra Leone tribunal, for instance, to reinforce the distinction between the judicial role in truth but not in reconciliation.

what consequences the evidence will invite for the central trial determinations. Rarely in current trial practice is fact-finding or evidence settling achieved for its sake alone. With restorative justice and its international manifestations, truth-telling is the primary purpose of facts and evidence. The manner in which truth is extracted or the conditions under which it is offered may then, in conventional evidentiary terms, make it unsuitable as a foundation for guilt. But this is not its purpose in so many restorative settings. Truth, and the acceptance of responsibility, and even the shaming and reconciliation which results from its revelation, may not have been possible in an adversarial argument. In such a circumstance the story may be concealed through adversarial tactics or simply go untold. Recognizing the sometimes different processes and purposes around truth-telling there will be occasions where truth and actionable evidence are not incompatible for the purposes of retributive determinations. It is just that this will not be necessary as an outcome for the transformed trial to succeed.

This is a case where the normative framework of the adversarial trial in particular will need to be repositioned. The determination of truth rather than the proof of a particular case (or the achievement of an evidentiary standard) will become the principal concern for the transformed international trial. This in turn will lead to new conditions on fact-finding, new rules for the treatment of evidence and new functions for facts as evidence of truth rather, than adversarial dominance.

Coexistence of mediation and adversarial contest/inquisition

Adversarial trial is supported by structures such as state prosecution, professional representation, rules of evidence connected to a presumption of innocence, etc. Inquisitorial trials still test the veracity of the prosecution case by state professionals who act on behalf of victim/offender interests. Mediation might still employ the professional/representational context, but for purposes not essentially bound to which side wins or loses the argument. Mediation of its very nature requires decision-making geared to compromise outcomes rather than dominant argument. In the transformed trial there will be a place for both forms of decision-making, perhaps not on the same issue but certainly as options within a single process. Obviously, the choice for one may preclude the other. The judge directing the process down one decision-path in preference to the other may be in recognition of the widest potential for a satisfactory if not comprehensive outcome.

Potency of judicial discretion

This proposed trend is contrary to recent attempts in many Western common-law jurisdictions to limit the scope of judicial independence through the restriction of judicial discretion (Zdenkowski 2000). The political logic behind such developments is to complement an intensely retributive community conscience where leniency is perceived as inconsistency and harsh sentencing is equated with victim's justice. It would appear from the climate of ICJ victim communities that the retributive spirit is not so predictable and uniform. In any case we believe that inclusive justice will be better ensured through the strong and creative exercise of judicial discretion, accountable through the inclusion of larger communities of justice. Also, the activation of choice from different paradigms within the trial requires the consistent and professional management of the central adjudicator if competing rights are to be balanced and accountability simplified.

Integration of civil and criminal remedies

The distinction between civil and criminal jurisdictions in the international justice setting is already confused and somewhat unconvincing.[10] It is a distinction having largely broken down in the operation of alternative and less formal justice settings. This is as a result of the natural connections in the minds of victims in particular between the determination of truth, the apportionment of responsibility and the settling of compensation. Where community reconciliation is concerned, the victim and the community become claimants and the accused is no longer simply a defendant but is brought into the compensation cycle as one of the first stages of re-acceptance. The challenge will be for the rights afforded parties in civil and criminal settings, and their consequent obligations and responsibilities to be made more compatible without compromising principles such as the presumption of innocence now crucial to trial justice.

Application of restorative truth-telling to facilitate determinations of responsibility

New voices will appear in the transformed trial. Those who view it against the background of current trial formality may see at once a more fluid, communicative, animated and accessible process of

---

10   Even in domestic jurisdictions such as Italy (as discussed in Chapter 4) the victim can become a civil claimant within the criminal trial.

conversation. As a narrative of the conflict under adjudication and potential mediation, the transformed trial will be more revealing and intuitive because of its concern for establishing the truth. This then becomes a process and an outcome of the transformed trial; a process and an outcome on which a variety of choices then can be made sense of.

De-emphasis of guilt and penalty

In suggesting this change, retributive justice and its utility are not sidelined. In fact, there may be occasions where retribution is more effectively produced as a consequence of the assumption of responsibility, rather than the imposition of guilt. In talking of a lesser significance for guilt and penalty, trial decision-making need no longer be bound to a narrow track towards a dichotomous determination. It is also consistent with the suggestion that evidence and fact-finding should now be directed more to the establishment of truth, than the victory for one side of an adversarial context.

The retributive and restorative purposes may be achieved down a new path to responsibility. Restorative justice largely relies for its activation on the accused accepting responsibility, rather than after its disputed proof. There may be occasions where apportioning responsibility is more important than the punishment to follow. Here the immunities offered in the restorative scenario may bring about an open acceptance of responsibility and the civil remedies to follow which an adversarial contest may not have satisfied. The retributive desire for allocating responsibility is thus achieved. The sacrifice may be penality, but if sanction is seen more broadly as to include civil restitution then responsibility comes with a price.

Repositioning of diversion

In current criminal justice models diversion is largely employed to remove the offender (and to a lesser extent the victim) out of the formal process into an alternative justice paradigm which may be more successful or at least less destructive than formal agency intervention. Therefore, diversion is a route out of one justice paradigm because of its inappropriateness or inadequacy. The transformed trial will merge alternatives, take down some barriers between investigation and trial, integrate more justice interests and instrumentalities within the trial, and thereby cure some reasons for escaping the trial's dead hand. In such a setting diversion will be from one alternative pathway of influence within the trial to another.

These decision contexts or relationships ripe for change will transform and be transformed by dynamic pathways of influence. The components of these pathways (identified in Chapters 3, 6 and 7) will also change as will their power to influence the relationships which produce trial decisions. An example of this is the new status of the victim and the manner in which this will require professional representation in order to achieve the greatest level of inclusion within judicial determinations. As the trial is an inter-related process of decision-making, then the interconnection between changing pathways of influence will be the map for trial transformation. In the judge/victim example it will require a new place for victims in the determination process facilitated by an expanded judicial discretion. It will also demand a hereto underdeveloped relationship between the victim and his or her professional advocate (lawyer or otherwise).

Along with fields for change there needs to be as part of the transformation impetus some consideration of the contextual preconditions for change. These contextual preconditions require the acceptance of certain repositioned moral imperatives such as the value of victim focus, which we argued for in the preceding chapter. Whilst the essential ideology of a just trial is confirmed and reinforced in this proposed transformation, it is to encapsulate a range of new and important constituencies which themselves will bring strain to the limited notion of fairness which the present trial protections confirm (see Findlay 2001c). It was always likely that in any major expansion of trial constituencies, competing interests and their ramifications for the determination of fairness would exacerbate. The answer to this is not to degenerate the 'rights basis' of the trial into some relativist confusion, but rather to incorporate an expanded notion of individual and collective rights, centrally within a new normative framework for international criminal trials which better accommodates both paradigms of ICJ. In this regard, context transforms essentially, reiterating important themes from the current trial, and aspirations for restorative justice, so that pathways of influence will transform to achieve any and all of the outcomes of the merged justice paradigms.

In discussing what is available and appropriate for change in the context of the transforming trial, the analysis will of necessity rehearse the difficulties associated with any restructuring of trial decision-making. As the section on 'challenges' reveals, to change processes and outcomes of decisions in the trial necessitates some conflict with the pre-existing order. Even with the toughest new normative framework, those working in trials currently with the benefit of status and influence will not be easily persuaded to relinquish their predominance in any pathway of influence simply for the common good. Relying as heavily as the trial does on individual discretion to achieve decisions, that discretion now largely vested in the individual and competing offices of trial professionals, it may be discretion which can subvert the transformation process unless it is focused and made openly accountable.

In terms of focus we later suggest that the judge (adjudicator) is crucial to the realization of trial transformation. This recognition promotes our preference for a centralization and enhancement of judicial discretion as a mechanism for both activating transformation in practice, and containing the reluctance to reform from other professionals which might be predicted. The assumption here is that accountability at least will be more easily achieved if the diversification of discretion throughout the main trial decision-making sites is centralized, and if the judge is made more responsible for the various pathways of influence that will remain. The normative framework governing the exercise of this expanded judicial discretion should be more effectively required to reflect the 'rights framework' which is a justification for the introduction of restorative justice into the trial process.

Having developed available process and outcome options in the transformed trial process, the judge (through advanced discretion and a more flexible normative framework) will be given the power to:

- direct diversion from one justice paradigm to another, within, or beyond the trial;

- determine whether the production of truth through trial 'conversations' best suits the purpose of restorative or retributive outcomes;

- in this, ensure that the access and inclusion of lay participants in particular are confirmed through the important stages of trial decision-making;

- adjudicate on motions by any participant in the trial to redirect the process from one justice paradigm to another;

- ensure that the service provided by trial professionals enhances access and inclusion for lay participants; and

- promote openness and accountability in the exercise of professional discretion.

Purpose for change

The trial has historically operated as an institution for processing complex and sometimes contradictory principles for punishment. It is at least inquisitorial in nature, often adversarial in argument, ruled by strict conventions of evidence and committed to determining liability and sanction. Its focus is individualized and it operates within a model reference about personal responsibility, community morality, normative obligation and state monopoly.

The function of the trial often appears to run contrary to the ideology justifying and driving it.[11] Trial process and outcomes are said to rest on and in turn represent the equality of the individual before the law and the uniform and certain application of justice. One morning in any trial court would disabuse the observer of these expectations. In this way trial justice is consistent with Pat O'Malley's observation that the incoherence and volatility of penal science arise out of the contradictory policies of criminal justice. The agenda for the trial as it now is, jurisdictionally and internationally suffers from just such incoherence and volatility in the context of ICJ in particular. Incoherence, for instance, arises out of the lay/professional participation paradox. Professional trial players are given a status which sets them apart from the accused, the witness and the victim. Their expertise is meant to facilitate representation and protect adversarial argument. In fact, it tends also to distance the lay participant from the process and its outcomes, as well as seeing the development of the process more to the advantage of the professional vocation. Volatility is a feature of trial decision-making, the more that the legitimate expectations of victim communities are recognized whilst remaining constrained within the parameters of retributive punishment.[12] Incoherence and volatility are constant consequences of the restrictions on real participatory access to trial justice by those who are most personally connected to the substance of its deliberations.

One of the important purposes for trial transformation is to open up trial access to those who might seek more from it than retributive outcomes alone. This is not only an effort for more and broader access,

---

11 The operation of the jury as fact-finder in a system in which it acts as both a powerful legitimator as well as a marginal force in overall justice decision-making. See Findlay and Duff (1982a).

12 This is one explanation for the rapid and erratic increase in the severity of imprisonment sentences in those jurisdictions where victim outrage against crimes such as collective sexual assault is recognized by sentencing judges as a legitimate consideration in setting a sentence.

but also access to more inclusive and productive justice as a result of the trial experience. We acknowledge that the trial already offers more than retributive justice in both process and determinations.[13] Rehabilitation already sits uncomfortably within the judge's remit, although a contemporary 'just deserts' policy prevalence in sentencing legislation makes recourse to individual reform strategies often an unbalanced marriage in sentencing practice.

The trial is not unfamiliar with managing and sometimes reconciling (or at least rationalizing) conflicting sentencing and punishment principles (see Norrie 1999b). What the trial is not comfortable with is the operation of essentially community-focused processes and outcomes such as restoration and restitution, which may in fact either challenge or supervene a retributive finality. A reason for this is the relationship between 'penal science' mythology (just deserts, deterrent sentencing, measuring dangerousness, predictive sentencing, etc.) and the dominance of the language and communication of the trial by the cast of professional players. As Cotterrell (1992) remarks, legal professionals cordon off the specialist knowledge on which law and justice is said to operate, through mystical language and ritual, only for the understanding of the initiated. Trial transformation must break down this mystique, with or without the co-operation of trial professionals. A way to ensure that at least some professionals are willing to negotiate their status, and level their pathways of influence, is through demonstrating the occupational utility and attractiveness of restorative diversions and outcomes within the transformed trial.

With the introduction of stronger community empathy, and the interests of victims in particular, into the trial as a consequence of transformation, the significance of penality may diminish as a crucial purpose for trial decision-making.[14] Along with this may come some challenge to the sovereignty of 'states' as the monopolists of punishment and the authority of trial justice. Garland talks of this in his assertion that criminal justice is now more about control (1985, 1990, 2001). However, none of these trends will simply follow in the international context and if they do they may be consistent with internationalization.

---

13 Criminal injuries compensation schemes and victim impact statement opportunities are designed to do more than simply feed into the retributive project.

14 In fact it is anticipated that, rather than being diminished by a rush to restorative trial practice, penality will assume a more balanced place in a range of available trial outcomes. Penality, and the proof of liability on which it rests, may be complemented and confirmed through some of the truth-finding phases of the restorative project.

The international trial is not legitimated merely by individual or collective state authority, as a product to some extent of international organizations. Perhaps one of the limitations over trial legitimacy in ICJ is the limited franchise offered by the sponsorship of removed political institutions.[15] A return of justice decision-making to the agents closer to the conflict deliberated (and its disputing communities) will distance the connection of the trial to political authority, while at the same time enhancing its broader based legitimacy. And it might also be argued that a rejuvenated trial process which incorporates restorative/ community justice within a more inclusive 'governmentally' sponsored institution (Braithwaite 2002a) can enhance the control potential of global governance agencies. A central purpose for trial transformation therefore is to restructure its authority foundations as a consequence of reintroducing community, and thereby sharpening its legitimacy and impact on ICJ.

In working towards trial transformation this is not simply a process of addressing tensions between ideology and function, or of practice and outcome. While recognizing the conflicts at the centre of criminal justice and control, well represented in jury trial, Garland, Norrie and O'Malley pose that these signal more complex contextual meanings better understood through exploring the individual contexts of trial decision-making. Tensions such as these are fermented, compromised and conciliated through the different pathways of influence within the trial and these are the best platforms for transforming justice paradox within the trial itself. It is not helpful to suggest trial transformation as the reconciliation of simple dichotomies such as:

- state or community-focused justice;
- retributive or restorative processes and outcomes;
- formal or less formal institutions; and
- professional or lay adjudication.

The justice that is proposed through trial transformation is an incorporation of these themes as they are part of the continuum of justice in the international setting.[16] This continuum recognizes the

---

15 This may particularly prove problematic when the whole institution such as the UN is constantly challenged by its most senior and powerful members, as does the USA. This has lead to rival justice paradigms in direct conflict with the operation of conventional ICJ institutions.

16 The notion of a continuum is meant to suggest that justice does not have to be considered in terms of dichotomies and opposed choices. In fact, victim communities in particular seek justice resolutions which are dynamic and fluid, to complement an array of transient needs.

various and varying aspirations for ICJ (in the transformed trial) harboured by different parties and negotiated through pathways of influence. Effectively to stimulate integration and a more collaborative effort at trial justice these pathways need to be relieved from the constraints binding retributive justice (such as guilt and innocence, sentencing and penalty), and should be offered the opportunity to engage with associated stages of justice along this continuum (restitution and sanction, for instance). This is a crucial purpose for transformation, and the most inclusive satisfaction of those who will benefit therefrom.

Along this continuum are represented opportunities for choice. Trial decision-making should be expanded by greater choice, in order to enhance its relevance against an international context where choice is demanded and denied for a new generation of justice claimants. Moreover these are the communities with the novel aspirations for ICJ (such as restitution for genocide and the truth behind ethnic cleansing) which justify its very existence.

The transformed trial should support *communities of justice* representing such novel claims. A community of justice is a sharp context for ICJ that should (but up until now has failed to) locate its legitimacy from the global community, a notion itself systematically underdeveloped (see Chapter 7). The transformed trial will be sustained by recognizing the communities it serves. Translated into trial decision-making processes these communities become active within expanded pathways of influence. A community of justice in this state incorporates victim interests, the agents of trial justice employed in facilitating the formal establishing and adjudication of these interests, and those who would challenge and deny their credibility. A community of justice can, therefore, exist within and beyond the trial, and thereby better bind the trial process to the communities it is said to serve.

For example, communities are bound together by a range of desires and obligations, and when it comes to ICJ these bonds are a fundamental justification for the need to intervene and the nature of the intervention. A community of justice may incorporate victims and their immediate support communities, those who identify and defend these victims, the perpetrators of their victimization and their supports, and further the agencies and institutions of war and of justice which interpret and adjudicate their conflicts.

The trial in many respects fails with its individualist focus to address communities and to confront the challenges posed by community interaction. The tragedy in this is that ICJ is about communities in transition often within post-conflict states, desperate for tranquil governance, and in more instances these communities seem to be avoiding the trial in favour of their own experiments with justice process. The trial will be left behind as a symbol of ICJ if it fails to engage with communitarian as well as individualist determinations. It also needs to take its place within communities of justice if it is to provide a forum for community justice resolution internationally.

Another important dimension for communities of justice is the recognition that they can facilitate and produce ICJ along with being its recipient. If trial transformation is to be empowering for its lay participants in particular then integration across the process of decision-making will feature. Integrative sentencing is now recognized as a way in which the victim's interest at least are better represented in trial sanctions. A problem experienced with this development is that when integration is more structural and imposed (as with victim impact statements) than collaborative and emergent, then the integration process itself may further entrench non-inclusive structures of professional status in particular.

Collaborative justice has been described (Findlay 1997a: 145) as a system where the formal, state-sponsored institutions join with community-centred justice initiatives in order to bring about more varied and wide-ranging justice delivery. The experience of introducing restorative justice into institutionalized and formal justice systems has required some collaboration (Findlay 1997a). However, in the case of the police and restorative juvenile justice, for instance, this has been considered by the former as a concession on their behalf, even in the face of their own failure to control juvenile crime. It becomes a case of the formal allowing space and jurisdiction for the informal, but always under its patronage. This has also meant that the community-based justice forms have been forced to sacrifice context and change activity in the process of incorporation within the formal justice model which may irrevocably harm its restorative potential. For example, where reconciliation is taken out of its community context and moved up to be a possible court determination in cases of domestic violence, it has the potential to exacerbate the abusive relationship, and the domination of the abuser, beyond community or court observation.[17] There is a warning in this for trial transformation.

Collaborative justice becomes a different negotiation in situations where customary or indigenous forms of justice prevail, and formal, state-sponsored justice is elite or limited in its coverage (see Findlay

---

17 Examples of this are developed in Findlay (1997a).

1999e). Here customary justice is more likely to retain its integrity even after integration because the formal processes and outcomes are seeking its legitimacy and are therefore more tied to its contexts and purposes. Interestingly, ICJ is just such a situation. Despite the symbolic significance of tribunals and trials in ICJ, recent experience reveals that restorative justice paradigms have greater victim coverage and community application by far. Once this has been recognized as the real context for collaboration in ICJ, the prospects for collaborative justice improve, and the safety of restorative justice within any such collaboration is confirmed. This is the consequence of formal ICJ needing to incorporate the wider legitimacy of restorative forms as a powerful purpose behind trial transformation.

Challenges for change

This section is concerned with confronting some fundamental problems for ICJ resulting from operationalizing the notion of the transformed trial. One such difficulty relates to the need to suggest ways in which the prevalent concept of individual criminal responsibility exemplified by international trial paradigms can be linked to notions of collective justice. In essence, this apparent disjunction between individual and collective responsibility raises a number of interconnected issues which go to the heart of the ideology and praxis of ICJ.

First, it challenges the legitimacy of justice in international criminal trials because it fails to suggest what linkage might exist between the moral positions individual citizens of the 'international community as a whole' might adopt regarding the appropriate principles for punishing gross violations of international humanitarian law, and the position taken by victims and communities crucially affected by these events. A Durkheimian notion of individualism lends itself to conceptualizing a shared moral basis for the internationalization of human rights norms. However, this is insufficient to suggest a unifying morality which might support globalized forms of moral action such as punishment, let alone ones that connect with particular communities of justice.[18] Furthermore, it is difficult to see how individualism as a notion of fairness and justice can be transformed at the level of international

18 Perhaps, as Cotterrell (1992: 227) speculates, there is a need to develop further Durkheim's ideas within conceptualizations or taxonomies of community (such as Weber's), in order to comprehend the complex subjectivities of social action and their significance.

penality into principles for punishment. This is because the validity of individualism as a conceptual vehicle for understanding the basis for shared moral values and the existence of evaluative notions such as justice and fairness depends on the prior identification of shared or unifying interests (Cotterrell 1999a: 114).

Secondly, at the normative level, despite vague assertions that legal accountability contributes to rehabilitation of the victim's dignity and the reconciliation of opposing factions, the foundation instruments of trial institutions actually fail to suggest how the achievement of a communitarian philosophy of punishment might be reached through discretionary decision-making in international criminal trials. If we accept the notion that law exists as an integrative mechanism (Cotterrell 1992: 71), this must imply an acknowledgement that legal norms reflect notions of justice compatible and supportive of ideology at several levels.[19] However, it also implies a Durkheimian imperative which suggests a need to provide interpretations and adopt practices that might allow us to make the link between the recognition of law as a representation of morality and the existence of forms of expressed morality in civil society as reflected in communities of justice. Thus, the moral legitimacy of the international penal regime is constituted through its capacity to reflect socially meaningful (i.e. pluralistic) conceptions of morally unacceptable behaviour and appropriate responses. This in turn requires an acknowledgement that it is the international criminal trial process itself which provides the trans-formative mechanism and supplies linkage between moral purpose, legal norms and the legitimacy of trial justice. However, as previously discussed, a fundamental problem with this conceptualization is the fact that there is a disjunction between international trial justices' depiction of a 'one culture' world community and reality; that this represents the antithesis of plurality. It also tends to diminish the plurality of expectations for justice which communities of victims may see beyond retributive trial.

Thirdly, since the normative objectivity of international humanitarian law and the complexities of legal justice do not resonate with the subjectification of punishment in the international community (especially victim communities), law, process and rights operate at a relative distance. This realization re-enforces the need to construct a meaningful model of justice for international trials which recognizes the relational quality of rights norms; one which appreciates the fact

---

19 Namely, global or regional, but also as suggestive of a morality of sanctioned punishment.

that process rights must relate to the legal and moral contexts of criminal action and punishment. As Norrie (2000) suggests, a relational model of justice is concerned to examine the connections between responsible individuals and communities so that punishment is envisaged as part of that shared experience. Rights conceived in these terms implies a sharing of the justice process; namely, that rights should no longer be conceived as a distinct set of normative constraints on process, but rather as an integral and inseparable component of relational justice. In effect, for international penality this conceptualization envisages a meaningful connection between the universality of rights and their application in context.

In summary, it is problematic to view international trial justice as a coherent and credible unilateral force which is capable of creating and facilitating opportunities for transforming moral principles that combine retributive and restorative aspirations into practice. It is also crucial to view the achievement of these objectives within the context of universally accepted rights paradigms which satisfy the functional requirement of legitimating the boundaries of international action against citizens and states. This requires a pluralistic vision of law which reaches beyond parochial state interests to reflect communitarian concerns at the international level. These concerns are not simply upgraded to the province of international organizations or dominant political coalitions. They need to connect with the civil stakeholders of ICJ.

Our proposed reconciliation of competing paradigms for international trial justice must therefore recognize these challenges and suggest how mobilizing discretionary power within a flexible transformed normative structure can address the strain between the collective and the individual. We see their interests recognized in the notion of communities of justice. Such communities then become the legitimate (and legitimating) constituencies for trial justice.

How can processual norms help to transform trial ideology into outcomes which have moral legitimacy for communities of justice when the focus of the trial remains that of establishing the guilt and individual responsibility of selected individuals? Since we accept that the legitimacy of the international trial will be transformed through repositioning its rationality and constituency, we envisage an integrated trial structure that will have as its normative focus the reconciliation of competing demands for justice. Whilst the prosecution of individual perpetrators remains the sole concern of international criminal trials, the collective morality of states or other identifiable social groups involved in social conflict and war who bear collective responsibility, can nevertheless be impugned through international penality by refocusing the transformed trial towards the achievement of outcomes that are regarded as legitimate by those demanding justice. Hence, the use of discretionary power within the transformed trial will be in order to achieve justice for the international community, and recognized as legitimate precisely because it facilitates linkage between individual and collective moral accountability.

The transformed trial will not be concerned to provide a normative structure that automatically equates responsibility with liability, since its purpose will be to work towards outcomes that maximize the establishment of truth and to facilitate ways in which responsibility for that truth can lead to peace and reconciliation. Notions of criminality as destruction, disintegration, conflict and social breakdown demand that we move beyond traditional process models providing solutions which simply equate crime with individual responsibility. Instead, they must lead directly to imperatives for reconstruction and reparation compatible with restorative justice principles aimed at increasing understanding, empowering victims and citizens and sharpening their potential for participation and the resolution of conflict. Facilitating restorative justice outcomes is seen as potentially capable of re-empowering victims and a force for social cohesion. Consequently, the nature and operation of the transformed process will determine the appropriate evidentiary satisfaction for liability as well as truth for responsibility. This will be possible because each stage of the transformed trial will be informed by an ideology designed to give effect to the objectives of reconciling conflicting penal aspirations, and working towards solutions to encourage strategies that will bring about reconciliation and peace in post-conflict societies.

Dimensions of change

Having advocated a multidimensional conceptualization of trial process for CCA in our earlier discussions of theory and method, we argue that this approach provides a crucial conceptual paradigm for transforming context through the outcomes produced by trial trans-formation. In other words, we regard the transformation process delivered through the trial as one which seeks to engage with the different contextual components of trial justice. In so doing processual decision-making is seen as a potential mediator of different justice contexts reflected against the ideological, jurisdictional, institutional and interactional dimensions of a transformed trial process.

Ideological context

The ideolological context of trial transformation refers to the moral legitimacy of the ideology which informs structure. This ideology needs to be based on trust in justice and its institutions, which in turn depends on symbolic and instrumental relevance and engagement at the most inclusive community levels. A transformed ideology must enhance the legitimacy of ICJ through and for inclusivity. Translated by the process of policy formulation, this should be determined by political and pragmatic values which go beyond states and on to communities.

Transformation requires will (of communities, of international organizations, of sponsors of rights instruments and of trial professionals). Such will should not be reflective of a desire for hegemony or self-preservation; it is more to do with intrinsic and morally incorporative notions such as truth determination, peacemaking and good governance. More particularly, establishing a trial ideology which seeks to engage with notions of collaborative justice implies that it should strive to become recognized as an essential component of the system of global governance. The difficulties remain of reconciling moral claims for justice within a transformed trial process. Allied with this is the challenge of incorporating alternative justice paradigms whilst enhancing and not compromising them. Preferred community justice outcomes will assist this.

The transformed trial will become the ultimate determinant of inclusion and exclusion as evidenced by the extent to which the ideology is translated into a rights-based practice. In short, fair trial means access; access leads to inclusion; inclusion must in part involve voluntary participation and this relies on legitimacy; legitimacy through relevance and a broader restorative process and outcomes.

As we argue, discretion is the medium for the translation of ideology into practice. Hence, accountability is to a new normative framework and new communities of interest (communities of justice). Ideological transformation is key to repositioning the pathways of influence between professional and lay players. Correspondingly, this will reposition the authority of the trial process, its place in ICJ and delineate its role in global governance.

Jurisdictional context

We regard this context as moving beyond time and space, and normative and institutional frameworks. Jurisdiction is not simply about whether the new trial straddles the civil and criminal in its possible processes and outcomes. It also requires a discussion of the trial without the constraints of its particular normative framework. Consequently, the transformed trial will, of necessity, involve an expansion of decision-making boundaries. The throughput of process in terms of information, involvement and decision outcomes anticipated will pose a challenge to conventional jurisdictional paradigms based on power and authority. The dynamic and transitional context of the 'international' should not be foreign to this. Similarly, in determining the structural conditions for inclusivity, these will no longer be internal to fair trial alone. It will be necessary to go outside and consider the collaboration of the trial with other legitimate procedural and outcome expectations.

Within jurisdictional contexts ideology will be operationalized through the normative structures of foundation instruments, teleological interpretation, professional conduct norms and rights paradigms. We argue for CCA here (justice paradigm to justice paradigm) as the crucial methodology for delivering a common language for transformation and justice delivery.

What is best for truth determination will depend on the particular purpose in any trial decision site for uncovering and applying truth. Hence, for example, existing or new trial styles may be deployed, or process diverted by trial professionals (subject to judicial sanction) towards this end; evidential and decision-making norms could be aimed at facilitating retributive as well as restorative outcomes. This will require that they and their critical determinants fundamentally transform. Above all, this context should engage with the rationale and normative implications of truth determination. This means that we should consider why and how trial facts can support truth-finding, and how judges should be looking for resolutions beyond penality. Context will also determine particular ramifications for normative frameworks, professional practice, decision-making and the exercise of discretion. For example, greater movement towards adoption of the civil law model for the gathering and preliminary testing of evidence should be evaluated within the framework for collaborative justice. In other words, we should question whether such remodelling leads to greater inclusion and consider what is sacrificed in terms of accountability and trial rights, for some parties at least.

Restorative and diversionary options which consider how legitimate expectations for justice can be best fulfilled (including amnesty) should occur within the trial at any suitable time, to be determined by the judge on application or direction. We would argue against the adoption of a discrete jurisdictional approach to remedies. Instead, we favour a uniform justice approach which for wider community satisfaction incorporates civil and criminal remedies. In this sense, collaborative justice has jurisdictional as well as institutional and expectational dimensions. Our view is that movement away from an exclusive focus on guilt and proof burden should facilitate this approach and produce a redefinition of liability towards responsibility consistent with restorative justice. For example, trial evidence could be informed by particular levels of probative value to reflect its sources, nature and possible utility. This alone would effectively uncouple the retributive dynamic which drives the production of facts for trial consumption in most Western justice paradigms and thereby facilitate the repositioning of rationales for action.

Institutional context

This context suggests a structured framework for transformation envisaging the trial as a facilitator of inclusivity; facilitating decision-making processes that are flexible enough to accommodate restorative outcomes. However, we would argue against exclusive adherence to structural change and institutional context. We regard decision sites, relationships and pathways of influence in a rights context as instrumental facilitators of inclusivity. A pervading theme of this book has been how human agency is the essential force that determines the recursive reality of trial process; how the instrumentality of discretionary decision-making within the context of trial relationships and perceived structural constraints is responsible for adding value to facts that determine trial outcomes (see Chapter 6 in particular). Therefore values of collaborative justice can only be forged and driven forward where institutional agents and participants in trial process are free to manipulate normative boundaries and barriers in ways which favour the production of restorative outcomes when these are considered appropriate. Freeing up normative boundaries also includes removing potential obstacles to flexibility such as professional status when it proves an obstacle to inclusion rather than a rights guarantee. It also involves confronting the nature of trial reasoning and language and the role of discretion in decision-making, and developing them flexible enough to accommodate restorative outcomes. This may mean at one time, expansion and contraction of different discretion contexts.

While acknowledging the paradox of relying on professional discretion but at the same time advocating a degree of professional disestablishment, we suggest a collaborative approach to changing communication structures and bureaucratic/managerial variables to facilitate change. Clearly, it is important for the structural framework to be operated in a manner conducive to negotiation and compromise, whilst retaining the essentials of a trial framework: its decision-making and its structures. We suggest the following features of inclusivity integral to the transformed institutional trial context:

1 *Communication* – open questioning should be encouraged and the evidential emphasis on probity should be relaxed, with the important caveat that this should not be allowed to impact irresponsibly on rights protection and accountability.

2 *Environment* – the nature and context of information delivery should be changed. More especially, the two-stage process (verdict/ sentence) should be collapsed, whilst maintaining a clear separation between fact-finding and verdict where this is the preferred outcome. Intermediate stages should be considered and outcomes merged to become part of a process towards individualized justice for a broader community of interest.

All this has important repercussions for the normative framework, especially in terms of delineating the appropriate parameters for dis-cretionary decision-making, and the provision of constant information and feedback to trial participants. Without doubt, in order to deliver an institutional trial model that is reflective and dynamic demands particular emphasis on increased transparency and victim feedback. Furthermore, trial dynamism will be reflected through processual interaction by all participants within these normative constraints. What will shape this as a process rather than simply a structural or normative entity will be the instrumental discretionary power released to participating human actors to infuse trial decision-making with a culture aimed at achieving individualized justice for identifiable victim communities.

Interactive context

Processual interaction is the crucial context which will govern the operation of pathways of influence. The exact nature of discretionary decision-making as social reality will depend on the repositioning of player variables/professional relationships and professional goals as we have described. Such changes will influence trial practice to the extent that decision-making will be redirected towards transformation. This will happen through positioning the decision-making process within a normative framework where the patterning of activities and the social reality of discretion is achieved within changed, expanded and identifiable decision pathways. However, decision-making will not be circumscribed by the values and norms of legal practice where expertise, monopolization, brute force and language are deployed as routine aspects of legal professionalism (Cotterrell 1992: 200). This is where the tone of transformation needs to reflect the new way of thinking about trial justice: conciliation rather than conflict. Both lawyers and judges, as interpreters and mediators of legal ideology, will gradually develop new techniques for rationalizing law and legal knowledge within the transformed ideological context of the international trial through their involvement and participation in seeking alternative and more constructive trial outcomes to satisfy communities of justice.

Trial interactions should also exploit the collective nature of discretionary decision-making (avoiding *in camera* deliberations) in order to maintain the reality of collaborative justice and public accountability. Critical will be the retraining of the judiciary and other trial professionals, without which the intuitive reasoning and patterned decision-making necessary for trial transformation will not be effective in practice. Particularly significant are the problems of recruiting and training a real global judiciary reflecting the international context and in touch with global victim communities. But this is a problem whatever justice paradigm is employed for the trial. A reshaping of the judicial role through community collaboration thus becomes a crucial component of this trial dimension.

Looking at each dimension (framework/context) in turn reveals a number of interconnected critical themes which may in fact argue against the discrete utility of any particular context. This phenomenon is consistent with our conceptualization of processual reality and the development of the methodology of CCA with its capacity to conceptualize social processes across time and space: within and between contexts, and to accommodate different levels of analysis at different levels of abstraction, thus facilitating our understanding of the linkage between ideology, power and policy as social processes.

Themes for the transformation trial practice

The transformed trial will require a new normative framework reliant on repositioned judicial discretion. Within this context judicial discretion will facilitate the adoption of pathways designed to promote outcomes compatible with the perceived demands for the varied justice of interested parties. The issue of judicial activation and supervision is not just a question of processual control and accountability. It is crucially about the possibility of transformation by discretionary activation of procedural norms. Changing the normative context of discretionary decision-making will transform the objective focus for trial professionals and provide an environment designed to bring representatives of outside agencies directly into a redirected process aimed at a specific outcome. Such determinations will help forge normative links between retributive and restorative trial justice imperatives.

Let us begin by considering the broader sociological context for promoting constructive outcomes through operationalizing discretion within the transformed trial. As Tulkens (2002: 678) has argued, evidence suggests that legal rules and procedures merely serve to reenforce existing inequalities of condition and position which inevitably undermine the credibility and legitimacy of the processes of negotiation and compromise that may be initiated and conducted within the prevailing paradigms of distributive justice. This is so whether they are grounded in adversarial, inquisitorial or hybridized normative paradigms for trial practice. In the context of international trial justice we have noted how such inequalities are reflected in the continued disenfranchisement of the victim and victim communities. Whilst some commentators, such as Braithwaite (2002a), regard regulatory legal frameworks as incompatible with the objectives of truth-finding and reconciliation, others (such as Dignan 2002) are prepared to countenance the blending of retributive and restorative alternatives within reconstituted paradigms for trial justice.

We would argue that trial processes take on different contextual significance when operationalized for transformation, and may need to be reconceptualized in assessing their relevance for the operation of discretionary power. Processual activity within the trial cannot be divorced from its social context; paradoxically, processual activity is itself contextualized social action. Action and interaction in the form of mediation, negotiation and conciliation depend on discretion within relationships being directed towards such objectives. Trial professionals and others participating in a social process must therefore perceive normative constraints as favourable to their achievement. Consequently, the repositioning of judicial discretion as an instrumental facilitator of constructive consequentialist outcomes for international trial process must come within a normative context where procedure is seen as potentially productive for promoting peace and reconciliation. Such an aspiration can only be realized through the development of procedural norms infused with the potential for judicial discretion to facilitate constructive solutions for individual cases within the broader context of satisfying conflicting global and local demands for justice. This means that trial procedure must:

- recognize relative weakness in the negotiating positions of defendants and victims as citizens of subjugated states;
- provide clear guidelines concerning the appropriateness of negotiation at specific stages in the trial process;
- clarify the extent to which trial participants and other agents should engage in negotiations;
- ensure that cultural misunderstandings in trial procedure and its effects are minimized;
- clarify how procedures based on expediency can engage with issues of trial justice; and
- seek to minimize obfuscation and lack of transparency regarding the nature of the process and its effects on the calculation of sentence.

In addition to these fundamental issues adequate attention should also be directed at the following concerns:

1 Since we advocate an integrated trial process, it is important that opportunities for the various outcomes that might be acceptable to the parties (as satisfying the demands for global and local justice) are continually exploited, beginning with a reconceived function for pre-trial review. Instead, this should be a process directed by the judiciary whereby aspirations for the process are detailed by participants, and an outline provided of the evidence which they propose to mobilize in support of the achievement of these objectives. In this context, judicial discretion will be directed towards using the trial process as a forum which will allow the establishment of responsibility provided through the testing of evidence to be used to build constructive outcomes.

2 It will be a judicial task to ensure that the balance of advantage is controlled by the court and that the interests of all parties are equally represented, both in terms of their ability to participate in the process itself and in the outcome. This means that findings of responsibility and the attribution of blame will not purely be seen as individually disadvantageous. They will instead be recognized as contributing to the construction of a broader truth about the reasons for the conflict that produced the behaviour in question, and how that truth can be used to provide an outcome for the process that will promote healing within victim communities.

3 The idea that process bargaining is an anathema to truth and the protection of human rights is misconceived. The propensity for actors to manipulate norms and structures to their own advantage is a facet of human nature which should be acknowledged. The important point is that it is perception of context and outcome that determines the motives and direction for action. For example, plea bargaining in the context of adversarial trial is generally challenged by those who regard it as compromising the concept of a fair trial on the basis that it is duplicitous. Thus, remorse is seen as a rationalization used by sentencers to conceal the true nature of the transaction being undertaken, i.e. bargaining away or buying off the defendant's due process rights in return for the economy of a low trial rate and/or absolving victims and witnesses from the ordeal of oral testimony.

If bargaining is transposed into a context dedicated to the objective of using truth-finding as a route to reconciliation then judicial discretion can be utilized to motivate bargaining decisions in that direction. Again, taking remorse, Bagaric and Amarasekara (2001a) have recently argued that it does not fit easily into philosophical categories. In a conventional retributive paradigm it may be argued that punishment must be assessed objectively on the basis of the degree of harm and the offender's blameworthiness (Hirsch 1993: 72). Remorse may then be seen as relevant (or not) only at the sentencing stage. On the other hand, utilitarian philosophy might regard the notion of a sentencing or confession reward as something which is compatible with utilitarian considerations such as the prevention of future crime, thereby, justifying the adoption of a more humane approach to the offender. Remorse may even be seen as a punishment in itself and, therefore, justifying mitigation of sentence on the basis that the net cost in suffering would equal that of the non-repentant offender serving a longer sentence.

The transformation of context we advocate would allow discretion to be employed as a pragmatic tool because factors such as remorse, contrition and confessions would be evaluated within a philosophical paradigm that accommodates (*inter alia*) retributive and restorative objectives. Hence, if truth-finding is the driver for process and the truth so revealed can be used to satisfy retributive and restorative demands for justice, the fact of remorse may be approached flexibly and used to make a positive contribution towards achieving the aspirations for justice which interested participants have promoted. The normative structure and the discretionary power it confers on the judiciary would facilitate this aim and accord it real value.

4 Finally, consideration should be given to the relative demands of trial participants in terms of reconciling the extent of their participation with the promotion of the trial for the achievements of the objectives they have put forward for the trial. Here the instrumental use of discretionary power must be exercised within a normative framework which ensures adequate rights protection for all parties. This will be a consequence of achieving constructive and legitimate levels of access and inclusion in the process and its outcomes.

Broader issues concerning governance and accountability will necessarily have a major influence on the normative model of discretionary intervention. The integration of retributive and restorative strategies within a transformed conceptualization of the international trial raises crucial questions about how judicial discretion will be used in order to reconcile aspirations for global and local justice. At one level, we have argued for a convergence of interests to reflect the fact that the ideology of the trial process will be repositioned to accommodate the possibility of pursuing constructive outcomes for victims and victim communities. Whilst this may be a universal aspiration for the transformed trial, it is pragmatic and based on our view that the moral legitimacy of ICJ depends upon it. However, it is manifestly insufficient to argue that the reconciliation and repositioning of retributive and restorative themes to satisfy demands for local justice provide a satisfactory normative control on decision-making.

The search for truth in the transformed trial is a bridge between the purposes for ICJ and the moralities behind global conflict resolution. Some of the themes for trial transformation which endorse truth-finding as its central purpose will work down from the meta to the more micro concerns of process and outcome. These include the following:

- *Dealing with the mechanics of truth-seeking in the transformed trial.* This supports the introduction of restorative process but at the same time may necessarily diminish retributive concerns about guilt. A way to incorporate these concerns is through a specific reconsideration of the role of 'facts' (evidence) in establishing truth and apportioning guilt/responsibility, leading on to sentence. The purpose of facts in the new trial and their evidentiary status may mean an expansion of the trial particularly into what we see at present as pre-trial concerns. For instance, trial facts may now indicate the contributory nature of liability rather than individual guilt. This then might suggest collective responsibility and a more mediated and conditional trial outcome.

- *Lay/professional relationships of influence.* The importance of authority structures in the trial decision-making process cannot be denied. A repositioning of those structures to allow for renegotiated pathways of influence will mean that the nature of trial decision-making will change, and sometimes radically. The manner in which the professional will be reinvented will pose several paradoxes which only individual trial practice may resolve. An example is with legal representation and the manner in which it is said to protect the rights of lay participants, whilst at the same time being accused of distancing the lay voice from crucial decision processes. The personality of the professional and the persistence of the lay client will be important factors in the development of more sensitive and inclusive representation experiences.

- *New normative framework reliant on repositioned judicial discretion.* We have touched on this theme as essential for the initiation and perpetuation of trial transformation. The expansion of discretion it will invite requires specific counterbalances of individual and institutional accountability. The discretion of trial participants will be supervised through the discretion of the judge. This in turn must be conditional upon open reliance back to the observation and satisfaction of communities of justice.

  In this way discretion becomes the focus for accountability as well as a mechanism for its achievement. The normative framework for the transformed trial shall be specific in the discretionary powers it expands and creates against the interests of new trial constituencies such as victim communities.

  Discretion is also important when we look at the link between retributive and restorative trial justice in the transformed trial. The transformation process itself will rely on the discretionary activation of procedural norms which bring representatives of outside agencies directly into a redirected decision-making process aimed at a selected outcome which could be both restorative and retributive. Victim compensation through offender contribution is a good example of this.

- *Ramifications for process of a move away from the resolution of guilt and innocence, towards truth and responsibility.* Transformed trial practice will need a regular relationship between the processes and outcomes of retribution and restoration. We have argued that such a relationship is both appropriate and possible if the pathways to achieving either outcome are more compatible and tolerant. Truth through mediation may bring an acceptance of liability and a possibility of contrition. This may mean, however, that the truth on hand may not support punishment but compensation. Case by case the judge will have to prioritize the processes for truth-telling, and select and augment the various compatible outcomes on offer.

Three possibilities for the nature of any such relationship on offer in a particular trial may be that:

1 retribution can be better achieved with the assistance of restorative processes (diversion) – (see the establishment of truth and the use of amnesties);

2 there is a mix of both retributive and restorative processes, and where progressive components of both give a better overall satisfaction of client interest (victim compensation rather than state sanction); and

3 one takes precedence over the other, largely determined against more exclusionary client interest.

Realizing new justice expectations

It is clear that trial transformation is dependent on atmospheres of collaboration and trust. Justice paradigms which are currently so often opposed, professional and lay participants who work at arm's length, and constituent communities and their expectations foreign to each other need to find ground for integration. It is similar ground to some extent as that on which peacemaking and governance initiatives advance. It depends on trust from which will emerge common purpose.

The transformed trial process is envisaged as representing increased constituent access, greater lay inclusion and the accountability of significant interests in trial decision-making. Accountability will hopefully provide the confirmation and reiteration of trust. As collaborative justice protected through this new trial institution gives greater legitimacy to ICJ, then it will move from a symbolic to a sharply practical influence for good governance particularly in post-conflict states.

Clearly, accountability and governance, whether at the macro or micro level, depend upon reflecting relationships of dependency, trust and social control against the realities of globalization and its consequences for ICJ. Consequently, such relationships between individual human actors (regardless of state or group affiliation) and global structures such as international criminal courts and tribunals must be based upon a unifying moral principle which supports a conceptualization of ICJ that favours the restoration of social stability, and promotes flexible models of conflict resolution.[20] We do not, however, argue for universalized principles of equity or fairness; these must remain morally relative in satisfying legitimate expectations for justice. Rather we suggest that their instantiation as principles for distributive justice which promote conflict resolution establishes a sufficient basis for accountability. In terms of governance, therefore, the norms of control established by the transformation of international trial process are in reality mechanisms for the management of morally unacceptable risks. In other words, the trial process itself implements strategies for the control of behaviour whose moral significance the international community wishes to mark; behaviour which threatens the peace and stability of nation-states.

In order to materialize the power of the transformed trial to affirm these powerful and universal moralities crucial for the realization of good governance internationally, then the outcomes of the trial need to merit greater legitimacy and community confidence. Whilst recognizing the place of the present retributive drivers for trial justice it is necessary, as we have so far argued, to enhance the scope and style of trial outcomes through severing the essential connection between truth-finding and verdict, verdict and trial determination. Once this has been achieved through a more flexible normative framework for trial decision-making, then the selection of different processes for truth-finding, and outcomes which are mediated or determined, will become possible and practised.

Important to the achievement of new outcomes for the trial, and not just for their application, is the redesigning of responsibility within the trial. We have talked at length about new roles for trial professionals and a rebalancing of pathways of influence relating to lay and professional decision-makers. Also, the vital significance of the judge in ensuring such a repositioning and its smooth functioning will also necessitate new roles, powers and purposes for trial adjudicators. Much of this can be achieved through the goodwill and common purpose essential for collaborative justice. However, in order to give form and impetus to this collaboration, new normative frameworks for trial decision-making will require determination.

---

20 This universal principle embraces the possibility of various philosophical justifications for penality.

The new normative framework will do more than create the opportunity for novel trial processes and outcomes. It will also disengage from existing principles and distinctions which make harmonization of alternative justice paradigms difficult to achieve. In this respect the new normative framework is also more than an enunciation of a new morality for trial justice, one which better links to the concerns for reconciliation, conflict resolution and mutuality. It will require a practical dimension in order to, for example, redefine the connection between responsibility and liability. It will need to reveal how these notions do not always, as they often do now, follow on from a particular process. Aligned to this consideration is the resolution of commitments to non-impunity against pressures for amnesty. The preferential interpretation within this normative framework, of the purpose of the transformed trial now being the determination of truth and responsibility ahead of guilt and liability, will better accord with moralities of mediation and conflict resolution.

Policy of ICJ transformation and potential for global governance

Not being a definitive exploration of new world orders, this book can only conclude with several indicative policy directions for the relationship between ICJ and global governance. At present, if such a relationship is claimed, we see the international trial as a significant theatre where victor's justice is played out. But this is justice for the few. Its impact is intensely political. Beyond its symbolic resonance and its potential for closure, there is not much in this justice style for expansive victim communities or post-conflict states faced with community reintegration.

For the relationship to have a more practical significance it will need to rely on these assumptions:

1 The transformed trial will generate greater legitimacy for itself.

2 Because of the continued centrality of the trial within ICJ this enhanced legitimacy will flow over to ICJ more generally.

3 An enhanced and expanded constituency (particularly of victim communities) for the international trial will further validate and expand the relevance of ICJ.

4 Particularly for post-conflict states, the transformed trial with its potential for restorative justice in a solid 'rights framework' will act as an essential component for conflict resolution.

5 Trial outcomes which come from a mediation model will be appropriate for wider conflict resolution and the process from which they emerge may be translated into wider peacemaking agendas.

Based on such assumptions ICJ and its transformed trial process will more likely give:

• justice outcomes compatible with social inclusion and community reconciliation;
• justice outcomes which may also declare moral boundaries and wider community denunciation;
• justice processes which resolve rather than reward conflict;
• justice processes which represent rather than retard inclusive decision-making;
• justice ethics centrally adjudicated, accountably administered and collectively relevant; and
• justice ethics which confirm rather than contradict governance from peace and not conflict.

In terms of whether the transformed trial is able to sustain a 'pathway of influence' through ICJ and on to global governance, the overarching satisfaction of communities of justice will be the guide. Measures of justice satisfaction will also be drawn from both justice paradigms which have become the harmonized substance of the transformed trial. The activation of different paradigms within the trial and their priority will give indication of transformation practice and will provide the starting point for any actual influence trial to governance (beyond political symbolism).

Perhaps the most important argument for the trial as the universal institutional presence for collaborative ICJ is the way in which the trial can incorporate local agendas in post-conflict societies, and transform these into adjudicated resolutions for the best interests of communities of justice. At the same time, the central place of the transformed trial within ICJ requires it to recognize and advance global concerns for justice. The pathway of influence local/global over important decision sites will provide a mechanism where restorative justice subjectivities can be evaluated against more common retributive requirements.

Ultimately, we argue that international trial transformation may be pivotal in influencing the future role of ICJ in global governance. If there is one lesson that has been learned in the recent history of international trial justice it is that partial and symbolic justice is an inadequate response to the control of global threats to peace and global security. We suggest that within a paradigm which envisages a constructive and strategic role for trial justice in the healing and rebuilding of broken communities and lives, lies the real route to a credible ideology and practice for the control and management of war and social conflict. In this we would agree with Braithwaite (2002a: 207) that to fulfil the potential for restorative justice is a bottom-up process of engaging civil society in the institutional renewal necessary to forge just and permanent solutions for peace. However, in this book we have taken this aspiration one step further in suggesting how the transformation of international trial justice can move towards this end and help confirm ICJ as a credible force for global governance.

References

Ahmed, E., Harris, N., Braithwaite, J. and Braithwaite, V. (2001) *Shame Management through Reintegration*. Melbourne: Cambridge University Press.

Albrecht, H.-J. (2001) 'Post-adjudication dispositions in comparative perspective', in M. Tonry and R. Frase (eds) *Sentencing and Sanctions in Western Countries*. Oxford: Oxford University Press.

Alder, J. and Wundersitz, J. (eds) (1994) *Family Conferencing and Juvenile Justice: The Way forward or Misplaced Optimism*. Canberra: Australian Institute of Criminology.

Alldridge, P. and Chrisje, B. (2001) *Personal Autonomy: The Private Sphere and Criminal Law: A Comparative Study*. Oxford: Hart.

Alvarez, J. (1998) 'Rush to closure: lessons of the Tadic judgment', *Michigan Law Review*, 96: 2031.

Alvarez, J. (1999) 'Crimes of states/crimes of hate: lessons from Rwanda', *Yale Journal of International Law*, 24: 365.

Amann, D. (2000) 'Harmonic convergence? Constitutional criminal procedure in an international context', *Indiana Law Journal*, 75: 809. (http://cilp.nellco.org/cilp/2000/cilp0811.pdf).

Amann, D. (2002) 'Group mentality, expressivism and genocide', *International Criminal Law Review*, 2: 93.

Amnesty International (1999) *The International Criminal Court: Ensuring an Effective Role for Victims* (AI index: IOR 40/10/99).

Anderson, T. and Twining, W. (1991) *Analysis of Evidence: How to do Things with Facts*. London: Weidenfeld & Nicolson.

Aprile, E. (2001) *La competenza penale del giudice di pace*. Milano: Giuffre.

Ashworth, A. (1983) *Sentencing and Penal Policy*. London: Weidenfeld & Nicolson.

Ashworth, A. (1989a) 'Criminal justice and deserved sentences', *Criminal Law Review*, 340 (http://wwwserver.law.wits.ac.za/salc/issue/ip11.html).

Ashworth, A. (1989b) 'Techniques for reducing subjective disparity in sentencing', in Council of Europe, *Disparities in Sentencing: Causes and Solutions. Collected Studies in Criminological Research, Vol. XXVI.* Strasbourg: Council of Europe, 101–31.

Ashworth, A. (1993) 'Victim impact statements and sentencing', *Criminal Law Review*, 40: 498.

Ashworth, A. (1994) *The Criminal Process: An Evaluative Study* (1st edn). Oxford: Oxford University Press.

Ashworth, A. (1996) 'Crime, community and creeping consequentialism', *Criminal Law Review*, 43: 220.

Ashworth, A. (1998) *The Criminal Process: An Evaluative Study* (2nd edn). Oxford: Oxford University Press.

Ashworth, A. (1999) *Principles of Criminal Law* (3rd edn). Oxford: Oxford University Press.

Ashworth, A. (2000a) *Sentencing and Criminal Justice* (3rd edn). London: Butterworths.

Ashworth, A. (2000b) 'Victims' rights, defendants' rights and criminal procedure', in A. Crawford and J. Goodey (eds) *Integrating a Victim Perspective within Criminal Justice*. Aldershot: Ashgate, 185–204.

Ashworth, A. (2001) 'Criminal proceedings after the Human Rights Act: the first year', *Criminal Law Review*: 855.

Ashworth, A. (2002) *Human Rights, Serious Crimes and Criminal Procedure*. London: Sweet & Maxwell.

Ashworth, A. (2002b) 'Responsibilities, rights and criminal justice', *British Journal of Criminology*, 42: 578.

Ashworth, A. (2003) *Principles of Criminal Law* (4th edn). Oxford: Oxford University Press.

Ashworth, A. *et al.* (2001) *Criminal Litigation and Sentencing*. London: Blackstone.

Ashworth, A., Von Hirsch, A., Bottoms, A. and Wasik, M. (1995) 'Bespoke tailoring won't suit community sentences', *New Law Journal*, 6702: 970.

Ashworth, A. and Wasik, M. (eds) (1998) *Fundamentals of Sentencing Theory*. Oxford: Oxford University Press.

Auld, Lord Justice (2001) *Review of the Criminal Courts of England and Wales by the Right Honourable Lord Justice Auld* (http://www.criminal-courts-review.org.uk/).

Ayers, E. (1984) *Vengeance and Justice: Crime and Punishment in the 19th-Century American South*. New York: Oxford University Press.

Bagaric, M. (2001) *Punishment and Sentencing: A Rational Approach*. London: Cavendish.

Bagaric, M. and Amarasekara, K. (2000) 'The errors of retributivism', *Melbourne University Law Review*, 24 (http://www.austlii.edu.au/au/journals/MULR/2000/5.html).

Bagaric, M. and Amarasekara, K. (2001) 'Feeling sorry? Tell someone who cares: the irrelevance of remorse in sentencing', *Howard Journal of Criminal Justice*, 40: 364 (http://www.deakin.edu.au/sch_law_research/otherlegal/dlsarticles.php).

Bagaric, M. and Amarasekara, K. (2001) 'The prejudice against similar fact evidence', *International Journal of Evidence and Proof*, 5: 71.

Baker, E. and Clarkson, C. (2002) 'Making punishments work? An evaluation of the Halliday Report on sentencing in England and Wales', *Criminal Law Review*: 81.

Baldwin, J. and McConville, M. (1979) *Jury Trials*. Oxford: Clarendon Press.

Ball, C. (2000) 'The Youth Justice and Criminal Evidence Act 1999, Part I: a significant move towards restorative justice, or a recipe for unintended consequences', *Criminal Law Review*: 211.

Ball, H. (2004) 'US opposition to the ICC: a political perspective on international criminal justice', paper presented to Third International Conference *International Criminal Justice: A Transatlantic Dialogue* at the European Parliament and the Royal Flemish Academy for Sciences and Arts, Brussels, May.

Bankowski, Z. and Mungham, G. (1976) *Images of Law*. London: Routledge & Kegan Paul.

Bankowski, Z. and Mungham, G. (eds) (1980) *Essays in Law and Society*. London: Routledge & Kegan Paul.

Bassiouni, M.C. (1998a) *International Criminal Law* (2nd edn). Ardsley: Transnational Publishers.

Bassiouni, M.C. (1998b) 'The normative framework of international humanitarian law: overlaps, gaps and ambiguities', *Transnational Law and Contemporary Problems*, 8: 199.

Bassiouni, M.C. (1998c) *The Statute of the International Criminal Court: A Documentary History*. Ardsley: Transnational Publishers.

Bassiouni, M.C. (2001) 'Searching for peace and achieving justice: the need for accountability', *Law and Contemporary Problems*, 59: 9 (http://www.booksmatter.com/b0754622401.htm).

Bassiouni, M.C. and Manakas, P. (1996) *The Law of the International Criminal Tribunal of the Former Yugoslavia*. Irvington-on-Hudson, NY: Transnational Publishers.

Bauman, Z. (2000) 'Social uses of law and order', in D. Garland and R. Sparks (eds) *Criminology and Social Theory*. Oxford: Oxford University Press, 23–45.

Bayles, M. (1990) *Procedural Justice: Allocating to Individuals*. Dordrecht: Kluwer.

Beccaria, C. (1764) *On Crimes and Punishment (Dei Delitti e delle Pene)* (trans. H. Paolucci). Indianapolis, IN: Bobbs-Merrill (1963).

Becker, H. (1973) *Outsiders* (2nd edn). New York, NY: Free Press.

Behrens, H.-J. (1998) 'Investigation, trial and appeal in the International Criminal Court Statute (Parts V, VI, VIII)', *European Journal of Crime, Criminal Law and Criminal Justice*, 6: 429.

Beirne, P. (1983) 'Generalisation and its discontents', in E. Johnson amd I. Barak-Glantz (eds) *Comparative Criminology*. Beverly Hills, CA: Sage.

Bell, J. (2001) *French Legal Cultures*. London: Butterworths.

Bennett, W., Feldman, L. and Martha, S. (1981) *Reconstructing Reality in the Courtroom: Justice and Judgment in American Culture*. London: Tavistock.

Beresford, S. (2002) 'Unshackling the paper tiger: the sentencing practices of the ad hoc international criminal tribunals for the former Yugoslavia and Rwanda', *International Criminal Law Review*, 1: 33.

Berger, H. *et al.* (eds) (1989) *Handbuch der Sozialistischen: Forschung Methodologie, Method*. Berlin: Technicken, Akademie Verlag.

Bianchi, H. (1994) *Justice as Sanctuary: Toward a New System of Crime Control*. Bloomington, IN: Indiana University Press.

Blumberg, A. (1967) *Criminal Justice* (2nd edn). New York, NY: New Viewpoints.

Bohlander, M. (2000) 'Prosecutor v. Dusko Tadic: waiting to exhale', *Criminal Law Forum*, 11: 217.

Bohlander, M. (2001) 'The direct application of international criminal law in Kosovo', *Kosovo Legal Studies*, 1: 7.

Bohlander, M. (2003) 'Last exit Bosnia: transferring war crimes prosecution from the International Tribunal to domestic courts', *Criminal Law Forum*, 14: 59.

Bohlander, M. and Findlay, M. (2002) 'The use of domestic sources as a basis for international criminal law principles', *Global Community Yearbook of International Law and Jurisprudence*, 1: 3–26.

Bottoms, A. (1998) 'Five puzzles in von Hirsch's theory of punishment', in A. Ashworth and M. Wasik (eds) *Fundamentals of Sentencing Theory*. Oxford: Clarendon Press, 53–100.

Bottoms, A. (2003) 'Some sociological reflections on restorative justice', in A. von Hirsch *et al.* (eds) *Restorative Justice and Criminal Justice: Competing or Reconcilable Paradigms?*. Oxford: Hart.

Bottoms, A. and Brownsword, R. (1982) 'Incapacitaton as a strategy for crime control: possibilities and pitfalls', *British Journal of Criminology*, 22: 229.

Bottoms, A., Knapp, M. and Fenyo, A. (1995) *Intensive Community Supervision for Young Offenders: Outcome, Process and Cost*. Cambridge: University of Cambridge Institute of Criminology.

Bourdieu, P. (1977) *Outline of a Theory of Practice*. Cambridge: Cambridge University Press.

Box, S. (1983) *Power, Crime and Mystification*. London: Routledge.

Box, S. (1987) *Recession, Crime and Punishment*. Basingstoke: Palgrave Macmillan.

Braithwaite, J. (1989a) *Crime, Shame and Reintegration*. Cambridge: Cambridge University Press.

Braithwaite, J. (1989b) 'Criminological theory and organizational crime', *Justice Quarterly*, 6: 401.

Braithwaite, J. (1989c) 'The state of criminology: theoretical decay or renaissance', *Australian and New Zealand Journal of Criminology*, 22: 129.

Braithwaite, J. (1994) 'Thinking harder about democratising social control', in J. Alder and J. Wundersitz (eds) *Family Conferencing and Juvenile Justice: The Way forward or Misplaced Optimism*. Canberra: Australian Institute of Criminology.

Braithwaite, J. (1999) 'Restorative justice: assessing optimistic and pessimistic accounts', *Crime and Justice: A Review of Research*, 25: 1.

Braithwaite, J. (2001a) 'Crime in a convict republic', *Modern Law Review*, 64: 11.

Braithwaite, J. (2001b) 'Youth development circles', *Oxford Review of Education*, 27: 239.

Braithwaite, J. (2001c) 'Restorative justice and a new criminal law of substance abuse', *Youth and Society*, 33: 227.

Braithwaite, J. (2002a) *Restorative Justice and Responsive Regulation*. Oxford: Oxford University Press.

Braithwaite, J. (2002b) 'Rules and principles: a theory of legal certainty', *Australian Journal of Legal Philosophy*, 27: 47.

Braithwaite, J. and Pettit, P. (1990) *Not Just Deserts*. Oxford: Oxford University Press.

Brants, C. and Field, S. (1995) 'Discretion and accountability in prosecution: a comparative perspective on keeping crime out of court', in P. Fennell *et al.* (eds) *Criminal Justice in Europe: A Comparative Study*. Oxford: Clarendon Press.

Brants, C. and Field, S. (2000) 'Legal cultures, political cultures and procedural traditions: towards a comparative interpretation of covert and proactive policing in England and Wales and the Netherlands', in D. Nelken (ed.) *Contrasting Criminal Justice. Getting from Here to There*. Aldershot: Ashgate.

Brennan, C. (2001) 'The victim personal statement: who is the victim?' *Web Journal of Current Legal Issues*, 4: 3.

Bricola, F. (1965) *La discretzionalita nel diritto penale*. Milano: Giuffre.

British Journal of Criminology (2002) 'Special issue: practice, performance and prospects for restorative justice', *British Journal of Criminology*, 42.

Brittan, A. and Maynard, M. (1984) *Sexism, Racism and Oppression*. Oxford: Blackwell.

Bronzo, P. (ed) (2001) *La cometenza penale del giudice di pace: D Lgs 28 agosto 2000, n 274*. Milano: IPSOA.

Brown, M. and Pratt, J. (eds) (2000) *Dangerous Offenders: Punishment and Social Order*. London: Routledge.

Brunelli, D. (2001) 'Il congedo dalla pena detentiva nel microsistema integrato del diritto penale "mite"', in A. Salfati (ed.) *Il giudice di pace. Un nuovo modello di giustizia penale*. Padova: Cedam, 401ff.

Bryman, A. (1992) 'Quantitative and qualitative research: further reflections on their integration', in J. Brannon (ed.) *Mixing Methods: Qualitative and Quantitative Research*. Aldershot: Avebury.

Burke-White, W. (2001) 'Reframing impunity: applying liberal international law theory to an analysis of amnesty legislation', *Harvard International Law Journal*, 42: 467.

Burke-White, W. (2002) 'A community of courts: towards a system of international criminal law enforcement', *Michigan Journal of International Law*, 24: 1 (http://www.jsmp.minihub.org/Reports/otherresources/Burke-White%20ITP2.pdf).

Burke-White, W. (2003a) 'The International Criminal Court and the future of legal accountability', *ILSA Journal of International and Comparative Law*, 10: 195.

Burke-White, W. (2003b) 'Regionalization of international criminal law enforcement: a preliminary exploration', *Texas International Law Journal*, 38: 729.

Bush, R. and Fogler, J. (1994) *The Promise of Mediation: Responding to Conflict through Empowerment and Recognition*, San Francisco, CA: Jossey-Bass.

Campbell, E. (1999) 'Towards a sociological theory of discretion', *International Journal of the Sociology of Law*, 27: 79.

Campbell, T. (1999) 'Human rights. A culture of controversy', *Journal of Law and Society*, 26: 6.

Canepa, G. and Merlos, S. (2002) *Manuale di diritto penitenziario*. Milano: Giuffre.

Caplan, M. (2001) 'International criminal court sounds a wake up call', *The Times*, 10 April.

Carcano, A. (2002) 'Sentencing and the gravity of the offence in international criminal law', *International and Comparative Law Quarterly*, 51: 583.

Carlen, P. (1976) *Magistrates' Justice?*. Oxford: Martin Robertson.

Carlen, P. (1983) *Women's Imprisonment: A Study in Social Control*. London: Routledge & Kegan Paul.

Carlen, P. (1990) *Alternatives to Women's Imprisonment*. Milton Keynes: Open University Press.

Carlen, P. and Frankenberg R. (eds) (1994) *Race, Gender and Ideology*. Oxford: Blackwell.

Carlen, P. and Worrall, A. (eds) (1987) *Gender, Crime and Justice*. Milton Keynes: Open University Press.

Carsten, S. (2001) 'Current development: accommodating individual criminal responsibility and national reconciliation: the UN Truth Commission for East Timor', *American Journal of International Law*, 95: 952.

Casanovas, P. (1999) 'Pragmatic legal contexts', paper presented at the International Pragmatics Conference on *Pragmatics and Negotiation*, Tel Aviv University/Hebrew University of Jerusalem, 13–16 June.

Cassese, A. (1999) 'The statute of the international criminal court: some preliminary reflections', *European Journal of International Law*, 10: 144.

Cavadino, M. and Dignan, J. (1997) 'Reparation, retribution and rights', *International Review of Victimology*, 4: 233.

Cavadino, M. and Dignan, J. (2002) *The Penal System: An Introduction* (3rd edn). London: Sage.

Ceretti, A. (1996) *Come pensa il tribunale per i minorenni*. Milano: Giuffre.

Certoma, G. (1985) *The Italian Legal System*. London: Butterworths.

Chambliss, W. (1969) *Crime and the Legal Process*. New York, NY: Wiley.

Chambliss, W. (ed.) (1984) *Criminal Law in Action* (2nd edn). New York, NY: Wiley.

Chambliss, W. and Mankoff, M. (1976) *Whose Law? What Order? A Conflict Approach to Criminology*. New York, NY: Wiley.

Chambliss, W. and Seidman, R. (1982) *Law, Order and Power*. Reading, MA: Addison-Wesley.

Chiavario, M. (2002) 'Private parties: the rights of the defendant and the victim', in M. Delmas-Marty and J. Spencer (eds) *European Criminal Procedures*. Cambridge: Cambridge University Press, 541–93.

Chinkin, C. (1997) 'Due process and witness anonymity', *American Journal of International Law*, 91: 75.

Christie, N. (1977) 'Conflicts as property', *British Journal of Criminology*, 17: 1.

Christie, N. (2000) 'Dangerous states', in M. Brown and J. Pratt (eds) *Dangerous Offenders: Punishment and Social Order*. London: Routledge.

Christodoulidis, E. (2000) 'Truth and reconciliation as risks', *Social and Legal Studies*, 9: 179.

Cicourel, A. (1968) *The Social Organisation of Juvenile Justice*. New York, NY: Wiley.

Cockayne, J. (2001) 'Procedural and processual synthesis in the international tribunals. Part 1. The context of synthesis.' Unpublished working paper.

Cockayne, J. (2002a) 'A survey of recent criminal procedural reform in Italy, France and Spain: evidence of internationalisation.' Unpublished working paper.

Cockayne, J. (2002b) 'Conference report for the International Criminal Trial Project', prepared for the conference *Internationalised Criminal Courts and Tribunals: Practice and Prospects*, Universiteit van Amsterdam, the Netherlands, 25–26 January.

Cockayne, J. (2004) 'Stephen C. Neff: the rights and duties of neutrals: a general history', *Leiden Journal of International Law*, 17: 203.

Cockayne, J. and Huckerby, J. (2004) 'Special court for Sierra Leone: Truth and Reconciliation Commission applications for hearings with Samuel Hinga Norman and Augustine Ghao'. Unpublished casenote.

Cohen, S. (1985) *Visions of Social Control*. Cambridge: Polity Press.

Cohen, S. (1993) 'Human rights and crimes of the state: the culture of denial', *Australian and New Zealand Journal of Criminology*, 26: 97.

Cohen, S. (1995) 'State crimes of previous regimes: knowledge, accountability and the policing of the past', *Law and Social Inquiry*, 20: 7.

Condorelli, L. and Villalpando, S. (2002) 'Relationship of the court with the United Nations', in A. Cassese *et al.* (eds) *The Rome Statute of the International Criminal Court: A Commentary*. Oxford and New York, NY: Oxford University Press.

Conso, G. and Grevi, V. (1977) *Commentario al nuova codice di procedura penale*. Padova: Cedam.

Cordero, F. (2001) *Procedura penale*. Milano: Giuffre.

Correra, M. and Riponti, D. (1990) *La vittima nel sistema italiano della giustizia penale*. Padova: Cedam.

Corso, P. (1993) 'Sistema processuale penale italiano', in C. Van Den Wyngaert *et al.* (eds) *Criminal Procedure Systems in the European Community*. London: Butterworths, 239.

Cotterrell, R. (1992) *The Sociology of Law: An Introduction* (2nd edn). London: Butterworths.

Cotterrell, R. (1995) *Law's Community: Legal Theory in Sociological Perspective*. Oxford: Clarendon Press.

Cotterrell, R. (1997) 'A legal concept of community', *Canadian Journal of Law and Society*, 12: 75.

Cotterrell, R. (1998a) 'Law and community: a new relationship in legal theory at the end of the millennium?', *Current Legal Problems*, 51: 367.

Cotterrell, R. (1998b) 'Why must legal ideas be interpreted sociologically?', *Journal of Law and Society*, 25: 171.

Cotterrell, R. (1999a) *Emile Durkheim: Law in a Moral Domain*. Edinburgh: Edinburgh University Press.

Cotterrell, R. (1999b) 'Transparency, mass media, ideology and community', *Cultural Values*, 3: 414.

Cotterrell, R. (2002a) 'Global law in a moral domain', *Socio-legal Newsletter*, 37: 6.

Cotterrell, R. (2002b) 'Seeking similarity, appreciating difference: comparative law and communities', in A. Harding and E. Orucu (eds) *Comparative Law in the 21st Century*. The Hague: Kluwer, 35–54.

Cotterrell, R. (2002c) 'Subverting orthodoxy, making law central: a view of socio-legal studies', *Journal of Law and Society*, 29: 632.

Cottingham, J. (1979) 'Varieties of retributivism', *Philosophical Quarterly*, 29: 238 (http://uwp.edu/~zaibert/punishmentSp04.htm).

Council of Europe (1989) *Disparities in Sentencing: Causes and Solutions Collected Studies in Criminological Research. Vol. XXVI*. Strasbourg: Council of Europe.

Council of Europe (1993) *Consistency in Sentencing. Recommendation R (92) 17*. Strasbourg: Council of Europe Press.

Crawford, A. (2000) 'Contrasts in victim–offender mediation and appeals to community in France and England', in D. Nelken (ed.) *Contrasting Criminal Justice*. Aldershot: Ashgate, 205–29.

Crawford, A. and Goodey J. (eds) (2000) *Integrating a Victim Perspective within Criminal Justice*. Aldershot: Ashgate.

Crawford, A. and Newburn, T. (2003) *Youth Offending and Restorative Justice: Implementing Reform in Youth Justice*. Cullompton: Willan Publishing.

Crocker, L. (1995) 'The upper limit of just punishment', *Emory Law Journal*, 41: 1059.

Daly, E. (2002) 'Between punitive and reconstructive justice: the Gacaca Courts in Rwanda', *New York University Journal of International Law and Politics*, 34: 355.

Daly, K. (1994) *Gender, Crime and Punishment*. New Haven, CT: Yale University Press.

Daly, K. (1998) 'Restorative justice: moving past the caricatures', paper prepared for Institute of Criminology, Sydney Law School (http://www.gu.edu.au/school/ccj/kdaly_docs/kdpaper2.pdf).

Daly, K. (2000) 'Restorative justice in diverse and unequal societies', paper presented at Flinders University symposium on Criminal Justice in Diverse Societies, Adelaide, December (*Law in Context*, 17 (2000): 167–90).

Damaska, M. (1976) *The Faces of Justice and State Authority*. New Haven, CT: Yale University Press.

Davies, M. (2002) *Asking the Law Question: The Dissolution of Legal Theory*. Sydney and London.

Davies, M., Croall, H. and Tyrer, J. (2004) *Criminal Justice: An Introduction to the Criminal Justice System in England and Wales*. London: Pearson Education.

Davies, P., Francis, P. and Jupp, V. (2003) *Victimisation: Theory, Research and Policy*. Basingstoke: Palgrave Macmillan.

de Haan, W. (1990) *The Politics of Redress: Crime, Punishment and Penal Abolition*. London: Unwin Hyman.

Delmas-Marty, M. (ed.) (1996), *What Kind of Criminal Policy for Europe?* The Hague and London: Kluwer Law International.

Delmas-Marty, M. (2002) 'Global crime calls for global justice', *European Journal of Crime, Criminal Law and Criminal Justice*, 10: 286.

Delmas-Marty M. (2003) 'The contribution of comparative law to a pluralist conception of international criminal law', *Journal of International Criminal Justice*, 1: 13.

Delmas-Marty, M. and Spencer, J. (eds) (2002) *European Criminal Procedures. Cambridge Studies in International and Comparative Law*. Cambridge: Cambridge University Press.

Dennis, I. (ed.) (1987) *Criminal Law and Justice*. London: Sweet & Maxwell.

Dennis, I. (1997) 'Human rights and evidence in adversarial criminal procedure: the advancement of international standards', in J. Nijboer and C. Reijntjes (eds) *Proceedings of the First World Conference on New Trends in Criminal Investigation and Evidence* (http://www.panteion.gr/uk/departments/sociology/postgrad/

teaching_staff.html; http://www.uniadrion.unibo.it/judge/Course/ Outlines/Sijercic.htm).

Dennis, J. (2001) 'Judicial power and the administrative state', *Louisiana Law Review*, 62: 59.

de Sousa Santos, B. (1995) *Towards a New Common Sense: Law, Science and Politics in the Paradigmatic Transition*. New York, NY, and London: Routledge.

Dezelay, Y. and Garth, B. (1996) *Dealing in Virtue: International Commercial Arbitration and the Construction of Transnational Legal Order*. Chicago, IL: University of Chicago Press.

Dignan, J. (1999a) 'Restorative crime prevention in theory and practice', *Prison Service Journal*, 123: 2.

Dignan, J. (1999b) 'The Crime and Disorder Act and the prospects for restorative justice', *Criminal Law Review*: 48.

Dignan, J. (2002) 'Towards a systemic model of criminal justice', in A. von Hirsch *et al.* (eds) *Restorative Justice and Criminal Justice: Competing or Reconcilable Paradigms?* Oxford: Hart.

Dignan, J. and Cavadino, M. (1996) 'Towards a framework for conceptualising and evaluating models of criminal justice from a victims' perspective', *International Review of Victimology*, 4: 153.

Dolcini, E. (1979) *La commisurazione della pena*. Padova: Cedam.

Dolinko, D. (1991) 'Some thoughts about retributivism', *Ethics*, 101: 537.

Dolinko, D. (1997) 'Retributivism, consequentialism and the intrinsic goodness of punishment', *Law and Philosophy*, 16: 507.

Douzinas, C. (1996) 'Justice and human rights in postmodernity', in C. Gearty and A. Tomkins (eds) *Understanding Human Rights*. London: Mansell, 115–37.

Downes, D. and Rock, P. (1995) *Understanding Deviance: A Guide to the Sociology of Crime and Rule Breaking*. Oxford: Oxford University Press.

Drumbl, M. (2000a) 'Legal issues', in United Nations Association of the USA, *A Global Agenda: Issues before the 55th General Assembly of the United Nations*. New York, NY: Rowman & Littlefield, 225–70.

Drumbl, M. (2000b) 'Punishment goes global: international criminal law, conflict zones, and gender (in)equality', *Canadian Women Studies*, 19: 22.

Drumbl, M. (2000c) 'Punishment, postgenocide: from guilt to shame to *Civis* in Rwanda', *New York University Law Review*, 75: 1221.

Drumbl, M. (2000d) 'International human rights, international humanitarian law and environmental security: can the international criminal court bridge the gaps?', *ILSA Journal of International and Comparative Law*, 6: 305.

Drumbl, M. (2000e) 'Waging war against the world: a crime?', in J.E. Austin and C.E. Bruch *Environmental Consequences of War: Legal, Economic and Scientific Perspectives*. Cambridge: Cambridge University Press, 620–46.

Drumbl, M.A. (2001) 'The (al)lure of the genocide trial: justice, reconciliation, and reconstruction in Rwanda', in D. Barnhitzer (ed.) *Effective Strategies for Protecting Human Rights*. Aldershot: Ashgate.

Drumbl, M. (2002) 'Sclerosis: retributive justice and the Rwandan genocide', *Punishment and Society*, 2/3: 287.

Drumbl, M. (2003) *Towards a Criminology of International Crime*. Washington and Lee University Public Law and Legal Theory Research Paper Series, Working paper No. 03–07, May.

Dubber, M. (2001) 'Policing possession: the war on crime and the end of criminal law', *Journal of Criminal Law and Criminology*, 91: 829.

Dubois, F. (2000) 'Nothing but the truth: the SA alternative to dilemmas of corrective justice in transitions to democracy', in S. Veitch and E. Christodoulides (eds) *Lethe's Law: Justice, Law and Ethics in Reconciliation*. Oxford: Hart, 91–114.

Duff, P. and Findlay, M. (1997) 'Jury reform: of myths and moral panics', *International Journal of the Sociology of Law*, 25: 363.

Duff, P. and Findlay, M. (1982) 'The jury: ideology and practice', *International Journal of the Sociology of Law*, 10: 253.

Duff, R. (1986) *Trials and Punishments*. Cambridge: Cambridge University Press.

Duff, R. (1996) 'Punishment, citizenship and responsibility', in H. Tam (ed.) *Punishment, Excuses and Moral Development*. Aldershot: Avebury, 17–34.

Duff, R. (1998) 'Desert and penance', in A. von Hirsch and A. Ashworth (eds) *Principled Sentencing: Readings on Theory and Policy* (2nd edn). Oxford: Hart, 161–79.

Duff, R. (2001) *Punishment, Communication, and Community*. New York, NY: Oxford University Press.

Duff, A. and Garland, D. (1994a) 'Introduction: thinking about punishment', in *A Reader on Punishment*. Oxford: Oxford University Press, 1–43.

Duff, R. and Garland, D. (eds) (1994b) *A Reader on Punishment*. Oxford: Oxford University Press.

Durkheim, E. (1982) *The Rules of Sociological Method and Selected Texts on Sociology and its Method* (trans. W.D. Halls). London: Macmillan.

Durkheim, E. (1984) 'Two laws of penal evolution', in S. Lukes and A. Scull (eds.) *Durkheim and the Law*. Oxford: Blackwell, 102–32.

Dworkin, R. (1977) *Taking Rights Seriously*. London: Duckworth.

Edwards, I. (2001) 'Victim participation in sentencing: the problem of incoherence' *Howard Journal of Criminal Justice*, 40: 39.

Edwards, I. (2002) 'The place of victim's preferences in the sentencing of "their" offenders', *Criminal Law Review*: 689.

Eisnaugle, C. and Neibur, J. (2003) 'An international "truth commission": utilizing restorative justice as an alternative to retribution', *Vanderbilt Journal of Transnational Law*, 36: 209.

Eley, S., Malloch, M., McIvor, G., Yates, R. and Brown, A. (2002) *The Glasgow Drug Court in Action: The First Six Months* (www.scotland.gov.uk/library5/social/gdca-00.as).

Emerson, R. (1969) *Judging Delinquents: Context and Process in Juvenile Court*. Chicago, IL: Aldine.

Emmerson, B. and Ashworth, A. (2001) *Human Rights and Criminal Justice*. London: Sweet & Maxwell.

Erez, E. (1994) 'Victim participation in sentencing: and the debate goes on', *International Review of Victimology*, 3: 17.

Erez, E. (1999) 'Who's afraid of the big bad victim? Victim impact statements as victim empowerment *and* enhancement of justice', *Criminal Law Review*: 545.

Erez, E. *et al*. (1994) *Victim Impact Statements in South Australia: An Evaluation*. Adelaide: Office of Crime Statistics.

Erez, E. and Roger L. (1993) 'Crime impact v victim impact: victim impact statements in South Australia', *Criminology Australia*, 6: 3.

Erez, E. and Rogers, L. (1999) 'The effects of victim impact statements on criminal justice outcomes and processes: the perspectives of legal professionals', *British Journal of Criminology*, 39: 216.

Erez, E. and Tontodonato, P. (1990) 'The effect of victim participation in sentencing on sentence outcome', *Criminology*, 28: 451.

Erickson, M., Gibbs, J. and Jenson, G. (1977) 'The deterrence doctrine and the perceived certainty of legal punishment', *American Sociological Review*, 42: 305.

Evered, T. (1994) 'An international criminal court: recent proposals and American concerns', *Pace International Law Review*, 6: 121.

Ewald, W. (1998) 'The jurispurdential approach to comparatvie law: a field guide to "rats"', *American Journal of Comparative Law*, 46: 701.

Exner, F. (1949) *Kriminologie*. Berlin: Springer Verlag.

Fassler, L.J. (1991) 'The Italian Procedure Code: an adversarial system of criminal procedure in continental Europe', *Columbia Journal of Transnational Law*, 29: 245.

Feeley, M. (1979) *The Process is the Punishment: Handling Cases in a Lower Criminal Court*. New York, NY: Russell Sage Foundation.

Feeley, M. and Simon, J. (1992) 'The new penology: notes on the emerging strategy of corrections and its implications', *Criminology*, 30: 449.

Feinberg, J. (ed.) (1970) *Doing and Deserving: Essays on the Theory of Responsibility*. Princeton, NJ: Princeton University Press.

Feinberg, J. (1984) *Harm to Others*. Oxford: Oxford University Press.

Fenwick, H. (1995) 'Rights of victims in the criminal justice process: rhetoric or reality?' *Criminal Law Review*: 843.

Fenwick, H. (1997) 'Procedural rights of victims of crime: public or private ordering of the criminal justice process', *Modern Law Review*, 60: 317.

Findlay, M. (1991) 'Juror comprehension and complexity: strategies to enhance understanding', *British Journal of Criminology*, 41: 56.

Findlay, M. (1994a) *Jury Management in NSW*. Melbourne: AIJA.

Findlay, M. (1994b) 'The ambiguity of accountability: deaths in custody and regulation of police power', *Current Issues in Criminal Justice*, 6: 234.

Findlay, M. (1997a) 'Crime, community penalty and integration with legal formalism in the South Pacific', *Journal of Pacific Studies*, 21: 145.

Findlay, M. (1997b) 'The globalisation of crime', paper presented at the 15th *International Symposium on Economic Crime*, Cambridge.

Findlay, M. (1999a) *The Globalisation of Crime: Understanding Transitional Relationships in Context*. Cambridge: Cambridge University Press.

Findlay, M. (1999b) 'Lay participation in justice in transitional cultures' paper presented at the *Lay Participation in the Criminal Trial in 21st Century* conference, Siracusa.

Findlay, M. (1999c) 'The international criminal trial project', *Nottingham Law Journal*, 8: 121.

Findlay, M. (1999d) 'Relating crime and globalisation', *Australian Quarterly*, 71: 23.

Findlay, M. (1999e) 'Decolonizing restoration and justice: restoration in transitional cultures', paper presented at the *Restorative Justice and Civil Society* Conference, ANU, Canberra.

Findlay, M. (2000a) 'Decolonising restoration and justice: restoration in transitional cultures', *Howard Journal of Criminal Justice*, 39: 398.

Findlay, M. (2000b) *The Criminal Laws of the South Pacific* (2nd edn). Suva: IJALS (also Buffalo, NY: William S. Hein).

Findlay, M. (2000c) 'Decolonising restoration and justice: restoration in transitional cultures', in H. Strang and J. Braithwaite (eds) *Restorative Justice: Philosophy to Practice*. Aldershot: Ashgate, 185–202.

Findlay, M. (2000d) 'Juror comprehension and complexity: strategies to enhance understanding', *British Journal of Criminology*, 41: 56.

Findlay, M. (2001a) 'Synthesis in trial procedures? The experience of the international criminal tribunals', *International and Comparative Law Quarterly*, 50: 26.

Findlay, M. (2001b) *The Problem with Criminal Law*. Melbourne: Oxford University Press.

Findlay, M. (2001c) 'The costs of globalized crime: new methods of control', *International Journal of Comparative Criminology*, 1: 109.

Findlay, M. (2002a) 'The international and comparative criminal trial project', *International Criminal Law Review*, 2: 47.

Findlay, M. (2002b) 'Internationalised criminal trial and access to justice', *International Criminal Law Review*, 2: 237.

Findlay, M. (2003a) *Review of the Crimes (Forensic Procedures) Act NSW*. Report commissioned by the Department of the Attorney General, Sydney.

Findlay, M. (2003b) 'Crime, terror and transitional cultures in a contracting globe', in C. Dauvergne (ed.) *Jurisprudence for an Interconnected Globe*. Aldershot: Ashgate, 231–47.

Findlay, M. (2003c) 'The Pacific', in Transparency International (eds) *Global Corruption Report 2003*. Berlin: Transparency International, 115–28.

Findlay, M. and Duff, P. (1982a) 'The jury: ideology and practice', *International Journal of the Sociology of Law*, 10: 253.

Findlay, M. and Duff, P. (1982b) 'Jury vetting – ideology of the jury in transition', *Criminal Law Journal*, 6: 138.

Findlay, M. and Duff, P. (1988) *The Jury under Attack*. London and Sydney: Butterworths.

Findlay, M. and Henham, R. (2001) 'Methodology and the comparative contextual analysis of trial process: a preliminary analysis' (http://www.nls.ntu.ac.uk/clr/ictp/Publications/workingpapers/workingpaperspage.htm).

Findlay, M. and Henham, R. (2003a) 'Integrating theory and methodology in the comparative contextual analysis of trial process', paper presented at the workshop on *Socio-legal Research Methods*, International Institute for the Sociology of Law, Onati, Spain, April.

Findlay, M. and Henham, R. (2003b) Presentation at the colloquium on the *International and Comparative Criminal Trial Project*, Max Planck Institute for Foreign and International Criminal Law, Freiburg, Germany, September.

Findlay, M. and Henham, R. (forthcoming) 'Integrating theory and method in the comparative contextual analysis of trial process', in R. Banakar and M. Travers (eds) *Theory and Method in Socio-legal Research*. Oxford: Hart.

Findlay, M. and Zvekic, U. (1988) *Informal Mechanisms of Crime Control – a Cross Cultural Perspective*. Rome: UNSDRI.

Findlay, M. and Zvekic, U. (1993) *Alternative Policing Styles: Cross Cultural Perspectives*. Deventer: Kluwer.

Finnis, J. (1980) *Natural Law and Natural Rights*. Oxford: Oxford University Press.

Fionda, J. (1999) 'New Labour, old hat: youth justice and the Crime and Disorder Act 1998', *Criminal Law Review*: 36.

Fitzpatrick, P. (1992) *The Mythology of Modern Law*. London: Routledge.

Fitzpatrick, P. (2001) *Modernism and the Grounds of Law*. Cambridge: Cambridge University Press.

Floud, J. and Young, W. (1981) *Dangerousness and Criminal Justice*. London: Heinemann.

Forsythe, D. (1994) 'Politics and the International Tribunal for the Former Yugoslavia', *Criminal Law Forum*, 5: 401. (http://www.polisci.ucla.edu/faculty/trachtenberg/syllabi,lists/harvard/slaughter.pdf).

Forti, G. (2000) *L'immane concretezza*. Milano: Cortina.

Foucault, M. (1977a) *Discipline and Punish: The Birth of the Prison* (trans. A. Sheridan). London: Allen Lane.

Foucault, M. (1977b) *Language, Counter-memory, Practice: Selected Essays and Interviews*, D.F. Bouchard (ed.) (trans. D.F. Bouchard and S. Simon). Ithaca, NY: Cornell University Press.

Foucault, M. (1980) *Power/Knowledge: Selected Interviews and other writings, 1972–1977*. Brighton: Harvester.

Frase, R. (1998) 'Comparative criminal justice policy', in *Comparative Criminal Justice Systems: From Diversity to Rapprochment. Proceedings of the International Conference for the 25th Anniversary of the International Institute of Higher Studies in Criminal Sciences*, Siracusa, Italy, 16–20 December 1997 (*Nouvelles Etudes Penales* 17. International Association of Penal Law, Toulouse: Editions Eres), 109.

Freccero, S. (1994) 'An introduction to the new Italian criminal procedure', *American Journal of Criminal Law*, 21: 345.

Frulli, M. (2001) 'Are crimes against humanity more serious than war crimes?' *European Journal of International Law*, 12: 329.

Fuller, L.L. (1969) *The Morality of Law* (2nd edn). New Haven, CT: Yale University Press.

Gardner, J. (1998) 'Crime: in proportion and in perspective', in A. Ashworth and M. Wasik (eds) *Fundamentals of Sentencing Theory*. Oxford: Clarendon Press, 31–52.

Garfinkel, A. (1981) *Forms of Explanation: Rethinking the Questions in Social Theory*. New Haven: Yale University Press.

Garfinkel, H. (1956) 'Conditions of successful degradation ceremonies', *American Journal of Sociology*, 6: 420.

Garfinkel, H. (1967) *Studies in Ethnomethodology*. Englewood Cliffs, NJ: Prentice Hall.

Garfinkel, H. (ed.) (1986) *Ethnomethodological Studies of Work*. London and New York: Routledge and Kegan Paul.

Garfinkel, H. (2002) *Ethnomethodology's Program: Working out Durkheim's Aphorism*. Lanham, MD, and Oxford: Rowman & Littlefield.

Garkawe, S. (2003) 'The South African Truth and Reconciliation Commission: a suitable model to enhance the role and rights of the victims of gross violations of human rights', *Melbourne University Law Review*, 27: 334.

Garland, D. (1985) *Punishment and Welfare: A History of Penal Strategies*. Aldershot: Gower.

Garland, D. (1989) *Punishment and Society: A Study in Social Theory*. Chicago, IL: University of Chicago Press.

Garland, D. (1990) *Punishment and Modern Society*. Oxford: Oxford University Press.

Garland, D. (1996) 'The limits of the sovereign state: strategies of crime control in contemporary society', *British Journal of Criminology*, 36: 445.

Garland, D. (2001) *The Culture of Control: Crime and Social Order in Contemporary Society*. Oxford: Oxford University Press.

Gavron, J. (2002) 'Amnesties in the light of developments in international law and the establishment of the international criminal court', *International and Comparative Law Quarterly*, 51: 91.

Geula, M. (2000) 'Note: South Africa's Truth and Reconciliation Commission as an alternative means of addressing transitional government conflict in a divided society', *Boston University International Law Journal*, 18: 57.

Giarda, A. and Spangher, G. (eds) (2001) *Codici di procedura penale commentato*. Milano: Ipsoa.

Giddens, A. (1977) *Studies in Social and Political Theory*. London: Macmillan.

Giddens, A. (1979) *Central Problems in Social Theory*. London: Macmillan.

Giddens, A. (1982) *Profiles and Critiques in Social Theory*. London: Macmillan.

Giddens, A. (1984) *The Constitution of Society: Outlines of a Theory of Structuration*. Cambridge: Polity Press.

Giostra, G. and Illuminati, G. (2001) *Il giudice di pace nella giurisdizione penale*. Torino: Giappichelli.

Glaser, B. and Strauss, A. (1967) *The Discovery of Grounded Theory: Strategies for Qualitative Research*. Chicago, IL: Aldine.

Gobert, J. and Mugnai, E. (2002) 'Coping with corporate criminality – some lessons from Italy', *Criminal Law Review*: 619.

Goffman, E. (1961) *Encounters: Two Studies in the Sociology of Interaction*. Indianapolis: Bobbs-Merrill.

Goffman, E. (1969a) *Strategic Interaction*. Philadelphia, PA: University of Pennsylvania Press.

Goffman, E. (1969b) 'The insanity of place', *Psychiatry: Journal of Interpersonal Relations*, 32: 357.

Goffman, E. (1969c) *Where the Action Is: Three Essays*. London: Allen Lane.

Goffman, E. (1969d) *The Presentation of Self in Everyday Life*. London: Allen Lane.

Goldman, A. (1982) 'Toward a new theory of punishment', *Law and Philosophy*, 1: 57.

Göppinger, H.E. (1980) *Kriminologie* (4th edn). Munich: Beck.

Green, E. (1961) *Judicial Attitudes in Sentencing*. London: Macmillan.

Greer, S. (1995) 'Review of Ashworth (1994)', *British Journal of Criminology*, 35: 647.

Groenhuijsen, M. (1996) 'Conflicts of victims' interests and offenders' rights in the criminal justice system – a European perspective', in C. Sumner *et al.* (eds) *International Victimology: Selected Papers from the 8th International Symposium: Proceedings of a Symposium, 21–26 August 1994*. Canberra: Australian Institute of Criminology, 163–76.

Gross, H. and Hirsch, A. von (1985) *Sentencing*. Oxford: Oxford University Press.

Grosselfinger, N. (1998) 'Sentencing in the international court', paper presented at the American Society of Criminology annual meeting, Washington, DC, 12 November.

Gualtieri, P. (1995) 'Soggetto persona offesa e danneggiato dal reato: profili differenziale', *Rivista Italiana di diritto e procedura penale*: 1071.

Guest, J. (1999) 'Aboriginal legal theory and restorative justice. Part two', *Justice as Healing*, 4 (http://www.usask.ca/nativelaw/publications/jah/guest2.html).

Habermas, J. (1981) *The Theory of Communicative Action*. Cambridge: Polity Press.

Hall, C. (1998) 'The Fifth Session of the UN Preparatory Committee on the Establishment of an International Criminal Court', *American Journal of International Law*, 92: 331.

Halliday Report (2001) *Making Punishments Work: Review of the Sentencing Framework for England and Wales* (http://www.homeoffice.gov.uk/docs/halliday.html).

Hampton, J. (1988) 'The retributive idea', in J. Murphy and J. Hampton (eds) *Forgiveness and Mercy*. Cambridge: Cambridge University Press, 111–62.

Hart, H.L.A. (1961) *The Concept of Law*. Oxford: Oxford University Press.

Hart, H.L.A. (1968) *Punishment and Responsibility: Essays in the Philosophy of Law*. Oxford: Clarendon Press.

Hart, H.L.A. (1994) *The Concept of Law* (2nd edn). Oxford: Clarendon Press.

Harvard Law Review (2001) 'Developments in the law – international criminal law. II. The promises of international prosecution', 114 (May): 1943.

Hayner, P. (2001) 'Truth commissions and national courts', paper presented to the international conference *From a Culture of Immunity to a Culture of Accountability: International Criminal Tribunals, the International Criminal Court, and Human Rights Protection*, University of Utrecht, the Netherlands, 26–28 November.

Heffernan, W. and Kleinig, J. (2000) *From Social Justice to Criminal Justice*. New York, NY: Oxford University Press.

Henham, R. (1990) *Sentencing Principles and Magistrates' Sentencing Behaviour*. Aldershot: Avebury.

Henham, R. (1994) 'Attorney General's references and sentencing policy', *Criminal Law Review*: 499.

Henham, R. (1995a) 'Sentencing policy and mentally abnormal offenders', *The Criminal Lawyer*, 60: 4.

Henham, R. (1995b) 'Dangerous trends in the sentencing of mentally abnormal offenders', *Howard Journal of Criminal Justice*, 34: 10.

Henham, R. (1995c) 'Sentencing policy and the Court of Appeal', *Howard Journal of Criminal Justice*, 34: 218.

Henham, R. (1995d) 'Due process, procedural justice and sentencing policy', *International Journal of the Sociology of Law*, 23: 233.

Henham, R. (1995e) 'Criminal justice and the trial and sentencing of white collar offenders', *Journal of Criminal Law*, 59: 83.

Henham, R. (1995f) 'Cumulative sentencing and penal policy', *Journal of Criminal Law*, 59: 420.

Henham, R. (1995g) 'Review of Munro and Wasik (eds), *Sentencing, Judicial Discretion and Training*', *International Journal of the Sociology of Law*, 23: 161.

Henham, R. (1995h) 'Sentencing policy for drug offenders', paper presented at the British Society of Criminology conference, Loughborough University, July.

Henham, R. (1997a) 'Anglo-American approaches to cumulative sentencing and the implications for UK sentencing policy', *Howard Journal of Criminal Justice*, 36: 261.

Henham, R. (1997b) 'Protective sentences: ethics, rights and sentencing policy, *International Journal of the Sociology of Law*, 25: 45.

Henham, R. (1998) 'Human rights, due process and sentencing', *British Journal of Criminology*, 38: 592.

Henham, R. (1999a) 'Theory, rights and sentencing policy', *International Journal of the Sociology of Law*, 27: 167.

Henham, R. (1999b) 'Bargain justice or justice denied? Sentence discounts and the criminal process', *Modern Law Review*, 62: 515.

Henham, R. (2000a) 'Problems of theorising sentencing research', *International Journal of the Sociology of Law*, 28: 15.

Henham, R. (2000b) 'Reconciling process and policy: sentence discounts in the magistrates' courts', *Criminal Law Review*, 48: 436.

Henham, R. (2000c) 'Sentencing theory, proportionality and pragmatism', *International Journal of the Sociology of Law*, 28: 239.

Henham, R. (2001a) 'Theory and contextual analysis in sentencing', *International Journal of the Sociology of Law*, 29: 253.

Henham, R. (2001b) 'Social theory, rights and criminal justice', paper presented at the Australian and New Zealand Society of Criminology, 15th annual conference, University of Melbourne, February.

Henham, R. (2001c) 'Developing a theoretical framework for the contextual analysis of the relationship between sentencing law and policy', paper presented at the European Society of Criminology conference, University of Lausanne, Switzerland, September.

Henham, R. (2002a) 'Developing theory and methodology for understanding international penality'. Unpublished working paper.

Henham, R. (2002b) 'The internationalisation of sentencing: reality or myth?', *International Journal of the Sociology of Law*, 30: 265.

Henham, R. (2003a) 'Some issues for sentencing in the international criminal court', *International and Comparative Law Quarterly*, 52: 81.

Henham, R. (2003b) 'The philosophical foundations of international sentencing', *Journal of International Criminal Justice*, 1: 64.

Henham, R. (2003c) 'The policy and practice of protective sentencing', *Criminal Justice*, 3: 57.

Henham, R. (2004) 'Conceptualising access to justice and victims' rights in international sentencing', *Social and Legal Studies*, 13: 21.

Henham, R. and Findlay, M. (2001a) 'Theory and methodology in the comparative contextual analysis of trial process', paper presented at the expert seminar, London, March.

Henham, R. and Findlay, M. (2001b) 'Developing theory for the comparative contextual analysis of trial process.' Working paper derived from 'Theory and methodology in the comparative contextual analysis of trial process' (http://www.nls.ntu.ac.uk/clr/ictp/Publications/workingpapers/Theory%20and%20Methodology%20-%20Draft%2010.pdf).

Henham, R. and Findlay, M. (2001c) 'Theory and methodology in the comparative contextual analysis of trial process.' Unpublished working paper (http://www.nls.ntu.ac.uk/CLR/ICTP/index.htm).

Henham, R. and Findlay, M. (2002) 'Criminal justice modeling and the comparative contextual analysis of trial process', *International Journal of Comparative Criminology*, 2: 262.

Henham, R. and Findlay, M. (2003a) 'Developing theory for the contextual analysis of trial process', paper presented at the *Socio-legal Studies Association annual conference*, Nottingham Trent University, April.

Henham, R. and Findlay, M. (2003b) 'Integrating theory and methodology in the comparative contextual analysis of trial process', paper presented at the workshop *Socio-legal Research Methods*, International Institute for the Sociology of Law, Onati, Spain, April.

Henham, R. and Mannozzi, G. (2003) 'Victim participation and sentencing in England and Italy: a legal and policy analysis', *European Journal of Crime, Criminal Law and Criminal Justice*, 11: 278.

Hirsch, A. von (1976) *Doing Justice: The Choice of Punishments*. Boston, MA: Northeastern University Press.

Hirsch, A. von (1979) *The Question of Parole: Retention, Reform or Abolition?* Cambridge, MA: Ballinger.

Hirsch, A. von (1985) *Deservedness and Dangerousness in the Sentencing of Criminals*. New Brunswick, NJ: Rutgers University Press.

Hirsch, A. von (1993) *Censure and Sanctions*. Oxford: Oxford University Press.

Hirsch, A. von (1997) 'Beware of punishment: on *The Utility and Futility of the Criminal Law*, ed. by Annika Snare', *British Journal of Criminology*, 37: 686.

Hirsch, A. von (1999) 'Punishment, penance and the state', in M. Matravers (ed.) *Punishment and Political Theory*. Oxford: Hart, 69–82.

Hirsch, A. von and Ashworth, A. (1992) *Principled Sentencing*. Boston, MA: Northeastern University Press.

Hirsch, A. von and Ashworth, A. (eds) (1998) *Principled Sentencing: Readings on Theory and Policy*. Oxford: Hart.

Hirsch, A. von and Roberts, J. (1997) 'Racial disparity in sentencing: reflections on the Hood study', *Howard Journal of Criminal Justice*, 36: 227.

Hirsch, A. von and Wasik, M. (1997) 'Civil disqualifications attending conviction', *Cambridge Law Journal*, 56: 599.

Hirsch, A. von, Garland, D. and Wakefield, A. (eds) (2000) *Ethical and Social Perspectives on Situational Crime Prevention*. Oxford: Hart.

Hirsch, A. von, Roberts, J., Bottoms, A., Schiff, M. and Roach, K (2003) *Restorative Justice and Criminal Justice: Competing or Reconcilable Paradigms*. Oxford: Hart.

Hodgson, J. (2000) 'Comparing legal cultures: the comparativist as participant observer', in D. Nelken (ed.) *Contrasting Criminal Justice: Getting from Here to There*. Aldershot: Ashgate, 139–56.

Hodgson, J. (2001) 'The police, the prosecutor and the *Juge d'Instruction*: judicial supervision in France, theory and practice', *British Journal of Criminology*, 141: 342.

Hogarth, J. (1971) *Sentencing as a Human Process*. Toronto: University of Toronto Press.

Home Office (1996) *The Victim's Charter: A Statement of Service Standards for Victims of Crime*. London: HMSO.

Home Office (1997) *No More Excuses – a New Approach to Tackling Youth Crime in England and Wales* (CM 3809). London: HMSO.

Home Office (2000) 'Home Secretary announces national victims statements', press release 147/2000.

Home Office (2001a) *Criminal Justice: The Way Ahead* (CM 5074). London: HSMO.

Home Office (2001b) *Making Punishments Work: Report of a Review of the Sentencing Framework for England and Wales*. London: Home Office Communication Directorate.

Home Office (2001c) *Victim Personal Statements* (Circular 35/2001), August.

Honore, T. (2002) 'The necessary connection between law and morality', *Oxford Journal of Legal Studies*, 22: 489.

Hood, R. (1972) *Sentencing the Motoring Offender*. London: Heinemann.

Hood, R. (1992) *Race and Sentencing*. Oxford: Oxford University Press.

Horowitz, J. (2003) 'Racial (re)construction: the case of the South African Truth and Reconciliation Commission', *National Black Law Journal*, 17: 67.

Horton, J. (1992) *Political Obligation*. London: Macmillan.

Howland, T. and Calathes, W. (1998) 'The UN's International Criminal Tribunal, is it justice or jingoism for Rwanda? A call for transformation', *Virginia Journal of International Law*, 39: 135.

Hoyle, C. *et al.* (1998) *Evaluation of the 'One Stop Shop' and Victim Statement Pilot Projects. Home Office Research, Development and Statistics Directorate Report*. London: Home Office.

Hoyle, C. *et al.* (1999) *The Victim's Charter – an Evaluation of Pilot Projects. Home Office Research, Development and Statistics Directorate Research Findings* 107. London: Home Office.

Hoyle, C. and Young, R. (eds) (2002) *New Visions of Crime Control*. Oxford: Hart.

Hudson, B. (1987) *Justice through Punishment: A Critique of the 'Justice Model' of Corrections*. Basingstoke: Macmillan.

Hudson, B. (2003a) *Understanding Justice: An Introduction to Ideas, Perspectives and Controversies in Modern Penal Theory* (2nd edn). Buckingham: Open University Press.

Hudson, B. (2003b) 'Punishment, justice and responsibility'. *Punishment and Society*, 5: 215.

Hulsman, L. (1996) 'Critical criminology and the concept of crime', *Contemporary Crises*, 10: 63.

Hunt, A. (1993) *Explorations in Law and Society: Towards a Constitutive Theory of Law*. New York, NY: Routledge.

Hutton, N. (1995) 'Sentencing, rationality and computer technology', *Journal of Law and Society*, 22: 549.

Jackson, B.S. (1988) *Law, Fact and Narrative Coherence.* Liverpool: Deborah Charles.

Johnstone, G. (2002) *Restorative Justice: Ideas, Values, Debates.* Cullompton: Willan Publishing.

Johnstone, G. (ed.) (2003) *A Restorative Justice Reader: Texts, Sources, Context.* Cullompton: Willan Publishing.

Jorda, C. and De Hemptinne, J. (2002) 'The status and role of the victim', in A. Cassese *et al.* (eds) *The Rome Statute of the International Criminal Court: A Commentary.* Oxford: Oxford University Press, 1387–419.

Jörg, N., Brants, C. and Field, S. (1995) 'Are inquisitorial and adversarial systems converging?' in C. Harding *et al.* (eds) *Criminal Justice in Europe. A Comparative Study.* Oxford: Clarendon Press, 41 –56.

Jung, H. (1997) 'Plea bargaining and its repercussions on the theory of criminal procedure', *European Journal of Crime, Criminal Law and Criminal Justice,* 5: 112.

Kamenka, E. (1979) 'What is justice?', in E. Kamenka and A.E.-S. Tay (eds) *Justice.* London: Edward Arnold.

Katzenstein, S. (2003) 'Hybrid tribunals: searching for justice in East Timor', *Harvard Human Rights Journal,* 16: 245.

King, M. (1978) 'A status passage analysis of the defendant's passage through the magistrates' court', *Law and Human Behaviour,* 2: 187.

King, M. (1993) 'The truth about autopoiesis', *Journal of Law and Society,* 20: 218.

Kittichaisaree, K. (2001) *International Criminal Law.* Melbourne: Oxford University Press.

Lacey, N. (1987) 'Discretion and due process at the post-conviction stage', in I.H. Dennis (ed.) *Criminal Law and Justice.* London: Sweet & Maxwell, 221–35.

Lacey, N. (1988) *State Punishment.* London and New York, NY: Routledge.

Lacey, N. (1994) 'Government as manager, citizen and consumer: the case of the Criminal Justice Act 1991', *Modern Law Review,* 57: 534.

LaPrairie, C. (1995) 'Conferencing in Aboriginal communities in Canada: finding middle ground in criminal justice', *Criminal Law Forum,* 6: 576.

Larizza, S. (1992) *Criminalita minorile e ruola residuale del diritto penale.* Pavia.

Layder, D. (1994), *Understanding Social Theory.* London: Sage.

Leigh, L. (1997) 'Liberty and efficiency in the criminal process – the significance of models', *International and Comparative Law Quarterly,* 26: 516.

Lemert, E. (1972) *Human Deviance, Social Problems and Social Control* (2nd edn). Englewood Cliffs, NJ: Prentice Hall.

Linton, S. (2001a) 'Cambodia, East Timor and Sierra Leone: experiments in international criminal justice', *Criminal Law Forum,* 12: 185.

Linton, S. (2001b) 'Rising from the ashes: the creation of a viable criminal justice system in East Timor', *Melbourne University Law Review,* 25: 122.

Llewellyn, J. and Howse, R. (1998) *Restorative Justice – a Conceptual Framework*. Prepared for the Law Commission of Canada (http://www.lcc.gc.ca/en/themes/sr/rj/howse/howse_main.asp).

Llewellyn, K. (1960) *The Common Law Tradition: Deciding Appeals*. Boston, MA, and Toronto: Little Brown & Co.

Loughlin, M. (2001) 'Rights, democracy and law', in T. Campbell *et al.* (eds) *Sceptical Essays on Human Rights*. Oxford: Oxford University Press, 41–60.

Lovegrove, A. (1989) *Judicial Decision Making, Sentencing Policy, and Numerical Guidance*. New York, NY, and London: Springer-Verlag.

Lovegrove, A. (1997) *The Framework of Judicial Sentencing: A Study in Legal Decision Making*. Cambridge: Cambridge University Press.

Low, C. (1978) 'The sociology of criminal justice: progress and prospects', in J. Baldwin and A. Bottoms (eds) *Criminal Justice: Selected Readings*. Oxford: Martin Robertson.

Luhmann, N. (1985) *A Sociological Theory of Law*. London: Routledge.

Lukes, S. and Scull, A. (eds) (1995) *Durkheim and the Law*. Stanford, CA: Stanford University Press.

MacCormick, N. and Garland, D. (1998) 'Sovereign states and vengeful victims: the problem of the right to punish', in A. Ashworth and M. Wasik (eds) *Fundamentals of Sentencing Theory*. Oxford: Oxford University Press.

Mackie J. (1982) 'Morality and the retributive emotions' *Criminal Justice Ethics*, 1: 3–9.

Macrae S., Maguire N. and Milbourne L. (2003) 'Social exclusion: exclusion from school', *International Journal of Inclusive Education*, 7: 89.

Maguire, M., Morgan, R. and Reiner, R. (eds) (2002) *The Oxford Handbook of Criminology*. Oxford: Oxford University Press.

Maher, G. (1988) 'The verdict of the jury', in M. Findlay and P. Duff (eds) *The Jury under Attack*. Sydney and London: Butterworths.

Malsch, M. and Nijboer, J. (eds) (1999) *Complex Cases: Perspectives on the Netherlands Criminal Justice System*. Amsterdam: Thela Thesis.

Mann, M. (1988) *The Sources of Social Power. Vol. 1*. Cambridge: Cambridge University Press.

Mannozzi, G. (1996) *Razionalità e 'giustizia', nella commisurazione della pena*. Cedam: Padova.

Mannozzi, G. (1999) 'Are guided sentencing and plea bargaining incompatible? Perspectives of reform in the Italian legal system', paper presented at the *Sentencing and Society* international conference, University of Strathclyde.

Mannozzi G. (2002a) 'From the "Sword" to dialogue: towards a "dialectic" basis for Penal Mediation', in E.G.M. Weitekamp and H.-J. Jurgen (eds) *Restorative Justice: Theoretical Foundations*. Cullompton: Willan Publishing, 224–46.

Mannozzi, G. (2002b) 'Are guided sentencing and plea bargaining incompatible? Perspectives of reform in the Italian sentencing system', in

C. Tata and N. Hutton (eds) *Sentencing and Society: International Perspectives*. Aldershot: Ashgate, 110–32.

Mannozzi, G. (2003) 'Positioning mediation in the criminal justice system', in L. Walgrave (ed.) *Repositioning Restorative Justice: Restorative Justice, Criminal Justice and Social Justice*. Cullompton: Willan Publishing, 284–95.

Mannozzi, G. (2003) 'Victim participation and sentencing in England and Italy: a legal and policy analysis' (http://216.239.59.104/search?q=cache:MYbjpPnB60MJ:www.iuscrim.mpg.de/info/aktuell/docs/simon03_ej_version2.pdf+freccero+%2Bccp&hl=en).

Maogoto, J. (2001) 'International justice for Rwanda missing the point: questioning the relevance of classical criminal law theory', *Bond Law Review*, 13: 190.

Mashaw, J. (1987) 'Dignitory process: a political psychology of liberal democratic citizenship', *University of Florida Law Review*, 39: 433.

Mathiesen, T. (1974) *The Politics of Abolition*. London: Martin Robertson.

Mathiesen, T. (1990) *Prison on Trial*. London: Sage.

Matravers, M. (ed.) (1999) *Punishment and Political Theory*. Oxford: Oxford University Press.

Matza, D. (1964) *Delinquency and Drift*. New York, NY: John Wiley.

McBarnet, D. (1981a) *Magistrates' Courts and the Ideology of Justice*. Oxford: Martin Robertson.

McBarnet, D. (1981b) *Conviction: Law, the State and the Construction of Justice*. London: Macmillan.

McCold, P. and Wachtel, B. (2003) 'Community is not a place: a new look at community justice initiatives', in G. Johnstone (ed.), *A Restorative Justice Reader: Text, Sources, Context*. Cullompton: Willan Publishing.

McConville, M. (1998) 'Plea bargaining: ethics and politics', *Journal of Law and Society*, 25: 562.

McCoy, C. (1994) 'What we say and what they do: prosecutors' and judges' sentencing decisions at guilty plea versus trial', paper presented at the American Society of Criminology annual meeting, New Orleans, November.

McCoy, C. (2001) 'Searching for our lost rights', *Newark Star-Ledger (New Jersey)*, 18 April: 17.

McCoy, C. and Cohen, T. (2001) 'Mandatory minimum sentencing laws', in *Encyclopedia of Crime and Justice*. NJ: Macmillan/Prentice Hall.

McCoy, C. and Henham, R. (2004) 'Guilty plea discounts in American and English courts: an empirical description and ethical critique of the trial penalty' (http://www.nls.ntu.ac.uk/CLR/ICTP/index.htm).

McEwan, J. (2000) *Evidence and the Adversarial Process: The Modern Law* (2nd edn). Oxford: Hart.

McGoldrick, D. (1999) 'The permanent international criminal court: an end to the culture of impunity', *Criminal Law Review*: 644.

McLaughlin, E. and Muncie, J. (eds) (2001) *Controlling Crime*. London: Sage.

Meron, T. (2004) 'Procedural evolution in the ICTY', *Journal of International Criminal Justice*, 2: 520.

Miller, J. (1990) 'Plea bargaining and its analogues under the Italian criminal procedure code and in the United States: towards a new understanding of comparative criminal procedure', *New York University Journal of International Law and Practice*, 22: 215.

Miller, S. and Schacter, M. (2000) 'From restorative justice to restorative governance', *Canadian Journal of Criminology*, 42: 405.

Minow, M. and Spelman, E. (1990) 'In context', *Southern California Law Review*, 63: 1597.

Moghalu, K. (2001) 'The role of international criminal/humanitarian law in conflict settlement and reconciliation', paper presented to the international conference, *From a Culture of Immunity to a Culture of Accountability: International Criminal Tribunals, the International Criminal Court, and Human Rights Protection*, University of Utrecht, the Netherlands, 26–28 November.

Monaco, L. (1984) *Prosptective dell'idea dello 'scopo' nello teoria della pena*. Napoli: Jovene.

Monteverde, L. (1999) 'Mediazione e riparazione dope il giudizio: l'esperienza della magistratura di sorveglianza', *Minori et Giustizia*: 86.

Moore, M. (ed.) (1985) *Dangerous Offenders: The Elusive Target of Justice*. Cambridge, Mass: Harvard University Press.

Moore, M. (1987) 'The moral worth of retribution', in F. Schoerman (ed.) *Responsibility, Character and the Emotions*. Cambridge: Cambridge University Press, 179–219.

Morgan, R. (1996) 'The process is the rule and the punishment is the process', *Modern Law Review*, 59: 306.

Morgan, R. and Sanders, A. (1999) *The Uses to which Victim Statements are Put. Home Office Research, Development and Statistics Directorate Report*. London: Home Office.

Moro, A. (2000) *Manuale di diritto penale minorile*. Bologna: Zanichelli.

Morris, A. (2002) 'Critiquing the critics: a brief response to critics of restorative justice', *British Journal of Criminology*, 42: 578.

Morris, A. and Gelsthorne, L. (2000) 'Something old, something borrowed, something blue, but something new? A comment on the prospects for restorative justice under the Crime and Disorder Act 1998', *Criminal Law Review*: 18.

Morris, C. (1991) 'Punishment and loss of moral standing', *Canadian Journal of Philosophy*, 21: 53.

Morris, N. and Rothman. D. (eds) (1995) *The Oxford History of Prison: The Practice of Punishment in Western Society*. New York, NY: Oxford University Press.

Morris, N. and Tonry, M. (1990a) *Between Prison and Probation: Intermediate Punishments in a Rational Sentencing System*. New York, NY, and Oxford: Oxford University Press.

Morris, N. and Tonry, M. (eds) (1990b) *Crime and Justice: A Review of Research. Vol. 12.* Chicago, IL, and London: University of Chicago Press.

Morris, V. and Scharf, M. (1995) *An Insider's Guide to the International Criminal Tribunal for the Former Yugoslavia.* Irvington-on-Hudson, NY: Transnational Publishers.

Munro, C. and Wasik, M. (1992) *Sentencing, Judicial Discretion and Training.* London: Sweet & Maxwell.

Murphy, J. (1979) *Retribution, Justice and Therapy: Essays on the Philosophy of Law.* Dordrecht: Kluwer.

Nagel, T. (1972) 'War and massacre', *Philosophy and Public Affairs*, 1: 123.

Nappi, A. (2001) *La procedura penale per il giudice di pace.* Milano: Giuffre.

Narayan, U. (1993) 'Appropriate responses and preventative benefits: justifying censure and hard treatment in legal punishment', *Oxford Journal of Legal Studies*, 13: 166.

Nelken, D. (1994) 'The future of comparative criminology', in D. Nelken (ed.) *The Futures of Criminology.* London: Sage.

Nelken, D. (ed.) (1995) 'Legal culture, diversity and globalisation', in *Social and Legal Studies*, 4 (special issue).

Nelken, D. (ed.) (1997a) *Comparing Legal Cultures.* Aldershot: Dartmouth.

Nelken, D. (1997b) 'Understanding criminal justice comparatively', in M. Maguire *et al.* (eds) *The Oxford Handbook of Criminology* (2nd edn). Oxford: Oxford University Press.

Nelken, D. (1998) 'Blinding insights? The limits of a reflective sociology of law', *Journal of Law and Society*, 25: 407.

Nelken, D. (2000) 'Telling difference: of crime and criminal justice in Italy', in D. Nelken (ed.) *Contrasting Criminal Justice.* Aldershot: Ashgate.

Nelken, D. (2002) 'Legal transplants and beyond: of disciplines and metaphors', in A. Harding and E. Orucu (eds) *Comparative Law in the 21st Century.* The Hague: Kluwer, 19–34.

Nelken, D. and Feest, J. (eds) (2001) *Adapting Legal Cultures.* Oxford: Hart.

Nemitz, J. and Wirth, S. (1999) 'Some observations on the law of sentencing of the ICC' (http://www.ishr.org/ice/detail/nemitz.htm).

Newburn, T. (2003) *Crime and Criminal Justice Policy* (2nd edn). Harlow: Pearson Longman.

Nobles, R. and Schiff, D. (1995) 'Miscarriages of justice: a systems approach', *Modern Law Review*, 58: 299.

Norrie, A. (1991) *Law, Ideology and Punishment: Retrieval and Critique of the Liberal Idea of Criminal Justice.* Dordrecht and London: Kluwer Academic.

Norrie, A. (ed) (1993) *Closure or Critique: New Directions in Legal Theory.* Edinburgh: Edinburgh University Press.

Norrie, A. (1996a) 'The limits of justice: finding fault in the criminal law', *Modern Law Review*, 59: 540.

Norrie, A. (1996b) 'From law to popular justice: beyond antinomialism', in *Social and Legal Studies*, 5: 384.

Norrie, A. (1999a) 'Michael Moore's deviation ', *Oxford Journal of Legal Studies*, 19: 111.

Norrie, A. (1999b) 'Subjectivity, morality and criminal law', *Edinburgh Law Review*, 3: 359.

Norrie, A. (2000) *Punishment, Responsibility and Justice: A Relational Critique*. Oxford: Oxford University Press.

Norrie, A. (2001) *Crime, Reason and History: A Critical Introduction to Criminal Law* (2nd edn). London: Butterworths.

Nozick, R. (1981) *Philosophical Explanations*. Oxford: Clarendon Press.

O'Malley, P. (ed.) (1998) *Crime and the Risk Society*. Aldershot: Dartmouth.

O'Malley, P. (ed.) (2000) *Configurations of Risk*. Abingdon: Routledge.

O'Malley, P. and Sutton, A. (eds) (1997) *Crime Prevention in Australia: Issues in Policy and Research*. Sydney: Federation Press.

Oppeln, C. von (2002) 'Victim's protection in international law: the normative basis and a look into the practice', *European Journal of Crime, Criminal Law and Criminal Justice*, 10: 233.

Orentlicher, D. (1991) 'Settling accounts: the duty to prosecute human rights violations of a prior regime', *Yale Law Journal*, 100: 2537.

Osiel, M. (1995) 'Legal remembrance of administrative massacre', *University of Pennsylvania Law Review*, 144: 463.

Owens, M. (1995) 'California's three strikes law: desperate times require desperate measures – but will it work?' *Pacific Law Journal*, 26: 881.

Packer, H. (1968) *The Limits of the Criminal Sanction*. Stanford, CA: Stanford University Press.

Pakes, F. (2001) 'Styles of trial procedure at the International Criminal Tribunal for the Former Yugoslavia', paper presented at the European Society of Criminology conference, University of Lausanne, Switzerland, September.

Parker, I. (1992) *Discourse Dynamics*. London: Routledge.

Parmentier, S. (2003) 'Global justice in the aftermath of mass violence: the role of the international criminal court in dealing with political crimes', *International Annals of Criminology*, 41: 203.

Pennisi, A. (2001) 'Commentary on Art. 90', in A. Giarda and G. Spangher (eds) *Codici di procedura penale commentato*. Milano: Ipsoa.

Peroni, R. (1999) *La sentenza di patteggeamendo*. Padova: Cedam.

Pickard, D. (1997) 'Proposed sentencing guidelines for the international criminal court', *Loyola of Los Angeles International and Comparative Law Review*, 20: 123.

Picotti, L. and Spangher, G. (eds) (2002) *Verso una giustizia penale 'conciliativa'*. Milano: Giuffre.

Piergallini, C. (2001) 'Sistema sanzionatorio e reati previsit dal codice penale', *Diritto penale e processo*: 1353.

Pizzi, W. and Marafioti, L. (1992) 'The new Italian Code of Criminal Procedure: the difficulties of building an adversarial trial system on a civil law foundation', *Yale Journal of International Law*, 17: 1.

Polat, N. (1999) 'International law, the inherent instability of the international system, and international violence', *Oxford Journal of Legal Studies*, 19: 51.

Pollard, C. (2000) 'Victims and the criminal justice system: a new vision', *Criminal Law Review*: 5.

Ponti, G. (ed.) (1995) *Tutela della vittima e mediazione penale*. Milano: Giuffre.

Popovski, V. (2000) 'The international criminal court: a synthesis of retributive and restorative justice', *International Relations*, 15: 1.

Postema, G. (1986) *Bentham and the Common Law Tradition*. Oxford: Oxford University Press.

Practice Direction (1998) *Custodial Sentences*, 22 January.

Pratt, J. (1995) 'Dangerousness, risk and technologies of power', *Australian and New Zealand Journal of Criminology*, 28: 3.

Pratt, J. (1998) 'Towards the "decivilizing of punishment"', *Social and Legal Studies*, 7: 487.

Pratt, J. (2000) 'Emotive and ostentatious punishment: its decline and resurgence in modern society', *Punishment and Society*, 2: 417.

Presutti, A. (2002) 'Attori e strumenti della giurisdizione concilliativa: il ruolo del giudice e della persona offesa', in L. Picotti and G. Spangher (eds) *Verso una giustizia penale 'conciliativa*. Milano: Giuffre, 181.

Punch, K. (1998) *Introduction to Social Research: Quantitative and Qualitative Approaches*. London: Sage.

Radzinowicz, L. (1966) *Ideology and Crime*. London: Heinemann.

Radzinowicz, L. (1999) *Adventures in Criminology*. London and New York, NY: Routledge.

Radzinowicz, L. and Hood, R. (1979) 'Judicial discretion and sentencing standards: Victorian attempts to solve a perennial problem', *University of Pennsylvania Law Review*, 127: 1288.

Radzinowicz, L. and Joan, K. (1979) *The Growth of Crime: The International Experience*. Harmondsworth: Penguin Books.

Ratner, S. (2003) 'Belgium's war crimes statute: a post-mortem', *American Journal of International Law*, 97: 888.

Retzinger, S. and Scheff, T. (1996) 'Strategy for community conferences: emotions and social bonds', in B. Galaway and J. Hudson (eds) *Restorative Justice: International Perspectives*. Monsey, NY: Criminal Justice Press, 315–36.

Rex, S. (1998) 'Applying desert principles to community sentences: lessons from two criminal justice acts', *Criminal Law Review*: 381.

Rex, S. and Tonry, M. (eds) (2002) *Reform and Punishment: The Future of Sentencing*. Cullompton: Willan Publishing.

Richardson, P. (ed.), Thomas, D.A. (sentencing ed.), Bowes, M. *et al.* (contributing eds) (1999) *Criminal Pleading, Evidence and Practice: Archbold*. London: Sweet & Maxwell.

Roberts, P. (2002) 'On method: the ascent of comparative criminal justice', *Oxford Journal of Legal Studies*, 22: 539.

Roberts, P. (2003) 'Restoration and retribution in international criminal justice: an exploratory analysis', in A. von Hirsch *et al.* (eds) *Restorative Justice and Criminal Justice: Competing or Reconcilable Paradigms?*. Oxford: Hart, 115–34.

Roberts, P. and Zuckerman, A. (2004) *Criminal Evidence*. Oxford: Oxford University Press.

Rock, P. 'Phenomenalism and essentialism in deviancy theory', *Sociology*, 7: 12.

Rogers, L. and Erez, E. (1999) 'The contextuality of objectivity in sentencing among legal professionals in South Australia', *International Journal of the Sociology of Law*, 27: 267.

Roht-Arriaza, N. (1999) 'Institutions of international justice', *Journal of International Affairs*, 52: 473.

Romano, M. and Grasso, G. (1990) *Commentario sistematico del codice penale*. Milano: Giuffre.

Rostain, T. (2000) 'Educating *Homo economicus*: cautionary notes on the new behavioural law and economics movement', *Law and Society Review*, 34: 973.

Rubin, A. (2001) 'The international criminal court: possibilities for prosecutorial abuse', *Law and Contemporary Problems*, 64: 153.

Rusche, G. and Kirscheimer, O (1939/2003) *Punishment and Social Structure*. New Brunswick, NJ: Transaction Press.

Ryan, A. (1970) *The Philosophy of Social Science*. London: Macmillan.

Salfati, A. (ed.) (2001) *Il giudice di pace. Un nuovo modello di giustizia penale*. Padova: Cedam.

Salter, M. (1996) 'The impossibility of human rights within a post-modern account of law and justice', *Journal of Civil Liberties*, 1: 29.

Sanders, A. (2002a) 'Ad ius criminale humanius: essays in criminology, criminal justice and public policy by Inkeri Anttila', *Criminal Justice Matters*, 49: 46.

Sanders, A. (2002b) 'The system of prosecution', in M. McConville and G. Wilson (eds) *The Handbook of the Criminal Justice Process*. Oxford: Oxford University Press.

Sanders, A. (2002c) 'Magistrates' injustice: the recommendations of the Auld Review would result in less expertise – and less justice – in magistrates' courts', *Criminal Justice Matters*, 46: 12.

Sanders, A. (2002d) 'Victim participation in criminal justice', *Criminal Justice Matters*, 49: 30.

Sanders, A. (2002e) 'Victim participation in an exclusionary criminal justice system', in C. Hoyle and R. Young (eds) *New Visions of Crime Control*. Oxford: Hart.

Sanders, A. and Young, R. (2000) *Criminal Justice* (2nd edn). London: Butterworths.

Sanders, A., Hoyle, C., Morgan, R. and Cape, E. (2001) 'Victim impact statements: don't work, can't work', *Criminal Law Review*: 447.

Sandland, R. (1995) 'Review of Ashworth (1994)', *Criminal Law Review*: 679.

Sank, D., Caplan, D., Firschein, D. and Sank, D. (eds) (1991) *To Be a Victim: Encounters with Crime and Injustice*. New York, NY: Plenum Press, Insight Books.

Saphire, R. (1978) 'Specifying due process values: towards a more responsive approach to procedural protection', *University of Pennsylvania Law Review*, 127: 1114.

Sarantakos, S. (1993) *Social Research*. Basingstoke: Macmillan.

Schabas, W. (1997) 'Sentencing and the international tribunals: for a human rights approach', *Duke Journal of International and Comparative Law*, 7: 461. (http://www.law.duke.edu/journals/djcil/articles/djcil7p461.htm).

Schabas, W. (2001a) 'Protective measures for victims and witnesses versus the rights of the defendants', paper presented to the international conference *From a Culture of Immunity to a Culture of Accountability: International Criminal Tribunals, the International Criminal Court and Human Rights Protection*, University of Utrecht, the Netherlands, November.

Schabas, W. (2001b) *An Introduction to the International Criminal Court*. Cambridge: Cambridge University Press.

Schabas, W. (2002) 'Towards a universal criminal justice system', paper presented at the conference *Internationalised Criminal Courts and Tribunals: Practice and Prospects*, Universiteit van Amsterdcam, the Netherlands, January.

Schabas, W. (2003a) 'Indirect abolition: capital punishment's role in extradition law and practice', *Loyola of Los Angeles International and Comparative Law Review*, 25: 581.

Schabas, W. (2003b) 'Mens rea and the International Criminal Tribunal for the Former Yugoslavia', *New England Law Review*, 37: 1015.

Schabas. W. (2003c) 'The relationship between truth commissions and international courts: the case of Sierra Leone', *Human Rights Quarterly*, 25: 1035.

Schabas, W. (2003d) 'Punishment of non-state actors in non-international armed conflict', *Fordham International Law Journal*, 26: 907.

Schabas, W. (2004) *An Introduction to the International Criminal Court* (2nd edn). Cambridge: Cambridge University Press.

Schabas, W., May, R. and Wierda, M. (2003) 'International criminal evidence', *Michigan Journal of International Law*, 24: 887.

Scharf, M. (1999) 'The politics behind the US opposition to the international criminal court', *New England International and Comparative Law*, 5: 214.

Schiff, M. (1996) 'Parallels between restorative and retributive justice frameworks: are they really so different?', paper presented at the American Society of Criminology annual meeting, Chicago, 20–23 November.

Schur, E. (1968) *Law and Society: A Sociological View*. New York, NY: Random House.

Schur, E. (1971) *Labelling Deviant Behaviour: Its Sociological Implications*. New York, NY: Harper & Row.

Schur, E. (1973) *Radical Non-intervention: Rethinking the Delinquency Problem*. Englewood Cliffs, NJ: Prentice Hall.

Schur, E. (1979) *Interpreting Deviance: A Sociological Introduction*. New York, NY: Harper & Row.

Schur, E. (1980) *The Politics of Deviance: Stigma Contests and the Uses of Power*. Englewood Cliffs, NJ: Prentice Hall.

Schweisfurth, M., Davies, L. and Harber C. (2002) 'Learning democracy and citizenship: international experiences', paper presented at the Oxford symposium.

Searle, J. (1995) *The Construction of Social Reality*. London: Allen Lane.

Shearing, C. (2001) 'Punishment and the changing face of the governance', *Punishment and Society*, 3: 203.

Shriver, D. (2001) 'Truth commissions and judicial trials: complementary or antagonistic servants of public justice?', *Journal of Law and Religion*, 16: 21.

Sieber, U. (2003) *The Punishment of Serious Crimes: A Comparative Analysis of Sentencing Law and Practice. Vol. 1 Expert Report. Vol. 2. Country Reports*. Freiburg im Breisgau: Max Planck Institute for Foreign and International Criminal Law.

Skolnick, J. (1966) *Justice without Trial*. New York, NY: Wiley.

Slaughter, A. and Burke-White, W. (2002a) 'An international constitutional moment', *Harvard International Law Journal*, 43: 1.

Slaughter, A. and Burke-White, W. (2002b) 'Protecting the rights of civilians', *Harvard International Review*, 24: 66.

Smith, A. and Blumberg, A. (1967) 'The problem of objectivity in judicial decision-making', *Social Forces*, 46: 96.

Smith, J. (2002) *Smith and Hogan Criminal Law* (10th edn). London: Butterworths.

Snyder, L. and Caplan, A. (eds) (2002) *Assisted Suicide: Finding Common Ground*. Bloomington, IN: Indiana University Press.

Spierenburg, P. (1995) 'The body and the state: early modern Europe', in N. Morris and D. Rothman (eds) *The Oxford History of the Prison: The Practice of Punishment in Modern Society*. Oxford: Oxford University Press: 49–78.

Sprack, J. (2002) *Emmins on Criminal Procedure* (10th edn). Oxford: Oxford University Press.

Sriram, C. (2004) 'Globalising justice: from universal jurisdiction to mixed tribunals', *Netherlands Quarterly of Human Rights*, 22: 7. (http://www.ppl.nl/bibliographies/all/showresults. php? bibliography=icl& code=007&topic=Mixed%20models%20of%20international%20 criminal%20justice.

Steiner, H. (1999) 'Do human rights require a particular form of democracy?', in E. Cotran and A. Sherif (eds) *Democracy, the Rule of Law and Islam*, London: Kluwer Law International.

Strang, H. and Braithwaite, J. (eds) (2000) *Restorative Justice: Philosophy to Practice*. Aldershot: Ashgate Dartmouth.

Strang, H. and Braithwaite, J. (eds) (2001) *Restorative Justice and Civil Society*. Cambridge: Cambridge University Press.

Strauss, A. (1987) *Qualitative Analysis for Social Scientists*. New York, NY: Cambridge University Press.

Strina, E. and Bernasconi, S. (2001) *Persona offesa, parte civile*. Milano.

Strohmeyer, H. (2001) 'Collapse and reconstruction of a judicial system: the United States mission in Kosovo and East Timor', *American Journal of International Law*, 95: 46.

Sudnow, D. (1965) 'Normal crimes: sociological features of the penal code in a public defender office', *Social Problems*, 12: 255.

Summer, C. and Chambliss, W. (2003) *The Blackwell Companion to Criminology*. Oxford: Blackwell.

Sykes, G. and Matza, D. (1957) 'Techniques of neutralisation: a theory of delinquency', *American Sociological Review*, 22: 664.

Sztompka, P. (1990) 'Conceptual frameworks in comparative inquiry: divergent or convergent?', in M. Albrow and E. King (eds) *Globalisation, Knowledge and Society*. London: Sage.

Tamanaha, B. (1997) *Realistic Socio-legal Theory*. Oxford: Clarendon Press.

Tamanaha, B. (2001) *A General Jurisprudence of Law and Society*. Oxford: Oxford University Press.

Tantalo, M. and Colafiglio, A. (1995) 'La "nuova" vittima collectiva. Riflessioni su di paradosso risarcitorio', in G. Ponti (ed.) *Tutela della vittima e mediazione penale*. Milano: Giuffre.

Tarling, R., Huber, B., Puglia, R. and Ashworth, A. (1982) *The Future of Sentencing*. Cambridge: University of Cambridge, Institute of Criminology.

Tata, C. (1997) 'Conceptions and representations of the sentencing decision process', *Journal of Law and Society*, 24: 395.

Tata, C. (2002) 'So what does "and society" mean?', in C. Tata and N. Hutton (eds) *Sentencing and Society: International Perspectives*. Aldershot: Ashgate.

Thomas, D. (1979) *Principles of Sentencing* (2nd edn). London: Heinemann.

Thomas, D. (1982) *Current Sentencing Practice*. London: Sweet & Maxwell.

Thomas, D. (1998a) 'Viewpoint', *Sentencing News*, 2: 12.

Thomas, D. (1998b) 'Honesty in sentencing', *Sentencing News*, 1.

Thomas, D. (1999) *Sentencing Referencer 1999*. London: Sweet & Maxwell.

Thomas D. (2000) 'Commentary on *R v Turner*', *Criminal Law Review*: 48.

Thomas, D. (2004) 'The Criminal Justice Act: custodial sentences', *Criminal Law Review*: 702.

Times, The (2000) 'Statutory sentence offends court's sense of justice. Court of Appeal. Criminal Division. Published April 4, 2000. Regina v Turner (Ian). Before Lord Justice Mantell, Mr Justice Rougier and Judge Francis Allen', 4 April.

Tochilovsky, V. (1998) 'Trial in international criminal jurisdictions: battle or scrutiny?', *European Journal of Crime, Criminal Law and Criminal Justice*, 6: 55.

Tonry, M. (1992) 'Selective incapacitation: the debate over its ethics', in A. Von Hirsch and A. Ashworth (eds) *Principled Sentencing*. Edinburgh: Edinburgh University Press, 165–80.

Tonry, M. (ed.) (1998) *The Handbook of Crime and Punishment*. New York, NY: Oxford University Press.

Tulkens, F. (2002) 'Negotiated justice', in M. Delmas-Marty and J. Spencer (eds) *European Criminal Procedures*. Cambridge: Cambridge University Press, 641–87.

Tully, L. (2003) 'Note. Human rights compliance and the Gacaca jurisdictions in Rwanda', *Boston College International and Comparative Law Review*, 26: 385.

Twining, W. (1999) 'Narrative and generalizations in argumentation about questions of fact', *South Texas Law Review*, 40: 351.

United Kingdom Government (2002) *Justice for All* (white paper) (Cm 5563). London: HMSO.

United Nations (2000) *Basic Principles on the Use of Restorative Justice Programmes in Criminal Matters* (www.restorativejustice.org/.ents/ UNDecBasicPrinciplesofRJ.htm).

United Nations, Commission on Crime Prevention and Criminal Justice (2002) *Basic Principles on Restorative Justice*, Eleventh Session, Vienna, 16–25 April (www.restorativejustice.ca/NationalConsultation/ BasicPrinciplesBody.htm) (http://www.restorativejustice.org/rj3/ UNBasicPrinciples/CanadianResolutionDraft.htm).

Van der Vyver, J. (2000) 'National experiences with international criminal justice: universal jurisdiction. Unpublished conference paper.

Van der Vyver J. (2004) 'National experiences in international criminal justice: truth commissions', paper presented to Third International Conference *International Criminal Justice: A Transatlantic Dialogue* at the European Parliament and the Royal Flemish Academy for Sciences and Arts, Brussels, May.

Van Ness, D. (1998) 'Restorative justice: international trends', paper presented at Victoria University Wellington, New Zealand, 7 October (http://www.restorativejustice.org/rj3/Full-text/dan/Victoriatalk.pdf).

Van Roermund, B. (2001) 'Rubbing off and rubbing on: the grammar of reconciliation', in E.A. Christodoulidis and S. Veitch (eds) *Lethe's Law*. Oxford: Hart, 175–90.

Van Zyl, P. (2000) 'Justice without punishment: guaranteeing human rights in transitional societies', in C. Villa-Vicencio and W. Verwoerd (eds) *Looking Back, Reaching Forward: Reflections on the Truth and Reconciliation Commission in South Africa*. Cape Town and London: University of Cape Town Press and Zed Books.

Van Zyl Smit, D. (1999) 'Life imprisonment as an ultimate penalty in international law: a human rights perspective', *Criminal Law Forum*, 10: 1.

Van Zyl Smit, D. (2002) 'Punishment and human rights in international criminal justice', Inaugural Lecture as Professor of Comparative and International Penal Law in the University of Nottingham, 30 January.

Vaughan, B. (2001) 'Handle with care: on the use of structuration theory within criminology', *British Journal of Criminology*, 41: 185.

Viet-Wilson, J. (1998) *Setting Adequacy Standards*. Bristol: Policy Press.

Vigoni, D. (2002) *L'applicazione della pena su richiesta delle parti*. Milano: Giuffre.

Villa-Vicencio, C. (2000) 'Why perpetrators should not always be prosecuted: where the international criminal court and truth commissions meet', *Emory Law Journal*, 49: 205.

Villa-Vicencio, C. and Verwoerd, W. (2000) *Looking Back Reaching Forward: Reflections on the Truth and Reconciliation Commission of South Africa*. Cape Town and London: University of Cape Town Press and Zed Books.

Vogler, R. (1996), 'Criminal procedure in France', in J. Hatchard, B. Huber and R. Vogler (eds) *Comparative Criminal Procedure*. London: British Institute of International and Comparative Law.

Vogler, R. (2000) 'Three-dimensional justice: towards a comparative theory of criminal process'. Unpublished conference paper.

Wacquant, L. (2001) 'Deadly symbiosis', *Punishment and Society*, 3: 95.

Walgrave, L. (ed.) (2002) *Restorative Justice and the Law*. Cullompton: Willan Publishing.

Walgrave, L. (ed.) (2003) *Repositioning Restorative Justice*. Cullompton: Willan Publishing.

Walker, N. (1965) *Crime and Punishment in Britain: An Analysis of the Penal System in Theory, Law and Practice*. Edinburgh: Edinburgh University Press.

Walker, N. (1966) *The Aims of a Penal System*. Edinburgh: Edinburgh University Press.

Walker, N. (1972) *Sentencing in a Rational Society*. Harmondsworth: Penguin.

Walker, N. (1985) *Sentencing: Theory, Law and Practice*. London: Butterworths.

Walker, N. (1991) *Why Punish?* Oxford: Oxford University Press.

Walker, N. and Hough, M. (eds) (1988) *Public Attitudes to Sentencing: Surveys from Five Countries.* Aldershot: Gower.

Wasik, M. (1999) 'Reparation: sentencing and the victim', *Criminal Law Review*: 470.

Weisberg, R. (2003) 'Norms and criminal law and the norms of criminal law scholarship', *Journal of Criminal Law and Criminology*, 93: 467.

Weisberg, R. (2003) 'Restorative justice and the danger of "community"', *Utah Law Review*, 1: 343.

Wells, C. (1990) 'Situated decision-making', *Southern California Law Review*, 63: 1728.

Wexler, L. (1996) 'The proposed permanent international criminal court: an appraisal', *Cornell International Law Journal*, 29: 665.

Williams, G. (1961) *Criminal Law: The General Part* (2nd edn). London: Stevens.

Wood, D. (1998) 'Dangerous offenders and the morality of protective sentencing', *Criminal Law Review*: 424.

Wright-Mills, C. (1970) *The Sociological Imagination.* Harmondsworth: Penguin Books.

Wu, H. (2004) 'Accountability and justice: the binding agents of international criminal law'. Unpublished working paper.

Young, L. (1999) *The Exclusive Society: Social Exclusion, Crime and Difference in Late Modernity.* London: Sage.

Zappala, S. (1997) 'Le procès pénal italien: entre système inquisitoire et système accusatoire', *Revue Internationale de Droit Pénal*, 68: 111.

Zappala, S. (2003) *Human Rights in International Criminal Proceedings.* Oxford: Oxford University Press.

Zdenkowski, G. (2000) 'Sentencing trends: past, present and prospective', in D. Chappell and P. Wilson (eds) *Crime and the Criminal Justice System in Australia: 2000 and Beyond.* Sydney: Butterworths, 161.

Zedner, L. (1994) 'Reparation and retribution: are they reconcilable?', *Modern Law Review*, 57: 228.

Zedner, L. (1995) 'In pursuit of the vernacular: comparing law and order discourse in Britain and Germany', *Social and Legal Studies*, 4: 517.

Zedner, L. (1997) 'Victims', in M. Maguire, R. Morgan and R. Reiner (eds) *The Oxford Handbook of Criminology* (2nd edn). Oxford: Oxford University Press.

Zehr, H. (1990) *Changing Lenses: A New Focus for Crime and Justice.* Scottdale, PA, and Waterloo, Ontario: Herald Press.

Index

abstraction 24, 36
  levels and context 19
accepted knowledge 56–7, 59
access xx, 260, 264–7, 270
  by lay participants to the trial
    system 278–9
  expansion 326
  as a feature of fair trial 229
  for the purposes of survey 104–5
  to trial narrative 99
  to trial rights xxxvi
  in transformed trials xxxix–xl,
    333–4
  see also inclusion; participation
accountability 270, 282, 283
  and the transformed trial xli–xlii,
    332, 352–3
  and TRCs 287
  see also legal accountability
accused 170–1
action
  link to concept of power 20
  relationship between narrative
    and 29–30
  see also law in action; moral
    action; social action
'action in context' 16
adjudicators 353

role of judges as 326–7
  see also judges
admissibility 165
  challenges 135f
  see also materiality
admission of guilt 259, 260
advantage, balance of 348
adversarial trial styles xxx, 318
  coexistence with mediation 328
  distinction between inquisitorial
    and 10, 129
  in the English sentencing
    narrative 211
  introduction in Italy 248, 250,
    251
  operation of evidential rules 323
  roles of trial professionals 221
  tensions 253–4
advocacy, styles of 219
agency
  potential for changing outcomes
    317
  relationship between structure
    and 23, 36
  see also human agency
American realists 48
amnesties 282, 354
analytical universals 29